WOMEN, THE STATE, AND WELFARE

Women, the State, and Welfare

Edited by

LINDA GORDON

The University of Wisconsin Press

19.95

The University of Wisconsin Press
2537 Daniels Street
Madison, Wisconsin 53718

3 Henrietta Street
London WC2E 8LU, England

Copyright © 1990
The Board of Regents of the University of Wisconsin System
All rights reserved

10   9   8   7   6   5

Printed in the United States of America

Library of Congress Cataloging-in-Publication Data
Women, the state, and welfare / edited by Linda Gordon.
      324 pp.   cm.
   Includes bibliographical references and index.
   1. Public welfare—United States—History.   2. Poor women—United States—
History.   3. United States—Social policy—History.   4. Feminism—United States.
5. Women in politics—United States.   I. Gordon, Linda.
HV95.W66   1990
362.83'0973—dc20   90-50089
ISBN 0-299-12660-9   CIP
ISBN 0-299-12664-1 (pbk.)

Contents

v

Preface

This anthology began as a joint project with Rosalind Pollack Petchesky. At a very early stage, when we had only just begun to discuss what might be included, she had to leave me alone with the project because of her new and very demanding job. I am keenly aware that the benefit of her intellectual rigor and knowledge, combined with the mutual learning that can occur in such a team project, would have made this a better book.

My own thinking on this subject, as reflected in my first essay and in the choice of articles, has been influenced not only by Ros Petchesky but also by many other friends and colleagues with whom I have discussed these issues, at levels of abstraction ranging from a discussion about "the state" with graduate students here at the University of Wisconsin to mutterings about the daily news. I would like particularly to thank Rosalyn Fraad Baxandall, Johanna Brenner, Lisa Brush, Elizabeth Ewen, Stuart Ewen, Martha Fineman, Nancy Fraser, Ed Friedman, Susan Stanford Friedman, Allen Hunter, Nancy Isenberg, Alice Kessler-Harris, Judith Walzer Leavitt, Gerda Lerner, Sara McLanahan, Nancy MacLean, Ann Orloff, Kathryn Sklar, Susan Smith, Susan Traverso, Susan Ware, and Ann Withorn. To some authors whose work is included here I have special debts: Nancy Fraser, Jane Jenson, and Gwendolyn Mink rewrote their articles for this anthology. Elizabeth Schneider allowed me to cut her article drastically. Jane Jenson allowed me to lop off a theoretical introduction that was very dear to her and turned herself into an American historian at my pleading. Teresa Amott produced her essay especially for this collection. Frances Fox Piven and Richard Cloward, unintentionally, gave me, in their impressive *oeuvre* on welfare, not only a model of committed scholarship but an argument against which I was able to develop my own feminist analysis.

Acknowledgments

Grateful acknowledgment is made to the following publishers and journals for permission to reprint this material:

"The Gender Basis of American Social Policy," by Virginia Sapiro. Reprinted by permission of the author and the publisher from *Political Science Quarterly* 101, No. 2 (1986): 221–38.

"The Domestication of Politics: Women and American Political Society, 1780–1920," by Paula Baker. Reprinted by permission of the author and the publisher from *American Historical Review* 89 (June 1984): 620–47.

"The Origins of the Two-Channel Welfare State: Workmen's Compensation and Mothers' Aid," by Barbara Nelson. A different version of this article appeared in *Women, Change, and Politics*, ed. Louise Tilly and Patricia Gurin (New York: Russell Sage Foundation, 1989).

"Representations of Gender: Policies to 'Protect' Women Workers and Infants in France and the USA Before 1914," by Jane Jenson. A different version of this appeared in *Canadian Journal of Political Science* 22 (June 1989): 235–58.

"Family Violence, Feminism, and Social Control," by Linda Gordon. Reprinted by permission of the author and the publisher from *Feminist Studies* 12 (Fall 1986): 453–78.

"Struggle over Needs: Outline of a Socialist-Feminist Critical Theory of Late-Capitalist Political Culture," by Nancy Fraser. Reprinted by permission of the author and the publisher, the University of Minnesota Press. Copyright © 1989 by the Regents of the University of Minnesota.

"The Dialectic of Rights and Politics: Perspectives from the Women's Movement," by Elizabeth M. Schneider. A different version of this article appeared in *New York Law Review* 61 (Oct. 1986): 589–652.

"Ideology and the State: Women, Power and the Welfare State." Reprinted by permission of the author and the publisher from *Socialist Review* 74 (March–April 1984): 13–19.

"Welfare is Not *for* Women: The War on Poverty, Legal Services, and an Alternative Model of Advocacy for Poor Women," by Diana Pearce. Reprinted by permission of the author and the publisher from *Clearinghouse Review* 14 Special Issue (Summer 1985): 412–18.

Contributors

Teresa Amott is on the faculty of Bucknell University in Pennsylvania. She is author, along with Julie Matthaei, of *Race, Gender, and Work: A Multicultural Economic History of Women in the United States* (1990). She has been active in the welfare rights movement for many years.

Paula Baker is an assistant professor of history at the University of Massachusetts at Amherst, where she teaches United States women's and political history. She is the author of *The Moral Frameworks of Public Life: Gender, Politics, and Government in Rural New York, 1870–1930* (1989).

Nancy Fraser teaches philosophy, comparative literature and theory, and women's studies at Northwestern University. She is the author of *Unruly Practices: Power, Discourse and Gender in Contemporary Social Theory* (1989).

Linda Gordon is Florence Kelley Professor of History at the University of Wisconsin at Madison. She is the author of *Woman's Body, Woman's Right: A Social History of Birth Control in the U.S.* (originally 1976, revised edition 1990) and *Heroes of Their Own Lives: The Politics and History of Family Violence* (1988) and editor of *America's Working Women: A Documentary History* (1976).

Jane Jenson is professor of political science, Carleton University, Ottawa, Canada, and a research affiliate of the Center for European Studies, Harvard University. She is coauthor of *The View from Inside: A French Communist Cell in Crisis* (1984), *Absent Mandate: The Politics of Discontent in Canada* (1984), and *Crisis, Challenge and Change: Party and Class in Canada Revisited* (1988). She is coeditor of *Behind the Lines: Gender and the Two World Wars* (1987) and *Feminization of the Labor Force: Paradoxes and Promises* (1988).

Gwendolyn Mink is associate professor of politics at the University of California, Santa Cruz. Her first book, *Old Labor and New Immigrants in American Political Development*, dealt with the political consequences of racism and nativism in the American Federation of Labor. She is now writing a book on the gender and race bases of pre-New Deal welfare state politics, to be published by Cornell University Press.

Barbara J. Nelson, professor at the Hubert H. Humphrey Institute of Public Affairs, University of Minnesota, is a political scientist with interests in social policy and social movements. She is the author of *Making an Issue of Child Abuse: Political Agenda Setting for Social Problems* (1984), *American Women and Policies: A Selected Bibliography and Resource Guide* (1984), and *Wage Justice: Comparable Worth and the Paradox of Technocratic Reform* (with Sara M. Evans) (1989).

Diana Pearce has written and spoken widely on the "feminization of poverty," a concept she introduced to the lexicon of scholars and activists in her 1978 article on women, work, and welfare. In addition to ongoing research on women's economic inequality, Dr. Pearce's current work focuses on welfare reform at the national, state, and local levels and the housing needs of women who head families. She currently directs the Woman and Poverty Project at Wider Opportunities for Women in Washington, D.C.

Frances Fox Piven, coauthor of *Regulating the Poor*, *Poor Peoples' Movements*, *The New Class War*, *The Mean Season*, and most recently, *Why Americans Don't Vote*, is professor of political science at the Graduate School and University Center, City University of New York.

Virginia Sapiro is professor of political science at the University of Wisconsin at Madison, where she has also been chair of the Women's Studies Program. She is the author of *Women in American Society* and *The Political Integration of Women*.

Elizabeth M. Schneider is professor of law at Brooklyn Law School. She clerked for United States District Judge Constance Baker Motley of the Southern District of New York in 1973, has been Staff Attorney at the Center for Constitutional Rights in New York City, and Administrative Director of the Constitutional Litigation Clinic at Rutgers Law School–Newark. She has been a long-time feminist activist and lawyer in the women's rights movement and has written widely in the fields of women's and civil rights.

WOMEN, THE STATE, AND WELFARE

Introduction: How to Read This Book

This book collects, for the first time under one cover, a group of the best essays about women and the United States welfare state, chosen to offer different disciplinary and theoretical perspectives. It aims also to encourage scholarship on this topic through an interdisciplinary and academic-nonacademic cross-pollination, with the view that by placing various approaches in contact we can increase the overall creativity and fertility on this topic. Most of these articles have been published but often in academic, disciplinary journals that are unlikely to be read by nonspecialists, especially given the quantity and, now, specialization of feminist writing in the United States. Although the authors do not all agree, the reader will find remarkable evidence of a collective process in the development of a gender analysis that incorporates divisions of class and race. Each essay stands on its own and no previous reading is required to understand any one of them. Nevertheless, the anthology is also designed to be read as a book, from beginning to end. The order of the essays represents a compromise between a roughly chronological history and a tracing of the intellectual development of this collective feminist scholarly thinking over the last decade.

In the introductory essay I review recent attempts to conceptualize the welfare state in two sections. First I discuss the limitations of ways of thinking that do not use gender as a category of analysis. Then I discuss the new feminist scholarship on the subject. The notes to this essay may serve as a useful guide to additional reading. But this should not be read as a bibliographical essay; it is far less comprehensive and much more opinionated. It criticizes what I take to be inadequate, overly simple, or ahistorical perspectives on the state and welfare and concludes with a rumination about the direction I think welfare thinking ought to take.

The book continues with four historical essays, ironically most of them not by historians but by historically minded political scientists—a wave of the future, I hope. Virginia Sapiro argues that the basic outlines of the development of modern social policy only make sense on the basis of a gender analysis. Otherwise key generalizations do not work; for example, if the Protestant work ethic and a laissez-faire political economy were so central a part of our heritage, why did they seem to apply to less than half the population? And, if the system was so oppressive to women, why were some of the early "turning point" policies apparently aimed to help women? She outlines the historical interconnections between movements to help the needy and women's movements and identifies the contradiction that while our welfare system has in theory been designed to maximize independence this has never been its goal for women. Rather than simply document these discriminatory assumptions, she explores the need for a new appraisal of the values and meanings of dependence and independence.

Historian Paula Baker places in a long perspective—a century and a half—the track of women's political influence. Published originally in 1984, her article shows that while the political parties that grew up around universal white male suffrage in the United States were deeply and quintessentially fraternal in their character and purposes, disenfranchised white women were nevertheless developing their own political culture. She uses the concept of political culture to assess the impact of women's activism on American politics *before* female suffrage. She shows that by the end of her story, in the Progressive era, these women had amassed substantial political power, enough not only to affect social policy in some areas but also, more important, to redraw the boundary of the political sphere, making the public welfare a governmental responsibility. Her article was influential among women's historians in challenging a view of women as passive or as exclusively the object of politics. It should be equally important in challenging models of the welfare state in which women function only as recipients of aid and/or victims.

Gwendolyn Mink opens a new perspective on this long history, emphasizing the racial origins of United States programs for social provision. She argues that while in Europe welfare programs grew out of struggles for political and social equality primarily within homogeneous ethnic groups, the "nub" of United States welfare state formation was "the clash between racial diversity and an idealized American citizenry." The gendered content of these programs —both from the perspective of those men who ruled and of those women who campaigned for a welfare state—must be seen as equally racial, reflecting the particular gender patterns of a white privileged group. This is a vital corrective to a tendency to read the term "racial" as referring to people of color and to perceive whites as without race. Mink argues that what appears as a motherhood track was actually "gender-based solutions to what was widely perceived to be a racial problem."

Barbara Nelson then offers a more detailed example of the welfare double standard through her comparison of two nearly simultaneous welfare reforms, workmen's compensation and mothers' "pension" or aid programs, both adopted for the first time around 1910–11. Two channels—a motherhood and a wage-work stream—directed but did not wholly determine the later development of the welfare state. Nelson also interrogates the concepts being used, such as labor and welfare policy, and shows the necessity for integrating gender into political-science scholarship about the development of state administrative capacity.

Jane Jenson, a political scientist whose work has focused on modern France, has contributed the only comparative study in this volume. Her article is motivated by dissatisfaction with several early theoretical models of subjecting the state to a gender analysis: a "dual systems" structuralist analysis that examines the intersection of patriarchy and capitalism; a Marxist analysis that understands the state to regulate the labor force; and a more purely feminist analysis that subordinates capitalism to patriarchy as the primary system. Rejecting all these functionalist analyses, Jenson uses international comparison to identify the influence of specific political struggles. Her comparison of policies to "protect" women workers and infants in France and the United States has important implications for how we understand the processes by which social policies are made. France is not a country particularly notable for the high status of women: the women's movement was historically weaker there than in the United States, women won political rights later there, and women appear generally to have had less social power and freedom there in some spheres. Nevertheless, due to the stronger participation of women in the labor force and in labor/socialist movements in the nineteenth century, the French adopted policies recognizing women, and even married women, workers as legitimate and permanent members of the labor force and went much further towards providing needed services for women workers than did the United States. The two-track welfare system of the United States, defined by Nelson but noticed also by many other scholars, was not replicated in France. Jenson's article challenges universal and determinist notions about gender systems and suggests how strongly welfare policies may be influenced by different political cultures and social movements.

My own article on family violence and social control has several points of intersection with the problems of conceptualizing the welfare state. First, it reminds us that welfare policy includes not only the giving of material goods but also regulation—of the market and the family in particular. Second, it shows in a microcosmic way what Jenson's work implies on a broader scale: that actual policies are the results of contestation, not only between organized political forces but also between individuals at the level of "social work" encounters. Third, it protests the understanding of social control (discussed more fully in the first essay) as exclusively a form of domination, arguing rather that women of many social groups have sometimes been able to use the state in their own interest against more personal oppressions.

The next two articles, by philosopher Nancy Fraser and lawyer Elizabeth M. Schneider, call our attention to the ways in which people make claims for social provision or protection. Like my own article, both are concerned with the political activism not only of organized groups but also of individuals. Nancy Fraser's essay incorporates several critical perspectives in its intervention into political theory: it deviates from the objectivistic and technocratic spirit of mainstream Anglo-American theory by using discourse analysis to theorize needs as interpreted and contested; it breaks with androcentric neomarxian theory by rejecting functionalism and treating terms such as "economic," "political," and "domestic" as ideological labels; yet it also represents a critique of forms of discourse analysis that posit a single, seamless "symbolic order" without contestation or political agency. Fraser calls our attention directly to the contestedness of welfare policy by considering how we speak about these services. She elaborates, first, the meanings of the sphere called "social," in contrast to "political" and "domestic," and how the boundaries of these "spheres" shift as a result of discursive struggles. Fraser argues that the notion of the "social" expresses not only a particular form of late-capitalist economy but also the rise of particular forms of (social) movements—that is, movements outside the sphere of conventionally defined political (electoral, party) activity. Then she identifies the increasing usage of the rhetoric of "needs" in a late-capitalist culture and how this needs talk is used by one group to depoliticize policies and transform them into matters requiring expert, supposedly nonpolitical, administration. But she resists a pessimistic, determinist reading of needs talk and instead offers examples of resistant, even subversive, discourses about needs. She suggests that these more democratic uses of the concept of needs occur when needs claims are translated into social rights.

Elizabeth Schneider offers a defense of the discourse of rights from another perspective. Many critical legal scholars have argued that rights language is inevitably and hopelessly individualistic and ideologically pluralist. This attack on rights has been challenged from many perspectives, notably by women and minorities. Writing from her extensive experience as a women's rights litigator and activist, she argues that while rights talk has the potential both to "advance and obscure political growth and vision," it has in fact helped women illuminate their common experience and build a collective identity. In other words, she argues, rights claims need not be individualistic; when the source of the rights claims was women's experience itself, liberal "rights language was not simply 'occupied' " but modified to offer a more interdependent, communal vision of women's possibilities.

The last three articles in this collection focus more directly on contemporary welfare controversies and strategies. They share themes found in the historical and theoretical articles preceding and argue the relevance of these feminist critiques to immediate political conflicts. Frances Fox Piven's essay was originally written in the early 1980s, as the idea of a "gender gap" in American politics began to attract the attention of political commentators. Taking the emergence of a distinctive women's politics as her premise, she examined the complex sources of that politics. Her perspective shares with that of earlier articles the critique of regarding welfare recipients as uniquely "dependent," the argument that the welfare state was in part constructed "from below," and the argument that the welfare state has been strengthening to many women. She argues that the contemporary gender gap is being shaped by the interaction of the traditional "caring" orientations of women and their decidedly new circumstances in the family and labor market. Fox Piven argues that the state has benefited women not only as a provider of welfare benefits but also as employer, and she discusses one of women's relations with the state not previously emphasized in this anthology and often entirely neglected from feminist work about welfare: electoral power. She believes that women have the potential to move into "the forefront of electoral calculations," in which case the gender gap about military and welfare policies will be particularly salient. Above all she calls our attention to the opportunity that the welfare state creates for community and social movements among welfare recipients, so important fifteen to twenty years ago, and potentially powerful again.

Sociologist Diana Pearce will be known to many readers as the author of the by now famous phrase "the feminization of poverty." She offers here a different version of the two-track model of welfare programs from that used by Nelson: for Pearce both streams of welfare provision are male models, and the War on Poverty continued the male assumption that joblessness was the major cause of poverty and full employment its solution. Pearce argues, to the contrary, that female poverty is unique, because of women's responsibility for children and discrimination in the labor market, so that employment cannot be the only solution for women. Most important she shows the dialectical relation between the welfare system and women's poverty: women are poor because of the discriminatory sexual division of labor, in the family as in the labor market; while the welfare system reinforces women's disadvantaged position in both areas. Thus she believes that a real welfare reform cannot be gender neutral nor restricted to welfare provision itself but must challenge gender inequality in employment and family relations as well.

Economist Teresa Amott focuses an examination of contemporary welfare issues on the much-publicized rise in single-mother families among African-Americans. She demonstrates that family structure is a poor explanation for poverty and welfare clientage, since the overwhelming number of poor black single mothers were in poverty *before* they became mothers. She shows

the inadequacy of several hypotheses about why the number of black single mothers is high and increasing, criticizing the "Moynihan" theory about
black family pathology, the conservative theory that welfare availability causes
single-mother families, and William J. Wilson's reduction of the problem to
lack of "marriageable"—that is, employed—black men. She traces the history
of aid to single mothers since the 1940s, a history that supports the view that
expansion of the welfare rolls has been as much a sign of women's political
empowerment as of impoverishment. She concludes with a skeptical reading
of the likelihood of success of the Family Security Act of 1988, the newest
form of "workfare."

I hope that this anthology, by allowing readers to immerse themselves in a
range of thinking about women and the welfare state, will help to bring gender
into the center of welfare scholarship and policy making and welfare issues
into the center of feminist thinking and activism.

CHAPTER 1

The New Feminist Scholarship on the Welfare State

LINDA GORDON

If the state were a family, it would be assumed that welfare is a woman's affair. Even in families with shared domestic responsibilities, women are in charge of the welfare of family members. In fact, in the actual, nonfamily state, women constitute most of the recipients and providers of "welfare." Most Americans think of women—single mothers—when they think of "welfare." Nevertheless, when experts, and especially scholars, have examined welfare they have either described it as an ungendered program or as if the sex of those involved in it made no difference.

Even the rich new feminist scholarship in the United States is just beginning to address the welfare state. Although women's studies began earlier in the United States and has proliferated more than in many other countries, on this topic we are retarded in comparison to the greater quantity of scholarship from other countries.[1] Perhaps this is because the U.S. welfare state has been relatively weak and, even more important, less visible than its European counterparts—because of its decentralization through a federal system and because of the mystification accomplished through labeling as "welfare" only some of those state programs that contribute to citizens' well-being. Also contributing to the disinterest of U.S. feminist scholars has been the tradition of hostility towards the state, which marked the women's liberation movement here, influenced as it was by the New Left.

Disinterest is no longer the case, and feminist appraisals of the welfare state are increasing. They are able to draw upon the voluminous production of feminist thinking and activism in a variety of fields: history, literary criticism, philosophy, sociology, economics, and politics, as well as the older traditions of liberal and Left scholarship on social welfare. Indeed the feminist consideration of the welfare state stands in a complex dialogue with the older scholarship: bewildered and critical because of its inexcusable neglect

9

of women and gender, sharing the general perspective of support for state responsibility for the public welfare, and appreciating also the contrasting tradition of suspicion of the controlling power the state gains in the very act of assuming that responsibility. These authors are also in a critical dialogue with other feminist scholars and activists, complaining about their neglect of the state and criticizing them for their avoidance of politics. There are many silent presences in this discourse: British academic and political defenders of the Labour Party's welfare programs such as T. H. Marshall and R. M. Titmuss; Marxist political economists (Ian Gough, Claus Offe, and James O'Connor might be mentioned); critical historians and social workers (such as James Weinstein, Anthony Platt, Michael Katz, Clarke Chambers, and Jeffry Galper) who deflated claims about the altruistic purposes of welfare provision; the Afro-American scholars, feminist and nonfeminist, from W. E. B. Du Bois to William J. Wilson, who taught white feminists so much about discrimination, domination, and control of the state; hundreds of feminist writers who rendered visible women's work, women's nurturance, and women's aspirations.

Most of the articles in this collection are documented, but, especially in an anthology, footnotes cannot adequately describe traditions of debate and/or the inheritance of shared values. In this essay I want to trace some of those missing lines of connection. I hope to help the reader place what follows on a map of welfare-state and feminist scholarship. My map is, like all maps, only a projection, a representation of how people have interpreted geography, and makes no claims to "objective" presentation of this world of thought. My "projection," like all projections, is designed to highlight what is salient for me: historical scholarship and U.S. scholarship.[2]

THE GENDER-BLIND WELFARE-STATE SCHOLARSHIP

Most scholarship about the welfare state simply does not use gender as a category of analysis (by contrast most do understand welfare to reflect and form the class system).[3] Some of the more recent historians of the United States welfare state, such as Robert Bremner, James Patterson, Walter Trattner, John Ehrenreich, David Rochefort, and Michael Katz, do notice and specify women's particular welfare situation at times, but they do not consider it a major organizing principle of the system.[4]

The omission of a gender analysis distorts our understanding of the welfare state through many levels. Sometimes it obscures the existence of a policy altogether, since the policy is not spelled out at a general level but emerges from the intersection of many constrictions on women's lives. One author, for example, recently concluded that the United States has no policy towards pregnancy,[5] a mistake that results from the tendency to perceive women's reproductive activity as "natural," from the failure to understand that policy is as much constructed by denials of needs as by meeting them, and, because of the nature of the state in the United States, from the difficulty of identifying policy that is constructed of the practices of private employers, educational institutions, medical insurance carriers, town, country, state, and federal taxation, employment, welfare, and family law. In this volume the article by Nancy Fraser calls our attention to the varying languages of policy. For example, an examination of United States policy towards pregnancy would have to consider the period in which pregnant women were excluded from certain jobs, such as teaching, and the evolution towards a standard that no longer considers pregnant women as symbols of or stimuli for immorality; the fact that United States employers today provide virtually no paid and few unpaid maternity leaves; and the fact that public funds will pay for childbirth but not for abortion.

Several authors in this volume, notably Barbara Nelson and Diana Pearce, show that there is a double standard of welfare provision for men and women. One source of this differential treatment is our gender system, including norms that women, especially mothers, should be primarily domestic and supported by men. The failure of several decades of "workfare" programs can only be explained in terms of fundamental ambivalence on the part of legislatures, welfare professionals, and voters about whether public support of single mothers is better or worse than sending mothers into the labor force. As waves of recent welfare reform have tried to get AFDC recipients to "work"—that is, take wage-labor employment—the lack of gender analysis obscures the labor-market sex segregation that makes it difficult for women to get jobs that provide even as good an income as welfare provision. Lack of gender analysis has also hidden the fact that even identical welfare programs would have different meanings and consequences for women, especially mothers, who already do the vast majority of parenting and housework, which must then be added to whatever wage work they do. Assumptions about masculinity have equally affected the welfare system, as it has been mainly unthinkable for able male welfare recipients not to work, while welfare workers made it a priority to protect men's egos from the damages of being unable to support a family.

Moreover, gender distinctions helped create the meanings of welfare. In an insightful study of German welfare history, Heide Gerstenberger showed that just as welfare rested on a worthy/unworthy distinction, so it helped define the bounds of the "respectable," drawing a circle that excluded those who needed help.[6] There has been too little examination of the gender sources of the stigma attached, both for men and for women, to receiving welfare.[7] Since so many women's major work is taking care of children, it has been harder to define, perhaps, whether AFDC recipients are working or malingering; since their singleness usually involves an appearance of sexual freedom, the sexual double standard is easily exploited to label them immoral. Definitions of "respectability" have been deeply gendered, and there appears to be some sexual content to taxpayers' hostility to independent women. For example, in my own recent study of the history of family violence, I found that although social work agencies accepted in theory a deserving/undeserving distinction that put widows in the former and illegitimate mothers in the latter category, in practice they did not necessarily treat the widows better than the "immoral" women. This was because in practice *any* female-headed family seemed to them to threaten immorality.[8]

Even more fundamentally, lack of gender analysis obscures the *roots* of poverty, the inequitable distribution and production that create the need for welfare programs in the first place. Much of our welfare expenditure goes to AFDC, which is a program founded on the principle that the norm is for mothers and children to be supported by men; that norm is, of course, the product of our particular sex/gender system—it is not a biological or divine given. A different sex/gender system might require men and women to share in child care and in earning; yet another might assume that the state should take all responsibility for the financial support of children. The sex/gender system is responsible for women's low wage rates and segregation in low-status jobs.

The contemporary discussion of the underclass in the United States is dulled by lack of a gender analysis. "Underclass" is of course a vague and highly ideological term used in a variety of ways: stirring up fears of crime, supporting the "war" on drugs, but also uncritically mixing into this amalgam hostilities to minorities, single-mother families, taxes, and welfare provision in general. There are serious and answerable questions about whether there is a shift among the very poor towards more criminal, self-destructive, exploitive, sexually irresponsible behavior. It is difficult in any case to examine a topic about which there is so much hysteria, but lack of sex distinctions makes the discussion even more murky. Criminality, drug business, and sexual and physical violence are overwhelmingly male; more, they are associated specifically with assertions of masculinity. When women participate in these behaviors it is usually as followers of men, a pattern associated precisely with one sense of feminity as being both nurturant and loyal to men. Thus it is reasonable to hypothesize that this kind of increasing underclass, if it exists, is associated with crises of gender identity. Meanwhile many women, particularly single mothers, are often included in generalizations about the underclass even though they do not engage in violent or criminal behavior; they are so categorized either because they are welfare recipients or because they are single mothers, making the "underclass" just another rhetorical device in the attack on social provision and depriving us of categories that might illuminate specific problems.

Not only problem definitions but also their solutions have been gendered. Most welfare programs have been designed to shore up male-breadwinner families or to compensate—temporarily—for their collapse. But welfare clients must work to collect their entitlements, and women do a disproportionate amount of this work too. Medical aid, aid for the disabled, programs for children with special needs, indeed educational institutions altogether assume that women will be available to make it possible for the aid to be delivered: to drive, to care, to be at home for visits, to come to welfare offices. Just as in the market economy women translate between the paycheck—that is, money as an abstract token of exchange—and the meeting of material needs of their families—for example, buying the food, cooking it, cleaning so that new food can be cooked the next day—so too in the "welfare" economy women translate between the entitlement and the actual giving of nurture.[9]

Blindness to gender exists in a sometimes contradictory but nevertheless mutually reinforcing relation to ignorance of the racial bases of the modern welfare state. This is particularly true in the United States, where, as Gwendolyn Mink argues in this volume, economy and government have been from the beginning of the state organized around black subordination and the expropriation of Native Americans and Mexicans. The assumptions and priorities that guided the welfare system here, since the seventeenth century, have been as fundamentally white as they have been male. The vision of republicanism that underlies both U.S. resistance to public welfare programs and the design of those programs was based not only on "manly" definitions of dignity and independence but also on coexistence with a slave society, with black servitude as a foil against which (white) citizenship and self-respect were defined. In the New Deal period, for example, the exclusion of Afro-Americans from welfare benefits was not peripheral to the new federal programs but a fundamental part of their construction,[10] part of the basic political realignment that created the New Deal. Most good-quality welfare programs were designed as emergency wage-replacement provisions for those accustomed to (at least) upper-working-class wages. For different reasons and in different ways, virtually all but white men were excluded from these jobs and thereby from the better welfare programs.

The relation of the welfare state to both gender and race as fundamental social divisions is bilateral. These divisions have helped create the need for welfare by creating poverty, and then shaped its nature and distribution, but the welfare programs in turn have influenced the nature of the divisions. The situation of women and of minority men has been affected, for better and for worse, by the structure of the welfare state. Indeed the very meanings of femininity, masculinity, and blackness and other racial stereotypes in the United States today derive in part from the shape and administration of these programs. The exclusions and limits of unemployment insurance, which thereby force many onto general relief or AFDC, create negative attitudes about the high levels of minority unemployment, for example. The definition of masculinity as breadwinning and independent is reinforced by the assumption, long present in AFDC, for example, that men should be responsible for the children of the women they live with. The consensus about women's normative domesticity has been shaped in a double-binding way by the structure of AFDC (keeping women at home but inadequately supported, thereby forcing them into the underground wage labor market, but declining to provide for child care).

Similarly contradictory is the rhetoric that welfare represents deplorable "dependence," while women's subordination to husbands is not registered as unseemly. This contradiction should not be surprising, for the concept of dependence is an ideological one that reflects particular modes of production. For example, in traditional societies only men of substantial property were considered independent, and not only women and children but all men who worked for others were considered dependents. Only in the modern era, where wage labor became the norm for men and voting rights were extended to all men, did employed men begin to be "independent." Women, for whom wage labor was not the majority experience until recently, and whose earnings are on average much less than men's, continued to be considered as dependent. Indeed, women's dependence (e.g., their unpaid domestic labor) contributed to men's "independence." Only in the last half-century has the term "dependent" begun to refer specifically to adult recipients of public aid, while women who depend on husbands are no longer labeled as dependents (except, of course, for purposes of the IRS). There is also a class double standard for women: the prosperous are encouraged to be dependent on their husbands, the poor to become "independent." [11] Public dependence, of course, is paid for by taxes, yet it is interesting that there is no objection to allowing husbands tax exemptions for their dependent wives. As Virginia Sapiro points out in this volume, the antidependence ideology then penalizes those who care for the inevitably dependent—the young, the sick—who are, of course, disportionately unpaid women and low-paid service workers. In fact, the entire discourse about dependence masks the evident interdependence of vast numbers of the population in modern societies.

The gendered design of welfare programs is by no means simply a matter of male policy makers keeping women subordinate. Few scholars have noted the disproportionate influence of women in envisioning, lobbying for, and then administering welfare programs, especially at the state and local levels where most programs are located. This is not only a matter of giving recognition where it is due, although that is in itself important to compensate for patterns of systematically depriving women of credit for their work. It also requires incorporating the fact that women have often been influential in campaigning for welfare provisions that turned out to be quite discriminatory against women, as in the case of protective legislation or AFDC itself. An analysis of women's activism requires understanding the complex relation that women, especially reformers, have had to conventional gender and family arrangements—often seizing upon what is beneficial to women in those arrangements, often distancing themselves from and seeking to control the needy quite as much as did men, often negotiating delicate compromises hoping to shift slightly the sexual balance of political and economic power.

Meanwhile theoretical debates about the nature of modern welfare states have been similarly impoverished by the lack of gender analysis. Among historians two rather polarized perspectives competed throughout much of the mid-twentieth century. One is affectionately known to those who use a British model as Whig history,[12] although the American Talcott Parsons was an able advocate of it. Jill Quadagno characterizes this view thus: "As industrialization proceeds, it . . . reduc[es] the functions of the traditional family and . . . [dislocates] certain categories of individuals whose labor becomes surplus— the very young, the old, the sick, and the disabled."[13] Quadagno is here correct to leave out women, for the theories she is describing do so. And yet without women the theory is mushy, to say the least. These lost "functions" of the "traditional" family were mainly women's labor, and modern welfare systems do not in fact replace them with anything except differently organized women's labor: women are the main workers in the welfare system, still badly underpaid, performing labor that the current tax system could not support if living wages prevailed; and women continue to do the work of consuming welfare, always vastly underestimated—waiting in lines, making phone calls, processing applications, scrimping when checks are late, begging help and favors when checks are inadequate, etc.

This Whig view often assumed a gradual and conflict–free progress that specified no agent, other than sympathetic and wise legislators. A social-democratic version specified organized labor as the agent,[14] but this was rarely argued *historically*. This argument was based on static sociological operations that correlated welfare programs with union membership or some similar index of labor strength; it did not offer an actual historical narrative of union campaigns for welfare programs. Moreover, without taking gender into consideration, none of this scholarship is correct. In the United States and probably elsewhere as well, organized women, feminist and nonfeminist, devoted more energy to campaigning for welfare programs than did unions, and in certain periods—for example, the Progressive era—they were more influential. Furthermore a gender analysis *of* trade union activity is needed to determine which unionists made welfare high priority and which programs aroused the most union support.

Opposing the Whig interpretation were both left- and right-wing criticisms of welfare programs as controlling: suppressing individual freedom, weakening resistance, and/or distracting the citizenry from the fundamental issues of power. The Left version of this "social-control" argument, discussed in my essay in this volume, views welfare provisions (like higher wages) as encouraging workers to accept the capitalist economy and the liberal governmental system, essentially trading political power for a higher standard of living.[15] This perspective has many problems but foremost is its hidden assumption that the workers making this bad bargain are male. Frances Fox Piven and I both argue in this volume that working-class women, who received much less money from the welfare system, actually gained more power from it, because they could use different systems against each other—for example, the welfare system against domestic male supremacy.[16]

Both these perspectives, as Theda Skocpol has argued, tended to remove politics from consideration and to render the state merely an abstraction or at best a homogeneous and passive tool of larger interests. In the last two decades there has been a renascence of theorizing about the state, particularly among Marxists,[17] and some of this argumentation is directly relevant to welfare and gender issues. Ralph Miliband argued an important modification of instrumentalist theory, the relative autonomy of the state, showing that the capitalist class, if it does not literally staff the state, nevertheless retains power to influence it from without.[18] But what has great explanatory power about class relations by no means works equally well for gender. If we attempt to insert gender into this model we meet trouble: it is difficult to specify what "male" interests are, and if we argue that "men" (a dubious category as a universal) have the preservation of women as their long-term interest and will therefore support measures at least to keep them alive, then the theory becomes so vague as to be not disprovable.[19]

Nicos Poulantzas met some of these objections with his functionalist view, arguing that direct participation of capitalists is not crucial in understanding state functions, but that the state is *objectively* bourgeois and *definitionally* committed to maintaining those values and structures. Here the state becomes abstract; it has no necessary connection with any particular capitalists at all but serves to retain unity among them (and to promote disunity among the working class).[20] Can gender be added to this model? It has indeed been argued that the maleness of the state comes not only from its personnel but is imbedded in its nature, in bureaucratic and hierarchical forms. And in fact Poulantzas's emphasis on unity would find more evidence if it were understood as a class and gendered unity. But to argue that the state objectively functions to maintain male dominance *either* suggests that women have never advanced their position, that we are no better off now than a century ago, which is patently counterexperiential, *or* defines male supremacy in such a way as to include all concessions to women, in which case the premise is tautological.

Those interested in gender analysis would do better to work with a conflict model of the state such as that suggested in Fred Block's class-struggle approach. He postulates a group of state managers, separate from capitalists;

but the managers' fortunes depend on a healthy economy, which, given the real alternatives available to managers, can only be capitalist. Block rejects the view that the state can become a tool of working-class goals, as in the social-democratic model of the welfare state, but he also rejects "social-control" theories on the grounds that capitalists are usually far too short-sighted to trade concessions for long-term stability. Instead these concessions represent victories for workers; but in making them, managers accumulate more power for the state, which then, in periods of working-class weakness, allows it to reform these concessions into structures that support the economic as well as the political system.[21] Organized feminists, too, have won major concessions, only to have these reshaped in periods of feminist decline. But of course those concerned with gender must also consider the possibility that the group of managers, being male and being influenced by its maleness, is in that respect similar to the ruling group, also male. Furthermore, Block's theory involves a fairly economistic, mechanistic determination of when the "working class" will be weak and when strong, and certainly there is no such model for predictions with respect to gender relations.

"State-centered" theories of welfare state development are most associated with Theda Skocpol, who has argued for the influence of particular political configurations. Theoretically it is not difficult to acknowledge the importance of such political factors on policy development, and historians in particular welcome this directive to return to narrative, detailed, causal explanations. Unfortunately in Skocpol's own historical work, the notion of state "capacity" and the study of the decision-making processes of its operators—bureaucrats and politicians—tends to occlude evidence of nongovernmental activism.[22] Skocpol wavers in how much she claims for her politics-centered approach: to the extent that it calls for a more complex explanatory theory, adding political complications to simplified class models, it is evidently reasonable; but in other places Skocpol seems to want to substitute politicians for class (or gender, or race), political conflict for social struggle; her work seems to erase the labor movement from the history of the New Deal, for example. Since there has been little previous acknowledgement of the role of organized women, or of social change with respect to gender, in the history of welfare programs, here she is not erasing but merely continuing to paint around big blank spots.

Another set of relevant debates took place in England among those directly involved in the establishment of its welfare programs.[23] The reformer often most credited for the British welfare state, Beveridge, assumed women's domesticity and dependence on the male ("family") wage, but acknowledged a need to compensate for the failure or inadequacies of that system. T. H. Marshall, a political theorist justifying these welfare innovations, constructed an influential theory of the evolution of citizenship rights, arguing that "social" citizenship, what Franklin D. Roosevelt called "freedom from want," was a third stage following the guarantee of political citizenship, that is, the vote. Marshall's theory did not challenge women's dependence on the male wage. As Gillian Pascall has argued, according to Marshall women's marital dependency should be called feudal because it is an ascribed rather than an achieved status, a relic that subverts his theory of the development of citizenship rights.[24] Marshall's periodization also ignores the history of women's relation to the state. His stages of citizenship (first due process rights, then political rights, or the franchise, then social citizenship, or welfare entitlements) only describe the male experience; throughout the world women won important "social" rights from the state *before* they got the vote.

The British welfare discourse was transformed by the work of Titmuss, in which women were clearly visible. Rejecting grand theorizing, he went in for empirical examination of the welfare services and the needs for them and observed the gendered relations in both.[25] Nevertheless Titmuss was Whiggish in his view that industrialization was responsible for (temporary) family problems, which could be corrected by a good welfare system; he saw women but did not see male supremacy.

THE NEW FEMINIST SCHOLARSHIP

With the renascence of women's studies in the 1970s, feminist thinking turned to welfare. There has been a remarkably international coherence to the scholarship—if not the activism—as will be evidenced by the many references that follow to foreign, especially British and Australian, work. The lowest common denominator of this new work shows that the premise with which I (deliberately) began, that previous scholarship about welfare had been gender-blind, is too simple. However "blind," that scholarship was hardly disabled, for it functioned effectively to mystify and thus defend a gendered and unequal society. In exposing that defensive function, the new feminist scholarship about welfare moved through discernable stages, albeit they are not neatly consecutive and the "progress" involves no consensus but disagreement. These "stages" exist only as analytic categories but perhaps useful ones.

First there was a great deal of work that demonstrated the *discriminatory* character of welfare programs and their function to reinforce sexist arrangements in domestic and public life.[26] In a rich article on the British poor laws in the nineteenth century, Pat Thane showed how the traditional distinction between the deserving and the undeserving poor was drawn for women in terms of their relations to men: widows were always deserving, deserted or unmarried mothers nearly always condemned.[27] We have learned how Social Security discriminates against women,[28] and how many women have been excluded from unemployment compensation because of the kinds of jobs they do, for example.[29] Analysts learned to recognize policies where they seemed invisible, such as Irene Diamond's work on discrimination against women in housing.[30]

The critique of discrimination quickly developed into a structural critique of welfare, in what I consider a second stage of development of the feminist scholarship. A recent sustained example of this sort of approach is Mimi Abramovitz's *Regulating the Lives of Women*, the first book-length feminist analysis of the history of welfare to appear in the United States. Abramovitz moves beyond concern with discrimination to demonstrate how welfare policy functioned to reinforce the entire social system of women's subordination, particularly their constriction within the family and dependence on men.[31] Barbara Nelson's article in this volume continues this kind of analysis still further; through a close study of two welfare programs, she shows that gender assumptions about women's dependence were part of the historical bases of welfare policy. Several scholars have noted the existence of inequalities within the welfare system, most commonly described as a double standard between privileged and nonstigmatized programs such as Old Age and Survivors Insurance (commonly called Social Security) and stingy and humiliating ones such as AFDC, but most have viewed these as class divisions.[32] Others, such as Hace Sorel Tishler, thought the mothers' aid payments were small because the group of "dependent mothers" was insignificant in comparison to unemployed or injured men or the aged—a myth based on the social invisibility of single mothers.[33] Several feminist scholars have interpreted these inequalities in gender terms, including both Nelson and Pearce in this volume.

Nelson's work is part of a new school of analysis that sees welfare programs as having the function not only of keeping women subordinate, but, perhaps more important, of supporting a whole social system. I prefer to call this system the family wage, since it rests on a familial organization in which the husband/father is supposed to be the exclusive breadwinner and the wife/mother responsible for the large quantities of unpaid domestic labor that are essential to every aspect of human life, including the continuation of the economic system.[34] Internationally, feminist analyses have noted that the only explanation that can make sense of seemingly contradictory welfare policies is their function to keep this system (women's economic dependence on men, men's economic dependence on wages and personal dependence on women) in place. Many students of welfare policy, including Jill Roe writing about Australia, Hilary Land, Jane Lewis, and Mary McIntosh writing about Britain, and Mimi Abramowitz and myself writing about the United States, have all argued this perspective.[35] Indeed, in England where family allowance programs were adopted after World War II, the payments were originally made to male heads of families and women could collect them only after considerable feminist campaigning.

Making the family-wage assumptions behind welfare programs even more pernicious is the fact that few men have ever *actually* been able to earn a family wage, that is, a wage large enough single-handedly to support a family. Full dependence on husbands has actually been a "privilege" of a minority of women. Thus negotiations between women and welfare givers have become ritualized exchanges of fictional slogans, with both parties aware that women's likelihood of stable reliance on male wages is not great. Furthermore, women may be coerced by welfare requirements into following paths of action that are least conducive to achieving ultimate independence of welfare—by pursuing men instead of their own upward mobility or by accepting low-wage, unskilled, part-time jobs with terrible working conditions instead of holding out for education, good-quality child care, and better jobs.

The family-wage assumption on which the welfare system has been predicated expresses some of the economic assumptions of industrial capitalism. In this century government intervention into stabilizing relations of productions has been more widely accepted—as in workmen's and unemployment compensation, industrial health and safety laws, agricultural stabilization programs, and even labor relations acts guaranteeing union recognition, for example—while the domestic sphere remains ideologically "private."[36] In fact, as I will argue, domestic, reproductive life is indeed governmentally regulated, with certain forms of it supported and others penalized. Michael Walzer has argued slightly differently: that in the United States governmental regulation of distribution—that is, welfare—is more accepted than is governmental control of production.[37] This is true ideologically only, because in fact there is extensive state control of production. The differences concern the degree to which such controls are mystified and the distributional results of both—not only in cash benefits but in power. With respect to welfare, the ideology of the privateness of reproduction is itself an influence, and one disadvantageous to those who do reproductive work, for it undermines their formation of a sense of entitlement to public help.

In its most extreme form, women's responsibility for domestic, reproductive work has deprived them of citizenship. Carole Pateman has argued that in liberal theory, the first criterion for "citizenship," as that concept evolved, was some form of "independence," defined in terms of the characteristic male experience—for example, property ownership, bearing arms, and self-employment. Hegel was one of many who found a way to acknowledge women's membership in the human and national community without attributing to them citizenship by viewing women as members of families, that is, nonindependent members.[38] The very concept of modern citizenship (in contrast to that of the rights of the subject) arose along with the public/private distinction that ideologically separated women from public life. Of course women were rarely effectively cut off from public activity, and they were active political and commercial figures long before the beginning of legal citizenship entitlements in the nineteenth century. Nevertheless the view of women as private, noncitizens, added to the expectation that they should be the dependents of men, made it difficult to conceive that they should have entitlements to state support.

Some versions of these critiques of the welfare state looked more to its contemporary functions than to its original assumptions, and they adopted and adapted the New Left social-control model. They reflect the antistatist, anti-expert, participatory-democracy values characteristic of the late 1960s/early 1970s women's liberation movement, originating in the New Left but also in individualist values and middle-class experience of many women's liberation theorists and in the anger of the welfare rights movement. A classic example was Barbara Ehrenreich's and Deirdre English's *For Her Own Good*, an indictment of physicians, psychoanalysts, child psychologists, and home economists for usurping women's traditional autonomous skills and then using their newly professional "expertise" to control women's work and even identity.[39] Another is Alicia Frohman's analysis of day care. Following James O'Connor's *The Fiscal Crisis of the State*, which argues that such services function to regulate the labor market, subsidize the costs of production, legitimize the system ideologically, and provide social control, Frohman denies that day-care programs serve women in any way. Rather she relies on a reserve-army-of-labor theory to explain that such programs emerge when needs for women's labor are paramount and contract at other times.[40] Others used social-control assumptions to challenge the Whiggish view that the state functioned to protect the weaker social groups: for example, Diana Leonard Barker's article on the regulation of marriage argues that the primary effect of marriage law is to perpetuate the exploitive entitlements of the stronger spouse, the husband.[41] A more complex form of social-control argument, and one that made many feminists uncomfortable, called attention to the role women reformers played in disciplining men and to women's influence in definitions of "respectability," recognizing the socially conservative content of some feminist reform work.[42] Equally unsettling to a simple social-control model has been the evidence of women's *choice* in the family-wage system—not only accepting it but agitating for it. Patricia Tulloch, writing about Australia, concluded that care-giving was often women's chosen preference, notwithstanding its disadvantaged economic consequences.[43] (In scholarship outside the area of welfare—in labor history, for example—a great deal of evidence has accumulated that working-class married women would have preferred a family-wage system had it been available, because they preferred a chance to devote themselves full-time to domestic labor.)

A common feminist theorization of the social control inherent in the welfare system was the notion of a public or state patriarchy as opposed to private, familial patriarchy. This perspective rested in part on the interpretations of

Talcott Parsons, influential in most sociology of the family several decades ago, that family functions had been transferred to the state. Parsons and his predecessors such as W. I. Thomas had been positive about this transfer, for they believed that the state could provide experts who were needed to socialize citizens in our modern, complex societies; and indeed the strongest critique of this transfer-of-functions tendency came from those, Left, liberal, or Right, who sought to support a family erroneously identified as traditional and who did not notice, or mind, the suppression of women it entailed. Feminists, by contrast, attacked both old and new forms. Carol Brown argued that patriarchy is an umbrella system in which there are public aspects, controlled by men collectively, and private aspects, run by men individually. Since male-headed families are no longer needed to maintain the overall patriarchy, men's individual powers in familial matters have been increasingly delegated, so to speak, to the state.[44] Political theorist Zillah Eisenstein has conceptualized a "capitalist patriarchal state." States are patriarchal, she argues, because the "distinction between public (male) and private (female) life has been inherent in the formation of state societies."[45] She too describes a transition from husband/father's control to state control but sees the nature of the social control of women as continuous and essentially similar.

The "state patriarchy" analysis was extremely useful in pointing to the growing independence of some women from fathers and husbands, but its way of seeing the state did not hold up in the face of mounting historical scholarship about women and family. In the first place, this school of analysis relied on the feminist appropriation of the word "patriarchy" from an older and richer historical usage. Deriving from the Greek, the first English usage, in the sixteenth century, referred to an ecclesiastical hierarchy. By the early seventeenth century "patriarchy" was being used to describe a societal form whose organization was based on, and analogous to, a father's control over his family. It is of course logical that this meaning of the word developed precisely as patriarchal society was beginning to erode in the face of commercial capitalism and the individualist values it promoted. By using a word so filled with fatherly, familial, organic, fixed hierarchical relations to describe today's male supremacy, situated in a nonfamilial, inorganic, meritocratic society, we lose much of its power and nuance, and we mask significant historical change. In the second place, the emphasis on the continuity of "patriarchy" obscures from view the gains of women, or, at best, represents them as an inevitable epiphenomenon of modernization or secularization rather than as the result of collective political struggle, that is, of feminism.

Another feminist scholar of the welfare state, Eli Zaretsky, broke with the emphasis on the continuity of patriarchy and argued, to the contrary, the transformative effect of capitalism on gender, through inventing the public/private distinction. Following from the important insight that only in modern society do we find intense subjectivity and consciousness of private life, Zaretsky argued (like Abramovitz and Nelson and many others) that the welfare state served to reinforce, not to subvert, the private family. Indeed, the very inadequacies of welfare programs, as my own article in this collection shows, grew from the reluctance of welfare agencies and their leaders to undermine the male-headed nuclear family.[46] As Zaretsky noticed, the form of the welfare state—bureaucratized provision for strangers—is public, but its content—individual family "independence" and women's responsibility for child raising and domestic work—private; the result was an alienated public life and an alienated private life.[47] But while Zaretsky recognized historical change, he too argued primarily functionally, neglecting the political struggles over welfare policy and particularly the influence of organized women on the growth of welfare policies, the notion of the private, and the resultant alienation.

All these structural critiques of welfare policy, emphasizing social control, share a major limitation: they rely only on functionalist argumentation, focusing on the rationality of welfare programs for those in power. This is a limitation, not a defect; functionalist analyses are often illuminating. Just as any good detective must ask, "Who benefits?", so that question when posed historically is often an important step towards an explanation. But functionalist explanations assume that welfare policy is coherently beneficial to some group or groups. Thus they cannot explain its often contradictory, even self-defeating aspects. These emerge both from the fragmented and inconsistent goals of policy makers, but also, most important, from the fact that most welfare policies represent the jerry-built compromises that are the artifacts of political and social conflict.

It is not surprising then that the major critique of this social-control model came from scholars looking at welfare historically. Carole Pateman, for example, despite her insistence on the patriarchal nature of welfare, recognizes that dependence on the state may be preferable to dependence on individual men; since women do not "live with the state" as they do with men, they are better able to make collective struggles about their entitlements.[48] Frances Fox Piven in this volume points out a remarkable and constructive contradiction in the welfare system: that this form of support for "dependent" women has in fact made many of them "independent" by giving them employment in the welfare system.

At a certain point the efflorescence of empirical, historical scholarship about welfare created a third "stage," documenting *women's political activism and influence* in the making of that system. At first this work, unlike the critical theoretical work, was primarily celebratory, and rightly so. Historians, on the basis of archival research, uncovered a virtually lost history of women's leadership in welfare, arising from such organizations as the National Consumers' League, the Women's Trade Union League, the National Association

of Colored Women, and the YWCA. But much of the feminist critique of these
Progressive-era liberal programs was lost in this work. Paula Baker's article in
this anthology was one of the first to transcend the celebratory model, to synthesize the effects and meanings of this intense, committed work by thousands
of women, and then to examine its meanings. She illuminates with historical specificity some of the male aspects of the state, such as the fraternalism
of political parties. She argues that women engaged in political activity long
before they won suffrage, a point that adds to a growing theoretical understanding that we must enlarge what counts as politics and the political far
beyond electoral activity.[49] But Baker, synthesizing a great deal of historical
scholarship about women, in fact argues much more: that this women's politics fundamentally changed the nature of the state. She concludes that in the
Progressive era, reaping the harvest from their cultivation of a new kind of
state responsibility, women's very successes permanently ended the separate
male and female political cultures that had characterized the previous centuries
of United States history. In the early twentieth century middle-class men also
began to take up single-issue, extraelectoral agitating and lobbying campaigns
around welfare issues and, indeed, soon came to dominate at least the leadership of this politics.

At first this history, written by white women, recognized only white
women's contributions. This omission was not only a matter of undervalu-
ing the history of minorities, but resulted from the very definitions of what
constituted welfare and welfarist work, developed from the white experience.
A more complex, nonexclusive historical understanding of welfarist work is
beginning to emerge, especially about that of Afro-Americans thanks to the
development of black women's historical scholarship; the histories of Asian-
American, Hispanic-American, and Native American women are also gaining
momentum. The new historical scholarship suggests that women played a
particularly influential role among Afro-Americans, as among whites, in providing for the public welfare, but with considerable differences in form and
content.

White women's strategies were often based on the substantial political influence, economic resources, and social mobility that many had, relying on
wealth and connections to lobby for legislation and win administrative power
through jobs and appointment to committees and commissions. Minority
women, especially women of color, usually lacking influence on government at
any level, had to turn to "private" welfare provision. (Ultimately, studying this
activity may contribute to an expanded and developed theory of the state, as
constituting more than government.) Excluded from private and governmental
white welfare programs, minority welfare activity was often indistinguishable
from civil rights activity.[50]

Out of the minority experience also came different welfare priorities. Particularly influential was the fact that black women were more likely to be employed than white women, black mothers especially more than white mothers; statistically black women were less able and possibly less willing to depend on male wages than were whites. Minority women in general worked in very different jobs than whites, as domestics, agricultural laborers, and laundresses, for example. These limits and choices were partly shared by working-class and other poor white women, but there were also considerable cultural differences. Afro-American reformers were also committed to the family wage ideal, but minority women activists were considerably more likely than whites to accept women's and even mothers' employment as a long-term reality and to seek programs that would make it easier, such as child-care facilities or protection against sexual harassment. This history suggests how racially specific have been what whites regard as mainstream welfare proposals; how deeply our welfare debates have taken place within a uniquely white set of political, economic, and familial assumptions. Moreover, the white women's welfarist activity played a role in maintaining, even reinforcing, class and race exclusions. Their organizations remained all white, not only because they had little interest in or sensitivity to women in other circumstances, but because on occasion they acted to exclude black women. Equally important, the white vision of public welfare—aid to needy children, replacement of male wages for dependent wives, protection for working women in industrial and urban enterprises—took as given the structures that not only excluded blacks but confirmed them in subordination.[51]

For white, even working-class white, women, the history of their work for public welfare confirms the notion that they were struggling within a masculine state, leaving aside the issue of how that maleness was structured and expressed. Even poor, immigrant white women were often operating in cities in which their men were organized, albeit as vassals, into party politics. For black women it is not clear that this conceptualization—a male state—holds. The modifier "white," as in a white male state, was in fact far more than a modifier; it was an absolutely fundamental structuring principle, as Gwendolyn Mink argues in this volume.

Historians have more often recognized the influence in welfare policy of a class perspective—that of the charity workers who were the direct antecedents of today's welfare policy makers. This is a perspective that, as Michael Katz puts it in his recent book, *The Undeserving Poor*, sees the poor as "them" rather than "us."[52] From Charles Loring Brace and the "rescue" or "kidnapping" of poor children (depending on one's point of view) in the 1870s to today's concern of large agribusiness employers for their migrant labor force, welfare policies have been powerfully influenced by the needs of capital and capital/labor relations. However, in the United States this class "otherness" became by the late nineteenth century indivisible from an ethnic/religious/

"racial" otherness because of the heavy immigration of southern and eastern Europeans coincident with peak rates of urbanization and impoverishment. Thus even the class character of a welfare system will be more fully revealed by the growth of scholarship about minorities. Scholarship about class differences in women's visions of and campaigns for social provision is even less developed than that about race. The standard view regarding working-class views on welfare in the welfare-state histories relies on Gompers's pronouncements in opposition to governmental programs; the opinions of rank-and-file unionists remain unexplored and evidence that union locals often supported welfare campaigns neglected. Working-class women, unionized and not, seem unlikely to have been faithful devotees of Gompers's anti-public-welfare attitudes.

These class, race, and gender structures have been constantly contested. A framework for understanding the historical development of the welfare state, if it is to have actual explanatory power, must keep in focus not only the powerlessness but also the challenges and occasionally power of the resistant and sometimes organized subordinates. Moreover, these subordinates are not a homogeneous group: some are controlling, some controlled; alliances among these various subordinated groups may be tactical and shifting, dependent on momentary common enmities to those with more power who are also divided. This approach has at times yielded conclusions that are unexpected and, to some feminists, even threatening, for if women's power is to be recognized, their responsibility must be also; and not only distinctions but even relations of domination among women become influential. Nancy Hewitt's study of women's activism in nineteenth-century Rochester, New York, is a good example of feminist critique of the universality of sisterhood and the often dominant influence of women's class allegiances in their reform activity.[53] Similarly, my studies of family violence showed women charity and caseworkers as controllers of poor women, cast doubt on whether there were any distinctions between the approaches of male and female child protectors, and showed women "clients" actively struggling against efforts to "help" them by their wealthier, altruistic "sisters." [54]

Lisa Peattie and Martin Rein have offered a conceptual approach to welfare contestation that makes gender central, and their perspective is valuable and underrecognized. They want to develop a notion of claims (to goods, services, resources) that does not privilege wages but considers the wage form merely one variety of claiming. Industrial societies have, they argue, three realms within which claims are generated: family, economy, and government.[55] These have different logics: family claims rest on assumptions of what they call "solidarity;" wage claims on assumptions of exchange; and the basis of claims on government is precisely the subject of dispute. Women's methods of claiming have been based more on familial assumptions—not literally kinship solidarity but acceptance of interdependence—because family work has been more important and wage labor less important in most women's histories. The Peattie/Rein approach rejects the dominant view of wages or "earnings" as somehow naturally deserved, but it tries to situate wages as one among several potentially legitimate claims for goods and services, such as those arising from kinship or friendship obligations or from a welfare system. Peattie and Rein's discussion has the particular value of identifying what has been a Marxist, liberal, and conservative consensus in privileging the wage form as *the* means of providing for the citizenry and the implications of this assumption for welfare and for women: dependence on men, with welfare functioning to replace the male wage when it is not forthcoming. (Most feminists who have recognized and criticized this assumption have concluded from this critique that women were *only* victims, missing the mixture of women's support for the family wage system and their resistance to it, and especially missing women's successes.)

Peattie and Rein's concept of solidarity-based claims has something in common with the new discourse of "needs," discussed by Nancy Fraser in this volume. Neither are based on principles of exact exchange or meritocracy. Both Marxist and conservative social critics have remained suspicious of needs as a base of political struggle, because they are so obviously constructed historically by hegemonic cultural and economic powers.[56] Feminists are only just beginning to examine how a "needs" discourse can remain a democratic, oppositional one. The Italian sociologist Laura Balbo is one who has recognized the importance of women in the creation of a "needs-oriented culture," and that women have gained thereby a position of unprecedented strategic political strength and public importance.[57]

But Peattie's and Rein's perspective, although coming from a very different intellectual tradition, has some of the weaknesses of Foucault, another interpreter of welfare measures. In his work on prisons, for example, Foucault was a member of the social-control group of theorists; in other respects —notably in the work on sexuality—Foucault argues for a multiplicity of competing discourses constructing needs. The Peattie and Rein view of competing claims is like Foucault's view of swirling discourses, tending towards pluralism, suggesting at times an indeterminacy so total as to deny the possibility of identifying any particular structures of hegemonic power. (In fact at other times Foucault returns to a quite conventional Marxist view that specific discourses express the material relations of specific historical stages.) The historical evidence will not confirm such an open-ended, power-agnostic view. *Not* everything is possible at every historical moment. Just as definitions of poverty have changed as minimal standards of living grew, so too aspirations and expectations of entitlement have grown. One hundred years ago many single mothers accepted—albeit with agony and fury—that they might have to lose their children in order to support them. Today single mothers feel entitled to raise their own children. This transformation of hopes, indeed of "needs," is a historical artifact, explicable through the study of social and political movements. Histories that trace only legislation and political alliances, and explanations on the basis of some abstract "modernization," are not adequate to chart such transformations.

TOWARDS A NEW WELFARE HISTORY

Gender is thus also involved in welfare history through the personal and collective transformation of its recipients, that is, their increased aspirations. These higher hopes developed, in turn, both from large-scale socioeconomic change, which brought more women into wage earning and independence from men, and from women's movements, which formulated new experiences into greater demands for power and autonomy. The scholars who examine welfare arrangements, in this volume and elsewhere, are also affected by these changes. That is, the critical view of welfare reflects our own high aspirations for ourselves and other women. Histories of welfare lack explanatory power if they do not include the surrounding context of options for women—contraception; deindustrialization and the relative increase in low-wage, unskilled service jobs; the masses of women now in higher education; the conservative and religious revival, which threatens many women's rights and benefits.

It is clear that an accurate welfare history must not only incorporate racial and gender relations of power as fundamental but must also register the agency of these subordinated groups in the construction of programs and policies. It must recognize the "relative autonomy" of the welfare state from direct control by a unified ruling group and register instead that the state is an arena of conflict with a particularly influential role played by social service professionals. The 1988 welfare reform reflects, indeed, a strange and novel combination of conservative motives (tax cutting, hostility to single mothers and women's sexual and reproductive independence, racism) with an acceptance of women's employment. Indeed, the newest reform rests on an alliance between those who believe that employment and reliance on wages is on the whole strengthening to women and those who would use employment as a punishment for deviant women. Diana Pearce, in this volume, argues that the liberal as well as the conservative perspective is potentially injurious to women, based as they are on two alternative models, both male: woman as dependent or woman as second-class worker. The only effective and just reform of welfare would require as preconditions an entirely different valuation of the work of child raising and nurturance of dependents, an end to discrimination against women and minorities in the labor force, *and* a radical increase in employment opportunities overall.

Recent welfare reform should also be examined in the context of the decline of a welfare rights movement and a lack of unity among welfare "experts" about what should be the content of such rights if there are any. Oddly, welfare rights is a subject being discussed now not by historians but by legal scholars, and they examine not the social movements for welfare rights but their legal tracks. These "tracks" are ambiguous. Somewhere between the mothers' pensions of the early twentieth century and the workfare programs of today, recipients gained some kind of legal claim to this "welfare" and to judicial recourse if grants are denied without due process.[58] This recourse is of course largely theoretical, since most welfare recipients by their very need for welfare are unable to mount suits to claim the rights. Moreover some scholars, notably those identified with the "critical legal studies" movement, have taken a pejorative view of this rights discourse altogether, not only because the claimants are so often unable to make them real, but also because the claims are by nature individualized and individualizing, perhaps even antagonistic to collective action. A historical view belies that criticism, since there are many past instances of rights claims provoking, rather than dampening, collective militance. Elizabeth Schneider illustrates such cases in this volume while also constructing a general argument defending rights discourse. In the National Welfare Rights Organization, naming AFDC a right was important in shaping not only the political potential of welfare recipients—their sense of selves as citizens—but also their personal identities.[59] (Although an increasing cross-section of Left, feminist, and liberal welfare policy experts are calling for universal grants as a means of getting rid of the stigma attached to means-tested payments, such a reform seems unlikely in the absence of a strong movement of welfare recipients themselves.)

The most sophisticated studies of welfare will have to improve on what is now available in several respects. One need is a better specification of the balance between "structure and agency," that is, between the long-term economic and ideological patterns that organize societies and the more short-term influence of political elites and political subordinates. More particularly this will require synthesizing structural and functionalist critiques of the operation of welfare programs with detailed histories of their development. It will require rejecting determinist models of historical narrative that assume that final outcomes were somehow inevitable and that defeated proposals were *ipso facto* impossible;[60] it means writing history with foresight as well as hindsight, so to speak, from the vantage point of participants who did not already know the outcome. Another need in welfare scholarship is the fuller integration of activity among minority groups and the influence of racial attitudes and practices throughout the society. This must, furthermore, identify the important differences among the experiences of various minority groups; to the extent that we have made any progress in this area so far, it has been primarily about Afro-

Americans and there has been a tendency to use the terms "minority" and "black" interchangeably. These two needs in turn suggest a needed advance in gender analysis: examining not only the relationships between women and other family members, and between women and the state, but among women as well. Women are not only divided by class, race, and other "differences" but may enter actual conflicts of interest with other women that directly affect their views on welfare policy.[61] The concept of "difference" does not capture what is at issue because it implies a pluralist multiplicity of stories that benignly coexist or interact; it may obscure relations of inequality, domination, and even exploitation among women.

Specifying these goals for a more complex analytic framework should not diminish the need for more of the same as well. Gender-conscious scholarship on this topic is flourishing, but "gender-blind" (or really, gender-obscuring) scholarship is also. It will take a long time, perhaps even another whole "wave" of a women's movement and a women's-studies renascence, to teach everyone that welfare as an academic topic or a social issue cannot be understood without particular attention to the situation of women and the gender system of the society.

NOTES

1   There are already several collections of feminist articles on welfare from the U.K., Norway, and Australia, for example: Cora V. Baldock and Bettina Cass, *Women, Social Welfare, and the State in Australia* (Sydney: Allen and Unwin, 1983); H. Holter, ed., *Patriarchy in a Welfare Society* (Oslo: Universitetsforlaget, 1984); Jane Lewis, ed., *Women's Welfare Women's Rights* (London: Croom Helm, 1983); Jennifer Dale and Peggy Foster, *Feminists and the Welfare State* (London: Routledge and Kegan Paul, 1986). In Britain a stronger radical social work perspective has produced more feminist scholarship on social welfare. There are excellent books such as Gillian Pascall's *Social Policy: A Feminist Analysis* (London: Tavistock, 1986) and Elizabeth Wilson's *Women and the Welfare State* (London: Tavistock, 1977).

2   For an introduction offering a British social work perspective, see Pascall, *Social Policy*.

3   Jill Quadagno, "Theories of the Welfare State," *Annual Reviews in Sociology* 13 (1987): 109–28.

4   Robert Bremner, *From the Depths. The Discovery of Poverty in the United States* (New York: New York University Press, 1956); James T. Patterson, *America's Struggle Against Poverty 1900–1980* (Cambridge: Harvard University Press, 1981); Walter I. Trattner, *From Poor Law to Welfare State: A History of Social Welfare in America* (New York: Free Press, 1974, 1984); John Ehrenreich, *The Altruis-*

tic Imagination: A History of Social Work and Social Policy in the United States (Ithaca: Cornell University Press, 1985); David A. Rochefort, *American Social Welfare Policy: Dynamics of Formulation and Change* (Boulder & London: Westview Press, 1986); Michael B. Katz, *In the Shadow of the Poorhouse: A Social History of Welfare in America* (New York: Basic, 1986). This omission is primarily characteristic of liberals; conservatives have been more likely to talk openly about the fact that their goals include the maintenance of certain nonneutral gender patterns, especially the division of labor in the family. See Allen Hunter, "Children in the Service of Conservatism: Parent-Child Relations in the New Right's Pro-Family Rhetoric." University of Wisconsin Institute for Legal Studies Working Paper 2-8, April 1988. For references, see especially George Gilder, *Wealth and Poverty* (New York: Basic Books, 1981) and Charles Murray, *Losing Ground. American Social Policy, 1950–1980* (New York: Basic Books, 1984).

5 Patricia Huckle, "The Womb Factor: Pregnancy Policies and Employment of Women," in *Women, Power and Policy*, ed. Ellen Boneparth (New York: Pergamon, 1982), 144–61.

6 Heide Gerstenberger, "The Poor and the Respectable Worker: On the Introduction of Social Insurance in Germany," *Labour History* 48 (May 1985): 69–85.

7 For example, Patrich M. Horan and Patricia Lee Austin in "The Social Bases of Welfare Stigma," *Social Problems* 21 (1974): 648–57, virtually ignore gender.

8 Linda Gordon, *Heroes of Their Own Lives: The Politics and History of Family Violence, Boston, 1880–1960* (New York: Viking/Penguin, 1988), chap. 4.

9 For examples, see Emily I. Abel, "Adult Daughters and Care for the Elderly," *Feminist Studies* 12, no. 3 (Fall 1986): 479–97; Laura Balbo, "The Servicing Work of Women and the Capitalist State," in *Political Power and Social Theory*, ed. Maurice Zeitlin (Greenwich, Conn.: JAI Press, 1982), 251–70. On women as translating between money and needs, see Batya Weinbaum and Amy Bridges, "The Other Side of the Paycheck: Monopoly Capital and the Structure of Consumption," in *Capitalist Patriarchy and the Case for Socialist Feminism*, ed. Zillah Eisenstein (New York: Monthly Review Press, 1979), 190–205.

10 Jill Quadagno, "From Old Age Assistance to Supplemental Security Income: The Political Economy of Relief in the South 1935–1972," in *The Politics of Social Policy in the United States*, ed. Margaret Weir, Ann Shola Orloff, and Theda Skocpol (Princeton: Princeton University Press, 1988); Jerry Cates, *Insuring Inequality: Administrative Leadership in Social Security, 1935–1954* (Ann Arbor: University of Michigan, 1983); Harvard Sitkoff, *A New Deal for Blacks: The Emergence of Civil Rights as a National Issue, The Depression Decade* (New York: Oxford, 1978); Raymond Wolters, *Negroes and the Great Depression: The Problem of Economic Recovery* (Westport, Conn.: Greenwood, 1970); Wolters, "The New Deal and the Negro," in John Braeman et al., eds., *The New Deal: The National Level* (Columbus: Ohio State University Press, 1975).

11 Martha Ackelsberg, "Dependency, Resistance and the Welfare State. Contributions and Limits of Feminist Theory," in *Gender and the Origins of the Welfare State*. Proceedings of Conferences at the Harvard Center for European Studies, 1987–88.

12   The first to apply the characterization "Whig" to a view that the progress of repre-
     sentative government led inevitably to the welfare state was probably Asa Briggs
     in his "The Welfare State in Historical Perspective," *Archives Europeennes de
     Sociologie*, II, no. 2 (1961): 221–58.

13   Jill Quadagno, "Theories of the Welfare State," *American Review of Sociology* 13
     (1987), 112.

14   Michael Shalev, "The Social Democratic Model and Beyond: Two Generations
     of Comparative Research on the Welfare State," in *Comparative Social Research*
     (1983) 6, 315–51; Quadagno, "Theories of the Welfare State," 115.

15   This model is used by John Ehrenreich, *The Altruistic Imagination*.

16   This point is also extremely well argued in a review of my book by Ann Withorn,
     "Radicalizing History: Writing about Women's Lives and the State," *Radical
     America* 22, nos. 2–3 (1989): 45–51.

17   In the following discussion I am indebted to Theda Skocpol's "Political Response
     to Capitalist Crisis: Neo-Marxist Theories of the State and the Case of the New
     Deal," *Politics and Society* 10, no. 2 (1980): 155–201.

18   Ralph Miliband, *The State in Capitalist Society* (London: Weidenfield & Nicolson,
     1969).

19   The difficulty in positing a homogeneous set of interests among men has been a
     problem for all theorizing about "patriarchy" or male supremacy. This difficulty is
     one reason that I prefer a historical approach to conceptualizing male power, de-
     scribing its actual operations in specific historical circumstances, examining class
     and ethnic groups among men as well as particular relations between men and
     women.

20   Nicos Poulantzas, "The Problem of the Capitalist State," in *Ideology in Social
     Science*, ed. Robin Blackburn (New York: Random House, 1973).

21   Fred Block, "The Ruling Class Does Not Rule: Notes on the Marxist Theory of
     the State," in *Revising State Theory. Essays in Politics and Postindustrialism*, ed.
     Fred Block (Philadelphia: Temple, 1987), 51–68.

22   Theda Skocpol and John Ikenberry, "The Political Formation of the American
     Welfare State in Historical and Comparative Perspective," *Comparative Social
     Research* 6 (1983): 87–148, for example.

23   In the following discussion about British social-welfare theory I am indebted to
     Pascall, *Social Policy*.

24   Pascall, *Social Policy*, 9.

25   Hilary Rose, "Re-reading Titmuss: The Sexual Division of Welfare," *Journal of
     Social Policy* 10, no. 4 (1981): 477–502.

26   Sylvia Law, "Women, Work, Welfare, and the Preservation of Patriarchy," *Uni-
     versity of Pennsylvania Law Review* 131, no. 6 (May 1983): 1251–331; Joan Cum-
     mings, "Sexism in Social Welfare: Some Thoughts on Strategy for Structural
     Change," *Catalyst*, no. 8 (1980): 7–34; Hilary Land, "Women: Supporters or Sup-
     ported?" in *Sexual Divisions and Society: Process and Change*, ed. Diana Leonard
     Barker and Sheila Allen (London: Tavistock, 1979), 108–32; Hilary Land, "Who
     Still Cares for the Family? Recent Developments in Income Maintenance, Taxation
     and Family Law," in *Journal of Social Policy* 7, no. 3 (July 1978): 275–84.

27 Pat Thane, "Women and the Poor Law in Victorian and Edwardian England," *History Workshop: A Journal of Socialist Historians*, no. 6 (Autumn 1978): 29–51.

28 Gail Bushwalter King, "Women and Social Security: An Applied History Overview," in *Social Science History* 6, no. 2 (Spring 1982): 227–32.

29 Diana M. Pearce, "Toil and Trouble: Women Workers and Unemployment Compensation," *Signs* 10, no. 3 (Spring 1985): 439–59.

30 Irene Diamond, "Women and Housing: The Limitations of Liberal Reform," in *Women, Power and Policy*, ed. Ellen Boneparth (New York: Pergamon, 1982), 109–17.

31 Mimi Abramovitz, *Regulating the Lives of Women. Social Welfare Policy from Colonial Times to the Present* (Boston: South End Press, 1988).

32 For example, Katz, *In the Shadow of the Poorhouse*, 238–39.

33 Hace Sorel Tishler, *Self-Reliance and Social Security 1870–1917* (Port Washington, N.Y.: National University Publications, 1971), 142.

34 See Linda Gordon, "What Does Welfare Regulate?" *Social Research* 55, no. 4 (Winter 1988): 609–30.

35 Hilary Land, "The Family Wage," *Feminist Review* 6 (1980): 55–77; Jill Roe, "The End is Where We Start From: Women and Welfare Since 1901," in *Women, Social Welfare and the State in Australia*, ed. Cora V. Baldock and Bettina Cass (Boston: George Allen & Unwin, 1983), 1–19; Jane Lewis, "Dealing with Dependency: State Practices and Social Realities, 1870–1945," in *Women's Welfare, Women's Rights*, ed. Jane Lewis (London: Croom Helm, 1983), 17–37; Mary McIntosh, "The Welfare State and the Needs of the Dependent Family," in *Fit Work for Women*, ed. Sandra Burman (New York: St. Martin's Press, 1979), 153–72; Mimi Abramowitz, *Regulating the Lives of Women*, esp. chaps. 1 and 3; Linda Gordon, "What Does Welfare Regulate?"

36 Helene Silverberg, "Women, Welfare and the State," *Cornell Journal of Social Relations*, vol. 18 (Spring 1985): 1–12.

37 Michael Walzer, "Socializing the Welfare State," in *Democracy and the Welfare State*, ed. Amy Gutmann (Princeton: Princeton University Press, 1988), 13–26.

38 Carole Pateman, "The Patriarchal Welfare State," in *Democracy and the Welfare State*, ed. Gutmann, 231–60. See also her *The Sexual Contract* (Stanford: Stanford University Press, 1988). On issues of citizenship see also Susan Moller Okin, *Justice, Gender, and the Family* (New York: Basic Books, 1989).

39 Barbara Ehrenreich and Deirdre English, *For Her Own Good. 150 Years of the Experts' Advice to Women* (New York: Anchor/Doubleday, 1978).

40 Alicia Frohman, "Day Care and the Regulation of Women's Labor Force Participation," *Catalyst*, no. 2 (1978): 5–17. She does not seem aware that Ruth Milkman has demonstrated that the reserve-army-of-labor hypothesis does not work for women, because the labor market is so sexually segregated that it has little flexibility to exchange women's and men's jobs. See Ruth Milkman, "Women's Work and the Economic Crisis: Some Lessons from the Great Depression," *Review of Radical Political Economics* 8, no. 1 (Spring 1976): 73–97.

41 Diana Leonard Barker, "The Regulation of Marriage: Repressive Benevolence," in *Power and the State*, ed. Gary Littlejohn et al. (New York: St. Martin's Press,

1978), 239–66. Libba Gaje Moore's dissertation, "Mothers' Pensions: The Origins of the Relationship Between Women and the Welfare State," University of Massachusetts, 1986, comes to similar conclusions.

42   Ann Douglas, *The Feminization of American Culture* (New York: Knopf, 1977); William Leach, *True Love and Perfect Union: The Feminist Reform of Sex and Society* (New York: Basic Books, 1980); Ellen DuBois and Linda Gordon, "Seeking Ecstasy on the Battlefield: Nineteenth-Century Feminist Views of Sexuality," *Feminist Studies* 9, no. 1 (Spring 1983); Linda Gordon, *Heroes of Their Own Lives*; Linda Gordon, "Race and Class Divisions in Women's Welfare Activism," forthcoming.

43   Patricia Tulloch, "Gender and Dependency," in *Unfinished Business: Social Justice for Women in Australia* (Sydney: George Allen & Unwin, 1984), 19–37.

44   Carol Brown, "Mothers, Fathers and Children: From Private to Public Patriarchy," in *Women and Revolution*, ed. Lydia Sargent (Boston: South End Press, 1981), 239–67. Norwegian scholar Helga Maria Hernes conceptualizes this as a transition from private to public dependence; see her "Women and the Welfare State. The Transition from Private to Public Dependence," in *Patriarchy in a Welfare Society*, ed. H. Holter. United States feminist philosopher Ann Ferguson makes a finer and somewhat different distinction between "father patriarchy," "husband patriarchy" in the modern period, and "public (capitalist) patriarchy." See her "On Conceiving Motherhood and Sexuality: A Feminist Materialist Approach," in *Mothering. Essays in Feminist Theory*, ed. Joyce Trebilcot (Totowa, N.J.: Rowman & Allanheld, 1984), 153–82.

45   Zillah R. Eisenstein, *Feminism and Sexual Equality* (New York: Monthly Review Press, 1984), 89.

46   For more on this see Linda Gordon, "Single Mothers and Child Neglect," *American Quarterly* 37, no. 2 (Spring 1985): 173–92.

47   Eli Zaretsky, "The Place of the Family in the Origins of the Welfare State," in *Rethinking the Family. Some Feminist Questions*, ed. Barrie Thorne (New York: Longman, 1982), 188–224.

48   Pateman, "The Patriarchal Welfare State."

49   A welcome addition to Baker's work will be Theda Skocpol's *Protecting Soldiers and Mothers. The Politics of Social Provision in the United States, 1870s–1920s*, forthcoming. On enlarging the notion of the political, see Linda Gordon, "What Should Women's Historians Do: Politics, Social Theory, and Women's History," *Marxist Perspectives*, no. 3 (Fall 1978).

50   For a good overview of this activity, see Paula Giddings, *When and Where I Enter. The Impact of Black Women on Race and Sex in America* (New York: William Morrow, 1984).

51   Linda Gordon, "Race and Class Divisions in Women's Welfare Activism," forthcoming.

52   Michael Katz, *The Undeserving Poor: From the War on Poverty to the War on Welfare* (New York: Pantheon, 1989), epilogue.

53   Nancy Hewitt, *Women's Activism and Social Change. Rochester, New York 1822–1972* (Ithaca, N.Y.: Cornell Univesity Press, 1984).

54 Gordon, *Heroes of Their Own Lives*; Gordon, "The Frustrations of Family Violence Social Work: An Historical Critique," *Journal of Sociology and Social Welfare* XV, no. 4 (December 1988).

55 Lisa Peattie and Martin Rein, *Women's Claims: A Study in Political Economy* (Oxford: Oxford University Press, 1983), esp. p. 9ff.

56 See Agnes Heller, "Can 'True' and 'False' Needs be Posited?" in *The Power of Shame. A Rational Perspective* (London: Routledge, Kegan Paul, 1985), chap. 5, for just one example.

57 Laura Balbo, "Family, Women, and the State: Notes Towards A Typology of Family Roles and Public Intervention," in *Changing Boundaries of the Political*, ed. Charles S. Maier (Cambridge: Cambridge University Press, 1987), 201–19.

58 There is an interesting legal debate about *when* the rights claim emerged. Sylvia Law, "Women, Work, and Welfare"; Rand E. Rosenblatt, "Legal Entitlement and Welfare Benefits," in *The Politics of Law. A Progressive Critique*, ed. David Kairys (New York: Pantheon, 1982), 262–78; William H. Simon, "The Invention and Reinvention of Welfare Rights," *Maryland Law Review* 44, no. 1 (1985): 1–37; William H. Simon, "Rights and Redistribution in the Welfare System," *Stanford Law Review* 38, no. 143 (1986): 1431–516.

59 Guida West, *The National Welfare Rights Movement: The Social Protest of Poor Women* (New York: Praeger, 1981).

60 For an egregious example of this kind of thinking see Daniel Levine, *Poverty and Society: The Growth of the American Welfare State in International Comparison* (New Brunswick: Rutgers University Press, 1988).

61 For example, Deborah G. White, "Fettered Sisterhood: Class and Classism in Early Twentieth Century Black Women's History," forthcoming; Linda Gordon, "Race and Class Divisions in Women's Welfare Activism," forthcoming.

CHAPTER 2

The Gender Basis of American Social Policy

VIRGINIA SAPIRO

During the last quarter of the nineteenth century, women—thousands of them —became increasingly organized and active in the attempt to promote the general welfare, especially by helping the most vulnerable members of society. As individual leaders and as group participants they were instrumental in organizing and nationalizing movements for public health (mental and physical), poor relief, penal and other institutional reform, education for the previously uneducated, and child welfare. As the nineteenth century waned and the twentieth dawned, women were prominent among proponents of a principle that was hitherto nearly alien to American ideology but that has now, a century later, come to be an accepted part of our political views: the government and, they increasingly argued, the national government, have a responsibility to promote the general welfare actively by providing initiative and support where necessary. The degree and types of support remain, perhaps more now than then, matters of profound political contention, but in the late twentieth century even the most conservative ideologues tend to agree that government must provide a "safety net" for its people.

The late nineteenth and early twentieth centuries were also a time during which thousands of women, many of them the same as those involved in the general welfare movements, were agitating to promote women's welfare specifically.[1] The suffrage movement, aimed at providing women with what we now regard as the basic right of citizenship and the basic means of leverage within a democratic political system, is only the best-known facet of the women's movement of that era. As many historians have demonstrated, a large proportion of nineteenth-century feminists came to their concerns for women through their charitable and political efforts aimed at the needy.[2] Moreover, many nineteenth-century feminists conceived of their woman-directed activities as means to improve the lot not just of women but of women's families and communities.[3]

The development of American social welfare policy was heavily influenced by women, who often saw themselves acting on behalf of women. These women—many of them feminists—were instrumental in the development of the American social welfare state, such as it is: the efforts in the 1840s of Dorothea Dix to get Congress to provide money and land for the construction of mental institutions (the bill passed but President Franklin Pierce's veto was sustained); the establishment of the United States Sanitary Commission; Josephine Shaw Lowell's New York Charity Organization Society and its counterparts; the settlement movement; Florence Kelley's National Consumers' League; many Progressive leaders; the instigators of the Children's Bureau; and the authors and primary promoters of the 1921 Infancy and Maternity (Sheppard-Towner) Bill.

The history of movements for women's welfare and for the general welfare are virtually inseparable. But we can go further and argue that it is not possible to understand the underlying principles, structure, and effects of our social welfare system and policies without understanding their relationship to gender roles and gender ideology. Three examples suggest how important understanding this relationship is: widows' or mothers' pensions, protective labor legislation, and the Sheppard-Towner Act of 1921.

In 1911, Missouri became the first state to provide for cash assistance to widows with dependent children. By 1935, the date of the nationalization of this policy through Title IV (Aid to Dependent Children) of the Social Security Act, all states except South Carolina and Georgia had acted similarly. As Walter Trattner argues, "Widow's pension laws marked a definite turning point in the welfare policies of many states. In theory at least, they removed the stigma of charity for a large number of welfare recipients. They also broke down the nineteenth-century tradition against public home relief."[4] Before the advent of widows' pensions, public pensions were limited to military personnel or civil servants, people whose willingness to work for limited public salaries would be rewarded with security.[5] Widows' pensions were different in that they provided for needy private persons. The Social Security Act, through Aid to Dependent Children (ADC), did the same at the federal level.

Protective labor legislation offers another example of the role that gender differentiation played in promoting social welfare ideas within the United States. At the turn of the century, efforts to provide for public regulation of working conditions advocated by both trade unions and groups such as the National Consumers' League were turned back consistently on the grounds that they would conflict with the right of employers and employees to make contracts freely and unimpeded by forces outside the market. The major turning point in employment and workplace policy came in 1908 when the Supreme Court, in *Muller v. Oregon,* upheld the right of a state to limit the working hours of women.[6] Although protective labor legislation has been highly contentious among feminists from the first for reasons that will be discussed, the "thin edge of the wedge" for regulation of the workplace was provided by policies based on a particular construction of gender ideology.

A third example of the importance of gender in the expansion of American social policy is the Sheppard-Towner Bill, enacted in 1921 and in force until Herbert Hoover assured its demise in 1929. Sheppard-Towner provided for the first time for matching federal grants-in-aid to states for the purpose of promoting child and maternal health services. This was the first time the federal government provided grants for state welfare programs other than education,[7] and it provided the precedent for later efforts. The program was widely attacked as the first incursion of "bolshevism" into the United States and was the subject of the first major—but certainly not the last—campaign against "state medicine." [8] Anxiety over socialism was one of the major reasons for the demise of the pure laissez-faire system of labor contract in the marketplace. Sheppard-Towner put government, notably the federal government, in the business of providing the public with social services other than protective services and education.

These cases mark turning points in American political ideology. The notion that "that government governs best that governs least" was transformed, at least to the degree that the standard of what constitutes "least" was questioned. To the belief that people should be self-reliant, which meant providing for themselves and their families, was added the idea that it was good for private individuals to engage in charitable acts (although it was not good for individuals to expect to depend upon these acts), and also that government had some responsibility to provide. Government was now to promote the general welfare not just by assuring civil order but by providing for that welfare directly.

Of crucial importance here, women were the apparent beneficiaries of these policies. When these policies were first set in place, there was no intention on the part of most policy makers to set any precedents for other parallel reforms or, certainly, for more widespread changes in the structure or theoretical basis of political economy. Indeed, there was considerable opposition to these changes, specifically because they might turn out to be turning points and precedents, as some interest groups such as the labor and the Progressive movements hoped they might be. Why were women so central to these changes? What does this "coincidence" tell us about the development of gender ideology, political ideology, and social policy in the United States?

Unfortunately, the standard treatments of social policy offer little assistance in answering these questions because the relationships among gender, feminism, and the development of social welfare policy has generally been neglected outside of feminist scholarship. Marxists and non-Marxists alike have identified the development of the welfare state as a part of the political process of the development of capitalist industrialism; to the non-Marxist especially it is a part of the political transformation of societies into mass democracies. Within the standard view of the history of welfare states, as Peter Flora and Arnold J. Heidenheimer write, "one may interpret the welfare state as an answer to increasing demands for socioeconomic equality or as the institutionalization of social rights relative to the development of civil and political rights." [9] Just so; but academic analyses tend to focus on demands and rights specifically relevant to class conflicts within society, thus obscuring the roles of women and gender. This, interestingly, is the case as much for non-Marxists as for Marxists. A woman's economic interests are generally assumed to follow from a husband when the woman is married, and especially a homemaker, and to be defined adequately by standard class definitions in cases where women are employed. The problem is that standard views of economic interest and organization are defined primarily through male history and experience, and feminist activists have often been aware of these differences. [10]

Analysis of the theory and practice of social policy has rarely taken full account of the relevance of gender, and it often implicitly accepts without examination certain paternalistic and patriarchal assumptions about the nature of gender that are also embedded in the policies themselves. As a result, there is little understanding of how social policy affects women in particular and, more generally, how women's welfare is linked to general welfare.

The remainder of this article examines the relationship between women's welfare and the general welfare within the framework of American social policy, especially as it treats economic dependency. Women have been defined primarily as dependents, *because* others depend upon their dependency. American social policy, it shall be argued, not only assumes but helps to maintain this state of affairs. Further, many social policies that most affect women are not, in fact, aimed primarily *at* them but rather, in many sense, *through* them. Finally, analysis of the relationship between women and social policy does not teach us "only" about women and social policy but about our construction and understanding of social policy and the general welfare more broadly.

AMERICAN SOCIAL POLICY: THE STANDARD VERSION

Social policy is, as Albert Weale has written, "a deliberate attempt by governments to promote individual and social welfare in certain specific dimensions using any suitable policy instruments." [11] This definition is useful because it underscores the point that social policy is not a matter simply of social services or even more narrowly (and perhaps more commonly believed) social services for the poor. Social policy, in other words, is not always what it seems to be to the untrained eye. Some of the most important social services are not aimed at the poor (e.g., public universities), and many of the social policies that might do the most to promote individual and social welfare are not services (e.g., occupational safety and health regulations or benefits policies and nondiscrimination policies). Indeed it has been argued repeatedly that it is not easy and not always worthwhile to draw definite boundaries among social policy and fiscal or civil rights policies.[12]

For the first century and more of American history, social policy basically rested on the belief that the welfare of the society and its component parts could best be assured by allowing—encouraging—individuals to pursue their own interests freely. This notion was as much a moral as an economic belief. What came to be known as the "protestant work ethic" supported moral and policy distinctions made among the "just" desserts earned by the diligent well-off and the shiftless poor and the unfortunate "deserving" poor. As Robert Goodin has pointed out, the emphasis on self-reliance was, at its heart, a concern about the moral character of individuals. Conservatives continue to maintain, despite empirical evidence to the contrary,[13] that provision of welfare benefits makes individuals psychologically dependent and removes their motivation to pursue their interests in the marketplace and, therefore, short circuits the entire system. In other words, provision of welfare changes the character of individuals so as to make them bad and unproductive members of society.

In practical terms, therefore, the nation was to be composed of diligent hardworking individuals who competed in the marketplace (or, for the agrarian ideal of self-sufficiency, worked their land) to make something of themselves and to provide for themselves. With the growth of industrialism and the ascendency of a middle class, the principle of individualistic competition in a free market to assure self-sufficiency became a moral, social, political, and economic ideal. The implications of this set of beliefs for social welfare have been well summarized by Ramesh Mishra: "Paternalism—of the state but also of the employer—is frowned upon."

Not the bonds of status but those of contract between "free" men typifies the basic model of social relationship outside the family. Translating these generalities into patterns of welfare, we might say that the middle-class society is likely to develop a "residual" system of welfare. In the early states of industrialization neither state nor enterprise welfare is favored. Instead, friendly societies, voluntary organizations, charities, and market responses to the various problems and needs are encouraged.[14]

This is precisely what happened during the second half of the nineteenth century in the United States. There was an impressive growth of charity and social action (a growth especially among women) as the more negative by-products of industrialism became more obvious, but this "social action was largely a voluntary do-it-yourself arrangement among individuals with a common interest."[15]

Should individuals be in need of assistance or cooperation, such arrangements were to be made on a voluntary basis. There were clear hierarchies of responsibility or, as Michael Walzer puts it, spheres of justice.[16] The core in which assistance could be freely sought and in which others had the most responsibility to provide was the immediate family followed by more distant relatives. At the next stage were neighbors and others in the local community. As the public domain began to share in provision, the state was seen as more obliged than the federal government. Above all, aid and cooperation were to come from the private world rather than from government. As James Leiby notes, only in the twentieth century was "social welfare" rather than "charity and correction" widely used to label assistance. "Social welfare," he argues, connotes "a recognition of human interdependence . . . , a sense of mutual responsibilities and goals among [society's] classes and parts, and of the need for common policies to realize them." [17]

The earliest social policies fall into two general categories. The first, into which we might put social insurance (originally called "workingman's insurance") and pensions, were aimed at helping or providing some added security to those who were working to help themselves and their society. The second was assistance aimed at those who seemed most inevitably dependent: paupers without relatives to help, children and especially orphans, and "defectives" such as the insane and criminally inclined. Later a third type of social policy developed but did not really flower until the post–World War II era: social regulation or government intervention in the rules and procedures of the market. Above all, American social policy was developed with a continuing distaste for paternalism and an emphasis on allowing individuals, and by later policies helping individuals, compete as individuals in an open market in order to achieve self-sufficiency and self-reliance.

The previous paragraphs offer little more than a standard, albeit boiled down, rendition of American social policy thinking and practice. Turning our attention to the place of women in this story we find that this rendition is seriously flawed. It is written in apparently generic gender-neutral terms and, therefore, masks an extremely gender-based story.

THE REVISED VERSION: BEYOND GENDER NEUTRALITY

In order to see the fault in analysis of social policy and in social policy itself, let us look again at the main themes: dependence and self-reliance, individualism and paternalism. In fact, if we consider the subjects of policy not in the apparently gender-neutral terms (such as individual, worker, family) usually used but in the explicit terms of male and female, we find that the dominant ideology underlying social policy thinking and action has never stressed individualism pure and simple. It has never been uniformly opposed to either dependency or paternalism, and it has never supported a universal value of self-reliance, especially in economic terms. Instead, it has supported individualism, independence, and self-reliance for some people (primarily men) and dependence and reliance on paternalism for others (primarily women). This is largely because individuals have been viewed in terms of functional roles depending upon gender. Men are regarded as breadwinners for themselves and their families, and women are regarded as wives and mothers who are and should be economically dependent upon those breadwinners.

In order to understand the relationship of women to social policy, it is necessary to consider policy directly regarding the ability of women to provide for themselves. As we have seen, the primary purpose of most American social policy is supposed to be to allow "individuals" to provide for themselves, to reward those who have done so, and to provide a back-up for those who have not been able to do so because of circumstances beyond their own control. If, however, this really was "the" American approach to social policy, it should apply in a gender-neutral way. In fact, this view did not apply to women; indeed, throughout most of American history it has been contradictory to the predominant prescription for women.

Until the enactment of the Married Women's Property Acts in the 1840s, women could not own property, including that which they inherited or earned through their own labor, and they could not make contacts without their husband's consent. In other words, women were barred by law from engaging in the activities that were supposed to be the primary principle of political economy and the civil right most fiercely protected by American law up to the twentieth century—the right to contract freely to pursue one's economic interest. The reason was the common-law principle of *femme couverte*. Women's economic and political identities and interests were incorporated into (not with) those of their husbands. Women's only voluntary contract was the marriage contract, by which they were thought to be giving blanket tacit consent to most future decisions made by their husbands.[18]

Even when free women gained the right to own and manage property and to make contracts, they did not gain the right to provide for themselves. If employers wanted to bar women as a class from employment, their right to do so was protected by the principle of governmental noninterference in private contracts. Moreover, as women began to seek training and jobs outside the women's sphere of employment (domestic labor and sewing) states stepped in to help bar women's further progress.

The first Supreme Court case concerning women's economic rights was *Bradwell v. Illinois,* which in 1874 upheld a state's right to prohibit women's admission to the bar.[19] Although the main reason offered by the Court was the principle of state's rights, the concurring opinion expressed the paternalistic view that has been repeated in law and political argument numerous times:

"Man is, or should be, woman's protector and defender," and, therefore, must protect her from the world of work and individualistic competition. Further, "the harmony, not to say identity, of interests and views which belong, or should belong, to the family institution is repugnant to the idea of a woman adopting a distinct and independent career from that of her husband." Most telling of all, the prohibition covered not just married but all women, because women are defined by their actual or potential statuses as wives and mothers. "The paramount destiny and mission of women are to fulfill the noble and benign offices of wife and mother. This is the law of the Creator. And the rules of society must be adapted to the general constitution of things and cannot be based upon exceptional cases." Whereas the Protestant work ethic as applied to income-producing work was a moral and economic principle for men, economic dependency was a moral, God-given principle for women.

Government became increasingly involved in restricting women's abilities to provide for themselves and their families and even in denying women their own rights of citizenship separate from those of their husbands.[20] Public institutions of higher education, including the land grant colleges, were generally sex segregated and, therefore, kept women from the programs that might lead them to professional careers. Women were barred from certain job classifications and in some jobs such as teaching, they were refused employment if they were married or certainly, if they were pregnant. Female employees were fired if they got married or if they became pregnant. Government discriminated against women in pay. Even the National Industrial Recovery Act (NIRA) signed by Franklin Delano Roosevelt in 1933 provided for sex differences in pay despite intensive lobbying by women's groups and assurances by Eleanor Roosevelt and Labor Secretary Frances Perkins. Moreover, women's jobs were especially likely to be excluded from minimum wage regulations, and the Public Works Administration and Federal Emergency Relief Administration tended to emphasize projects that·involved male jobs.[21]

Not until nearly a century after *Bradwell,* in Title VII of the 1964 Civil Rights Act, did the federal government take a stand against sex discrimination in hiring; only in 1971 did the Supreme Court, in *Phillips v. Martin Marietta,* argue that employers may not discriminate against women, in this case women with children.[22] Following a case in which the Supreme Court upheld the right of an employer to discriminate against pregnant women in occupational benefits,[23] Congress passed the 1978 Pregnancy Discrimination Act, which incorporated into Title VII the principle of nondiscrimination against pregnant women.

Because social policy tends to be analyzed as a class issue, we tend to look to labor movements and unions as some of the primary instigators of progressive social policy insofar as their role is to pursue the interests of workers. Although women have benefited from labor organization in gender-specific ways (e.g., gender differentials in pay are lower among unionized than nonunionized workers), the early history of the labor movement shows considerable support for paternalistic and exclusionary treatment of women in the job market.[24] Although women constituted about 30 percent of printers by 1831 and 16 percent of newspaper compositors by 1850, for example, print unions would not accept women to full membership until 1873.[25] Other unions continued to bar women. Samuel Gompers, among other union activists, was opposed to women workers on the grounds that they took wages from men and destroyed the family. In 1898 he urged the government to prohibit women from federal employment.

The perspective of labor unions leads us back to specific consideration of social policy. The labor movement and its leaders such as Gompers were among the most committed supporters of protective labor legislation for women. Their reasons varied. Certainly some of the motivation was the desire to assist those in a relatively weak position in the labor market. As suggested earlier, unions saw woman-directed policies as the "thin edge of the wedge" of more widespread protections for all workers. But another major motivation in the United States as in other countries was to use legislation directed at women to protect male jobs and wages. Protective labor legislation for women could directly and indirectly keep women out of competition for "male" jobs and make them less desirable to employers. Indeed, "protection" has generally been applied less strenuously to "female" than to "male" jobs. Hours and weightlifting limits, for example, were never applied to domestic labor, paid or unpaid. Protective labor legislation made women more expensive to hire than they had been. As feminist observers have often remarked, this type of policy has served at least as much to keep women out of higher paying jobs as it has to improve their working conditions. This has been true of later types of protective legislation as well.[26]

Another early proposal of the labor and other movements concerned with workers was not just the provision of a *living* wage but of a family wage; that is, a wage that would give the (male) breadwinner the ability to support his family without needing to depend on a wage-earning wife. Again, the thinking did not simply concern the economic situation of a family but the character of those in the family. Women, it was thought, should not have to seek employment because their jobs were to care for the other members of the family. Men should not have to compete with women for jobs; after all, men need to support their families. Most important, "manhood" was defined in part by the ability of a man to support his family. Men were—and still to some degree are—taught to feel emasculated when they depend on women's wages. The goodness or badness of dependency depends on who is depending on whom. Husbands' economic dependence upon wives is bad. Wives' economic dependence upon husbands is good, in part because it is often thought to allow men to be more independent.[27]

Most social policy aimed at women has been designed explicitly to benefit them in their capacity as wives and mothers and more particularly, to benefit those who depend upon them for nurturance and domestic service: husbands, children, and elderly relatives. The widows' pensions and Sheppard-Towner Act mentioned previously are early examples. In an important sense, women have not been the main targets of these policies but rather, they were the main conduit of these policies, which were aimed at providing for children. The original construction of ADC provided for support of the children in one-parent families. Only later was support extended to the care giver.[28]

Social policy aimed at women has been designed to benefit them in their capacity as wives and mothers only in a limited sense. Its intention has been to enable them to *care* for their families and not, by and large, to *provide* for them in the sense that is expected of a breadwinner. Often, as in the case of ADC (and its later incarnation as AFDC (Aid to Families with Dependent Children)), it has been aimed at relieving mothers of the "need to work." Women were expected to remain economically dependent because of domestic responsibilities assigned to them. In contrast, the "man in the house" provisions, which allowed administrators to withhold funds if any evidence was found to indicate a man (related or not) was living in, or even a frequent visitor to the house, underscore the degree to which men were still regarded as responsible for economic support.

Only in the late 1960s and especially the 1970s were any serious efforts made to enable women to be economic providers for themselves and their families. Title VII of the Civil Rights Act was given some force in 1971 when the Equal Employment Opportunities Commission (EEOC) gained power to litigate. The growth of affirmative action programs signaled governmental support for improving the employment prospects of women, even if no employers were actually punished for failing to achieve hiring goals. The Work Incentive (WIN) Program established at the end of the 1960s began to suggest that even for women, "work goes with welfare." At first, however, men were given priority in WIN funding, followed by women on a first-come-first-served basis.[29] In 1971, AFDC regulation required for the first time that female recipients of AFDC funds with children over six years old should seek employment. Even the relatively meager efforts to provide women with the means and incentive to seek employment have remained controversial and, during the Reagan administration, were attacked and reduced.[30]

Even if there is more widespread support for the breakdown of familial gender roles in the marketplace, support for traditional gender roles within the home remain firm even, in a sense, with regard to families in which there is no adult male. Programs of employment incentives and supports for women have not included provision of child-care services, which remain the responsibility of mothers. A bill passed through Congress that would have provided federal funds for day-care centers was vetoed by Richard Nixon on the grounds that such services would break up "the family." Despite the pronationalist claims of recent administrations, the United States remains one of the few Organization for Economic Cooperation and Development (OECD) nations that lacks a maternity leave policy. It lags in other supports for pregnant women and families with children as well.

It is important to note that although women and children are supposed to depend upon a male breadwinner for financial support, public policy has not been vigorous in enforcing this goal. Marital law still assumes that husbands are responsible for financial support, but court cases continue to conclude that if a woman is actually residing with her husband that is proof enough that he is supporting her adequately regardless of what he provides or what he is capable of providing. This is an unwarranted assumption either that husbands provide adequate allowances to their wives or that married couples pool their resources in such a way as to allow each individual to draw on them freely. One of the major causes of poverty among women and children in recent decades has been the refusal of divorced husbands to comply with court orders for support payments. Only when the Reagan administration realized that considerable sums of AFDC money could be saved was a serious policy of enforcement initiated, but it was originally designed to encompass only women who were eligible for AFDC funding. The implication was that support of women by their husbands is a private matter of no concern to government unless or until women became public charges because of lack of spousal support. If for much of our history women's welfare was supposedly safeguarded by a husband, we are led to the deduction that for most of our history women's welfare has been of little concern to government, except insofar as it served instrumental purposes in providing care and services for others.

Women's primary relationship to the structure of the general welfare is to provide essential services that might otherwise cost money either to the private or public sector.[31] As many feminist observers have pointed out, when it is said that families have the primary responsibility to care for themselves, what one really means is that women have the primary responsibility to care for others in the family.[32] Given the continuing gender division of labor in the family, it is not the family as a unit but rather women in families who care for children, the elderly, and other dependents, including breadwinners, who are dependent upon these services for their own day-to-day maintenance. Of course, given gender divisions of labor in the marketplace, when people are employed to replace what has previously been women's domestic labor, these services continue to be rendered by women. A major and generally hidden question in social policy, therefore, is whether women should be required to provide for the general welfare in a way that often necessitates that they remain economically dependent and ultimately perhaps in need of social welfare provisions themselves. Or can women and others provide for the general welfare in a way that allows women to provide for themselves as well?

Women's contribution to the general welfare goes beyond the provision of services that need to be done. Even in the minority of cases in which women do not contribute wages to a household, they help determine the worth of the wages that are contributed by others. Again, because of the continuing gender division of domestic labor, women's efforts in shopping, cooking, and other household tasks affect the value of each dollar brought in. Although public pronouncements have often acknowledged the importance of women's contribution to the home, there has been little effort to give women a return. Only in this decade, for example, have courts begun to recognize women's investment in domestic labor as an economic contribution to be considered in dividing household assets following divorce. Homemakers do not receive their own Social Security benefits but rather are supposed to benefit through their husbands' contributions. In fact, only 54 percent of women receiving Social Security benefits make their claims on the basis of their own work records; the other 46 percent claim as wives.[33] In the case of divorced women, however, only those who qualify under very stringent conditions find that their years of contributing to their husband's maintenance and worth results in payment.

It is women's provision of care and the expectation that they should do so that does the most to make women dependent. Those who are most economically vulnerable are the women who do the most to fulfill a paternalistic and patriarchal gender ideology: they devote themselves full time to caring for their families. Any human capital investment they made in earlier years through education, training, or employment becomes devalued with each year they are homemakers,[34] and they lack the further benefits afforded by continuing job experience. They foresake both the independent security of employment and employment-related benefits including pensions, and they foresake a considerable amount of ability to provide for themselves should the need arise. Women's economic activities, however, cannot be regarded as choices in the full sense of the word. Our social policies assume that women are the primary caregivers, which means there is little assistance to be offered to women who are, in addition, breadwinners. Our social welfare system depends on women either being dependent or taking on what has become to be known as the "double burden." Even when women attempt to seek employment, they continue to face job discrimination based on this gender ideology. Although it is illegal for employers to take marital or maternal status into account, they continue to devalue women as employees because of the assumption that women's primary focus of attention is the home.

Reality contradicts the persistent view that women are not providers. The majority of women are now in the labor force, including the majority of women with children as young as two.[35] They now spend relatively few years out of the labor force. Women make important financial contributions to their households. Many people have noted that women who do not have a husband to help support themselves and their families are particularly likely to suffer from poverty. In 1983, more than one-quarter of all divorced and separated women were on welfare. Thirty-seven percent of single mothers with one child were poor, as were 85 percent of single mothers with four children. But married men are also poorer if they do not have a wife who makes financial contributions to the home. Among married white couples, 9 percent of the families in which the husband was the only earner were poor compared with 3 percent in which both spouses worked. The difference is even more stark among black families, where we find 24 percent were poor if only the husband was a wage earner compared with 4 percent if both were.

BEYOND GENDER-BIASED SOCIAL POLICY

Women constitute a majority of the beneficiaries of most major social welfare programs in existence today—with the exception of unemployment insurance. Among adults receiving AFDC, the largest single item in what is regarded as the welfare budget, over 80 percent of the beneficiaries are women. As Barbara Nelson reports, women constitute 70 percent of the housing beneficiaries, 65 percent of Medicare users, 62 percent of beneficiaries of Social Security (Old Age, Survivors and Disability Insurance or OASDI), 57 percent of food stamp recipients, and 56 percent of Medicaid users.[36] It is no wonder. These programs are intended primarily for the poor and aged, and women are a majority of both. Indeed, they are an increasing proportion of the poor (now roughly two thirds), a phenomenon known as the "feminization of poverty."

American social policies, including those targeted particularly at helping the economically vulnerable, are not simply part of the solution, they are part of the problem. They have helped women primarily in their capacity as wives or, especially, as mothers and not because any positive value has been placed on removing women from a dependent state. As Barbara Nelson observes, "The poorer a woman, the greater the likelihood that she makes a claim for benefits on the basis of her position as a wife or mother."[37] One of the reasons is that women's poverty is increased substantially by their economic dependence brought on by the dependence for care that others place on them. Here it must be reemphasized that those who depend on women's care include not just children and elderly relatives but able-bodied working husbands. Moreover, whereas the more obviously vulnerable such as children and elderly relatives depend on women's care and caring, husbands have also depended psychologically on women's dependency itself, a point made as long as a century ago by John Stuart Mill in his "Subjection of Women." [38] Although this point might suggest that gender divisions of labor make women and men mutually and, therefore, acceptably dependent upon each other, the dependency of men on women's dependency and the particular vulnerabilities of women created by others' dependence on them means we cannot properly say that the women and men in this relationship are truly interdependent, a term that would suggest more symmetry of power.[39]

Because of gender-role assumptions, the family presumption in caring—that those outside the family, and especially government, have only a residual role to play—is really a presumption that women should have the primary role in caring or offering personal services and only a secondary role in financial provision. Conversely, this outlook defines men's primary role as provision and their secondary role as caring. Contrary to the standard rendition of social policy, we do not assume a single line of responsibility for caring that runs from family to other private individuals and organizations to government. Predominant beliefs and attitudes encompass a dual hierarchy of responsibility, one for provision and one for caring. For provision the line extends from the male "head of the family" outward, in ideological terms skipping over the female adult on the grounds that it is less demoralizing for a man to be supported by outside males (or agencies) than to be supported by a woman. For caring, the line extends from the wife and mother outward, in ideological terms skipping over the male adult on the grounds that men are not competent at caring or that their primary role is provision. Here lies another interesting assumption: a man cannot provide *and* care, a combination of efforts faced by most married women today. The reality contradicts the belief; women do indeed provide. There has been somewhat less change in familial patterns of caring men; their assumption of the caring role has not increased as dramatically as has women's assumption of the provision role.

In order for our policies to cease supporting the dependency of women, it is necessary for society to cease depending on women as women; that is, it is necessary that we do not define women in terms of what have up to now been considered women's unique roles and propensities toward caring. This also requires that we no longer depend on men as men or, in other words, on the man's exclusive roles as provider.

The pressing policy question that arises from this discussion is: If we abandon the gender division of responsibility in the family, who will provide and, especially, who will care? Do we place the primary responsibility on governmental institutions? This is certainly the view taken by conservative critics of feminist arguments, who see women's apparent abandonment of exclusive domestic roles as both the cause of the need for social services and as a force that will weaken men's incentives to be providers. It has also been the suggestion of some early Marxist theorists, who called for the "socialization" of domestic labor, and of the influential Progressive Charlotte Perkins Gilman, who at the turn of the century offered a slightly different picture of taking domestic labor out of the home and out of the realm of women's familial responsibility.[40]

It would be a sad commentary on the human state if our acceptance of responsibility to help others is based only on a structure of gender inequality and power hierarchies. As Robert Goodin has argued, our fundamental moral responsibilities spring from the situation of being able to help those who are vulnerable and dependent, and especially those who are vulnerable to us.[41] We have these responsibilities regardless of gender. One cannot shirk moral responsibilities on the basis of a functionalism of gender.

Goodin's theory of responsibility and vulnerability is important, because it provides a way of analyzing and assessing our hierarchies of responsibility for others. It is in the intimacy of the family that we are most likely to find both vulnerability and ability to help that is linked to specific individuals, especially with respect to the kind of necessary caring that has been defined as women's responsibility. Responsibility does move outward to family, friends, community, and others most likely to be aware of the situation and have individual and mutual ties to those who need help. By emphasizing the notion of those who are next most responsible, Goodin draws the line of caring to the community as a whole and its administrative voice, government, which, he argues, has responsibility under three circumstances: "When no one has been assigned primary responsibility," when "those with primary responsibilities . . . prove unable to discharge them," and when "the persons with primary responsibilities prove unwilling to discharge them." [42]

This construction of the residual responsibility of government does not leave us where we started, with government providing only the barest of safety nets for those who have already fallen. We know, for example, that parents are unable to work at full-time jobs with inflexible schedules (as most have) and take care of dependent children at the same time. If we, as a community, know this to be a pattern in a significant proportion of economically active members of our society, we could argue that we as a community, through government, have a responsibility to help. Alternative means of assistance include workplace policies that mandate more flexible job schedules; parental leave policies that allow parents leave time without making them and their families more vulnerable through loss of pay, benefits, or career opportunities; and direct or indirect provision of child-care services. Goodin argues that the purpose of social policy is to protect the vulnerable and dependent. Protecting the vulnerable implies protecting those at particular risk, not just those who are already in trouble. It follows that social policy, in seeking to protect the vulnerable and dependent, should not at the same time create vulnerability and dependency. Our minimalist social policies up to this point have done just that.

Women have suffered, in a sense, from the tendency to make relatively rigid distinctions between *social* policies and *rights* policies. There is not a space here to repeat in full the arguments that claim that the distinctions are not great and that some social policies, including the provision of certain services, constitute rights.[43] Let us, rather, briefly consider one example that has served as a theme throughout this discussion. For most of our history, Americans have accepted the idea that women should be dependent upon their husbands and that they should not, if possible, provide for themselves through gainful employment. Following from this idea, men have been accorded higher priority in training and jobs, even when there were more qualified women available. In public debate today, policies aimed at securing education and jobs for women are labeled rights policies. If we also thought of them in terms of social policy, we would be more likely to define the goals of these policies as providing for the general welfare—that is, of providing the means whereby a significant portion of the society could become more economically secure and less dependent and vulnerable. We would then not only allow women to become self-reliant, we would encourage it.[44]

This is a call for collective as well as individual responsibility and it is a criticism of crass individualism, even if that individualism is softened with an overlay of voluntaristic altruism. Advocacy of collective responsibility does not, as some critics would argue, mean the demise of the individual as an agent in society. To the contrary, it is entirely consistent with Albert Weale's argument that "there is one overriding imperative to which government action ought to be subject to its authority. This principle of autonomy asserts that all persons are entitled to respect as deliberative and purposive agents capable of formulating their own projects, and that as part of this respect there is a governmental obligation to bring into being or preserve the conditions in which this autonomy can be realized."[45]

This is precisely what has been missing in social policy as it concerns women: the preservation of conditions of autonomy. In a sense this is true for men as well, because their roles also have been dictated by prescriptions that are made on the basis of sex. But for women the prescription is dependency including dependency of identity itself.[46] Social policy has assumed that women are not autonomous individuals and moral agents, but that they live contingent lives. With specific regard to their economic lives, their ability to provide for themselves and others is supposed to be contingent upon whether others around them need their caring services. Choice as a moral agent is missing. Women are defined as individuals who place themselves second. The irony is that this "altruism" often keeps them from helping not only themselves but others they would wish and feel obligated to help.

We are in great need of constructing more humane social policy for the future and also of reinterpreting what has gone before. Historically, for vast numbers of men the individualistic ideology of self-reliance has not worked. For women it never existed.[47]

NOTES

1   On women's movements of this period see Barbara Berg, *The Remembered Gate: Origins of American Feminism: Women and the City, 1800–60* (New York: Oxford University Press, 1978); Ellen DuBois, *Feminism and Suffrage: The Emergence of An Independent Women's Movement in America, 1848–69* (Ithaca, N.Y.: Cornell University Press, 1978); Eleanor Flexner, *Century of Struggle: The Women's Rights Movement in the United States* (Cambridge, Mass.: Harvard University Press, 1975); Stanley Lemons, *The Woman Citizen: Social Feminism in the 1920's* (Urbana: University of Illinois Press, 1972).

2   For example, Berg, *Remembered Gate*; and DuBois, *Feminism and Suffrage*.

3   For example, Linda Gordon, *Woman's Body, Woman's Right: A Social History of Birth Control in America* (New York: Viking Press, 1976).

4   Walter I. Trattner, *From Poor Law to Welfare State: A History of Social Welfare in America* (New York: Free Press, 1974), 190.

5   James Leiby, *A History of Social Welfare and Social Work in the United States* (New York: Columbia University Press, 1978), 212.

6   *Muller v. Oregon*, 208 U.S. 412, (1908).

7   Trattner, *From Poor Law to Welfare State*, 187.

8   Lemons, *Woman Citizen*.

9   Peter Flora and Arnold J. Heidenheimer, "The Historical Core and Changing Boundaries of the Welfare State," in *The Development of Welfare States in Europe and America* ed. Peter Flora and Arnold J. Heidenheimer (New Brunswick, N.J.: Transaction Books, 1981), 22.

10 For further discussion, see Christine Delphy, *Closer to Home: A Materialist Analysis of Women's Oppression* (Amherst: University of Massachusetts Press, 1984); Lydia Sargent, ed., *Women and Revolution: A Discussion of the Unhappy Marriage of Marxism and Feminism* (Boston: South End Press, 1981).

11 Albert Weale, *Political Theory and Social Policy* (London: Macmillan, 1983), 5.

12 Weale, *Political Theory and Social Policy*; Richard M. Titmuss, "The Social Division of Welfare: Some Reflections on the Search for Equity," in *Essays on the Welfare State*, ed. Richard M. Titmuss (London: Allen and Unwin, 1958), 34–55.

13 Robert E. Goodin, "Self-Reliance versus The Welfare State," *Journal of Social Policy* 14 (January 1985): 25–47.

14 Ramesh Mishra, *Society and Social Policy: Theories and Practice of Welfare* (London: Macmillan, 1981), 41.

15 Leiby, *A History of Social Welfare*, 33.

16 Michael Walzer, *Spheres of Justice* (New York: Basic Books, 1983).

17 Leiby, *A History of Social Welfare*, 2. For a parallel discussion of charity versus justice, see Robert E. Goodin, *Protecting the Vulnerable* (Chicago: University of Chicago Press, 1985), chap. 2.

18   Carole Pateman, "Women and Consent," *Political Theory* 8 (May 1980): 149–68; Virginia Sapiro, "Women, Citizenship, and Nationality: Immigration and Naturalization Policies in the United States," *Politics and Society* 13 (1984).

19   *Bradwell v. Illinois,* 83 U.S. 130, (1874).

20   Sapiro, "Women, Citizenship, and Nationality."

21   Lois Scharf, " 'The Forgotten Woman': Working Women, the New Deal, and Women's Organizations," in *Decades of Discontent: The Women's Movement, 1920–40,* ed. Lois Scharf and Joan M. Jensen (Westport, Conn.: Greenwood Press, 1983), 243–60. On women in the New Deal see also Susan D. Becker, *The Origins of the Equal Rights Amendment: American Feminism Between the Wars* (Westport, Conn.: Greenwood Press, 1981); Susan Ware, *Beyond Suffrage: Women in the New Deal* (Cambridge, Mass.: Harvard University Press, 1981).

22   *Phillips v. Martin Marietta,* 400 U.S. 542, (1971).

23   *General Electric v. Gilbert,* 429 U.S. 125, (1976).

24   Bettina Berch, *The Endless Day: The Political Economy of Women and Work* (New York: Harcourt, Brace, Jovanovich, 1982).

25   Maron Marzolf, *Up From the Footnote: A History of Women Journalists* (New York: Hastings House, 1977); DuBois, *Feminism and Suffrage.*

26   On occupational safety and health, for example, see Wendy Chavkin, ed., *Double Exposure: Women's Health Hazards on the Job and at Home* (New York: Monthly Review Press, 1984).

27   For an economic history that treats the changing psychology of gender divisions of labor, see Julie A. Matthaei, *An Economic History of Women in America: Women's Work, The Sexual Division of Labor, and The Development of Capitalism* (New York: Schocken, 1982).

28   Dorothy C. Miller, "AFDC: Mapping a Strategy for Tomorrow," *Social Service Review* 57 (December 1983): 599–613.

29   Sar A. Levitan, Martin Rein, and David Marwick, *Work and Welfare Go Together* (Baltimore: Johns Hopkins Press, 1972), 77.

30   Deborah K. Zinn and Rosemary C. Sarri, "Turning Back The Clock on Welfare," *Signs* 10 (Winter 1984): 355–70.

31   See, for example, Gerdt Sundström, "The Elderly, Women's Work, and Social Security Costs," *Acta Sociologica* 25 (1982): 21–38.

32   Michele Barrett and Mary McIntosh, *The Antisocial Family* (London: Verso, 1982).

33   Barbara J. Nelson, "Women's Poverty and Women's Citizenship: Some Political Consequences of Economic Marginality," *Signs* 10 (Winter 1984): 223.

34   Marnie Mueller, "Applying Human Capital Theory to Women's Changing Work Patterns," *Journal of Social Issues* 38 (Spring 1982): 89–96.

35   Elizabeth Waldman, "Labor Force Statistics from a Family Perspective," *Monthly Labor Review* 106 (December 1983): 16–20.

36   Nelson, "Women's Poverty and Women's Citizenship," 209–231.

37   Ibid., 223.

38   John Stuart Mill, "The Subjection of Women," in *Essays in Sex Equality,* ed. Alice Rossi (Chicago: University of Chicago Press, 1970), 123–242. For a psychoanalytically based attempt to explain this relationship, see Nancy Chodorow, *The*

Reproduction of Mothering: Psychoanalysis and the Sociology of Gender (Berkeley: University of California Press, 1978).

39   For more discussion of intrafamilial vulnerability and dependence see Goodin, *Protecting the Vulnerable*, chap. 4; Patricia Tulloch, "Gender and Dependency," in *Unfinished Business: Social Justice for Women in Australia*, ed. Dorothy Broom (Sydney, Australia: Allen and Unwin, 1984).

40   Charlotte Perkins Gilman, *Women and Economics* (New York: Harper & Row, 1966).

41   Goodin, *Protecting the Vulnerable*.

42   Ibid., 151–52.

43   See, for example, T. H. Marshall, "Citizenship and Social Class," in *Sociology At The Crossroads and Other Essays*, ed. T. H. Marshall (London: Heinemann, 1963); Mishra, *Society and Social Policy*.

44   For a parallel discussion of policies of toleration versus liberation, see Virginia Sapiro, *The Political Integration of Women: Roles, Socialization, and Politics* (Urbana: University of Illinois Press, 1983), chap. 8.

45   Weale, *Political Theory and Social Policy*, 42.

46   For the classic development of this theme, see Simone de Beauvoir, *The Second Sex* (New York: Knopf, 1953).

47   I would like to thank Graham Wilson and Bob Goodin for their helpful comments and criticisms.

CHAPTER 3

The Domestication of Politics: Women and American Political Society, 1780–1920

PAULA BAKER

On one subject all of the nineteenth-century antisuffragists and many suffragists agreed: a woman belonged in the home. From this domain, as wife, as daughter, and especially as mother, she exercised moral influence and insured national virtue and social order. Woman was selfless and sentimental, nurturing and pious. She was the perfect counterpoint to materialistic and competitive man, whose strength and rationality suited him for the rough and violent public world. Despite concurrence on the ideal of womanhood, antisuffragists and suffragists disagreed about how women could best use their power of moral superiority. Suffragists believed that the conduct and content of electoral politics—voting and office holding—would benefit from women's special talents. But for others, woman suffrage was not only inappropriate but dangerous. It represented a radical departure from the familiar world of separate spheres, a departure that would bring, they feared, social disorder, political disaster, and, most important, women's loss of position as society's moral arbiter and enforcer.[1]

The debates over female suffrage occurred while the very functions of government were changing. In the late nineteenth and early twentieth centuries, federal, state, and municipal governments increased their roles in social welfare and economic life. With a commitment to activism not seen since the first decades of the nineteenth century, Progressive-era policy makers sought ways to regulate and rationalize business and industry. They labored to improve schools, hospitals, and other public services. These efforts, halting and incomplete as they were, brought a tradition of women's involvement in government to public attention.[2] Indeed, from the time of the Revolution, women used,

55

and sometimes pioneered, methods for influencing government from outside electoral channels. They participated in crowd actions in colonial America and filled quasi-governmental positions in the nineteenth century; they circulated and presented petitions, founded reform organizations, and lobbied legislatures. Aiming their efforts at matters connected with the well-being of women, children, the home, and the community, women fashioned significant public roles by working from the private sphere.[3]

The themes of the debates—the ideology of domesticity, the suffrage fight, the reemergence of governmental activism, and the public involvement of nineteenth-century women—are familiar. But what are the connections among them? Historians have told us much about the lives of nineteenth-century women. They have explained how women gained political skills, a sense of consciousness as women, and feelings of competence and self-worth through their involvement in women's organizations. But as important as these activities were, women were also shaped by—and in turn affected—American government and politics. Attention to the interaction between women's political activities and the political system itself can tell us much about the position of women in the nineteenth century. In addition, it can provide a new understanding of the political society in which women worked—and that they helped change.[4]

In order to bring together the histories of women and of politics, we need a more inclusive definition of politics than is usually offered. "Politics" is used here in a relatively broad sense to include any action, formal or informal, taken to affect the course or behavior of government or the community.[5] Throughout the nineteenth century, gender was an important division in American politics. Men and women operated, for the most part, in distinct political subcultures, each with its own bases of power, modes of participation, and goals. In providing an intellectual and cultural interpretation of women and politics, this essay focuses on the experiences of middle-class women. There is much more we need to learn about the political involvement of women of all classes in the years prior to suffrage; this essay must, therefore, be speculative. Its purpose is to suggest a framework for analyzing women and politics and to outline the shape that a narrative history of the subject could take.

The basis and rationale for women's political involvement already existed by the time of the Revolution.[6] For both men and women in colonial America, geographically bounded communities provided the fundamental structures of social organization. The most important social ties, economic relationships, and political concerns of individuals were contained within spatially limited areas. Distinctions between the family and community were often vague; in many ways, the home and the community were one.[7] There were, to be sure, marked variations from place to place; community ties were weaker, for example, in colonial cities and in communities and regions with extensive commercial and market connections, such as parts of the South.[8] Still, clear separations existed between men and women in their work and standards of behavior, and most women probably saw their part in the life of the community as the less important. A little-changing round of household tasks dominated women's lives and created a routine that they found stifling. Women had limited opportunities for social contact, and those they had were almost exclusively with other women. They turned work into social occasions, and they passed the milestones of their lives in the supportive company of female friends and relatives. But, however confining, separation provided a basis for a female culture—though not yet for female politics.[9]

Differences between men's and women's political behavior were muted in the colonial period, compared with what they later became. In many places, men who did not own land could not vote because governments placed property restrictions on suffrage. Both men and women petitioned legislatures to gain specific privileges or legal changes. Citizens held deferential attitudes toward authority; elections were often community rituals embodying codes of social deference. A community's "best" men stood for election and were returned to office year after year, and voters expected candidates to "treat" potential supporters by providing food and drink before and on election day. Deferential politics, however, weakened by the middle of the eighteenth century. Economic hardship caused some men to question the reality of a harmony of interests among classes, and the Great Awakening taught others to question traditional authorities. Facing a growing scarcity of land, fathers could no longer promise to provide for their sons, which weakened parental control. This new willingness to question authority of all sorts was a precondition for the Revolution and was, in turn, given expression by republican thought.[10]

Republicanism stressed the dangers posed to liberty by power and extolled the advantages of mixed and balanced constitutions. In a successful republic, an independent, virtuous, watchful, and dispassionate citizenry guarded against the weakness and corruption that threatened liberty. Although interpreted by Americans in different ways, republicanism provided a framework and a rationale for the Revolution. It furnished prescriptions for citizenship and for the relationship between citizens and the state. And it helped unify a collection of local communities racked by internal divisions and pressures.[11]

While the ideology and process of the Revolution forced a rethinking of fundamental political concepts, this reevalution did not extend to the role of women. As Linda K. Kerber persuasively argued, writers and thinkers in the republican tradition were concerned more with criticizing a particular political administration than with examining traditional assumptions about the political role of all inhabitants. Given their narrow intentions, they were not obliged to reconsider the position of women in the state. The language of republicanism also tended to make less likely the inclusion of women. Good republicans were, after all, self-reliant, given to simple needs and tastes, decisive, and committed first to the public interest. These were all "masculine" qualities; indeed, "feminine" attributes—attraction to luxury, self-indulgence, timidity, dependence, passion—were linked to corruption and posed a threat to republicanism. Moreover, women did not usually own land—the basis for an independent citizenry and republican government.[12]

Despite their formal prepolitical status, women participated in the Revolution. They were central to the success of boycotts of imported products and, later, to the production of household manufactures. Their work on farms and in businesses in their husbands' absences was a vital and obvious contribution. Women's participation also took less conventional forms. Edward Countryman recounted instances in which groups of women, angered at what they saw as wartime price gouging, forced storekeepers to charge just prices. During and after the war, women also took part in urban crowd actions, organized petition campaigns, and formed groups to help soldiers and widows. Some even met with legislatures to press for individual demands.[13] Whatever their purposes, all of these activities were congruent with women's identification with the home, family, and community. In boycotts of foreign products and in domestic manufacture during the Revolution, women only expanded traditional activities. In operating farms and businesses, they stepped out of their sphere temporarily for the well-being of their families. Because separations between the home and community were ill defined in early America, women's participation in crowd actions can also be seen as a defense of the home. As Countryman and others pointed out, a communalist philosophy motivated the crowd actions of both men and women. Crowds aimed to redress the grievances of the whole community. Women and men acted not as individuals but as members of a community—and with the community's consent.[14]

Women's political participation took place in the context of the home, but the important point is that the home was a basis for political action. As Kerber and Mary Beth Norton have shown, the political involvement of women through the private sphere took new forms by the beginning of the nineteenth century. Women combined political activity, domesticity, and republican thought through motherhood. Although outside of formal politics, mothering was crucial: by raising civic-minded, virtuous sons, they insured the survival of the republic. On the basis of this important task, women argued for wider access to education and justified interest and involvement in public affairs. As mothers women were republicans; they possessed civic virtue and a concern for the public good. Their exclusion from traditionally defined politics and economics guaranteed their lack of interest in personal gain. Through motherhood, women attempted to compensate for their exclusion from the formal political world by translating moral authority into political influence. Their political demands, couched in these terms, did not violate the canons of domesticity to which many men and women held.[15]

During the nineteenth century, women expanded their ascribed sphere into community service and care of dependents, areas not fully within men's or women's politics. These tasks combined public roles and administration with nurturance and compassion. They were not fully part of either male electoral politics and formal governmental institutions or the female world of the home and family. Women made their most visible public contributions as founders, workers, and volunteers in social service organizations.[16] Together with the social separation of the sexes and women's informal methods of influencing politics, political domesticity provided the basis for a distinct nineteenth-century women's political culture.

Although the tradition, tactics, and ideology for the political involvement of women existed by the first decades of the nineteenth century, a separate political culture had not yet taken shape. Women's style of participation and their relationship to authority were not yet greatly different from those of many men. Until the 1820s—and in some states even later—property restrictions on suffrage disfranchised many men. Even for those granted the ballot, political interest and electoral turnout usually remained low.[17] During the early years of the republic, deferential political behavior was again commonplace. Retreating from the demands of the Revolutionary period, most citizens once again seemed content to accept the political decisions made by the community's most distinguished men. This pattern persisted until new divisions split communities and competing elites vied for voters' support.[18]

Changes in the form of male political participation were part of a larger transformation of social, economic, and political relationships in the early nineteenth century. The rise of parties and the reemergence of citizen interest in politics had a variety of specific sources. In some places, ethnic and religious tensions contributed to a new interest in politics and shaped partisan loyalties. Recently formed evangelical Protestant groups hoped to use government to impose their convictions about proper moral behavior on the community, a goal opposed by older Protestant groups and Catholics. Other kinds of issues—especially questions about the direction of the American political economy—led to political divisions. Citizens were deeply divided about the direction the economy ought to take and the roles government ought to play. They thought attempts to tie localities to new networks and markets in commerce and agriculture could lead to greater prosperity, but such endeavors also meant that economic decisions were no longer made locally and that both the social order and the values of republicanism could be in danger. Local party leaders linked these debates to national parties and leaders,[19] and the rise of working men's parties in urban areas seemed to spring from a similar set of questions and sense of unease about nineteenth-century capitalism.[20]

Whatever their origin, parties also served other less explicitly "political" purposes. The strength of antebellum parties lay in their ability to fuse communal and national loyalties. The major parties were national organizations, but they were locally based: local people organized rallies, printed ballots, and worked to gain the votes of their friends and neighbors. Through political activities in towns and cities, parties gained the support of men and translated their feelings into national allegiances.[21] Political organization provided a set pattern of responses to divisive questions, which raised problems to the national level and served to defuse potential community divisions. Indeed, by linking local concerns to national institutions and leaders, parties took national political questions out of the local context.[22] The local base of the Democrats and Whigs allowed them to take contradictory positions on issues in different places. Major party leaders searched for issues that enabled them to distinguish their own party from the opposition, while keeping their fragile constituencies intact. At the same time, local politics returned in most places to a search for consensual, nonpartisan solutions to community questions.[23]

The rise of a national two-party system in the 1820s and 1830s inaugurated a period of party government and strong partisan loyalties among voters that lasted until after the turn of the twentieth century. Parties, through the national and state governments, distributed resources to individuals and corporations and patronage to loyal partisans. Throughout most of the nineteenth century, roughly three-quarters of the eligible electorate cast their ballots in presidential elections. The organization and identity of the parties changed, but the preeminence of partisanship and government-by-party remained. Party identifications and the idea of partisanship passed from fathers to sons.[24]

Partisan politics characterized male political involvement, and its social elements help explain voters' enthusiastic participation. Parties and electoral politics united all white men, regardless of class or other differences, and provided entertainment, a definition of manhood, and the basis for a male ritual. Universal white manhood suffrage implied that, since all men shared the chance to participate in electoral politics, they possessed political equality. The right to vote was something important that men held in common. And, as class, geography, kinship, and community supplied less reliable sources of identification than they had at an earlier time, men could at least define themselves in reference to women. Parties were fraternal organizations that tied men together with others like themselves in their communities, and they brought men together as participants in the same partisan culture.[25]

Election campaigns celebrated old symbols of the republic and, indeed, manhood. Beginning as early as William Henry Harrison's log cabin campaign in 1840, parties conducted entertaining extravaganzas. Employing symbols that recalled glorious old causes (first, the Jacksonian period and, later, the Civil War), men advertised their partisanship. They took part in rallies, joined local organizations, placed wagers on election results, read partisan newspapers, and wore campaign paraphernalia. In large and small cities military-style marching companies paraded in support of their party's candidates, while in rural areas picnics and pole raisings served to express and foster partisan enthusiasm.[26]

Party leaders commonly used imagery drawn from the experience of war: parties were competing armies, elections were battles, and party workers were soldiers. They commented approvingly on candidates who waged manly campaigns, and they disparaged nonpartisan reformers as effeminate.[27] This language and the campaigns themselves gathered new intensity in the decades following the Civil War. The men who marched in torchlight parades recalled memories of the war and demonstrated loyalty to the nation and to their party. Women participated, too, by illuminating their windows and cheering on the men; sometimes the women marched alongside the men, dressed as patriotic figures like Miss Liberty.[28] The masculine character of electoral politics was reinforced on election day. Campaigns culminated in elections held in saloons, barbershops, and other places largely associated with men. Parties and electoral politics, in short, served private, sociable purposes.

Just as the practice and meaning of electoral politics changed in the early nineteenth century, so did the function of government. State and local governments gradually relinquished to the marketplace the tasks of regulating economic activity, setting fair prices, and determining product standards. State governments limited the practice of granting corporate charters on an individual basis and, instead, wrote uniform procedures that applied to all applicants. These governments also reduced, and finally halted, public control of businesses and private ventures in which state money had been invested. A spate of state constitutional revisions undertaken from the 1820s through the 1840s codified these changes in the role of government in economic life. In state after state, new constitutions limited the power of the legislatures. Some of this power was granted to the courts, but most authority passed to the entrepreneurs. This transformation in governance is just beginning to be reevaluated by political historians.[29] For our purposes, the important point is that governments largely gave up the tasks of regulating the economic and social behavior of the citizenry.

The rise of mass parties and characteristic forms of male political participation separated male and female politics. When states eliminated property qualifications for suffrage, women saw that their disfranchisement was based solely on sex. The idea of separate spheres had a venerable past, but it emerged in the early nineteenth century with a vengeance. Etiquette manuals written by both men and women prescribed more insistently the proper behavior for middle-class ladies. Woman's attributes—physical weakness, sentimentality, purity, meekness, piousness—were said to disqualify her for traditional public life. Motherhood was now described as woman's special calling—a "vocation," in Nancy Cott's term—that, if performed knowledgeably and faithfully, represented the culmination of a woman's life.[30] While a handicap for traditional politics, her emotional and guileless nature provided strengths in pursuing the important tasks of binding community divisions and upholding moral norms.

At the same time, political activity expanded in scope and form. New organizations for women proliferated in small and large cities and became forums for political action.[31] These organizations took on some of the tasks—the care of dependents and the enforcement of moral norms—that governments had abandoned. If not maintained by church, government, and community, the social order would be preserved by woman and the home. Women's positions outside traditionally defined politics and their elevated moral authority took on new importance and may have allowed men to pursue individual economic and social ends with less conflict. Through selfless activities in the home and community, women could provide stability.[32]

As historians of women have pointed out, one of the ironies of Jacksonian democracy was the simultaneous development of the "cult of true womanhood" and rhetoric celebrating the equality of men.[33] These developments were related and carried ramifications for both male politics and woman's political role. The notion of womanhood served as a sort of negative referent that united all white men. It might, indeed, have allowed partisan politics to function as a ritual, for it made gender, rather than other social or economic distinctions, the most salient political division. Men could see past other differences and find common ground with other men.

"Womanhood" was more than just a negative referent, for it assigned the continued safety of the republic to the hands of disinterested, selfless, moral women. In the vision of the framers of the Constitution, government was a self-regulating mechanism that required good institutions to run properly—not, as in classical republicanism, virtuous citizens. Men's baser instincts were more dependable than their better ones; hence, the framers made self-interest the basis for government. While politics and public life expressed selfish motives, private life—the home—maintained virtue. The republican vocabulary lingered into the nineteenth century, but key words gained new meanings that were related to private behavior. "Liberty," "independence," and "freedom" had economic as much as political connotations, while "virtue" and "selflessness" became attributes of women and the home. Because order was thought to be maintained by virtuous women, men could be partisans and could admit that community divisions existed.[34] At the same time, male electoral participation defined politics. As the idea of parties gained citizens' acceptance and other modes of participation were closed off or discouraged, electoral participation stood as the condoned means of political expression.

Women's political demands and actions that too closely approached male prerogatives met with resistance. Women fought hard—and sometimes successfully—in state legislatures to end legal discrimination. But even their victories had as much to do with male self-interest as with women's calls for justice.[35] Still, they slowly gained legal rights in many states. And since male politics determined what was public and political, most of those demands by women that fell short of suffrage were seen as private and apolitical. The political activities of women in clubs and in public institutions achieved a considerable degree of male support. Women reformers not only drew little visible opposition from men but often received male financial support. Women's moral nature gave them a reason for public action, and, since they did not have the vote, such action was considered "above" politics.

Ideas about womanhood and separate spheres, as well as forces as diverse as urbanization and the resurgence of revival religion, gave women's political activity a new prominence. But that female sphere had now grown. Men and women would probably have agreed that the "home" in a balanced social order was the place for women and children. But this definition became an expansive doctrine: home was anywhere women and children were. Influential women writers such as Catherine Beecher described a "domestic economy" in which women combined nurturance and some of the organizational methods of the new factory. system to run loving, yet efficient, homes. Others expanded the profession of motherhood to include all of society, an argument that stressed the beneficial results that an application of feminine qualities had on society as a whole.[36] This perspective on motherhood and the home included not only individual households but all women and children and the forces that affected their lives. And it had a lasting appeal. As late as 1910, feminist and journalist Rheta Childe Dorr asserted: "Woman's place is Home. . . . But Home is not contained within the four walls of an individual house. Home is the community. The city full of people is the Family. The public school is the real Nursery. And badly do the Home and Family need their mother." [37] Many nineteenth-century women found this vision of the home congenial: it encouraged a sense of community and responsibility toward all women, and it furnished a basis for political action.

Throughout the nineteenth century women participated in politics through organizations that worked to correct what they defined as injustices toward women and children. The ideas and institutions through which women acted, however, changed significantly over time. Early organizations, including moral reform societies and local benevolent organizations, based their political action on the notions of the moral superiority of women and an expansive woman's sphere. By the mid-nineteenth century, new groups rejected that vision. Early suffrage organizations insisted on rights for women and the independence to move outside of the woman's sphere. Although they by no means fully dismissed the notion of women's moral superiority, their tactics and ideology flowed from different sources, such as the abolition movement. Still later, a new generation of clubwomen returned to the idea of a woman's sphere but rejected sentimentality in favor of the scientific and historical vision of the Gilded Age. They stressed how scientific motherhood, if translated into efficient, nonpartisan, and tough-minded public action, could bring social progress. Temperance activists and suffragists in the late nineteenth century wanted political equality so that the special qualities of womanhood could be better expressed and exercised: femininity provided a sort of expertise needed in formal politics. Drawing on the growing body of works that recount the public activities of women, we can illustrate how the nineteenth-century female political culture operated.

Some of the earliest examples of women's organizations were benevolent and moral reform societies. These groups, usually located in cities, were staffed and managed by middle-class women.[38] Unable to believe that women voluntarily acted in ways that were in conflict with the strictures of the woman's sphere, they blamed their charges' misfortunes on male immorality. For example, the Female Benevolent Society and the Female Moral Reform Society, both in New York City and both most active in the 1830s, concentrated their efforts on eradicating moral lapses such as prostitution. Since no woman would choose such an unwomanly vocation, they reasoned, they blamed the moral inferiority of men and the scarcity of economic opportunities for women for this degradation of womanhood.

Such an analysis of the causes of unwomanly behavior encouraged women in benevolent groups to broaden their efforts and concerns. Organized women inaugurated employment services, trained women for work as seamstresses and housekeepers, and gathered funds to aid poor women. These reformers were also alarmed at the treatment of women in prisons; they feared these women were brutalized and immodestly mixed with male inmates. Hence they worked for prison reform and persuaded state and municipal governments to appoint female guards and police matrons, as well as to set up halfway houses and prisons for women. Other groups dedicated themselves to helping elderly women, poor women, children, and orphans. They were joined by clubwomen in working for dress reform, health and sex education, and education for women.[39] As their concerns widened, so did the variety of their tactics. One group published the names of prostitutes' clients that were gathered by members who held vigils outside of brothels. When moral suasion and shame seemed ineffective, they turned to law. Reformers lobbied legislators to pass measures that would

protect women, children, and the home. They also launched successful petition drives. A New York State group persuaded legislators to introduce a bill
that would make adultery and seduction punishable crimes. During the next
three years, they put pressure on assemblymen by publishing the names of representatives who voted against the measure. It passed. Members of charitable
organizations also worked to see legislation enacted that protected married
women's property.[40]

These demands, like all of the political actions of the antebellum groups,
were fully congruent with a broad vision of the woman's sphere. We should
recognize, too, that the vision of the home as embracing all women and
children had an important corollary: "woman" was a universal category in
the minds of organized women, as it was for others who held the doctrine
of separate spheres. Because all women shared certain qualities, and many
the experience of motherhood, what helped one group of women benefited
all. "Motherhood" and "womanhood" were powerful integrating forces that
allowed women to cross class, and perhaps even racial, lines.[41] They also
carried moral and political clout. Hence, women's groups celebrated the special moral nature of women, usually in contrast to men's capacity for immoral
behavior. The nature of woman simply suited her to ensure the moral and
social order, which sometimes necessitated the assistance of the state.

The culmination of this strain of female political culture was the Woman's
Parliament, convened by Sorosis, a professional women's club in New York
City, in 1869. Supporters envisioned creating a parallel government with
responsibilities complementing woman's nature: education, prisons, reform
schools, parks, recreation, political corruption, and social policy in general—
tasks that male partisan politics handled poorly, if at all. Participants intended
the parliament to be elected by all women at large, and, although it met only
once, the Woman's Parliament was the fullest expression of the transfer of
woman's sphere to politics.[42] Nonetheless, the members of the Woman's Parliament rejected woman suffrage, even though they were prepared to operate
a separate government. Suffrage represented the antithesis of the glorification
of separate spheres that lay behind the political activities of the early organizations. For these women and many men, suffrage was indeed a radical
demand.[43] By involving women in the male political arena, women's right to
vote threatened to end political separation. It implied—and suffragists argued
—that men and women should be treated as individuals, equal in abilities
and talents, and that neither men nor women were blessed with a special
nature. Women's suffrage threatened the fraternal, ritualistic character of male
politics, just as it promised to undercut female political culture.

The early suffrage movement developed from women's participation in
the abolition movement, particularly the Garrisonian wing, but there was no
simple connection between the two. Women, as Ellen DuBois pointed out, did

not need involvement in abolitionism to recognize their oppression. Rather, from their experience women gained political skills, an ideology distinct from the doctrine of separate spheres, and a set of tactics. They learned about political organization and public speaking, found humanism an attractive alternative to evangelical Protestantism and woman's special nature, and discovered Garrisonian moral suasion to be a useful way of making political demands. Abolitionism taught women how to turn women's rights into a political movement. Moreover, the rejection of their demands by the Radical Republicans showed them the unreliability of the established political parties and the necessity for an independent movement.[44] Yet the early suffrage movement was notably unsuccessful. The organization itself split over questions of tactics and purpose. A few western states passed woman suffrage amendments, but apparently for reasons other than women's demands. By the 1880s, many states allowed women to vote in school elections and even to serve on school boards. But, on the whole, the movement made little headway until the turn of the century.[45]

Neither the equality nor the liberal individualism promised by the early suffragists found a receptive audience in the nineteenth century. Throughout the late nineteenth and early twentieth centuries, women's political activities were characterized by voluntary, locally based moral and social reform efforts. Many women had a stake in maintaining the idea of separate spheres. It carried the force of tradition and was part of a feminine identity, both of which were devalued by the individualism that suffrage implied. Separate spheres allowed women to wield power of a sort. They could feel that their efforts showed some positive result and that public motherhood contributed to the common good. Moreover, men were unwilling to vote for suffrage amendments. The late nineteenth century was the golden age of partisan politics: at no time before or since did parties command the allegiance of a higher percentage of voters or have a greater hand in the operation of government. Indeed, in the extremes of political action of both men and women during the late nineteenth century—torchlight parades and the Woman's Parliament—there were hints of earnest efforts to hold together a social and political system that was slipping from control. At any rate, separate political cultures had nearly reached the end of existence.

Throughout the nineteenth century, the charitable work of women aimed to remedy problems like poverty, disease, and helplessness. But after the Civil War the ideas that informed women's efforts, as well as the scope of their work, markedly changed. New perceptions about the function of the state and a transformed vision of society came out of the experience of the war. It had illustrated the importance of loyalty, duty, centralization, and organization and encouraged a new sense of American nationality. Even as the federal government drew back from its wartime initiatives, many Americans were recognizing the shortcomings of limited government. Amid rapid urbanization and industrialization, the economic system nationalized and reached tighter forms of organization. Social thinkers and political activists discovered limits in the ability of traditional Protestantism, liberalism, or republicanism to explain their world. Some even questioned the idea of moral authority itself and turned to a positivistic interpretation of Spencerian sociology, which stressed the inevitability of historical progress and touted science as the height of human achievement. While the system had its critics, it more commonly was justified by a faith in historical progress.[46]

Women's political culture reflected these changes. The work of northern women in the Sanitary Commission illustrates some of the directions that their politics took. The commission, a voluntary but quasi-governmental organization founded by male philanthropists, set out to supply northern troops with supplies and medical care. Volunteers, they argued, were too often distracted by the suffering of individuals, and community-based relief got in the way. Unsentimental and scientific, the members of the commission felt they best understood the larger purpose and the proper way to deal with the magnitude of the casualties. Women served as nurses in the commission, as they did in army hospitals and voluntary community relief operations. They moved women's traditional roles of support, healing, and nurturance into the public sphere. At the same time, their experiences taught them the limits of sentiment and the need for discipline. Women such as Clara Barton, Dorthea Dix, Mary Livermore, and Mother Bickerdyke gained public acclaim for their services. Well-to-do northern women raised a substantial amount of money for the commission by running "Sanitary Fairs." They collected contributions, sold items donated by men and women, and publicly celebrated the Union's cause.[47]

The commission is an important example of women's participation in politics. The acceptance and expansion of the woman's sphere, professionalization, and the advancement of science over sentiment were repeated in other Gilded Age female organizations. Some middle-class groups saw socialism as the solution to heightened class tensions, and, for a time, such groups formed alliances with working-class and socialist organizations. In Chicago, the Illinois Woman's Alliance cooperated with the Trade and Labor Assembly on efforts to secure legislation of interest to both groups. Yet such alliances grew increasingly rare as socialists were discredited.[48]

Organized women found a more permanent method in social science. Especially in its early reformist stage, social science tied science to traditional concerns of women.[49] The methods and language of social science—data collection, detached observation, and an emphasis on prevention—influenced the political work of women. In the South, women in church and reform groups adopted these methods to address what they perceived as the important social dislocations created by the Civil War. Gilded Age "friendly visitors" spent time with the poor, gathering information and providing a presumably uplifting example. They did little more, since alms giving was bad for the poor because it discouraged work, and, by standing in the way of progress, it was also a detriment to the race. Even more "scientific," Progressive-era settlement workers later mocked the friendly visitors' pretensions. They saw the Gilded Age ladies as lacking in compassion and blind to the broader sources of poverty and, hence, the keys to its prevention. Later still, professional social workers, further removed from sentimentality, replaced the settlement workers and their approaches.[50] Yet in the Gilded Age, social science provided women with quasi-professional positions and an evolutionary argument for women's rights. It also contributed a logic for joining forces with formal governmental institutions, because social science taught the importance of cooperation, prevention, and expertise. This faith in the scientific method and in professionalism eventually led to a devaluation of voluntary work and to the relinquishment of social policy to experts in governmental bureaucracies.[51]

The temperance movement illustrates another way that women fused domesticity and politics. It engaged more women than any other nineteenth-century cause and shows how women could translate a narrow demand into a political movement with wide concerns. Temperance appealed to women because it addressed a real problem—one that victimized women—and because, as a social problem, it fell within the woman's sphere. The temperance movement developed through a number of stages and gained momentum especially during the Second Great Awakening. Its history as a women's movement, however, began with the temperance crusade during the years following the Civil War. In small cities and towns in the East and Midwest, groups of women staged marches and held vigils outside or conducted prayer meetings inside saloons, which sometimes coerced their owners to close. In some places, they successfully enlisted the aid of local governments. In most towns, however, the saloons reopened after a short period of "dry" enthusiasm.[52]

The Women's Christian Temperance Union was a descendant of the temperance crusade. It, too, relied on Protestant teachings, women's sense of moral outrage, and the belief in women's moral superiority. Throughout its history, the WCTU was involved in working for legislation such as high license fees and local option. But under the leadership of Frances Willard, the organization, while still defining temperance as its major goal, moved far beyond its initial concerns and closer to the Knights of Labor, the Populist party, and the Christian Socialists and away from the tactics and ideology of the temperance crusade. Like these Gilded Age protest movements, the WCTU turned a seemingly narrow demand of group interest into a critique of American society.[53] Indeed, the ability of the WCTU to cast the traditional concerns of women in terms of a broad vision and of the public good helps explain its success. But that success was in part the result of its flexible organization. Although centrally directed, the WCTU was locally organized, which allowed the branches to determine their own concerns and projets within the general directives of the leadership. Willard's WCTU inaugurated the "Do Everything" policy, which allowed local organizations to choose projects as they saw fit. The WCTU made temperance the basis of demands for a wide range of reforms. Alcohol abuse, they argued, was a symptom, not a cause, of poverty, crime, and injustices done to women. Therefore, the WCTU organized departments in areas such as labor, health, social purity, peace, education, and, eventually, suffrage. The locals were directly involved in electoral politics: small-town women worked for "dry" candidates, while the Chicago Union supported the Socialist party.[54]

The WCTU's call for the vote for women nearly split the organization. It supported suffrage not for the sake of individual rights but because the ballot could allow women to serve better the causes of temperance, the home, and the public good. American politics and economics in the late nineteenth century contained enough examples of the baneful results of unrestrained self-interest, from political corruption to avaricious corporations. The efforts of women to deal locally with social problems were no longer sufficient in a nation where the sources were extralocal and created by male, self-interested political and economic behavior. Woman's vote, they argued, would express her higher, selfless nature. The WCTU combined the woman's sphere with suffrage under the rubric of "Home Protection," an argument that implied feminine values belonged within traditionally defined politics. While taking traditional domestic concerns seriously, the WCTU taught women how to expand them into wider social concern and political action. With greater success than any other nineteenth-century women's group, it managed to forge the woman's sphere into a broadly based political movement.

Other groups—notably the second generation of woman suffragists and clubwomen—also attempted to combine the woman's sphere and women's rights. In this effort, woman suffrage remained divisive. As DuBois and Carl Degler have shown, the threat woman suffrage posed to the doctrine of separate spheres helps explain why the struggle was so long and bitterly fought. But an examination of the political context can provide further insights. The antisuffragists' most powerful argument was that suffrage was dangerous because it threatened the existence of separate spheres. If women voted, they would abandon the home and womanly virtues. The differences between the sexes would be obscured: men would lose their manhood and women would begin to act like men. Throughout the nineteenth century, those arguments struck a chord. Participation in electoral politics did define manhood. Women also had a stake in maintaining their sphere and the power it conferred. But by the end of the century profound social, economic, and political changes made that antisuffrage argument—and the separate male and female political cultures—less persuasive to many women—and many men.

The nature of electoral politics changed significantly during the early twentieth century. Gone were not only the torchlight parades but also most of the manifestations of the male political culture that those parades symbolized. Voter turnout began to decline, and men's allegiance to political parties waned. In the broadest sense, these changes can be traced to the effects of rapid urbanization and industrialization.[55] In the nineteenth century, partisan politics was a local experience, resting on certain sorts of community relationships. In the partisan press and campaigns, politics meant economic policy. Locally, such issues were handled in an individualistic, partisan manner; on the national level, abstract discussions of distant economic questions supplied the basis for a partisan faith.

But by the early twentieth century the communities in which voters' loyalties were formed had changed. Men's most important relationships were no longer contained solely within geographically defined localities but were instead scattered over distances. Their political ties were no longer exclusively with neighbors but also with people having similar economic or other interests. Male political participation began to reflect this shift. Men increasingly replaced or supplemented electoral participation with the sorts of single-issue, interest-group tactics that women had long employed. Moreover, political parties that dealt with problems on an individualistic basis now seemed less useful because economic and political problems demanded more than individualistic solutions.[56] The sum of these changes in nineteenth-century patterns of electoral participation was to lessen the importance of partisan politics for men. In hindsight, at least, woman suffrage presented less of a threat to a male political culture and to manhood.

Even more important, the antisuffragists could no longer argue so forcefully that the vote would take women out of the home. Government had assumed some of the substantive functions of the home by the early twentieth century. Politics and government in the nineteenth century had revolved almost entirely around questions of sectional, racial, and economic policies. To be sure, governments, especially at the state level, spent the largest portion of their budgets on supporting institutions like schools, asylums, and prisons.[57] But election campaigns and partisan political discussions largely excluded mention of these institutions. In the Progressive era, social policy—formerly the province of women's voluntary work—became public policy. Women themselves had much to do with this important transition—a transition that in turn changed their political behavior.

Women continued to exercise their older methods of political influence, but now they directed their efforts through new institutions. Women's clubs—

united in 1890 as the General Federation of Women's Clubs—were one important means. Beginning as self-improvement organizations, many clubs soon focused on social and cultural change. These women sought to bring the benefits of motherhood to the public sphere. They set up libraries, trade schools for girls, and university extension courses, and they worked to introduce home economics courses, to improve the physical environment of schools, and to elect women to school boards. They also sponsored legislation to eliminate sweatshops and provide tenement-house fire inspection. Clubwomen interested in sanitary reforms helped enact programs for clean water and better sewage disposal. In many cities, they raised money for parks and playgrounds. Clubs were also important in pressing for a juvenile court system and for federal public health legislation, such as the 1906 Pure Food and Drug Act.[58]

But by the Progressive period, these women recognized that their efforts—and even public motherhood—were not enough. The scope of these problems meant that reform had to be concerned with more than the care of women and children. Charity had real limits. Problems were not solvable, or even treatable, at the local level. Despite attempts to uplift them, the poor remained poor, and women began to identify the problem as having broader sources. The municipal housekeepers needed the help of the state: alone, they were powerless to remove the source of the problem, only to face the growing number of its victims. As Mary Beard explained in 1915:

It is the same development which has characterized all other public works—the growth from remedy to prevention, and the growth is stable for the reason that it represents economy in the former waste of money and effort and because popular education is leading to the demand for prevention and justice rather than charity. In this expansion of municipal functions there can be little dispute as to the importance of women. Their hearts touched in the beginning by human misery and their sentiments aroused, they have been led into manifold activities in attempts at amelioration, which have taught them the breeding places of disease, as well as of vice, crime, poverty, and misery. Having learned that effectively to "swat the fly" they must swat its nest, women have also learned that to swat disease they must swat poor housing, evil labor conditions, ignorance, and vicious interests.[59]

What Beard described was the process by which politics became domesticated. Women's charitable work had hardly made a dent in the social dislocations of industrial society. The problems were unsolvable at the local level because they were not local problems. And, since the goal of these women was to prevent abstract, general problems—to prevent poverty rather than to aid poor people —the methods of antebellum organizations would not suffice. Hence, the state —the only institution of sufficient scope—had to intervene. Women therefore turned their efforts toward securing legislation that addressed what they perceived to be the sources of social problems—laws to compensate victims of industrial accidents, to require better education, to provide adequate nutrition, and to establish factory and tenement inspection, for example.[60] Clubwomen pointed proudly to playgrounds that they had founded and later donated to local governments.[61] Thus women passed on to the state the work of social policy that they found increasingly unmanageable.

Historians have not yet explicitly addressed the questions of how and why governments took on these specific tasks. In the broadest sense, the willingness of government to accept these new responsibilities has to do with the transformation of liberalism in the early twentieth century. Liberalism came to be understood not as individualism and laissez faire but as a sense of social responsibility coupled with a more activist, bureaucratic, and "efficient" government. This understanding of government and politics meshed nicely with that of women's groups. Both emphasized social science ideas and methods, organization, and collective responsibility for social conditions. Thus there were grounds for cooperation, and the institutions that women created could easily be given over to government. Yet the character of collective action varied. The business corporation created the model for the new liberalism, while politically active women and some social thinkers took the family and small community as an ideal.[62] But whatever the mechanism, as governments took up social policy—in part because of women's lobbying—they became part of the private domain.

The domestication of politics, then, was in large part women's own handiwork. In turn, it contributed to the end of separate political cultures. First, it helped women gain the vote. Suffrage was no longer either a radical demand or a challenge to separate spheres, because the concerns of politics and of the home were inextricable. At the same time, it did not threaten the existence of a male political culture because that culture's hold had already attenuated. The domestication of politics was connected, too, with the changed ideas of citizens about what government and politics were for. Each of these developments, illustrating ties between transformations in politics and the role of women, merits further attention.

Recovering from a period of apathy and discouragement, the women's suffrage campaign enjoyed renewed energy in the early twentieth century. The second generation of suffragists included home protection in their arguments in favor of votes for women. They noted that the vote would not remove women from the home and that electoral politics involved the home and would benefit from women's talents. Suffragists argued that women's work in World War I proved their claims to good citizenship. They also took pains to point out what the vote would not do. Indeed, the suffragists made every conceivable argument, from equal rights to home protection to the need for an intelligent electorate. Such a wide array of practical claims did not necessarily represent a retreat from the radicalism of Elizabeth Cady Stanton's generation. Suffragists often presented arguments in response to accusations by the opposition. If opponents claimed that woman suffrage would destroy the home, suffragists replied that it would actually enhance family life. The suffragists' arguments, moreover, reflected a transition in political thought generally. Just as Stanton's contemporaries spoke in the language of Garrisonian abolitionism, the later suffragists framed their ideas in the language of science, racism, efficiency, and cooperation. This does not make their nativist or racist rhetoric any less objectionable, but it does mean that second-generation suffragists were working within a different cultural and intellectual environment.[63]

But organization, not argumentation, was the key to winning the vote for the second generation. They discarded a state-by-state strategy and concentrated on winning a national amendment. Under the leadership of Carrie Chapman Catt and others, suffragists patterned their organization after a political machine, mimicking male politics. The suffrage campaign featured a hierarchical organization, with workers on the district level who received guidance, funds, and speakers from the state organizations, which in turn were supported by the national organization. They conducted petition campaigns to illustrate the support that suffrage had from women and men. They held parades and pageants to demonstrate that support and gather publicity. To be sure, suffragists pointed to the positive results votes for women could bring. But most of all, they aimed to show that woman suffrage—whatever it meant—was inevitable.[64]

Suffragists considered the suffrage referenda in New York to be pivotal tests. Victory there would provide crucial publicity for the cause and lend credence to the notion of inevitability. In 1915 the referendum lost by a fairly wide margin in a fiercely fought campaign; only five scattered upstate counties supported the referendum. Two years later, woman suffrage was back on the ballot. This time, the suffragists concentrated their efforts on district work in major cities. Curiously, the election approached with much less fanfare than that of 1915. The suffragists apparently had won their battle of attrition. The amount and tone of the newspaper coverage suggest that woman suffrage was indeed considered inevitable, and the referendum passed, almost entirely because of the support it received in the cities. The election results point to important patterns. The woman suffrage referendum ran poorly in areas where the prohibition vote was high or where high voter turnout and other manifestations of the nineteenth-century culture of politics were still visible. Here, women's suffrage was still a threat. Conversely, it ran well in cities, especially in certain immigrant wards and places where the Socialist vote was high— where nineteenth-century political patterns had never taken hold or had already disappeared. Men who had no stake in maintaining the old culture of politics seemed more likely to support woman suffrage. In the South, where the right to vote was tied to both manhood and white supremacy, woman suffrage also met stiff resistance.[65]

That woman suffrage had little impact on women or politics has been consid-

ered almost axiomatic by historians. It failed to help women achieve equality.
It did not result in the disaster antisuffragists imagined. Women did not vote
as a reform bloc or, indeed, in any pattern different from men. Woman suffrage simply doubled the electorate. Historians have traced the reasons for the
negligible impact of woman suffrage to the conservative turn of the second-
generation suffragists, including their single-minded pursuit of the vote and
home protection arguments. But to dismiss woman suffrage as having no impact is to miss an important point. It represented the endpoint of nineteenth-
century womanhood and woman's political culture. In a sense, the antisuffragists were right. Women left the home, in a symbolic sense; they lost their
place above politics and their position as the force of moral order. No longer
treated as a political class, women ceased to act as one. At the same time,
politics was unsexed. Differences between the political involvement of men
and women decreased, and government increasingly took on the burden of
social and moral responsibility formerly assigned to the woman's sphere.

The victory of woman suffrage reflected women's gradual movement away
from a separate political culture. By the early twentieth century, the growing
number of women who worked for wages provided palpable examples of the
limits of notions about a woman's place. Certainly by the 1920s, the attachment of women to the home could not be taken for granted in the same way
it had in the nineteenth century, in part because by the 1920s the home was
something of an embarrassment. Many men and women rejected domesticity
as an ideal. The "new woman" of the 1920s discarded nineteenth-century
womanhood by adopting formerly male values and behavior.[66] To be sure,
most women probably did not meet the standard of the "new woman," but
that ideal was the cultural norm against which women now measured their
behavior. Women thus abandoned the home as a basis for a separate political
culture and as a set of values and way of life that all women shared.
    Women rejected the form and substance of nineteenth-century woman-
hood. Municipal housekeepers and charity workers saw that the responsibility
for social policy was not properly theirs: only government had the scope
and potentially the power to deal with national problems. Society seemed
too threatening and dangerous to leave important responsibilities to chance,
and women to whom municipal housekeeping was unknown seemed to sense
this. They also surrendered to government functions that had belonged to the
woman's sphere. Given the seemingly overwhelming complexities and possibilities of grievous errors, women were willing to take the advice of experts
and government aid in feeding their families and rearing and educating their
children. Tradition offered little guidance; the advice of their mothers, who
grew up during the mid- and late nineteenth century, could well have seemed
anachronistic in an urban and industrial society. Their own experiences could

lead to wrong decisions in a rapidly changing society. Moreover, abandoning the functions of the old-fashioned woman's sphere allowed a new independence. Women made some gains, but they also lost the basis for a separate political culture.[67]

Lacking a sense of common ground, women fragmented politically. Their rejection of the woman's sphere as an organizing principle discouraged women from acting as a separate political bloc. Without political segregation to unite them, differences among groups of women magnified. What benefited professional women might be superfluous, even damaging, to the interests of working-class women. Women did not vote as a bloc on "women's" issues because there were no such issues, just as there were no issues that reflected the common interests of all men. The commonality that women had derived from the home in the nineteenth century disappeared, leaving women to splinter into interest groups and political parties. Organizing a separate women's party held little appeal for women because they could not find issues on which to unite.[68] Women were also no longer "above" politics. Their political behavior benefited from neither the veneration of the home and the moral power it bestowed nor the aura of public concern that their older informal methods of participation communicated.

It almost goes without saying that women gained little real political power upon winning the vote. Men granted women the vote when the importance of the male culture of politics and the meaning of the vote changed. Electoral politics was no longer a male right or a ritual that dealt with questions that only men understood. Instead, it was a privilege exercised by intelligent citizens. Important positions in government and in the parties still went to men. Woman suffrage was adopted just at the time when the influence of parties and electoral politics on public policy was declining. By the early twentieth century, interest groups and the formation of public opinion were more effective ways to influence government, especially the new bureaucracies that were removed from direct voter accountability.[69]

As differences between political participation of men and women lessened in the early twentieth century, the role of government changed. Government now carried moral authority and the obligations it implied. That governments often chose not to use that authority is not the point. What matters is that citizens wanted more from government in the way of ethical political behavior and of policies that ensured economic and social stability. To exercise moral authority, government needed to behave in moral ways. Citizens expected office holders to separate their public actions from their private interests and wanted a civil service system to limit the distribution of public rewards for party work. Even in the 1920s, citizens held government responsible for encouraging a growing economy and social order. When the methods employed in the 1920s for accomplishing these goals—government orchestration of self-

regulating functional groups—proved lacking, government took a larger hand
in directing social and economic policy.[70]

Even more fundamentally, Americans' perceptions of the distinctions between the public and private spheres were transformed by the 1920s. Although
it has not received sufficient scholarly attention, some of the outlines of this
change are discernable. In the nineteenth century, social and cultural separations between what was public and what was private were well defined, at least
in theory. The public world included politics, economics, and work outside of
the home, while the private sphere meant the home and family. These sharp de-
lineations provided a sense of stability. The lines were often crossed: women,
for example, worked outside of the home. And, while women brought their
"private" concerns to the "public" sphere, men's political involvement served
private ends. This paradox suggests a rethinking of the meanings of public and
private in the nineteenth century, one that has implications for understanding
public life in the twentieth. Social definitions of public and private blurred
in the twentieth century, recreating an obfuscation similar to that of colonial America. In a sense, the existence of spheres was denied. The personal
was political and the political was evaluated in regard to personal fulfillment.
Citizens judged office holders on the basis of personality. Men and women
shunned the traditional public world of voting and holding office to concen-
trate their attention on private life. Although not a descent into confusion (the
separations between public and private had also been murky in the nineteenth
century), these changes pointed to a complex and vastly different understanding of the meaning of public and private from the one held by people in the
nineteenth century.[71]

Women played important, but different, parts in two major turning points in
American political history, transformations that coincided with changes in the
roles of women. In the Jacksonian period, the cultural assignment of republican virtues and moral authority to womanhood helped men embrace partisanship and understand electoral politics as social drama. The social service
work of female organizations filled some of the gaps created as governments
reduced the scope of their efforts. Two political cultures operated throughout
the remainder of the nineteenth century. The female culture was based on the
ideology of domesticity and involved continual expansion of the environs of
the "home." Women carried out social policy through voluntary action. They
practiced a kind of interest-group politics by directing their attention to specific issues and exercising influence through informal channels. Male politics
consisted of formal structures: the franchise, parties, and holding office. For
many men, this participation was as much social as it was political, and it
contributed to a definition of manhood.

Women had a more active part in the political changes of the Progressive period. They passed on their voluntary work—social policy—to govern-

ments. Men now sought to influence government through nonelectoral means, as women had long done. Electoral politics lost its masculine connotations, although it did not cease to be male dominated. Voting, ideally, had less to do with personal loyalties than with self-interested choices. Women voted. They did so in somewhat smaller numbers than men, and they held few important party or governmental positions. But sharp separations between men's and women's participation abated. In this process, individual women gained opportunities. "Woman," however, lost her ability to serve as a positive moral influence and to implement social policy.

Much work on women's political involvement is necessary before we can fully understand the connections between women's activities and American politics. But if either is to be understood, the two must be considered together. Gaining a broader understanding of "politics" is one way to begin doing so. This interpretation should consider the political system as a whole and include both formal and informal means of influence. It could thus embrace voluntary activities, protest movements, lobbying, and other ways in which people attempt to direct governmental decisions, together with electoral politics and policy making. In determining what activities might be termed "political" we might adapt John Dewey's definition of the "public." For Dewey, the "public as a state" included "all modes of associated behavior . . . [that] have exclusive and enduring consequences which involve others beyond those directly engaged in them." [72] This understanding suggests that the voluntary work of nineteenth-century women was part of the political system. Although directed at domestic concerns, the activities of women's organizations were meant to affect the behavior of others, as much as—or more than—were ballots cast for Grover Cleveland. Given such a definition of politics, political historians could come to different understandings of the changes in and connections between political participation and policy making. Historians of women could find new contexts in which to place their work. Students of both subjects need to go beyond the definition of "political" offered by nineteenth-century men.

NOTES

A number of individuals commented on earlier versions of this essay, including Dee Garrison, Kathleen W. Jones, Suzanne Lebsock, Richard L. McCormick, Wilson Carey McWilliams, John F. Reynolds, Thomas Slaughter, and Warren I. Susman. I am grateful for their criticism, advice, and encouragement.

1   Accounts of the suffrage campaign include William H. Chafe, *Women and Equality* (New York:Oxford University Press, 1977); Carl N. Degler, *At Odds: Women and the Family in America from the Revolution to the Present* (New York: Oxford University Press, 1980), chap. 14; Ellen Carol DuBois, *Feminism and Suffrage: The Emergence of an Independent Women's Movement in America, 1848–1869* (Ithaca,

N.Y.: Cornell University Press, 1978); Eleanor Flexner, *Century of Struggle: The Woman's Rights Movement in the United States* (Cambridge, Mass.: Harvard University Press, 1958); Alan P. Grimes, *The Puritan Ethic and Woman Suffrage* (New York: Greenwood, 1967); Aileen S. Kraditor, *The Ideas of the Woman Suffrage Movement, 1890–1920* (New York: Columbia University Press, 1965); David Morgan, *Suffragists and Democrats in America* (East Lansing, Mich.: Michigan State University Press, 1970); William L. O'Neill, *Everyone Was Brave: A History of American Feminism* (Chicago: Quadrangle, 1969); Ross Evan Paulson, *Woman's Suffrage and Prohibition* (Glenview, Ill.: Scott, Foresman and Co., 1973); Anne F. Scott and Andrew M. Scott, *One-Half of the People: The Fight for Woman's Suffrage* (Philadelphia: University of Illinois Press, 1975). Important treatments of the ideology of domesticity include Nancy F. Cott, *The Bonds of Womanhood: Woman's Sphere in New England, 1790–1835* (New Haven: Yale University Press, 1975); Daniel Scott Smith, "Family Limitation, Sexual Control, and Domestic Feminism in Victorian America," in *Clio's Consciousness Raised*, ed., Mary Hartman and Lois W. Banner (New York: Octagon, 1974), 119–33; Kathryn Kish Sklar, *Catherine Beecher: A Study in American Domesticity* (New Haven: Yale University Press, 1973); Barbara Welter, "The Cult of True Womanhood, 1820–1860," *American Quarterly* 18 (1966): 151–74.

2   Syntheses of the vast number of works on Progressive reform include John W. Chambers II, *The Tyranny of Change: America in the Progressive Era, 1900–1917* (New York: St. Martin, 1980); Otis L. Graham, *The Great Campaign: Reform and War in America, 1900–1928* (Englewood Cliffs, N.J.: Prentice Hall, 1971); Arthur S. Link and Richard L. McCormick, *Progressivism* (Arlington Heights, Ill.: Harlan Davidson, 1983); Samuel P. Hays, *The Response to Industrialism, 1885–1914* (Chicago: University of Chicago Press, 1957); William L. O'Neill, *The Progressive Years: America Comes of Age* (New York: Harper Row, 1975); Robert Wiebe, *The Search for Order, 1877–1920* (New York: Hill and Wang, 1967). For a good recent review essay, see Daniel T. Rodgers, "In Search of Progressivism," *Reviews in American History* 10 (1982): 113–32.

3   Numerous works have appeared over the past decade that deal with the public activities of middle-class women. These works most often examine particular groups and attempt to trace the development of a feminist consciousness in the nineteenth century. See, for example, Barbara Berg, *The Remembered Gate— Origins of American Feminism: Women and the City, 1800–1860* (New York: Oxford University Press, 1978); Karen Blair, *The Clubwoman as Feminist: True Womanhood Redefined, 1868–1914* (New York: Holmes & Meier, 1980); Ruth Bordin, *Woman and Temperance: The Quest for Power and Liberty, 1873–1900* (Philadelphia: Temple University Press, 1981); Mari Jo Buhle, *Women and American Socialism, 1870–1920* (Urbana, Ill.: University of Illinois Press, 1981); Cott, *The Bonds of Womanhood*; Barbara Leslie Epstein, *The Politics of Domesticity: Women, Evangelism, and Temperance in Nineteenth-Century America* (Middletown, Conn.: Wesleyan University Press, 1981); Estelle B. Freedman, "Separatism as Strategy: Female Institution-Building and American Feminism, 1870–1930," *Feminist Studies* 5 (1979): 512–29; Linda K. Kerber, *Women of the Republic: Intellect and Ideology in Revolutionary America* (Chapel Hill, N.C.: University of North Carolina Press, 1980); William Leach, *True Love and Perfect Union: The Feminist*

Reform of Sex and Society (New York: Basic, 1980); Gerda Lerner, "The Lady and the Mill Girl: Changes in the Status of Women in the Age of Jackson," 15–30, "Community Work of Black Club Women," 83–93, "Political Activities of Anti-Slavery Women," 94–111, and "Black and White Women in Confrontation and Interaction," 112–28, in her *The Majority Finds Its Past: Placing Women in History* (New York: Oxford University Press, 1979); J. Stanley Lemons, *The Woman Citizen: Social Feminism in the 1920s* (Urbana, Ill.: University of Illinois Press, 1973); Keith E. Melder, *Beginnings of Sisterhood: The American Woman's Rights Movement, 1800–1850* (New York: Schocken, 1977); Mary Beth Norton, *Liberty's Daughters: The Revolutionary Experience of American Women, 1750–1800* (Boston: Little, 1980); Mary P. Ryan, *Cradle of the Middle Class: The Family in Oneida County, New York, 1790–1865* (Cambridge, Mass.: Cambridge University Press, 1981); Anne Firor Scott, *The Southern Lady: From Pedestal to Politics, 1830–1930* (Chicago: University of Chicago Press, 1970). A number of contemporary accounts are especially useful. See Mary R. Beard, *Women's Work in Municipalities* (New York, 1915); Jane Cunningham Croly, *The History of the Women's Club Movement in America* (New York, 1898); Mary A. Livermore, *My Story of the War* (Hartford, Conn., 1896); "Women and the State," in *Women's Work in America*, ed. William Meyers (Hartford, Conn., 1889); Frances E. Willard, *Woman and Temperance: Or, the Work and Workers of the Women's Christian Temperance Union* (Hartford, Conn., 1883).

4   A number of studies examine the treatment of women in American political thought. These include Zillah Eisenstein, *The Radical Future of Liberal Feminism* (New York: Longman, 1981); Jean Bethke Elshtain, *Public Man, Private Woman: Women in Social and Political Thought* (Princeton, N.J.: Princeton University Press, 1981); Kerber, *Women of the Republic*; Susan Moller Okin, *Women in Western Political Thought* (Princeton, N.J.: Princeton University Press, 1979). Historical treatments of women in politics include William H. Chafe, *The American Woman: Her Changing Social, Economic, and Political Roles, 1920–1970* (New York: Oxford University Press, 1972), 24–47; Jane Gruenebaum, "Women in Politics," in *The Power to Govern: Assessing Reform in the United States*. Proceedings of the Academy of Political Science no. 34, ed. Richard M. Pious (New York, 1981), 104–20; Gerda Lerner, ed., *The Female Experience: An American Documentary* (Indianapolis: Bobbs-Merrill Co., Inc., 1977), 317–22; Sheila M. Rothman, *Woman's Proper Place: A History of Changing Ideals and Practices, 1870 to the Present* (New York: Basic, 1978), 102–32, 136–53.

5   "Government" refers to the formal institutions of the state and their functions. "Policy" includes efforts by those within these institutions as well as by those outside them to shape social or economic conditions with the support of "government."

6   Cott, *The Bonds of Womanhood*; Kerber, *Women of the Republic*; Norton, *Liberty's Daughters*; Ryan, *Cradle of the Middle Class*. Also see Linda Grant DePauw, *Founding Mothers: Women in the Revolutionary Era* (New York: Houghton Mifflin, 1975); Joan Hoff-Wilson, "The Illusion of Change: Women and the American Revolution," in *The American Revolution: Explorations in the History of American Radicalism*, Alfred H. Young, ed. (DeKalb, Ill.: Northern Illinois University Press, 1976), 383–444. Of these works, only Kerber's and Norton's explicitly set

out to answer questions about women and politics, and their analyses differ on important points. On the basis of an examination of women's diaries and other papers, Norton argued that the Revolution and republicanism significantly changed the role of women. Family relationships, for example, grew more egalitarian, and women developed a new appreciation of their competence and skills outside the home. Kerber's analysis of American political thought in relationship to women, however, suggests that neither republicanism nor the Revolution had a positive effect on the role of women. Rather, republican thought assumed women were apolitical. But by the early nineteenth century an ideology of motherhood allowed women to combine domesticity with political action.

7   Thomas Bender, *Community and Social Change in America* (New Brunswick, N.J.: Johns Hopkins Press, 1978), 68; Paul Boyer and Stephen Nissenbaum, *Salem Possessed: The Social Origins of Witchcraft* (Cambridge, Mass.: Harvard University Press, 1971), 151; Richard L. Bushman, *From Puritan to Yankee: Character and the Social Order in Connecticut, 1690–1765* (New York: Norton, 1970), chaps. 1, 2; John Demos, *A Little Commonwealth: Family Life in Plymouth Colony* (New York: Oxford University Press, 1970), 182–85, chap. 4; James Henretta, *The Evolution of American Society, 1700–1815: An Interdisciplinary Analysis* (Lexington, Mass.: Heath, D.C., and Co., 1973), 23–31; Ryan, *Cradle of the Middle Class*, chap. 1; Michael Zuckerman, *Peaceable Kingdoms: New England Towns in the Eighteenth Century* (New York: Greenwood, 1970).

8   Bender, *Community and Social Change*, 62–67; Michael Kammen, *Colonial New York* (New York: Kraus International, 1975), 290; Paul G. E. Clemens, *The Atlantic Economy and Colonial Maryland's Eastern Shore: From Tobacco to Grain* (Ithaca, N.Y.: Cornell University Press, 1980); James T. Lemon, *The Best Poor Man's Country: A Geographical Study of Early Southeastern Pennsylvania* (Baltimore: Johns Hopkins Press, 1972); Edmund S. Morgan, *American Slavery, American Freedom: The Ordeal of Colonial Virginia* (New York: Norton, 1975), 149–79; Darrett B. Rutman, *Winthrop's Boston* (Chapel Hill, N.C.: University of North Carolina Press, 1965); and Sam Bass Warner, Jr., *The Private City: Philadelphia in Three Periods of Its Growth* (Philadelphia: University of Pennsylvania Press, 1968), chap. 1.

9   Kerber, *Women of the Republic*, chap. 1; Norton, *Liberty's Daughters*, chaps. 1–3.

10 Among the many works on colonial political practices, see, for example, Charles S. Sydnor, *Gentlemen Freeholders: Political Practices in Washington's Virginia* (Chapel Hill, N.C.: University of North Carolina Press, 1952); Robert Zemsky, *Merchants, Farmers, and River Gods: An Essay on Eighteenth-Century Politics* (Boston: Gambit, 1971). On changing attitudes toward authority, see Bushman, *Puritan to Yankee*, 138–63, 264–87; Jay Fliegelman, *Prodigals and Pilgrims: The American Revolution against Patriarchal Authority, 1750–1800* (Cambridge, Mass.: Cambridge University Press, 1982); Philip J. Greven, Jr., *Four Generations: Population, Land, and Family in Colonial Andover, Massachusetts* (Ithaca, N.Y.: Cornell University Press, 1970), chaps. 7, 8; Robert A. Gross, *The Minutemen and Their World* (New York: Hill and Wang, 1976); Gary B. Nash, *The Urban Crucible: Social Change, Political Consciousness, and the Origins of the American Revolution* (Cambridge, Mass.: Harvard University Press, 1979).

11 Reviews of the literature on republicanism include Robert E. Shalhope, "Toward

a Republican Synthesis: The Emergence of an Understanding of Republicanism in American Historiography," *William and Mary Quarterly*, 3d ser., 29 (1972): 49–80; Robert E. Shalhope, "Republicanism and Early American Historiography," *William and Mary Quarterly* 39 (1982): 334–56. The articles in Young's *The American Revolution* illustrate divisions in the republican consensus.

12 Kerber, *Women of the Republic*, chap. 2.

13 Edward Countryman, *A People in Revolution: The American Revolution and Political Society in New York, 1760–1790* (Baltimore: Johns Hopkins University Press, 1981), 43–44; Kerber, *Women of the Republic*, chaps. 2–3; Nash, *The Urban Crucible*, chap. 7; Norton, *Liberty's Daughters*, chaps. 6–7; Julia Cherry Spruill, *Women's Life and Work in the Southern Colonies* (Chapel Hill, N.C.: University of North Carolina Press, 1938; reprint ed., New York, 1972), 232–45.

14 Countryman, *A People in Revolution*; Eric Foner, *Tom Paine and Revolutionary America* (New York: Oxford University Press, 1976), chaps. 2, 5; Pauline Maier, "Popular Uprisings and Civil Authority in Eighteenth-Century America," *William and Mary Quarterly*, 3d ser., 27 (1970): 3–35; E. P. Thompson, "The Moral Economy of the English Crowd in the Eighteenth Century," *Past & Present* 50 (1971): 76–136; Warner, *The Private City*, pt. 1.

15 Kerber, *Women of the Republic*, chaps. 7, 9; Norton, *Liberty's Daughters*, chap. 9. Some works suggest that republicanism was not a cause of more egalitarian family relationships, of new education for women to enhance their roles as better wives and mothers, or of women's use of the home to gain political influence. Jay Fliegelman, for example, persuasively argued that by the middle of the eighteenth century the older notion of the patriarchal family was under attack. It was being replaced by a new ideal—one drawn from Locke and the Scottish commonsense philosophers. Examining these writings and popular novels, he showed that the new model, which called for affectionate and egalitarian relationships with children and humane child rearing designed to prepare children for rational independence and self-sufficiency, was in place well before 1776. In fact, the rhetoric of the Revolution was replete with images portraying the importance of personal autonomy and of parental respect for the individuality of children who had come of age. Thus, a cultural revolution against patriarchal authority preceded the Revolution. (Fliegelman's analysis, however, chiefly concerns sons, not daughters, and it deals with questions not directly related to relationships between men and women.) Furthermore, the "republican mother" was not an ideal limited to America. Traian Stoianovich showed that an ideology of domesticity similar in content to republican motherhood had appeared in a systemized form in France by the late seventeenth century. See Fliegelman, *Prodigals and Pilgrims*; Stoianovitch, "Gender and Family: Myths, Models, and Ideologies," *History Teacher* 15 (1981): 70–84.

16 For the idea that women's political activity through organizations filled an undefined space in American government and politics, see Suzanne Lebsock, *The Free Women of Petersburg: Status and Culture in a Southern Town, 1784–1860* (New York: Norton, 1984), chap. 7.

17 On electoral participation in the early nineteenth century, see Ronald P. Formisano, "Deferential-Participant Politics: The Early Republic's Political Culture," *American Political Science Review* [hereafter, *APSR*] 68 (1974): 473–87; Paul Kleppner,

Who Voted? The Dynamics of Electoral Turnout, 1870–1980 (New York: Praeger Publishers, 1982), chap. 3: "The Era of Citizen Mobilization, 1840–1900." For a discussion of the increasing rates of participation, their timing, and their causes, see Richard P. McCormick, "New Perspectives on Jacksonian Politics," *AHR* 65 (1959–60): 288–301.

18 The rise and decline—indeed, the existence—of deference in male political behavior remains widely debated by political historians. Ronald P. Formisano has provided a good review of this literature in "Deferential-Participant Politics." A number of studies of individual communities illustrate the appearance of competing elites and new community divisions and citizens' demands. See Bender, *Community and Social Change*, 100–108; Michael Frisch, *Town into City: Springfield, Massachusetts, and the Meaning of Community, 1840–1880* (Cambridge, Mass.: Harvard University Press, 1972), 32–53, 179–201; Harry L. Watson, *Jacksonian Politics and Community Conflict: The Emergence of the Second Party System in Cumberland County, North Carolina* (Baton Rouge, La.: Louisiana University Press, 1981), 82–108.

19 I have drawn my discussion of the connections between economic issues and party formation from Watson's *Jacksonian Politics and Community Conflict*, which imaginatively blends many of the themes and approaches historians have most recently advanced to explain nineteenth-century political life. Watson combined a refurbished economic interpretation, the assumption that citizens cared deeply about economic issues, a concern for questions about political culture, attention to republican ideology and quantitative methods, and a social analysis of politics in his account of party formation. Although such assumptions, methods, and concerns will probably continue to influence political historians, a good deal of debate remains about the development of parties and the meaning of partisanship. Richard P. McCormick argued that the legal framework governing elections (as well as the revival of the contest for the presidency) best explains the rising pitch of partisan behavior and that parties were fundamentally electoral machines, unconcerned with issues. See McCormick, *The Second American Party System: Party Formation in the Jacksonian Era* (Chapel Hill, N.C.: University of North Carolina Press, 1966). Others, however, have found that ethnic and religious tensions among citizens can account for partisan divisions. See Lee Benson, *The Concept of Jacksonian Democracy: New York as a Test Case* (Princeton, N.J.: Princeton University Press, 1961); Ronald P. Formisano, *The Birth of Mass Political Parties: Michigan, 1827–1861* (Princeton, N.J.: Princeton University Press, 1971); Paul Kleppner, *The Cross of Culture: A Social Analysis of Midwestern Politics, 1850–1900* (New York: Free Press, 1970); Michael F. Holt, *Forging a Majority: The Formation of the Republican Party in Pittsburgh, 1848–1860* (New Haven, Conn.: Yale University Press, 1969). For recent historiographic analyses of Jacksonian politics, see Ronald P. Formisano, "Toward a Reorientation of Jacksonian Politics: A Review of the Literature, 1959–1975," *Journal of American History* [hereafter, *JAH*] 63 (1976–77): 42–65; Sean Wilentz, "On Class and Politics in Jacksonian America," *Reviews in American History* 10 (1982): 45–63. Richard L. McCormick evaluated the work of those offering an ethnic and religious interpretation. See McCormick, "Ethno-Cultural Interpretations of Nineteenth-Century American Voting Behavior," *Political Science Quarterly* 89 (1974): 351–77.

20   Discussions of working men's parties include Bruce Laurie, *Working People of Philadelphia, 1800–1850* (Philadelphia: Temple University Press, 1980); Edward Pessen, *Most Uncommon Jacksonians: The Political Leaders of the Early Labor Movement* (Albany, N.Y.: State University of New York Press, 1967), 11–33. The Antimasonic party, strongest in rural areas, offered a moral critique of American politics and society; see Benson, *The Concept of Jacksonian Democracy*, 14–38. Ronald P. Formisano provided an analysis of both parties; see *The Transformation of Political Culture: Massachusetts Parties, 1790s–1840s* (New York: Oxford University Press, 1983), 197–224.

21   See Jean H. Baker, *Affairs of Party: The Political Culture of Northern Democrats in the Mid-Nineteenth Century* (Ithaca, N.Y.: Cornell University Press, 1983), chaps. 1, 2; Benson, *The Concept of Jacksonian Democracy*; Formisano, *The Birth of Mass Political Parties*, chaps. 2, 7; Watson, *Jacksonian Politics and Community Conflict*, 151–86, 269–77, 297–99, 312–13.

22   For a discussion of the removal of national issues from local politics, see Bender, *Community and Social Change*, 104.

23   On the positions on issues taken by various parties, see McCormick, *Second American Party System*; Michael F. Holt, *The Political Crisis of the 1850s* (New York: Wiley, 1978). Richard P. McCormick's view that parties were primarily electoral machines conflicts with that of Holt, who argued that parties needed clear divisions between them to maintain the voters' interest. For consensual politics at the local level, especially in settled towns, see Hal S. Barron, "After the Great Transformation: The Social Processes of Settled Rural Life in the Nineteenth-Century North," in *The Countryside in the Age of Capitalist Transformation: Essays in the Social History of Rural America*, ed. Steven Hahn and Johnathan Prude (Chapel Hill, N.C.: University of North Carolina Press, 1985), 327–44. Bender, *Community and Social Change*, 104–5; Stuart Blumin, *The Urban Threshold: Growth and Change in a Nineteenth-Century Community* (Chicago: University of Chicago Press, 1976), 144, 148.

24   For discussions of nineteenth-century voting patterns, see Walter Dean Burnham, "The Changing Shape of the American Political Universe," *APSR* 59 (1965): 7–28; Paul Kleppner, *Who Voted*, chap. 3; and Richard L. McCormick, "The Party Period and Public Policy: An Exploratory Hypothesis," *JAH* 66 (1979–80): 279–98. Although they agree on a description of political behavior in the nineteenth century, these accounts differ on periodization, focus, and explanations for the demise of nineteenth-century patterns. I have adopted McCormick's emphases on the continuities of partisan behavior throughout most of the nineteenth century and the links between distribution and partisanship. For the best account of the connections between partisanship and family, see Baker, *Affairs of Party*, chap. 1.

25   Daniel Calhoun suggested that fears about gender replaced fears about tyranny in the political thought of the nineteenth century; Calhoun, *The Intelligence of a People* (Princeton, N.J.: Princeton University Press, 1973), 188–205. For a discussion of partisan politics as a way of recreating fraternal relations, see Wilson Carey McWilliams, *The Idea of Fraternity in America* (Berkeley and Los Angeles: University of California Press, 1973), chap. 3, 243–53. For an account from the Progressive era, see Mary Kingsbury Simkhovitch, "Friendship and Politics," *Political Science Quarterly* 17 (1902): 189–205.

26   Descriptions and analyses of campaign rituals include Robert Gray Gunderson, *The Log Cabin Campaign* (Lexington, Ky.: University of Kentucky Press, 1957), 1–11, 108–47, 210–18; Richard Jensen, *The Winning of the Midwest: Social and Political Conflict, 1888–1896* (Chicago: University of Chicago Press, 1971), 1–33; "Armies, Admen, and Crusaders: Types of Presidential Election Campaigns," *History Teacher* 2 (1969): 33–50; Michael E. McGerr, "Political Spectacle and Partisanship in New Haven, 1860–1900," paper presented at the Seventy-Fifth Annual Meeting of the Organization of American Historians, held in Philadelphia, April 1982; McCormick, *The Second American Party System*, 15–16, 30–31, 75–76, 88, 145, 157–58, 268–76. Lewis O. Saum, drawing on a vast number of diaries, documented citizens' participation in campaigns and their laconic reactions to antebellum politics; Saum, *The Popular Mood of Pre–Civil War America* (Westport, Conn.: Greenwood Press, 1980), 149–57.

27   Party politicians often spoke of reformers—those men outside of the party—in terms that questioned the reformers' masculinity. Most of all, reformers were seen as politically impotent. Men whose loyalty to a party was questionable were referred to, for example, as the "third sex" of American politics, "man-milliners," and "Miss-Nancys." This suggests that men, like women, were limited in the forms that their political participation could take. Works that note these charges of effeminacy include Lois W. Banner, *Elizabeth Cady Stanton: A Radical for Woman's Rights* (Boston: Little, Brown, 1980), 43; Geoffrey Blodgett, "Reform Thought and the Genteel Tradition," in *The Gilded Age*, 2d ed., ed. H. Wayne Morgan (Syracuse, N.Y.: Syracuse University Press, 1970), 56–57; Richard Hofstadter, *Anti-Intellectualism in American Life* (New York: Knopf, 1963), 179–91; Alan Trachtenberg, *The Incorporation of America: Culture and Society in the Gilded Age* (New York: Hill and Wang, 1982), 163–65. In addition to this language, phallic imagery and symbolism had an important place in nineteenth-century electoral politics. Psychohistorians might find a good deal of underlying meaning in the long ballot (reformers favored the short form) and pole raisings, for example, as well as in partisans' charges of sexual impotence. Political historians, however, have as yet failed to examine the rituals and symbols of partisan contests in regard to their sexual connotations.

28   Formisano, *Transformation of Political Culture*, 266; McGerr, "Political Spectacle and Partisanship"; Saum, *The Popular Mood of Pre–Civil War America*, 153.

29   On economic policy and constitutional revision, see Wallace D. Farnham, " 'The Weakened Spring of Government': A Study in Nineteenth-Century American History," *AHR* 68 (1962–63): 662–80; L. Ray Gunn, "Political Implications of General Incorporation Laws in New York to 1860," *Mid-America* 59 (1977): 171–91; Oscar Handlin and Mary Flug Handlin, *Commonwealth: A Study of the Role of Government in the American Economy—Massachusetts, 1774–1861* (New York: New York University Press, 1947); Louis Hartz, *Economic Policy and Democratic Thought: Pennsylvania, 1776–1850* (Cambridge, Mass.: Harvard University Press, 1948); James Willard Hurst, *Law and the Conditions of Freedom in the Nineteenth-Century United States* (Madison, Wisc.: University of Wisconsin Press, 1956), chaps. 1, 2; Morton Keller, *Affairs of State: Public Life in Late Nineteenth-Century America* (Cambridge, Mass.: Belknap Press of Harvard University Press, 1977), 71–81. On changes in social policy, see Jeremy P. Felt, *Hostages of Fortune:*

Child Labor Reform in New York State (Syracuse, N.Y.: Syracuse University Press, 1956), 17–37; Walter I. Trattner, *From Poor Law to Welfare State: A History of Social Welfare in America* (New York: Free Press, 1974), chaps. 2–4.

30 Cott, *The Bonds of Womanhood*, chap. 2; Berg, *The Remembered Gate*, chaps. 2–4; Degler, *At Odds*, chaps. 3–5; Ann Douglas, *The Feminization of American Culture* (New York: Knopf, 1977), 65–90, 107–11; Sklar, *Catherine Beecher*, 87, 151–67, 212–13; Mary P. Ryan, *Womanhood in America: From Colonial Times to the Present* (1975; 2d ed., New York: New Viewpoints, 1979), 142–74; Carroll Smith-Rosenberg, "Beauty, the Beast, and the Militant Woman: A Case Study in Sex Roles and Social Stress in Jacksonian America," *American Quarterly* 4 (1971): 562–84; Ryan, *Womanhood in America*, 85–92; Welter, "Cult of True Womanhood."

31 Mary P. Ryan argued that these new organizations prepared women for a domesticity confined to the conjugal family; *Cradle of the Middle Class*, esp. 9–18. Perhaps Berg made the strongest case for the political importance of early nineteenth-century women's organizations, for she contended that these early reform groups provided the groundwork for American feminism; *The Remembered Gate*, esp. 6–7, 174–75, 240–42.

32 Welter, "Cult of True Womanhood"; Sklar, *Catherine Beecher*, 126–29, 151–67, 172, 212–13.

33 The phrase is Welter's; see "The Cult of True Womanhood." Since the appearance of her work, historians of women have concentrated on questions different from those Welter asked about the concurrent rise of the woman's sphere and male egalitarianism. Welter explored the relationship between the two and found that the new insistence on woman's place compensated for the lack of restraint on male political and economic ambitions. Scholars have since focused on the impact of domesticity on feminism. Some historians, taking a "cultural" approach, have seen the roots of feminism in women's organizations and domesticity. Others, notably Ellen DuBois, have found this inadequate. They have argued that, in order to understand the origins of feminism, historians should pay closest attention to explicitly "political" concerns in the nineteenth century. For an introduction to this debate, see "Politics and Culture in Women's History: A Symposium," *Feminist Studies* 6 (1980): 26–54. Studies of the woman's sphere in the Jacksonian period include Berg, *The Remembered Gate*; Cott, *The Bonds of Womanhood*; Lerner, "The Lady and the Mill Girl"; Glenda Riley, "The Subtle Subversion: Changes in the Traditionalist Image of the American Woman," *Historian* 32 (1970): 210–27; Sklar, *Catherine Beecher*, esp. 134–36, 155–67; Smith-Rosenberg, "Beauty, the Beast, and the Militant Woman"; and Ryan, *Womanhood in America*, 85–92.

34 Gordon Wood, *The Creation of the American Republic, 1776–1787* (Chapel Hill, N.C.: University of North Carolina Press, 1969). For an economic understanding of the republican vocabulary, see Rowland Berthoff, "Independence and Attachment, Virtue and Interest: From Republican Citizen to Free Enterpriser, 1787–1837," in *Uprooted Americans: Essays to Honor Oscar Handlin*, ed. Richard Bushman et al. (Boston: Little, Brown, 1979), 97–124. In a related vein, Merle Curti discussed economic arguments for national loyalty; see Curti, *The Roots of American Loyalty* (New York: Columbia University Press, 1946), chap. 4. On connections between domesticity and Jacksonian democracy, see Lawrence J.

Friedman, *Inventors of the Promised Land* (New York: Knopf, 1975), chap. 4; Sklar, *Catherine Beecher*, 80–89, 155–63.

35 Degler, *At Odds*, 332–33; Suzanne D. Lebsock, "Radical Reconstruction and the Property Rights of Southern Women," *Journal of Southern History* 43 (1977): 195– 216. Lebsock noted that opposition to women speakers, along with new forms of ritual deference, appeared in the middle of the nineteenth century, and she suggested that men may have reacted to women's increasing power in the private sphere by encroaching on their public roles; *Free Women of Petersburg*, chap. 7.

36 Mary P. Ryan referred to women who wished to apply motherhood to the pub- lic sphere as "social housekeepers"; *Womanhood in America*, 142–47, 226–35. For other studies that consider the expansion and articulation of domesticity, see Cott, *The Bonds of Womanhood*; Linda Gordon, *Woman's Body, Woman's Right: A Social History of Birth Control* (New York: Grossman, 1976), 95–115, 126–36; Ryan, *Cradle of the Middle Class*; Sklar, *Catherine Beecher*, 80–89, 96, 135–37, 151–67, 193–94, 203, 221–22, 264–65.

37 Rheta Childe Dorr, *What Eighty Million Women Want* (Boston, 1919; reprint ed., New York, 1971), 327.

38 Berg, *The Remembered Gate*, esp. chap. 7; Degler, *At Odds*, 279–86, 298–316; Cott, *The Bonds of Womanhood*, 149–59; Melder, *Beginnings of Sisterhood*, 40– 43, 50–60, 64–76; Ryan, *Cradle of the Middle Class*, chap. 3; Smith-Rosenberg, "Beauty, the Beast, and the Militant Woman."

39 Both Berg and Melder stressed the antimale rhetoric of these early organizations; Melder, *Beginnings of Sisterhood*, chap. 4, esp. 55. Also see Riley, "Subtle Sub- version"; Mary P. Ryan, "The Power of Women's Networks: A Case Study of Female Moral Reform in Antebellum America," *Feminist Studies* 5 (1979): 66–85; Smith-Rosenberg, "Beauty, the Beast, and the Militant Woman"; Blair, *Club- woman as Feminist*; Estelle B. Freedman, *Their Sisters' Keepers: Women's Prison Reform in America, 1830–1930* (Ann Arbor, Mich.: University of Michigan Press, 1981), 22–35; and Leach, *True Love and Perfect Union*, chaps. 6–7.

40 Berg, *The Remembered Gate*, 183–85. For comparable examples, see Melder, *Beginnings of Sisterhood*, chap. 4; and Ryan, "The Power of Women's Networks."

41 On the possibility of racial cooperation, see Blanche Glassman Hersh, *The Slavery of Sex: Feminist Abolitionists in America* (Urbana, Ill.: University of Illinois Press, 1978). Gerda Lerner has explicated the difficulty of such cooperation; see "Black and White Women in Interaction and Confrontation."

42 On the Woman's Parliament, see Blair, *Clubwoman as Feminist*, 39–45, 73.

43 DuBois, *Feminism and Suffrage*. Also see Degler, *At Odds*, chap. 7; Scott and Scott, *One-Half the People*.

44 DuBois, *Feminism and Suffrage*.

45 Fourteen states admitted women to the electorate at least for school elections. Four states—Wyoming, Colorado, Idaho, and Utah—passed full woman suffrage amendments. On the conservative, nonfeminist motives behind the passage of woman suffrage in the western states, see Grimes, *Puritan Ethic and Woman Suffrage*. For Sarah Churske Stevens's account of her successful race for school superintendent in Markate County, Minnesota, in 1890, see Lerner, *Female Ex- perience*, 361–73.

46 George M. Fredrickson, *The Inner Civil War: Northern Intellectuals and the Crisis

of the Union (New York, 1965); James Gilbert, *Designing the Industrial State: The Intellectual Pursuit of Collectivism in America, 1880–1940* (Chicago: Quadrangle Books, 1972); Peter Dobkin Hall, *The Organization of American Culture, 1700–1900: Private Institutions, Elites, and the Origins of American Nationality* (New York: New York University Press, 1982), 218–70; Thomas L. Haskell, *The Emergence of Professional Social Science: The American Social Science Association and the Nineteenth-Century Crisis of Authority* (Urbana, Ill.: University of Illinois Press, 1977); Keller, *Affairs of State*; Leach, *True Love and Perfect Union*; and Trachtenberg, *The Incorporation of America*.

47 L. P. Brockett and Mary C. Vaughn, *Women's Work in the Civil War* (Philadelphia: Zeigler, McCurdy and Company, 1967); Ann Douglas, "The War Within: Women Nurses in the Union Army," *Civil War History* 18 (1972): 197–212; Fredrickson, *The Inner Civil War*, 98–112, 212–16; Livermore, *My Story of the War*; Rothman, *Woman's Proper Place*, 71–74; Ryan, *Womanhood in America*, 226–28.

48 Buhle, *Women and American Socialism*; Ann D. Gordon and Mari Jo Buhle, "Gender Politics and Class Conflict: Chicago in the Gilded Age." Paper presented at the Upstate Women's History Conference, held in Binghamton, New York, October 1981.

49 Social science was for Franklin Sanborn, a leader of the American Social Science Association, "the feminine gender of Political Economy, . . . very receptive of particulars but little capacity of general and aggregate matters." Sanborn, as quoted in Haskell, *Emergence of Professional Social Science*, 137.

50 On women and social science, see Gordon and Buhle, "Gender Politics and Class Conflict"; Leach, *True Love and Perfect Union*, 316–22, 324–46; Rothman, *Woman's Proper Place*, 108–12. Transitions in reform thought and tactics are traced in Paul Boyer, *Urban Masses and Moral Order, 1820–1920* (Cambridge, Mass.: Harvard University Press, 1978); Robert H. Bremner, *From the Depths: The Discovery of Poverty in the United States* (New York: New York University Press, 1956); Fredrickson, *The Inner Civil War*, 98–112, 119–216; Roy Lubove, *The Professional Altruist: The Emergence of Social Work as a Career, 1880–1930* (Cambridge, Mass.: Harvard University Press, 1965), 2–20, 81–82, 84; David P. Thelen, *The New Citizenship: The Origins of Progressivism in Wisconsin, 1885–1900* (Columbia, Mo.: University of Missouri Press, 1972). On the South, see James L. Leloudis II, "School Reform in the New South: The Women's Association for the Betterment of Public School Houses in North Carolina, 1902–1919," *JAH* 69 (1982–83): 886–909; Scott, *Southern Lady*, chap. 6.

51 For an examination of changing attitudes about voluntarism, see Kathleen D. McCarthy, *Noblesse Oblige: Charity and Cultural Philanthropy in Chicago, 1849–1929* (Chicago: University of Chicago Press, 1982), esp. 27–50.

52 On women's activity in early temperance organizations, see Jed Dannenbaum, "The Origins of Temperance Activism and Militancy among American Women," *Journal of Social History* 15 (1981–82): 235–52; Epstein, *The Politics of Domesticity*, 93–114; Eliza Daniel ("Mother") Stewart, *Memories of the Crusade: A Thrilling Account of the Great Uprising of the Women of Ohio in 1873 against the Liquor Crime* (Columbus, Ohio: Hubbard, 1889; reprint ed., New York: Arno Press, 1972).

53 Willard attempted to ally the WCTU with the Prohibitionists and later the Popu-

lists. For a time, she also considered supporting the Republican party but found it an unreliable partner. On Willard's relationship and that of the WCTU to the parties and reform movements of the Gilded Age, see Jack S. Blocker, Jr., "The Politics of Reform: Populists, Prohibitionists, and Woman Suffrage, 1891–1892," *Historian* 34 (1975): 614–32; Ruth Bordin, "Frances Willard and the Practice of Political Influence," paper presented at the Seventy-Sixth Annual Meeting of the Organization of American Historians, held in Cincinnati, Ohio, April 1983; Buhle, *Women and American Socialism*, 60–69, 80–89; Epstein, *The Politics of Domesticity*, 137–47; Joseph R. Gusfield, *Symbolic Crusade: Status Politics and the American Temperance Movement* (Urbana, Ill.: University of Illinois, 1963), 88–96.

54   Bordin, *Woman and Temperance*; Buhle, *Women and American Socialism*, 54–60, 70–89; Degler, *At Odds*, 338–39; Gordon and Buhle, "Gender Politics and Class Conflict"; Epstein, *The Politics of Domesticity*, chap. 5.

55   Historians and political scientists have devoted a good deal of attention to changing patterns of electoral politics in the early twentieth century. Still, much controversy remains. For different points of view, see Burnham, "The Changing Shape of the American Political Universe"; Philip E. Converse, "Change in the American Electorate," in *The Human Meaning of Social Change*, ed. Angus Campbell and Converse (New York: Russell Sage Foundation, 1972), 263–337; J. Morgan Kousser, *The Shaping of Southern Politics: Suffrage Restrictions and the Establishment of the One-Party South, 1880–1910* (New Haven, Conn.: Yale University Press, 1974); Jerrold G. Rusk, "The Effect of the Australian Ballot on Split-Ticket Voting," *APSR* 64 (1970): 1220–38. Other important works tie changes in electoral politics to the transformation of governance in the twentieth century. See Hays, *Response to Industrialism*; Paul Kleppner, *The Third Electoral System, 1853–1892: Parties, Voters, and Political Cultures* (Chapel Hill, N.C.: University of North Carolina Press, 1979), and *Who Voted*, chap. 4; Richard L. McCormick, "The Discovery That Business Corrupts Politics: A Reappraisal of the Origins of Progressivism," *AHR* 86 (1981): 247–74; Wiebe, *The Search for Order*. The interpretation offered here blends elements of these approaches along with the findings of studies of late nineteenth-century community life. It owes the most to Samuel P. Hays, "Political Parties and the Community-Society Continuum," in *The American Party Systems: Stages of Political Development*, 2d ed., ed. William Nisbet Chambers and Walter Dean Burnham (New York: Oxford University Press, 1975), 152–81.

56   On the connection between community change and partisan behavior, see Hays, "Political Parties and the Community-Society Continuum"; Kleppner, *Who Voted*; Paula Baker, "The Culture of Politics in the Late Nineteenth Century: Community and Political Behavior in Rural New York," *Journal of Social History* (Winter 1984–85): 167–93. The relationship between partisanship and forms of policy making is analyzed in McCormick, "The Party Period and Public Policy."

57   Gerald N. Grob, "The Political System and Social Policy in the Nineteenth Century: Legacy of the Revolution," *Mid-America* 58 (1976): 5–19.

58   Blair, *Clubwoman as Feminist*; Marlene Stein Wortman, "Domesticating the Nineteenth-Century American City," *Prospects: An Annual of American Cultural Studies* 3 (1977): 531–72; Rothman, *Woman's Proper Place*, 102–26, 112–27;

and Margaret Gibbons Wilson, *The American Woman in Transition: The Urban Influence, 1870–1920* (Westport, Conn.: Greenwood, 1979), 91–99. Women in the South engaged in similar work through women's clubs and church organizations; see Leloudis, "School Reform in the New South"; John Patrick McDowell, *The Social Gospel in the South: The Women's Home Mission Movement in the Methodist Episcopal Church, South, 1886–1939* (Baton Rouge, La.: Louisiana State University Press, 1982); Scott, *Southern Lady*, chap. 6. Middle-class black women worked through separate organizations in the nineteenth century. See Lynda F. Dickson, "The Early Club Movement among Black Women in Denver, 1890–1925" (Ph.D. dissertation, University of Colorado, 1982); Tullia Hamilton, "The National Association of Colored Women's Clubs" (Ph.D. dissertation, Emory University, 1978); Gerda Lerner, "Community Work of Black Women's Clubs," and "Black and White Women in Interaction and Confrontation." For clubwomen's descriptions of their work, see Croly, *History of the Women's Club Movement*; Gerda Lerner, ed., *Black Women in White America: A Documentary History* (New York: Pantheon, 1972), chap. 8; Mary I. Wood, *The History of the General Federation of Women's Clubs for the First Twenty-Two Years of Its Organization* (New York, 1912).

59 Beard, *Women's Work*, 221.

60 *Ibid.*, chap. 6–7; Wilson, *American Woman in Transition*; Rothman, *Woman's Proper Place*, 119–27; Wortman, "Domesticating the Nineteenth-Century American City."

61 Wortman, "Domesticating the Nineteenth-Century American City"; Leloudis, "School Reform in the New South." For contemporary accounts, see Beard, *Women's Work*, chaps. 9–11; Wood, *History of the General Federation*, 120–209; Dorr, *What Eighty Million Women Want*.

62 Among the many works that trace the transition in liberal thought, see Theodore J. Lowi, *The End of Liberalism: The Second Republic of the United States*, 2d ed. (New York: Norton, 1979), chaps. 1–3; R. Jeffrey Lustig, *Corporate Liberalism: The Origins of Modern American Political Theory, 1890–1920* (Berkeley and Los Angeles: University of California Press, 1982); William E. Nelson, *The Roots of American Bureaucracy, 1830–1900* (Cambridge, Mass.: Harvard University Press, 1982); James Weinstein, *The Corporate Ideal in the Liberal State, 1900–1918* (Boston: Beacon Press, 1968). Discussions of the family and the small community as a model are provided in Jean B. Quandt, *From the Small Town to the Great Community: The Social Thought of Progressive Intellectuals* (New Brunswick, N.J.: Rutgers University Press, 1970); Wortman, "Domesticating the Nineteenth-Century American City." Although historians have not yet fully described the mechanism by which government took on work that had been the responsibility of voluntary organizations, a few hypotheses seem safe. Municipal governments were undoubtedly responding to demands for better social services—ones in part created by women's attempts to form public opinion. Turning to existing institutions would have been a logical choice for municipal governments. Office holders may also have seen new opportunities for patronage—opportunities that gained importance as older sources (service contracts arranged with private businesses, for example) fell under attack.

63 The second generation has been presented as conservative even by those historians

who have regarded suffrage as a radical demand. See Degler, *At Odds*, 357–61; Ellen DuBois, ed., *Elizabeth Cady Stanton and Susan B. Anthony: Correspondence, Writings, Speeches* (New York: Schocken Books, 1981), 192–93. The most detailed analyses of the suffrage movement's conservative turn are Kraditor, *Ideas of the Woman Suffrage Movement*; O'Neill, *Everyone Was Brave*.

64 DuBois pointed out that the second-generation suffragists' insistence on nonpartisanship is an indication that the vote—rather than what women might do with it—was their major goal; *Elizabeth Cady Stanton and Susan B. Anthony*, 182–83. The suffragists' new campaign tactics owed a large debt to the publicity-gathering techniques of the Congressional Union. For a good account of the course of the suffrage campaign, see Carrie Chapman Catt, *Woman Suffrage and Politics: The Inner Story of the Suffrage Movement* (1923; 2d ed., New York, 1926), 189–91, 212, 284–99, 302–15. Also see Flexner, *Century of Struggle*, 262–65, 271, 285; Sharon Hartman Strom, "Leadership and Tactics in the American Woman Suffrage Movement: A New Perspective from Massachusetts," *JAH* 62 (1975–76): 296–315.

65 The counties that supported suffrage in 1915 were Chautauqua, Schenectady, Chemung, Broome, and Tompkins. The lowest support for the referenda in both 1915 and 1917—as low as 30 percent—occurred in the counties of Livingston, Yates, Ulster, Lewis, Albany, and Columbia. Preliminary calculations suggest that in places where women's groups had a long history of public action, where men's organizations (such as agricultural societies) had increasing involvement in interest-group politics, and where the Socialist vote was high voters were more likely to support suffrage. The southern-tier counties, for example, illustrate the first two hypotheses. Schenectady County, like certain wards in New York City, supported Socialist candidates. Rough calculations also suggest that comparatively high levels of turnout and low incidence of split-ticket voting occurred in places where suffrage was unpopular. Nearly half of New York's sixty-two counties supported suffrage in 1917, but the greatest gains were made in New York, Bronx, Kings, Richmond, and Westchester counties. For studies of the New York City campaign, see Doris Daniels, "Building a Winning Coalition: The Suffrage Fight in New York State," *New York History* 60 (1979): 59–88; Elinor Lerner, "Immigrant and Working-Class Involvement in the New York City Suffrage Movement, 1905–1917: A Study in Progressive Era Politics" (Ph.D. dissertation, University of California, Berkeley, 1981). Both Daniels and Lerner emphasized the support suffrage received from immigrant groups—especially Jewish voters—and Socialist voters. Lerner noted that men who voted for suffrage probably knew many women who were financially independent. Neither, however, put the race in the context of long-term political patterns.

66 Paula S. Fass, *The Damned and the Beautiful: American Youth in the 1920s* (New York: Oxford University Press, 1977). Ironically, motherhood was ritualized and glorified just as the domestic ideal declined. See Kathleen W. Jones, "Mother's Day: The Creation, Promotion, and Meaning of a New Holiday in the Progressive Era," *Texas Studies in Literature and Language* 22 (1980): 176–96. For a review of the work on women in the 1920s, see Estelle B. Freedman, "The New Woman: Changing Views of Women in the 1920s," *JAH* 61 (1974–75): 373–93.

Also useful is Freda Kirchwey, *Our Changing Morality: A Symposium* (New York: Albert and Charles Boni, 1924).

67   On the changed relationship between doctors and mothers, see Kathleen W. Jones, "Sentiment and Science: The Late Nineteenth-Century Pediatrician as Mother's Advisor," *Journal of Social History* 17 (1983–84): 79–96. Jones stressed the reciprocal relationship between women and professionals, noting that women initially sought experts' advice and helped shape the profession of pediatrics. For accounts of women as more passive recipients of expert intrusion, see Barbara Ehrenreich and Deidre English, *For Her Own Good: One Hundred Fifty Years of the Expert's Advice to Women* (Garden City, N.J.: Anchor Press, 1979); Christopher Lasch, *Haven in a Heartless World: The Family Besieged* (New York: Basic Books, 1977); Rothman, *Woman's Proper Place*.

68   Felice Dosik Gordon, "After Winning: The New Jersey Suffragists, 1910–1947" (Ph.D. dissertation, Rutgers University, 1982). In an important recent article, Estelle B. Freedman has argued that women's separate institutions provided a degree of influence lost when women joined organizations that included both sexes; see "Separatism as Strategy."

69   On the rise of interest groups in politics, see Richard L. McCormick, *From Realignment to Reform: Political Change in New York State, 1893–1910* (Ithaca, N.Y.: Cornell University Press, 1981), 151–55, 173–77, 264–71; Herbert F. Margulies, *The Decline of the Progressive Movement in Wisconsin, 1890–1920* (Madison: University of Wisconsin Press, 1968); Mansel G. Blackford, *The Politics of Business in California, 1890–1920* (Columbus, Ohio: Ohio State University Press, 1977). The image of the intelligent client—in this case, the voter—was common in the late nineteenth and early twentieth centuries. It applied even to motherhood. See Jones, "Sentiment and Science"; Rothman, *Woman's Proper Place*, 97–99. A classic study that illustrates men's adoption of women's political tactics is Peter H. Odegard, *Pressure Politics: The Story of the Anti-Saloon League* (New York: Columbia University Press, 1928).

70   Ellis Hawley, *The Great War and the Search for a Modern Order: A History of the American People and Their Institutions, 1917–1933* (New York: St. Martin's Press, 1979), 80–109; Louis Galambos, *Competition and Cooperation: The Emergence of a National Trade Association* (Baltimore: Johns Hopkins University Press, 1966).

71   Christopher Lasch, *The Culture of Narcissism: American Life in an Age of Diminishing Expectations* (New York: Warner Books, 1979); Richard Sennett, *The Fall of Public Man: On the Social Psychology of Capitalism* (1974; 2d ed., New York: Vintage, 1976). On the transition from "character" to "personality" in twentieth-century culture, a transition that has important implications for the study of politics, see Warren I. Susman, " 'Personality' and the Making of Twentieth-Century Culture," in *New Directions in American Intellectual History*, ed. John Higham and Paul K. Conkin (Baltimore: Johns Hopkins University Press, 1979), 212–26.

72   John Dewey, *The Public and Its Problems* (New York: Henry Holt and Company, 1927), 27. As a refinement, "consequences" might be considered political only if they represent attempts to change prescriptions for behaviors and attitudes that are enshrined in law or custom, whether done through legal or informal means.

CHAPTER 4

The Lady and the Tramp: Gender, Race, and the Origins of the American Welfare State

GWENDOLYN MINK

> One of the results of this leaning toward social service is that Americans have lost all sincere convictions concerning the equality of all men, for they undoubtedly despise the blacks, the Mediterraneans, and many other races.
>
> —Andre Siegfried, *America Comes of Age* (1927)

CITIZENSHIP AND SOCIAL REFORM

Classic theories of the rise of welfare states take European experience as the model and class dynamics as the mainspring for social provision. Different theories weigh differently the causal role of capital, labor, and the state in bringing political attention to the social welfare. But they commonly assume that class politics provided the template for social policy innovation, and they commonly conclude that the resulting worker-directed reforms and benefits mediated capitalist relations, purchased labor's loyalty to established political arrangements, and expanded citizenship. The classic welfare state provided a solvent for the antagonism between capital and labor, for the contradiction between class and citizenship, and for the tension between capitalism and democracy.

The American welfare state, too, developed at the contested intersection of capitalism, citizenship, and democracy. But where the nub of European developments was the struggle for political and social equality, the nub of American welfare state formation was the clash between racial diversity and an idealized American citizenry.[1] Beginning with Bismarck, European governments experimented with social policies to offset the political effects of market inequality. These policies—for example, labor standards, social insurance— were aimed at the citizen-worker. Beginning with the first Roosevelt, munici- pal, state, and federal governments in the United States designed policies to offset the political effects of racial diversity. These policies were pitched to the citizen-mother.

The early American welfare state targeted women rather than workers in policies devised to uplift democratic character. Women's policies were the achievement of middle-class women's politics. Middle-class women's poli- tics linked the problem of racial order to the material and cultural quality of motherhood. Motherhood, in this view, held the key to vigor in the citizenry. But the only way mothers from new races could produce ideal American democrats would be through reform and reward of maternal practice. Women's politics won such reforms and rewards between 1900 and 1925: wages and hours protections for working women, mothers' pensions, and maternal and infant care programs. These policy victories socialized motherhood rather than citizenship.

The socialization of motherhood found its logic in the prevailing gender ide- ology and found its force in the race anxieties of what, in practice, was white men's democracy. Both gender ideology and white men's democracy sprang from the core of American republicanism. Gender ideology held women apart from the political community, but for reasons that would ultimately establish women's significance to the political community: namely, as the makers of men, as the wives and mothers of citizens. White men's democracy deployed an idealized republican citizenship as ideological ballast against the political incorporation of diverse peoples—blacks, Asians, eastern and southern Euro- peans. American thinking about citizenship and the republican order staked citizenship to manhood and manhood to virtue, industry, and independence. This made political life a masculine affair and denied women a public political identity. It also racialized manhood and bred a moral politics excited by dis- tinctions of character rather than distinctions of class. It struck a chord with old-stock working men, intellectuals, and politicians. It paved the way to the eventual political incorporation of white middle-class women.[2]

Race and gender interests in industrial America commonly clothed their claims in republican principles of manhood, motherhood, and citizenship. This common reliance on republican defenses developed from the demographic dynamics of nineteenth-century America: urbanization, emancipation, and im- migration. The movement of new peoples into the political community gelled the race interests of settled Americans. These race interests expressed anxieties about the purity and perpetuity of American democracy. They tied the future of American democracy to the demographic and political hegemony of the people who founded it—"the people made this government not government the people."[3] Old-stock, "Teutonic" Americans pursued their race interests by articulating a social geology of citizenship based on race. The social geology of citizenship in industrial America was grounded in republican instructions on independence, industry, and virtue. But these instructions were not explicitly racial: they were explicitly gendered.

Virtue demanded courage as well as willingness to sacrifice self-interest and risk life in defense of the republic. The capacity to soldier was thus the *sine qua non* of fearless and disinterested citizenship. Political education was preoccupied with this ethic between 1795 and 1860: schoolbooks treated American history as a sequence of military heroics.[4] Public policy enforced this ethic after the Civil War: the pension system for Union Army veterans tied America's first national social program to military service to the republic.[5] Such martial patriotism, celebrated in schools and rewarded by wages from the state, was by definition in the republican universe a masculine responsibility and achievement.[6]

Civic activity—participation in the political community—was a further requirement for public virtue. But women could not vote, serve on juries, or independently claim American identity throughout the nineteenth and early twentieth centuries by dint of Constitutional silence, judicial interpretation, and legislative choice: the Constitution reserved for the states the right to deny woman suffrage; the courts enforced an explicit doctrine of masculine citizenship beginning in 1875; and the Congress subsumed married women's nationality within that of husbands from 1855 until the 1930s.[7]

Industry—economic activity and productivity—required personal virtue of the ideal citizen and linked hard work to democratic character. The separation of home from work in developing American capitalism made industry a masculine virtue: separated from commercial productivity, home became a sanctuary from self-interest and competition and women's domestic labor became a matter of mission rather than work.[8] Popular opinion defended industry as men's sphere: as women moved into factory work the "cult of domesticity" gained fervor and social criticism stressed the desecrating effects of work on women's character.[9] Legal disabilities, too, ensured that women could not act as economic individuals.[10] Even as jurists and legislators began to relax common-law barriers to women's independent civil status—with passage of the mid-nineteenth-century Married Women's Property acts, for example— they continued to withhold from women basic weapons for economic activity —full control of property and earnings and the capacity to contract.[11]

At the core of the citizen ideal lay the ethic of independence. The work-ethic protestant and liberal inheritances of American republicanism made independence the goal of industry, while the resilience of an older republicanism made independence the precondition for public virtue.[12] Most important, the independence of citizens was widely regarded as the political community's best defense against tyranny: dependent people could be bought and bent to the will of another. "Dependence," wrote Jefferson, "begets subservience and venality, suffocates the germ of virtue, and prepares fit tools for the designs of ambition." [13]

Independence meant self-reliance, self-ownership, and autonomy. Because it required control of property, nineteenth-century Americans engaged in fierce struggles over the meaning of property.[14] But while American men debated the moral status of property in labor and property in things, women were denied the possibility of either. Law joined political theory to teach women's natural dependence.

Though manhood conferred citizenship, mere anatomy did not universalize men's political personality. Ideal citizenship was a moral construction: conformity to the ideal required personal and public virtue. From the revolutionary period onward, Americans fretted about maintaining a virtuous citizenry: their republican heritage taught that the health and greatness of the polity depended on the character of its people.[15] Character was tied to lineage: republican vigor demanded "sound republican stock." [16] The contingent relationship between character and lineage tied the moral future of the republic to the homogeneity of its people. Concerns about character and homogeneity nagged many Americans throughout the nineteenth century.

Many revolutionary-era Americans had urged "keeping separate from foreign mixtures . . . to keep . . . blood pure." [17] The legal order codified this advice in coercive matrimonial prohibitions: antimiscegenation laws and marital rights restrictions against slaves before the Civil War and against the mentally "unfit" after.[18] Reformers sought to enforce this advice through parental regulations: only those "who can give the world children with splendid physique, strong intellect, and high moral sentiment, may conscientiously take on themselves the responsibility of marriage and maternity" insisted Elizabeth Cady Stanton, for example.[19] Politicians worked to legislate homogeneity by regulating admission into American society. The sponsor of the Foran Act prohibiting the immigration of contract labor explained in 1884:

No matter how high a moral standard a community may attain, the introduction into that community of any considerable number of persons of a lower moral tone will cause a general moral deterioration just as sure as night follows day. . . . Let us lift our beloved America . . . so that she may move onward toward the shining heights which the hopes of her nativity foretold.[20]

Despite many efforts to defend the American citizenry against diversity, industrialization and the republican egalitarian ethos itself destroyed the homogeneity of the population. Laissez-faire capitalism emphasized price over virtue and the "free flow of labor" over protection of the "republican stock." At the same time that capitalism bred demographic change, persistent republicanism fired democratization. These synchronous developments secularized the political community. The extension of citizenship rights to adult white men by the Jacksonian period and to nonwhite men, at least in principle, after the Civil War leveled the moral distinctions upon which ideal citizenship rested. White manhood suffrage allowed unreformable men into the political community: drunkards, papists, paupers. Worse, universal manhood suffrage offered men incapable of manly virtue the rights of ideal citizenship: blacks, popularly regarded as incapable of self-possession, and new immigrants, widely viewed as incapable of self-reliance.[21]

The fact of racial and ethnic heterogeneity nourished anxieties about the future of the republic. Emancipation and industrialization distorted the American republican universe: it brought men whose poverty stigmatized them as dependent to the brink of political membership. The overlapping characteristics of race, poverty, and dependency among new citizens sharpened anxieties, breeding a moral politics aimed at reclaiming citizenship for old-stock white men only.[22] This politics made race and nationality the new moral ratchets of citizenship.

Republican gender ideology eased the development of a racialized citizenship. Gender ideology opposed manhood to womanhood, fastening manhood to productivity and independence and womanhood to servility and dependence. Old-stock Americans drew from this opposition the racial basis for political membership. By assigning feminine traits to ethnic men, old-stock Americans not only neutered allegedly servile and dependent men but marked them as a peril to republican liberty as well. For while woman's dependency was the mainspring of woman's virtue, men's dependency was the sign of men's inadequacy. The flip side of dependent womanhood was virtuous motherhood; the flip side of dependent manhood was the germ of tyranny. Thus the eastern or southern European immigrant was denounced as "the state-managed European laborer who declines to take care of himself in the American fashion;"[23] the "slavish" black man and the Asian "coolie" were deemed "by the unalterable structure of their intellectual being, voluntary slaves;" and all were ridiculed as "people who have never conceived the idea of independent manhood."[24] Samuel Gompers' apothegmatic title posed the problem directly: *Meat vs. Rice: American Manhood vs. Asiatic Coolieism: Which Shall Survive?*

By the late nineteenth century, democratic politics had become a politics of subordination and exclusion: through immigration restrictions, segregation, cultural regulation, barriers to suffrage, and exclusion from unions.[25] But these were only partial solutions to the problem of demographic change. Many new immigrants could vote, more were coming, and blacks could claim Constitutional protection—at least enough to force jurists to explain and justify segregation and disenfranchisement.[26] The "corruption of the Republic" had already begun.

While the American republican inheritance warned against such corruption, it also offered a defense against corruption. That defense was womanhood. For despite her political invisibility woman was nevertheless assigned a weighty political significance as the guardian of male virtue and reproducer of the (white) republican order.[27]

Woman's exile from the political community was premised on her natural vocation as wife and mother. According to the canons of republicanism and domesticity, woman's vocation gave her "the reins of government . . . [Mothers] give direction to the moral sentiments of our rising hopes, and contribute to form their moral state." [28] Woman's political assignment gave the winning edge to legal improvements in her civil status during the mid-nineteenth century: for example, married women's property protections and the maternal child custody preference.[29] It brought the state into proximity with the family: for homes are the "nurseries of the state" and "while with their interior administration, the State should interfere but little, it is obviously of the highest public concern that it should, by general laws adapted to the state of things around them, guard against disturbances from without." [30] It also gave women a wedge into the political community: from it some women would forge and claim woman's political identity, woman's distinctive relationship to the state, and woman's responsibility for national salvation.[31]

From her role in political reproduction woman promised perpetuity to the republican order. Yet in the context of demographic change, woman could not deliver on that promise simply by nurturing citizen-sons and correcting errant citizen-husbands: the citizen-race was at stake. "The home is the social workshop for the making of men"—and thus the linchpin of republican order—but poverty and demographic change put the American home at risk of dissolution.[32] Recognition of the reciprocal social obligations of home and political community pushed woman's sphere into the political community itself, where some women would receive from other women instructions on home and motherhood.

Industrial America's race challenge politicized womanhood and socialized woman's work. The women's politics that arose in response to this challenge accepted woman's place while transforming it. "Woman's place is Home," wrote suffragist Rheta Childe Dorr:

But Home is not contained within the four walls of an individual home. Home is the community. The city full of people is the Family. The public school is the real Nursery. And badly do the Home and the Family and the Nursery need their mother. . . . Woman's place is Home, and she must not be forbidden to dwell there. . . . For woman's work is race preservation, race improvement, and who opposes her, or interferes with her, simply fights nature, and nature never loses her battles.[33]

Women's politics was a democratizing politics, claiming full citizenship for women. It was also a gendered politics, staking woman's citizenship to woman's role—"Even their political liberty they want only because it will enable them to get other things . . . which tend to conserve the future mothers of children"—and forging a relationship between the state and woman's place— "If producing citizens to the State be the greatest service a woman citizen can perform, the State will ultimately recognize the right of the woman citizen to protection during her time of service".[34]

Women's politics was moreover a racial politics, tying the future of the republic to uplift of the citizenry. In the main, this politics was directed toward the new immigrant population—the eastern and southern Europeans who moved in droves into northern cities during the late nineteenth and early twentieth centuries. In the view of women reformers, the uplift of new Americans could be achieved through education: practice in "the art of thinking," in "right living," and in the organization of "their own activities for themselves" would help "combat successfully the deadliest foe of this Republic, the lowering of citizenship by industry."[35] As natural educators, mothers held the key to the rehabilitation of republican citizenship. Since all women were given this natural vocation, they shared a common identity that counterbalanced rigid social distinctions of race and ethnicity.

Still, uplift ultimately depended on "highly intelligent mothers" who met their "home responsibilities" to train future citizens.[36] Quality control of the conditions of motherhood as well as of mothers themselves thus became the focus of women's politics. Old-stock, middle-class women waged their politics in defense of motherhood and toward the end of political regeneration. When they did this they counterposed the possibility of racial assimilation to the politics of racial exclusion. And they quickened development of a welfare state by asserting a social right to the gender roles that defined woman's sphere.

GENDER, RACE, AND SOCIAL PROVISION

Gender politics does not by itself explain the American path to social provision. In western Europe, too, manhood and motherhood were important political paradigms. Democratizing movements were often confined to gender spheres: the language of rights indelibly associated full citizenship with manhood; while women's movements often grounded women's political identity and social claims in "mothers' needs."[37] Further, gender roles were typically encoded in social policies: early factory acts offered protections to women only; labor standards and income policies included maternity provisions; some social insurance schemes discriminated against women, for example, by denying married women independent coverage and by privileging skilled workers.[38] But despite its gender bias, European social policy sprang primarily from tensions between class and citizenship and linked work, need, and social entitlement.[39] Thus the politics of social policy has been a distributional politics;

its gender dimensions have revolved around the ways in which the social wage has assumed, reproduced, or intensified women's economic dependency.

What was distinctive about the American pattern was that it was drawn by race and mediated by gender. Where European social politics took place within a paradigm drawn by capitalism and democracy—class and citizenship —American social politics took place within a paradigm drawn by diversity and democracy. Where European social politics generated policies directed toward the conceptually genderless worker, American social politics generated policies directed toward the woman citizen and through her to the "well-being of the race."

This is not to say that capital, labor, and political elites in the United States did not debate worker-directed reform. Sectors of capital were instrumental in securing accident insurance; some segments of labor supported the idea of social insurance; Progressive political elites called for a broad array of social protections ranging from labor standards to pensions to health care. But in the main, capital preferred private sector management of the relations of distribution; unions stuck to their doctrine of voluntarism; while political elites ran up both against an intransigent judiciary and against a powerful ethic warning that material benefits would breed dependence in the citizenry. In combination these factors closed the state as the arena for elaborating a conceptually genderless social citizenship.[40]

But gender and race pressures on American democracy combined to open the state to elaborating woman's social citizenship. While men's citizenship and social protection could not be reconciled as long as democratic character was staked to independence, woman's citizenship required social protection because of woman's special responsibility for the future of the republic. Union labor—a likely voice for social provision in other settings—articulated this view of the gendered nature of citizenship and in so doing helped scuttle most national initiatives for worker-directed reform. American Federation of Labor leaders, most notably Samuel Gompers, counterposed dependence to independence, need to productivity, state-management to self-help, coercion to volition, "servility" to "red-blooded rugged independence and will power."[41] Though grounded in the ethic of fraternal associationalism, steeped in the exigencies of organizational self-interest, and driven by worries occasioned by courts and immigrants, the call to voluntarism was at its core an admonition to manly independence. American men eschewed social provision because the essence of their independence was the ability to do for themselves (and for their wives and children): through productive labor, the ownership of property in skill, and participation in voluntary and autonomous associations, such as unions. In this view, governmental interference in the realm of men's work was justified only to provide employment when the market did not (i.e., public works), to offer pensions as the deferred wages of military service (i.e.,

Civil War pensions and the proposed Old Age Home Guard of the United States Army), and to organize material support when manly independence was physically impaired in industrial accidents (i.e., workmen's compensation).[42]

Race politics heightened the perceived incompatibility between social provision and men's citizenship. If new immigrant and black men were not economically independent or were not adequate providers, this was because they were "servile," "slavish," "coolies," and "serfs." Social provision would validate debased manhood by servicing it: " 'public welfare' can have little place in a society of equals. . . . [It] has to do with the weak, the defective, the ineffective, the ignorant, and the incorrigible. . . . What can be the result of this . . . but the softening of the moral fibre of the people?" [43]

The idea that real men provided, rather than needed, meshed with ideas tying vigor in a democracy to the independence of its citizenry. If democratic vigor hung on the independence of citizens, then the future of the republic required reproduction of self-reliant and materially independent men. This gave both scientific and ethical authority to the punitive side of voluntarism: "Next to alcohol, and perhaps alongside it, the most pernicious fluid is indiscriminate soup." [44] Thus charities organizer Josephine Shaw Lowell advocated the teaching of values rather than the allocation of benefits: "It is cruel and cowardly of us in the extreme to make the path of dependence easy." Others worried that governmental response to social needs would lead to the elimination of the fit and the survival of the unfit and urged more drastic measures: "For every effort expended in care of the unfit individual, equal effort must be intelligently expended toward the eventual elimination of the unfit stock which produced the unfit individual." [45] The way to eliminate "unfit stock" was through immigration restriction, proper breeding, and removal from the political community.

Men's loss of economic independence in poverty problematized men's citizenship. Different segments of the political community responded to the coincident racial and economic geology of masculine America along a continuum ranging from admonition to subordination to exclusionism. Meanwhile women's lack of dependable men made woman's dependency a public problem. As woman's dependency took on public significance, woman's citizenship—woman's relationship to the state—was transformed. While men's work and men's families continued to be sealed from the state until the New Deal, women's work and fatherless families entered the protection of the state during the Progressive era. Protection carried benefits for women—minimum wages, maximum hours, mothers' pensions. But there were also costs. These policies placed women's needs and canons of womanhood at the core of woman's political personality.[46] And they made racial uplift rather than social equality the principle of women's social citizenship.

While gender difference was the cornerstone of the early American welfare state, the social geology of race in America drove the politics of welfare state building. The interaction between gendered citizenship and racial rehabilitation was mediated by early twentieth-century women's politics. Various middle-class reform movements dominated by women—suffrage, settlements, education, domestic science, temperance—comingled in a broader politics that seized the political space vacated by labor, capital, and the state on social welfare matters.

Seemingly by default, proponents of gender benefits tied to women's distinctive citizenship established the parameters for social provision during the first two and a half decades of the twentieth century. The policies developed within these parameters offered wages for motherhood through protections of women's "racial productiveness." [47] As they socialized motherhood, these policies also politicized woman's citizenship:

[Woman] has learnt to be a mother and a worker in her home; she begins to realize what new heights of achievement may be hers when she shall become also a worker and a mother in the world without. . . . When all doors are open to women . . . the qualities of conservation and careful building, of which I have spoken as belonging to motherhood, will be found to have a social value far too great to permit of further atrophy and disuse. . . . [A] very large part of the sedentary administrative and executive work of government offices and business enterprises, which now devolves upon men, will be performed by women, [so] that great numbers of men will thereby be left free for the more creative or physically energetic branches of work, to which they are temperamentally and bodily most suited.[48]

The labor and maternity legislation of the industrial period transformed women's relationships to the political realm. Though these policies hitched women's citizenship to gender principles, they affected individual women variably depending on race, class, and political position. Some middle-class, old-stock women became direct participants in politics and government—as members of commissions, school superintendents, health officers, social workers, and even as chiefs of the federal Children's and Women's Bureaus.[49] Meanwhile many working-class and poor ethnic women became political and governmental dependents subject to regulation by and supervision from courts, legislatures, and middle-class women.[50]

Women's policies turned on motherhood. Middle-class women reformers claimed woman's right to minimal conditions of motherhood and argued government's responsibility to respond to social needs on the basis of gender difference. According to Florence Kelley, leader of the National Consumers' League and champion of wages and hours protections for women:

The inescapable facts are . . . that men do not bear children, are free from the burdens of maternity and are not susceptible in the same measure as women, to the poisonous characteristic of certain industries. . . . The inherent differences are permanent. Women will always need many laws different from those needed by men.[51]

Under the leadership of women like Jane Addams, Josephine Goldmark, and Florence Kelley, women's politics pressed motherhood into the service of women's rights and women's wages. Their policy victories—*Muller v. Oregon*, mothers' pension legislation in many states, creation of the Women's Bureau, and the Sheppard-Towner Infant and Maternity Care Act of 1921—established reciprocal obligations between government and at least some of its citizens.

But by welding motherhood to woman's citizenship, women's politics problematized claims for gender equality. It further compromised the possibility of racial equality when it offered motherhood as the solvent for diversity in America. Arguing for policies tied to gender difference, women's politics interposed women reformers as managers of racial difference. This politics promoted an uplifted universal motherhood, one that would achieve both uplift and universality through the assimilation of Anglo-Saxon norms. Assimilated motherhood was women reformers' weapon against the blows to democracy dealt by poverty and multiculturalism.

Women's politics thus replayed the race anxieties of republican America. Race had long been a sticking point for the women's movement. During Reconstruction, suffragists had responded to the Fifteenth Amendment's guarantee of manhood suffrage by picking up the cudgel of race in their defense of women's claims.[52] Elizabeth Cady Stanton had raged in 1866 that:

In view of the fact that the Freedmen of the South and the millions of foreigners now crowding our shores, most of whom represent neither property, education, nor civilization, are all in the progress of events to be enfranchised, the best interests of the nation demand that we outweigh this incoming pauperism, ignorance and degradation, with the wealth, education, and refinement of the women of the republic.[53]

Stanton's linkage between race and republic was embellished by Susan B. Anthony several years later, when she harnessed masculinist republicanism's association of race and manhood for suffragist purposes:

While the dominant party have with one hand lifted up TWO MILLION BLACK MEN and crowned them with the honor and dignity of citizenship, with the other they have dethroned FIFTEEN MILLION WHITE WOMEN—their own mothers and sisters, their own wives and daughters—and cast them under the heel of the *lowest orders of manhood*.[54]

Similar racist appeals and racial reasons—regarding blacks in the South and new immigrants in the North—plagued the twentieth-century suffrage movement.[55] Many suffragists saw danger in the electoral power of the "lowest orders of manhood" and accordingly fashioned strategies to retract the political rights of "lesser men" while extending those rights to the "women of the republic." NAWSA (National American Woman Suffrage Association) proposals for educated suffrage bore more than a family resemblance to the literacy tests enacted contemporaneously in the South. As explained by one suffragist in 1906:

The National has always recognized the usefulness of woman suffrage as a counter-balance to the foreign vote, and as a means of legally preserving White supremacy in the South. In the campaign in South Carolina we . . . never hesitated to show that the White women's vote would give supremacy to the White race. And we have also freely used the same argument to the foreign-born vote.[56]

Racial concerns also figured prominently in the early twentieth-century social reform movement: in settlement houses, domestic science groups, mothers' clubs, consumers' leagues, and social work. But the issue for reformers was "race improvement" rather than white supremacy. Writing of the new immigrants serviced by Hull House, Jane Addams, for example, lamented: "Their ideas and resources are cramped. The desire for higher social pleasure is extinct. They have no share in the traditions and social energy which make for progress. Too often their only place of meeting is a saloon, their only host a bartender; a local demagogue forms their public opinion." So, Addams prescribed: "One thing seemed clear in regard to entertaining these foreigners: to preserve and keep for them whatever of value their past life contained and to bring them in contact with a better type of American."[57] Settlement houses and schools were key agents of this process of gradual assimilation: "An Italian girl who had had lessons in cooking . . . will help her mother to connect the entire family with American food and household habits."[58]

Though clearly race conscious, many of the leading women reformers rejected the harsh exclusionism of nativists, Southerners, and late nineteenth-century suffragists. The universality of the maternal vocation implied the possibility of a universal maternal virtue. This possibility combined with the fixed realities of poverty and diversity to produce prescriptions for women's uplift. Faith in uplift rooted in the universality of gender difference pushed women into a racial politics quite orthogonal to the political eugenics that dominated debates within white men's democracy.

The racial politics of women reformers found its logic in woman's distinctive citizenship. Political theory had divided the republican project into men's and women's spheres. Masculine citizenship was a political project, requiring defense of the republican order. Feminine citizenship was an educational project, requiring reproduction of the republican order: "The prime function of woman must ever be the perpetuation of the race."[59] Though concern for "sound republican stock" was shared across these spheres, for women reformers the educational ethic bore the idea of assimilation, located it in motherhood, and substituted it for the politics of exclusion.

The idea of assimilation blended the incipient—if ambivalent—racial liberalism espoused by Progressives like Theodore Roosevelt with the racial/ cultural regulatory prescriptions advanced by temperance women, charities organizers, and many birth-control advocates. Women reformers shared Roosevelt's premise that immigrant culture would yield to democratic habits, creating a distinctive American race: "Our object," he wrote, "is not to imitate one of the older racial types, but to maintain a new American type and then to secure loyalty to this type." [60] One way to achieve and secure the American type was through education. Another was to "dry up the pestilential social conditions in our great cities, where anarchistic organizations have their greatest possibility of growth." [61] Still another was to regulate the practice of motherhood, by linking social benefits to "right living" and Anglo-Saxon morality.

If the assimilationist impulse of women reformers resonated with Rooseveltian assumptions, the assimilationist methods of many of these women— child education advocates, settlement house workers, social workers—drew from the regulatory spirit of sister movements such as temperance. But women reformers resisted reproducing the stern prohibitions of temperance. Rather than forbid depraved cultural practices, they sought to educate newcomers to American habits and values:

What women must do . . . is to survey their national situation, not from the narrow point of view of reforming the surface morals of their countrymen, but from the standpoint of experts in race improvement. The world is in a mess, and the spectacle of women trying to extricate it from the mess by applying moral mustard plasters like anti-cigarette or even anti-liquor laws, makes me tired. . . . The first essential is more and better education . . . education of the bodies and souls, as well as the minds of people, to make them understand their place in the universe as efficient, useful, productive agents.[62]

When women reformers found their efforts to uplift frustrated by the extremes and immutability of poverty, they questioned economic conditions and in so doing socialized the problem of poverty. As Addams, Kelley, and others examined poverty, they introduced a new perspective on the relationship between poverty and race. For these reformers, poverty was not an indelible racial characteristic or a hereditary disqualification from citizenship. Rather, it was an impediment to racial uplift and thus to the rehabilitation of the citizenry. Many women reformers thus embraced efforts to treat the effects of poverty ("Shall I preach temperance to men whose homes are vile tenements?" wrote Florence Kelley) and to counter some of its causes (e.g., through minimum wage legislation). Alleviate the miseries of poverty, Kelley argued, for "this is the true work for the elevation of the race." [63] As another reformer explained in her study of blacks in Chicago:

While the morality of every young person is closely bound up with that of his family and his immediate environment, this is especially true of the sons and daughters of colored families who, because they continually find the door of opportunity shut in their faces, are more easily forced back into their early environment, however vicious it may have been.[64]

Reflecting this view, many white women reformers supported the NAACP and the National Urban League in their efforts to alleviate poverty and open opportunity.

These arguments took the edge off race thinking and identified an agenda for reform by political intervention. But women's reform agenda still assumed the idealized republican association between independence and worthy citizenship. Thus women reformers appealed to government to succor women's dependency rather than remedy economic inequality.

Women's reform agenda fitted well with the assumption that the presence in the citizenry of able-bodied poor men—either actually or potentially dependent—threatened the republic. The formal equality of dependent men aroused old fears of tyranny and corruption—fears of the perils posed to liberty by men who could be bought, and fears empirically grounded in the experience of patronage democracy. Though women reformers repudiated the view that poverty was a racial attribute—that some races were wholly unfit for independence—the persistent coincidence of race and poverty excited concerns about the compatibility of diversity and democracy.

So women reformers worked to turn ethnic men into American men—to enforce "the citizen's responsibilities of fatherhood." [65] They taught the work ethic and vocational skills to young boys, instructed poor or unemployed men to seek jobs rather than relief, and encouraged unionism.[66] Such lessons on productive and associational life—on the pursuit of manly independence—were the mainstay of assimilationist methods directed toward men. When assimilation worked, race diminished as a demarcation of citizenship. But masculine citizenship remained intact.

While women reformers sought to manage the effects of diversity on masculine citizenship through admonitions to self-help and self-discipline, they treated the effects of diversity on feminine citizenship through the socialization of motherhood. Individualized, characterological reform pursued by social servants rather than social benefits provided by the state held the key to making independent men of the able-bodied, racially different poor. One result was that the socialization of citizenship proceeded along gender tracks. Poor men, mainly of "lesser races," were thus put in problematic relationship to the expanding state.

Woman-directed reform took dependent womanhood as its premise and made the state the key to managing and mitigating that dependence. Gender difference anchored in a common maternal vocation universalized womanhood in a way that permitted women of "lesser races" to participate in the rehabilitation of American democracy. But this required intervention and direction to create republican mothers.

Education offered one route to reform—education in proper sanitation and nutrition, in prenatal and infant care, and in sewing, cooking and child rearing. Settlement houses, Progressive schools, social workers, and nurses could provide much of this instruction. But education of this type offered only a partial solution. It was largely remedial, directed towards correcting the habits of "ignorant mothers." More complete rehabilitation of immigrant, working-class motherhood required appropriate instruction for future mothers through the publicly managed school system. Thus women reformers pressed curricular reform:

> The schools may truthfully be said actively to divert the little daughters of wage-earning families from home life. . . . For the schools teach exactly those things which prepare girls to become at the earliest moment cash children and machine tenders: punctuality, regularity, attention, obedience, and a little reading and writing—excellent things in themselves, but wretched preparation either for domestic service as an alternative choice of occupations, or for homemaking a decade later on the lives of the pupils.[67]

One success on this front was achieved in New York, where promoters of domestic science introduced into the grade schools a syllabus that began with topics such as "the psychology of races—expression of the home ideal in races other than the Anglo-Saxon," "early social life of the Anglo-Saxon people," and "the home life of the Anglo-Saxon vs. the communistic family system." [68]

The rehabilitation of motherhood further required purposive government action to treat the effects of women's economic dependency. Poverty consigned many women (and children) to the world of work, impeding fulfillment of women's mission in the home. In poverty, motherhood was disgraced by need and squalor; at work, maternal capacities were impaired by physical strain and long hours.[69] This "denied women their birthright . . . [their] part in our common racial life." [70] At home, women's "racial productivity" was impeded by men who did not earn a family wage, could not find work, could not perform work, would not meet the obligations of fatherhood, or simply were not there.[71]

Dependent manhood did mischief to motherhood and through motherhood to republican order. Curing these mischiefs required alleviating women's poverty and regulating the conditions of women's work. From the standpoint of women reformers, amelioration of the conditions of motherhood could not be accomplished by mere education or moral uplift. The creation of republican motherhood was a public burden: woman's dependency placed the conditions of motherhood beyond individual women's control, and woman's role in political reproduction entitled her to public support. Recognition of the reciprocal obligations of mother and state encouraged a renegotiation of the location and import of woman's sphere.

This in turn transformed woman's relationship to the state. The struggle for women's political representation placed women in direct conversation with government, while the achievement of suffrage ended women's virtual representation through men. The quest for social support for motherhood encoded gender in state policy, while the success of gender-based reform formalized women's social dependency even as women achieved nominal political independence.

Women reformers tied their case for political rights to their social agenda, sometimes arguing that the absence of feminine virtues in politics prolonged social problems, other times citing legislative successs in woman suffrage states to demonstrate "the regenerative power of the ballot in service of the family." [72] As Jane Addams explained,

Woman's traditional function has been to make her dwelling-place both clean and fair. Is that dreariness in city life, that lack of domesticity . . . due to a withdrawal of one of the naturally cooperating forces? If women have been in any sense responsible for the gentler side of life which softens and blurs some of its harsher conditions, may they not have a duty to perform in our American cities? [73]

Elsewhere, she attributed the failures in "city housekeeping" to women's exclusion from what was properly women's political work: "The men of the city have been carelessly indifferent to much of this civic housekeeping, as they have always been indifferent to the details of the household . . . may we not say that city housekeeping has failed partly because women, the traditional housekeepers, have not been consulted as to its multiform activities?" [74]

Addams rested her arguments for women's representation on an analogy between city and household. For Addams as for other women reformers, this analogy ran much deeper than the metaphorical association between "housekeeping" and "sweeping out" vice and corruption in city politics. Much of women's traditional activities—as guardians of health, morals, and cleanliness —had been appropriated (and poorly pursued) by city governments. But these activities continued to belong to woman's sphere: if performed by government, then women belonged in government and politics.

These arguments fed into a feminization of political life. Appealing first to Plato, and then to history, Addams collapsed city and household, state and family, within the republican order. [75] She took the republican association of citizenship and the common defense, redefined it, and thereby expanded citizenship and government responsibility. Whereas a voice in the republic had once properly belonged to those who would bear arms to defend it, voices in the city now belonged to those who would protect and cleanse it. The enemies of the modern city were not external military foes but internal problems of pestilence, corruption, and decay. Women, Addams insisted, were essential to the defense of home and city against "the dangers incident to modern life":[76]

To test the elector's fitness to deal with this situation by his ability to bear arms, is absurd. . . . Certainly the military conception of society is remote from the functions of the school boards, whose concern it is that children be educated, that they be supplied with kindergartens and be given a decent place to play. The very multifariousness and complexity of a city government demands the help of minds accustomed to detail and variety of work, to a sense of obligation for the health and welfare of young children, and to a responsibility for the cleanliness and comfort of others.[77]

Thus Addams, Kelley, and others linked women's political rights and social reform. Implicit in this construction of woman's citizenship was the promise that women's political participation would clean up politics and industry; in return government would deliver support for the woman citizen.

Government conferred its support when it opened access to old-stock, middle-class women to investigate, lobby, and litigate for social reform. Women reformers used their access to investigate factory conditions and economic burdens that debased poor women's motherhood. They lobbied and litigated for wages and hours protections for women; though they had to wait until the 1930s to achieve wage guarantees, they won hours protection in the first decade of the twentieth century—a striking departure from laissez-faire constitutionalism and a breakthrough for social intervention by government.

But women's labor policy victories also entrenched the gendered readings of the Fourteenth Amendment that began with the *Bradwell* Court's declaration that "the paramount destiny and mission of woman are to fulfill the noble and benign offices of wife and mother." [78] Explicitly on the bases of motherhood and "the fact that woman has always been dependent upon man," women's labor standards traded women's liberty of contract for protection of the "well-being of woman . . . and the well-being of the race." [79] According to the logic of woman's separate citizenship, due process protections varied by gender and the general welfare was held to travel more directly through women than through men.[80] Borrowing the husband's prerogative to supervise woman's contract decisions, which underpinned the reasoning of *Bradwell*, the state claimed supervision of dependent motherhood when the Court affected women's labor contracts with a public purpose in *Muller*. This met the test posed by women reformers who held that "the state must be in its legislation and its political operation a supplement to the integrity and moral righteousness of the home, or it will inevitably disintegrate and become a destroyer of the home." [81]

Women reformers expanded the state's motherhood-enhancing and family-saving activities when they secured a federally funded program that directly reached maternity itself. A victory for Julia Lathrop, Florence Kelley, and a broad coalition of women's groups, the Sheppard-Towner Maternity and Infancy Protection Act of 1921 provided for professional instruction of expectant mothers in prenatal and infant care. Congress' overwhelming approval of the act testified to women's political significance both as policy advocates and as mothers. But "it seemed as though the women were just doing on a larger platform what women had been always supposed to do—care for women in childbirth, welcome the newborn and nurture the children." [82] The United States' first national social welfare measure, the Sheppard-Towner Act, tied health policy to motherhood and made social protection a gender benefit.

Similarly, the mothers' pension programs developed by the states extended social protection to woman's gender role. These policies enjoyed remarkable support: by 1915, only six years after the White House Conference on the Care of Dependent Children proposed social protection of "children of reasonably efficient and deserving mothers who are without the support of the normal breadwinner," twenty-nine states had instituted mothers' pension programs. By 1919, another ten states had followed suit.[83] Like labor and maternity legislation, mothers' pensions were conceived as a means to halt the erosions in motherhood wrought by work and poverty so that even poor women could "lead in the awakening of mankind to a sense of responsibilities resting upon the race, to provide each newborn soul with an environment which will foster its highest development." [84]

But unlike women's labor standards and maternity protections—which did not explicitly seek to remove women from waged work—mothers' pensions were predicated on the view that "family life in the home is sapped in its foundations when the mothers of young children work for wages." Because death or injury of husbands forced the breadwinning role upon mothers, public provision was needed to preserve the integrity of motherhood. Thus, for example, mothers' pensions were often seen as the corollary to workmen's compensation. As Florence Kelley explained:

> If a railroad has killed the breadwinner of a family, the railroad industry is not now legally the debtor of his widow during widowhood, and of the fatherless children even until the sixteenth birthday. If the breadwinner is not killed but disabled by an injury incident to his work, or by an industrial disease, transforming him from the breadwinner to a dragging burden upon his wife and children, they need not less but greater indemnification.[85]

This pathbreaking governmental intervention in affairs of distribution conditioned social provision on the absence of men, made manless women dependent on the state, and drew from women's dependence governmental prerogative to oversee and regulate motherhood. Mothers' pension legislation thereby added a coercive dimension to woman-centered reform. While labor and maternity legislation addressed the economic (and cultural) conditions of motherhood, mothers' pensions more directly and more rigidly policed and prescribed the moral qualities of motherhood. Most states conditioned assistance on the racially charged "moral fitness" of the individual mother as well as on her willingness to comply with restrictions on regular wage work. This brought motherhood under surveillance, as juvenile courts, local governments, and relief agencies investigated home conditions and women's morality.[86]

If mothers' assistance was a first step away from charity and toward entitlement,[87] that step was taken in the interest of race and republic. Women's benefits were consequently tied not to social rights but to political necessity. As one advocate explained:

The only chance that exists . . . of winning [the poor, husbandless, worthy mother] an environment in which she can maintain a home for herself and for her children as self-respecting as the home next door is to annex that home of hers to the public domain. . . . In the private domain, self-respect is, for her and for those whom she is training to democratic citizenship, permanently impossible.[88]

Recipients of mothers' pensions found themselves in something of a wage bargain, wherein "compensation" for motherhood was paid to women who met the terms of republican motherhood. Women's income support was conceived as remuneration for maternal work—as "payment of money . . . like the payment made by the state or nation to soldiers, sailors, or others who have rendered public service." [89] But that work was subject to quality control as a condition of remuneration, for the value of maternal work hung on mothers' contributions to the "racial welfare." [90] Thus in exchange for a meager stipend, a recipient had to be certified "a proper person, physically, mentally, and morally fit to bring up her children." [91]

"Moral fitness" was encoded with Anglo-Saxon biases—for temperance, nuclear-family households, American cooking. Though the criteria for moral fitness were sometimes delineated in pension legislation, wide discretion was ordinarily delegated to administrators and social workers—most of whom were white and middle class. Discretion allowed for the imposition of Anglo-Saxon criteria, as well as for racial exclusions where uplift was seen as either undesirable or impossible. Discretion meant, for example, that black mothers, barred from eligibility in some southern states, were elsewhere denied entitlement by policy managers.[92] Further, both law and discretion invited pension agencies to police their clients regularly to enforce fitness: evidence of smoking, lack of church attendance, poor hygiene, male boarders, or faulty budgeting could result in withdrawal of a mother's allowance. According to one agency, pensions were "a powerful lever to lift and keep mothers to a high standard of home care." [93] For mothers who did not meet the criteria of Anglo-Saxon morality, denial of pensions represented a form of political eugenics.

Mothers' assistance was the cornerstone of the American welfare state. Not only was it the first income security program, but it was the progenitor of a major pillar of the contemporary welfare state, aid to dependent children.[94] Grounded in the ideology of republican motherhood, mothers' pensions broke through the rigidities of laissez-faire capitalism to make the creation of "sound mothers" a social responsibility. At a time when the necessity of sound fathers was seen as men's burden—when the idea of social insurance pegged to waged work was heartily rejected in most quarters—the social contingency of motherhood won resounding consensus.

THE WAGES OF MOTHERHOOD

The origins of the American welfare state lay in gender-based solutions to what was widely perceived to be a racial problem. This left problematic legacies for the politics of social equality. Women were granted a kind of social citizenship but at the cost of equality both for themselves and for "lesser men." Hung on gender difference, women's citizenship justified women's separate—and disparate—treatment under law until the 1970s. And animated by the twin anxieties of race and republic, men's citizenship denied legitimacy to governmental mitigation of men's economic dependency. Meanwhile, the gender focus of early twentieth-century social provision made for neglect of reforms —educational expenditures, for example—that might have expanded men's citizenship even on its own terms.[95]

The gender-based solutions of the early twentieth century were carried forward in the New Deal. During the New Deal, the mothers' pension concept was federalized in Title IV (aid to dependent children) of the Social Security Act of 1935. This etched women's dependency in national policy and bound that dependency to discretionary regulation of mother's world. The Aid to Dependent Children program allowed the states to establish eligibility criteria, thus permitting continued regulation of women's personal lives. Such regulation often turned on racial considerations, most notably in the South, where criteria requiring "suitability" of the home and "propriety" of the parent allowed for discriminations in blacks' access to public assistance.[96]

Other New Deal measures, too, prescribed and enforced gender roles. The Sheppard-Towner Act, defunct after 1929, was resurrected, revised, and expanded in the maternal and child health provision, Title V, of the Social Security Act. New Deal labor market policies used motherhood as their rationale for limiting women's access to and protections in waged work. During the Depression, federal and local governments discharged married women: the federal government made the federally employed spouse of a federal employee a layoff priority, while twenty-six states legislated limitations on married women's employment.[97] The National Recovery Act set a lower minimum wage for women than for men. The Wagner Act reached fewer women than men: many unions excluded women, while some unions introduced discriminatory caveats—sex-based job classifications and wage differentials, as well as proscriptions against married women's employment—into their contracts.[98] The Fair Labor Standards Act excluded whole occupational categories mostly inhabited by women from its protections—seasonal workers, retail clerks in businesses not engaged in interstate commerce, domestic workers. Meanwhile the New Deal Court—remarkably on the eve of the enactment of the first national, universal wages and hours policy—upheld a state women's wage law on the grounds that "the protection of women is a legitimate end of the exercise of state power."[99]

New Deal income security policy also provided for women's dependency when it granted unearned old-age security benefits to wives and widows of insured workers. It assumed women's dependency when it treated women's wages as supplemental in its formulae for family old-age benefits limits and in its stipulations for survivor's benefits, and when it exempted major women's occupations—domestic and cannery workers and educational, charitable, and hospital personnel—from work-based Social Security entitlements.[100] And it reproduced women's dependency when it spelled out the funding formula for Aid to Dependent Children: mothers' monthly entitlement was half that of other categorical recipients of public assistance. Women earn only 59 cents to the male dollar in the contemporary labor market; they received only 50 cents of the male dollar in women-centered assistance in the New Deal welfare state.

Still, the "women first" strategy did bear fruit during the New Deal. A potentially genderless social insurance system was put in place with the enactment of old-age, unemployment, and accident insurance; however men's incorporation into the welfare state did not gender-neutralize social provision. Nor did it ease the tension between race and republic. The work-based mobilization of ethnic men into industrial unions, the coming of age of a generation of ethnic children whose mothers had been the targets of maternalist reform, and the significance of ethnic voters in the new Democratic majority eased a reconciliation between immigrant ethnicity and citizenship. The antinomy between race and republic was thereafter refocused around issues of color, as it had been under slavery and during the first waves of Asian and Mexican immigration. New Deal social policies reflected this focus, either in the constituencies they served directly (e.g., unionized labor) or in the interests they placated through delegation (e.g., the South). The old-age insurance program of the Social Security Act of 1935 virtually excluded blacks and latinos, for it excluded agricultural and domestic workers from coverage and marginalized low-wage workers.[101] Other provisions of the act—old-age assistance and aid to dependent children—handed implementation to the states, thereby opening the window of race-conscious discretion in determining eligibility and benefits levels. Moreover, men's benefits were generally tied to wages (old-age insurance), military service (the GI Bill), and unionism (health insurance) rather than need. Historically less well paid, less fully employed, and less unionized than white men, minority men were disadvantaged in a system pegged to earnings, economic independence, and political membership rather than to need and equality.

Far from socializing rights or universalizing benefits, the New Deal welfare state perpetuated gender and race distinctions among citizens by entrenching gender and race discriminations in entitlements. Women's entitlements and women's exclusions were tied to "mothers' needs" and women's economic dependence on men. Minority men's entitlements and exclusions varied with their conformity to the work, war, union, and income experience of white men. While mothers could receive public aid for their dependent children, they were written out of policies that either assumed or required potential economic independence. The GI Bill, for example—the first national educational assistance policy—reached a potential 78 percent of the civilian male population over the age of seventeen after World War II; "Rosie the Riveter" had no comparable avenue to higher education and economic opportunity opened for her.[102] While minority men were folded into the Social Security system and covered by New Deal labor policies if employed in covered occupations, they fell out of coverage disproportionately in comparison to white men because they could not meet occupational or minimum income eligibility criteria.[103]

Some discriminations have been corrected: New Deal labor policies have expanded their occupational coverage; the Civil Rights Act opened challenges to race- and gender-based employment discrimination; and in 1977 the woman wage earner secured for her family the same protections extended to the families of male wage earners under the Social Security Act.[104] But many discriminations persist. Minority men's claims on key contemporary social welfare programs are weaker than those of their white counterparts: "casual" or unstable work patterns are barriers to unemployment compensation, for example, and agricultural work is not protected by industrial health and safety provisions. Women's claims are weakened by the masculine premises of many policies: in most states, unemployment insurance, for example, takes the male worker as the norm, thereby ignoring the ways in which motherhood and waged work coexist in many women's lives. Many women are thus judged ineligible for a cushion against the loss of wages: some because they do not accumulate enough income to qualify as a result of low pay and part-time work; others because their loss of work is due to such practical realities as lack of child care during an assigned shift.[105] So while more than ten million men received work- and service-linked benefits in 1983—unemployment compensation, veteran's benefits, workers' compensation—only a little over five million women received one or more of these benefits.[106]

The distinctive relationship between women and the state charted by women's politics in early twentieth-century America yielded women's distinctive position in the New Deal welfare state and minority men's weak claim to social rights. The gender-biased social welfare innovations of the pre–New Deal period tackled problems of poverty through a focus on dependent motherhood and sought solutions to dilemmas of ethnic and racial diversity in the regulation of motherhood. The interweaving of race and gender during the process of the welfare state's formation gendered citizenship, produced maternalist policies that benefited some women, opened the state to other women, and allowed the assimilation of "lesser races" into the system while assuring their continued subordination within it. It created a welfare state that tied the woman citizen to woman's place and that institutionalized political ambivalence towards universal social citizenship. This skewed the politics of gender equality and willed race anxiety to another generation.

NOTES

1 I am using the term "race" as it figured in the politics of industrializing America. It refers to people of color and to white people we commonly refer to today as "ethnics." The Teutonic origins theory developed in the late nineteenth century established a racial hierarchy that separated eastern, central, and southern Europeans from northern and western (Teutonic) Europeans. Non-Teutonic Europeans were, along with blacks, Chinese, Japanese, Mexicans, etc., considered to be inferior racial stock.

2 On the "hybrid republican vision" see Drew McCoy, *The Elusive Republic: Political Economy in Jeffersonian America* (Chapel Hill: University of North Carolina Press, 1980); Isaac Kramnick, "The 'Great National Discussion': The Discourse of Politics in 1787," *William and Mary Quarterly* 45 (January 1988): 3–32. On the masculinism of American citizenship, see Linda Kerber, *Women of the Republic: Intellect and Ideology in Revolutionary America* (Chapel Hill: University of North Carolina Press, 1980); Linda Kerber, "The Republican Ideology of the Revolutionary Generation," *American Quarterly* 37 (Fall 1985): 474–95; Ruth Bloch, "The Gendered Meanings of Virtue in Revolutionary America," *Signs* 13 (Autumn 1987): 37–58; Jan Lewis, "The Republican Wife: Virtue and Seduction in the Early Republic," *William and Mary Quarterly* 44 (October 1987): 688–721.

3 Charles Francis Adams, quoted in Eric Foner, *Free Soil, Free Labor, Free Men* (New York: Oxford University Press, 1977), 228.

4 Jean H. Baker, *Affairs of Party: The Political Culture of Northern Democrats in the Mid-Nineteenth Century* (Ithaca: Cornell University Press, 1983), 84–85; Jean H. Baker, "From Belief into Culture: Republicanism in the Antebellum North," *American Quarterly* 37 (Fall 1985): 532–50.

5   Heywood Sanders, "Paying for the 'Bloody Shirt': The Politics of Civil War Pensions," in *Political Benefits*, ed. Barry Rundquist (Lexington, Mass.: Lexington Books, 1980): 137–59; Richard Bensel, *Sectionalism and American Political Development* (Madison: University of Wisconsin Press, 1984), 60–73.

6   Linda Kerber, " 'May All Our Citizens Be Soldiers and All Our Soldiers Citizens': The Ambiguities of Female Citizenship in the New Nation," in *Arms at Rest: Peacemaking and Peacekeeping in American History*, ed. Robert Beisner and Joan Challinor (New York: Greenwood Press, 1987).

7   On the Constitutional place of women see, among others, Linda Kerber, "From the Declaration of Independence to the Declaration of Sentiments: The Legal Status of Women in the Early Republic, 1776–1848," *Human Rights* 6 (1976–77): 115–24. On judicial regulation of women's citizenship, see *Minor v. Happersett*, 21 Wallace (1875); W. William Hodes, "Women and the Constitution: Some Legal History and a New Approach to the Nineteenth Amendment," *Rutgers Law Review* 25 (Fall 1970): 26–53. Notwithstanding passage of the Nineteenth Amendment, women's citizenship remained incomplete until only recently, when the Supreme Court, in *Billy Taylor v. Louisiana* 419 U.S. 522 (1975), declared women's representation on juries essential to construction of a "fair cross-section of the community." On women's dependent nationality see Sophonisba Breckenridge, *Marriage and the Civic Rights of Women: Separate Domicil and Independent Citizenship* (Chicago: University of Chicago Press, 1931), chaps. 2, 4, and 5; Virginia Sapiro, "Women, Citizenship, and Nationality: Immigration and Naturalization Policies in the United States," *Politics and Society* 13 (1984): 1–26. Married women's citizenship was not made fully independent until the revised Cable Act of 1931.

8   Nancy Cott, *The Bonds of Womanhood: "Women's Sphere" in New England, 1780–1835* (New Haven: Yale University Press, 1977), 64–70; Ruth Bloch, "American Feminine Ideals in Transition: The Rise of the Moral Mother, 1785–1815," *Feminist Studies* 4 (June 1978): 101–26.

9   Gerda Lerner, "The Lady and the Mill Girl: Changes in the Status of Women in the Age of Jackson," in *The Majority Finds Its Past: Placing Women in History*, ed. Gerda Lerner (New York: Oxford University Press, 1979), 15–30. For a contemporary response to popular opposition to women's movement into industry, see Elisha Bartlett, M.D., *A Vindication of the Character and Condition of the Females Employed in the Lowell Mills, Against the Charges Contained in the Boston Times, and the Boston Quarterly Review* (Lowell: L. Huntness Printer, 1841), esp. 15–21.

10 Norma Basch, *In the Eyes of the Law: Women, Marriage, and Property in Nineteenth Century New York* (Ithaca: Cornell University Press, 1982); Norma Basch, "Equity vs. Equality: Emerging Concepts of Womens' Political Status in the Age of Jackson," *Journal of the Early Republic* 3 (Fall 1983): 297–318; Wendy W. Williams, "The Equality Crisis: Some Reflection on Culture, Courts, and Feminism," *Women's Rights Law Reporter* 7 (Spring 1982): 176–78; Joan Hoff-Wilson, "The Legal Status of Women in the Late Nineteenth and Early Twentieth Centuries," *Human Rights* 6 (1976–77): 125–34.

11   In *Bradwell v. Illinois,* 16 (Wallace 130), 1873 the Supreme Court declared
      women incompetent to contract, reasoning that:

> The natural and proper timidity and delicacy which belongs to the female sex evidently
> unfits it for many of the occupations of civil life. . . . [The] divine ordinance as well as . . .
> the nature of things indicated the domestic sphere as that which properly belongs to the
> domain and functions of womanhood. The harmony, not to say identity, of interests and
> views which belong or should belong to the family institution, is repugnant to the idea of a
> woman adopting a distinct and independent career from that of her husband . . . a married
> woman is incapable, without her husband's consent, of making contracts which shall be
> binding on her or him.

Thirty-five years later the court reiterated its view, this time substituting the state
for the husband as the arbiter of woman's contract right. *Muller v. Oregon,* 208
U.S. 412 (1908).

12   Kramnick, "The 'Great National Discussion'," 16–23.
13   Edmund S. Morgan, *American Slavery, American Freedom: The Ordeal of Colo-
      nial Virginia* (New York: Norton, 1975), 384.
14   Sean Wilentz, *Chants Democratic: New York City and the Rise of the American
      Working Class, 1788–1850* (New York: Oxford University Press, 1984); Sean
      Wilentz, "Against Exceptionalism: Class Consciousness and the American Labor
      Movement," *International Labor and Working Class History* 26 (Fall 1984):
      1–24.
15   Gordon Wood, *Creation of the American Republic 1776–1787* (Chapel Hill: Uni-
      versity of North Carolina Press, 1969), 47–53.
16   Robert E. Shalhope, "Republicanism and Early American Historiography," *Wil-
      liam and Mary Quarterly* 39 (April 1982): 341.
17   "Letters of Agrippa," in *The Complete Anti-Federalist* 4, ed. Herbert Storing
      (Chicago: University of Chicago Press, 1981), 86.
18   Michael Grossberg, *Governing the Hearth: Law and the Family in Nineteenth
      Century America* (Chapel Hill: University of North Carolina Press, 1985), 103–
      39.
19   Ibid., 148. For the most part the legal order supported this view. Oliver Wendell
      Holmes' reasoning in *Buck v. Bell* 24 U.S. 200 (1927) was symptomatic:

> We have seen more than once that the public welfare may call upon the best citizens for
> their lives. It would be strange if it could not call upon those who already sap the strength
> of the State for these lesser sacrifices . . . in order to prevent our being swamped with
> incompetence. It is better for all the world, if instead of waiting to execute degenerate
> offspring for crime, or to let them starve for their imbecility, society can prevent those who
> are manifestly unfit from continuing their kind. . . . Three generations of imbeciles are
> enough.

20   *Congressional Record* (June 19, 1884), 5349–52.
21   The cultural and rhetorical symptoms of these views are described by Alexan-
      der Saxton, "Blackface Minstrelsy and Jacksonian Ideology," *American Quar-*

terly 27 (March 1975): 3–28; Thomas Gossett, *Race: The History of an Idea in America* (New York: Schocken Books, 1965). Francis Walker, "The Restriction of Immigration," *North American Review* (June 1896): 828; Woodrow Wilson, "Make Haste Slowly," *Selected Literary Papers* (1925): 30–39; and *History of the American People* 5 (1902), 212–13 are two contemporary presentations of these views.

22 By "old-stock" I am referring chiefly to the English, Welsh, Scots, Irish, and Germans. By artifice of late nineteenth-century scientific racialism, these groups were assigned the inherent democratic character of Teutonic peoples.

23 E.L. Godkin, quoted in Thomas Gossett, *Race: The History of an Idea in America* (1965), 268.

24 California State Senate, *Chinese Immigration: Its Social, Moral and Political Effect* (1878); *Congressional Record* (February 13, 1885), 1634.

25 On the contest between racial identity and universal political identity, see Eric Foner, *Politics and Ideology in the Age of the Civil War* (New York: Oxford University Press, 1980), chaps. 4, 5, and 6; Alexander Saxton, *The Indispensable Enemy: Labor and the Anti-Chinese Movement in California* (Berkeley: University of California Press, 1971), chap. 2. On the politics of racial exclusion, see Saxton, *The Indispensible Enemy*; Gwendolyn Mink, *Old Labor and New Immigrants in American Political Development: Union, Party, and State, 1875–1920* (Ithaca: Cornell University Press, 1986); George Frederickson, *White Supremacy: A Comparative Study in American and South African History* (New York: Oxford University Press, 1981); Richard Kluger, *Simple Justice* (New York: Vintage, 1977), chaps. 1–4.

26 For example, *Yick Wo v. Hopkins,* 118 U.S. 356 (1886); *Plessy v. Ferguson,* 163 U.S. 537 (1896); *Cumming v. Richmond County Board of Education,* 175 U.S. 528 (1899).

27 Linda Kerber, "The Republican Mother: Women and the Enlightenment: An American Perspective," *American Quarterly* 28 (Summer 1976): 187–205.

28 Reverend William Lyman, *A Virtuous Woman in the Bond of Domestic Union* (New London, 1802), 22.

29 Basch, *In the Eyes of the Law*; Grossberg, *Governing the Hearth*, chap. 7.

30 *Green v. State,* 58 Ala. 190 (1877), quoted in Grossberg, *Governing the Hearth*.

31 The ideology of republican motherhood and the canons of domesticity legitimized women's civic activity—especially for moral reform—throughout most of the nineteenth century. Cott, *The Bonds of Womanhood*; Caroll Smith-Rosenberg, "Beauty, the Beast, and the Militant Woman: A Case Study in Sex Roles and Social Stress in Jacksonian America," *American Quarterly* 23 (1971): 562–84; Nancy Hewitt, *Women's Activism and Social Change: Rochester, New York, 1822–1872* (Ithaca: Cornell University Press, 1984).

32 Barbara Ehrenreich and Deirdre English, "The Manufacture of Housework," *Socialist Revolution*, vol. 26 (1975): 12, 25.

33 Rheta Childe Dorr, *What Eight Million Women Want* (Boston: Small, Maynard and Company, 1910), 327, 330.

34 Ibid., 321–324.

35 Florence Kelley, *Modern Industry in Relation to the Family, Health, Education, Morality* (New York: Longmans, Green, and Co., 1914), 95–96.

36 Ibid., 52; Women's Bureau, Bulletin no. 23, *The Family Status of Breadwinning Women* (Washington, D.C., 1922), 42.

37 Mary Poovey, *The Proper Lady and the Woman Writer: Ideology as Style in the Works of Mary Wollstonecraft, Mary Shelley, and Jane Austen* (Chicago: University of Chicago Press, 1984); Sally Alexander, "Women, Class and Sexual Difference," *History Workshop Journal* 17 (Spring 1984): 125–49; Dorothy Thompson, *The Chartists: Popular Politics in the Industrial Revolution* (New York: Pantheon, 1984), chap. 6; Joan W. Scott, "On Language, Gender, and Working-Class History," *International Labor and Working-Class History* 31 (Spring 1987): 1–14; Ann Taylor Allen, "Mothers of the New Generation: Adele Schreiber, Helene Stocker, and the Evolution of a German Idea of Motherhood, 1900–1914," *Signs* 10 (Spring 1985): 412–38; Richard Evans, *Comrades and Sisters: Feminism, Socialism and Pacifism in Europe, 1870–1945* (New York: St. Martin's Press, 1987), 21–25, 55–57; Jane Jenson, "Struggling for Identity: The Women's Movement and the State in Western Europe," *West European Politics* 8 (October 1985): 5–18.

38 Mary Lyndon Shanley, "Suffrage, Protective Labor Legislation, and Married Women's Property Laws in England," *Signs* 12 (Autumn 1986): 62–77; Bentley Gilbert, *The Evolution of National Insurance in Britain* (1966), 331; Jane Jenson, "Both Friend and Foe: Women and State Welfare," in *Becoming Visible*, ed. Bridenthal and Koonz (Boston: Houghton Mifflin, 1987), 535–56; Elizabeth Wilson, *Women and the Welfare State* (1977), especially chap. 6.

39 Leonard Krieger, "The Idea of the Welfare State in Europe and the United States," *Journal of the History of Ideas* 24 (December 1963): 553–68; Peter Flora and Jens Alber, "Modernization, Democratization, and the Development of Welfare States in Western Europe," in *The Development of Welfare States in Europe and America*, ed. Peter Flora and Arnold J. Heidenheimer (New Brunswick: Transaction Books, 1981), 37–81; Mary Ruggie, *The State and Working Women: A Comparative Study of Britain and Sweden* (Princeton: Princeton University Press, 1984).

40 To be sure, some class-premised policies for social provision did win a hearing in the United States. Theodore Roosevelt, for example, raised the issue of health insurance in the 1912 presidential contest, the Progressive Party included a health plank on its platform, and in 1916 Congress considered health provision along with other proposals for social insurance. But business ambivalence toward socializing risks other than those already borne in tort liability (workmen's compensation), union labor interest in providing for its own constituency, and middle-class concern about the use of public benefits for patronage purposes (e.g., Civil War pensions and outdoor relief) generated powerful resistance to social provision. Daniel Nelson, *Unemployment Insurance: The American Experience* (Madison: University of Wisconsin Press, 1969), chaps. 2 and 3; Roy Lubove, *The Struggle for Social Security* (Pittsburgh: University of Pittsburgh Press, 1986); Jill Quadagno, *The Transformation of Old Age Security* (Chicago:

University of Chicago Press, 1988); Mink, *Old Labor and New Immigrants*; Sanders, "Paying for the 'Bloody Shirt';" Bensel, *Sectionalism*; John Gillin, *Poverty and Dependency* (New York: The Century Company, 1921), 153.

41 See, for example, Samuel Gompers in the *American Federationist* 22 (1915), 113.

42 On voluntarism, see Michael Rogin, "Voluntarism: The Political Functions of an Anti-Political Doctrine," *Industrial and Labor Relations Review* 15 (1962): 521–35; Mink, *Old Labor and New Immigrants*, chaps. 1, 5, and 7.

43 Samuel Gompers in the *American Federationist* 22 (1915), 113.

44 H.L. Wayland, *Baltimore Charities Conference* (1887), 18.

45 Joseph K. Hart, "Public Welfare and Our Democratic Institutions," American Academy of Political and Social Science *Annals* 105 (January 1923): 34.

46 Denise Riley makes a similar point about postwar British social policy in *War in the Nursery* (London: Virago, 1983), 194–95.

47 Beatrice Forbes-Robertson Hale, *What Women Want: An Interpretation of the Feminist Movement* (New York: Frederick A. Stokes, 1914), 180.

48 Ibid., 288–90.

49 Mary Ritter Beard, *Woman's Work in Municipalities* (New York: D. Appleton and Co., 1915); Judith Sealander, *As Minority Becomes Majority: Federal Reaction to the Phenomenon of Women in the Work Force* (Westport, Conn.: Greenwood Press, 1983).

50 The role of both women's politics and gender bias in building the American welfare state has been gaining in recognition: Stanley Lemons, *The Woman Citizen: Social Feminism in the 1920s* (Urbana: University of Illinois Press, 1973); Virginia Sapiro, "The Gender Basis of American Social Policy," in this volume; Sylvia Law, "Women, Work, Welfare, and the Preservation of Patriarchy," *University of Pennsylvania Law Review* 131 (May 1983): 1249–1339; Barbara J. Nelson, "The Origins of the Two-Channel Welfare State," in this volume, Kathryn Kish Sklar, "A Theoretical Framework for the Comparative Study of Women and Politics in the United States and Great Britain," paper presented at the Berkshire Women's History Conference, 1987; Barbara Ehrenreich and Frances Fox Piven, "Women and the Welfare State," in *Alternatives* ed. Irving Howe (New York: Longman, 1983) 41–60; Irene Diamond, ed., *Women, Families and Public Policy* (New York: Pantheon, 1984).

51 Florence Kelley, "Should Women be Treated Identically with Men by the Law?" *American Review* 3 (May–June 1923): 277.

52 Ellen DuBois, *Feminism and Suffrage* (Ithaca: Cornell University Press, 1978), chaps. 2 and 6.

53 Quoted in Paula Giddings, *When and Where I Enter* (New York: W. Morrow, 1984), 67.

54 Ibid., 66. My italics.

55 Aileen Kraditor, *Ideas of the Woman Suffrage Movement* (New York: Norton, 1965, 1981). Kraditor relates race appeals to the development of the suffragists' "expendiency" argument, wherein woman suffrage was urged as a means to reform rather than as a reform in itself.

56 Ibid., 138.

57   Jane Addams, *A Centennial Reader* (New York: Macmillan, 1960), 11, 16.
58   Jane Addams, *Twenty Years at Hull House* (New York: New American Library, 1960), 253.
59   Annie Marion MacLean, *Wage-Earning Women* (New York: Macmillan, 1910, 1974), 177.
60   Herman Hagedorn, ed., *The Works of Theodore Roosevelt* (1926–27), 18:402, 10:248; Theodore Roosevelt, *Winning of the West* (1917), 89.
61   James Richardson, ed., *Messages and Papers of the Presidents* 14 (New York: Bureau of National Literature, 1911), 6651–52.
62   Rheta Childe Dorr, quoted in "What Next?" *The Suffragist* (October 1920): 234.
63   Florence Kelley, "The Need of Theoretical Preparation for Philanthropic Work" (1887), quoted in Sheila Rothman, *Woman's Proper Place* (New York: Basic Books, 1978), 111–12. See also Jane Addams, "Why the Ward Boss Rules," *Outlook* 57 (April 18, 1892).
64   Louise de Koven Bowen, "The Colored People of Chicago: Where Their Opportunity Is Choked—Where Open," *The Survey*, reprinted in Beard, *Woman's Work*, 184.
65   A.E. Sheffield, "Administration of the Mothers' Aid Law in Massachusetts," *Survey* 31 (February 21, 1914): 644–45. Florence Kelley argued to the New York State Factory Investigation Commission that "a man ought to be held up by the community rigidly to his duty in supporting his wife and children." *Preliminary Report* 3 (1912), 1599.
66   Allen F. Davis, *Spearheads of Reform: The Social Settlements and the Progressive Movement* (New York: Oxford University Press, 1967).
67   Florence Kelley, *Modern Industry*, 97.
68   Quoted in Ehrenreich and English, "The Manufacture of Housework," 32.
69   Josephine Goldmark, *Fatigue and Efficiency* (New York: Charities Publication Committee, 1912).
70   Hale, *What Women Want*, 181.
71   Martha May, "Bread Before Roses: American Workingmen, Labor Unions and the Family Wage," in *Women, Work and Protest: A Century of U.S. Women's Labor History*, ed. Ruth Milkman (Boston: Routledge, Kegan Paul, 1985) 1–21; Florence Kelley, *Modern Industry*, 13, 32.
72   Florence Kelley, *Modern Industry*, 36.
73   Jane Addams, "Why Women Should Vote," *Ladies Home Journal* (January 1910).
74   Jane Addams, "Utilization of Women in City Government," in *Newer Ideals of Peace* (New York: Macmillan, 1907).
75   Jane Addams, "If Men Were Seeking the Franchise," reprinted in Addams, *A Centennial Reader*, 113.
76   Jane Addams, "Why Women Should Vote."
77   Jane Addams, "Utilization of Women in City Government."
78   *Bradwell v. Illinois,* 16 Wallace 130 (1873).
79   *Muller v. Oregon;* Sophonisba Breckenridge, "Legislative Control of Women's Work," *Journal of Political Economy* (February 1906), 107–9.
80   The court in *Muller v. Oregon* established the principle that legislation setting

the terms of women's labor contract is "for the benefit of all" and thus held such legislation to be within the scope of the police power. Three years earlier, in *Lochner v. New York,* 198 U.S. 45 (1905), the court applied more rigid scrutiny to legislation establishing maximum hours for bakers (a category including men), holding that the health of bakers was not a matter of the general welfare. While the Court found hours regulations for women in general to be appropriate, it found hours regulation for men Constitutional in rare occupational circumstances —when male workers were found to be unequal parties in the labor relations of hazardous industries (i.e., underground mining). *Holden v. Hardy,* 169 U.S. 366 (1898).

81   Lucinda Chandler quoted in William Leach, *True Love and Perfect Union* (New York: Basic Books, 1980), 89.

82   Sophonisba Breckenridge, *Women in the Twentieth Century: A Study of their Political, Social and Economic Activities* (New York, 1933), 264.

83   Mark Leff, "Consensus for Reform: The Mothers' Pension Movement in the Progressive Era," *Social Service Review* 47 (1973): 397–417.

84   Mrs. Theodore Birney, quoted in Rothman, *Woman's Proper Place,* 104.

85   Florence Kelley, *Modern Industry,* 16.

86   Gillin, *Poverty and Dependency,* 377.

87   Michael B. Katz. *In the Shadow of the Poorhouse* (New York: Basic Books, 1986), 129.

88   William Hard, "The Moral Necessity of 'State Funds to Mothers'," *Survey* 29 (March 1, 1913): 769–73.

89   "The Needy Mother and the Neglected Child," *Outlook* 104 (June 7, 1913): 280–83.

90   "Standardizing Service," *Equal Rights* (July 14, 1923): 172.

91   Pension rates varied among states; they averaged from nine to fifteen dollars per month for the first child, and from four to ten dollars per month for additional children. Pensions were allocated for children up to fourteen to sixteen years of age. U.S. Department of Labor, Children's Bureau, *Laws Relating to "Mother's Pensions" in the United States, Denmark, and New Zealand* (Washington, D.C., 1914).

92   Only 3 percent of mothers' assistance went to black mothers. See Leff, "Consensus for Reform" 414.

93   Leff, "Consensus for Reform," 412–14.

94   C.C. Carstens, "Social Security Through Aid for Dependent Children in Their Own Homes," *Law and Contemporary Problems* (April 1936): 246–52.

95   According to Andre Siegfried, while 51 percent of the South Carolina population was black, blacks only received 11 percent of public education monies. See also, Gavin Wright, *Old South, New South* (1985), 123; Robert A. Margo, *Disfranchisement, School Finance, and the Economics of Segregated Schools in the U.S. South, 1890–1910* (N.p., 1982).

96   Gunnar Myrdal, *An American Dilemma: The Negro Problem and Modern Democracy,* vol. 1 (New York: Harper & Row, 1962), chap. 15; Jill Quadagno, *The Transformation of Old Age Security,* 135.

97   Nancy Folbre, "The Pauperization of Motherhood: Patriarchy and Public Policy

in the United States," in *Families and Work*, eds. Naomi Gerstel and Harriet Engel Gross (Philadelphia: Temple University Press, 1987), 499.

98   Lois Scharf, *To Work and to Wed: Female Employment, Feminism, and the Great Depression* (Westport, Conn.: Greenwood Press, 1980), 130–31.

99   *West Coast Hotel v. Parrish,* 300 U.S. 379 (1937).

100 On specific measures, see Robert B. Stevens, *Statutory History of the United States: Income Security* (New York: Chelsea House, 1970), 117–19, 140–44. The benefits of insured wives, but not of insured husbands, were subject to reduction if combined benefits exceeded family benefit limits. Survivor's benefits were established for widows and their children; men's exclusion required judicial correction in the 1970s.

101 See Myrdal, *An American Dilemma*, chap. 15, fn. 65.

102 Veterans Administration, *Annual Report, 1984: America is #1 Thanks To Our Veterans* (Washington, D.C., 1984), 3.

103 For example, in 1935, 42 percent of black workers in occupations "covered" by social insurance earned incomes below the floor for eligibility established in the Social Security Act of the same year. Twenty-two percent of the white worker population in covered occupations earned incomes below the old-age insurance limit. See Wayne Caskey, "Workers with Annual Taxable Wages of Less than $200 in 1937–39," *Social Security Bulletin* (October 1931): 17–24.

104 *Califano v. Goldfarb,* 97 S.Ct. 1021 (1977).

105 Diana Pearce, "Toil and Trouble: Women Workers and Unemployment Compensation," *Signs* 3 (Spring 1985): 439–59.

106 Joan Acker, "Class, Gender, and the Relations of Distribution," *Signs* 13 (Spring 1988): 492.

CHAPTER 5

The Origins of the Two-Channel Welfare State: Workmen's Compensation and Mothers' Aid

BARBARA J. NELSON

The last decade has seen an outpouring of research on state formation[1] and more recently on the connection between state formation generally and the specifics of the creation of the welfare state in industrial democracies. The recent work on welfare state formation has been led by Theda Skocpol, Ann Shola Orloff, John Ikenberry, and Kenneth Finegold, among others.[2] One major conclusion of this body of research is that the relatively late emergence of the welfare state in the United States (during the New Deal) is in large part the result of earlier distrust of corrupt parties as the administrators of benefit programs and the lack of an alternative, neutral bureaucracy that could undertake this task. The sex, race, and class of the potential clients of new social programs do not figure importantly in the discussion of the emergence of a socially undifferentiated welfare state.

At the same time that the research on state formation was underway, feminist interpretations of power and politics, including feminist critiques of the welfare state, also developed. Feminist scholars examining the welfare state are much less unified in approach and topic. They include, among others, Mary McIntosh, Barbara Nelson, Lisa Peattie, Martin Rein, Virginia Sapiro, Jennifer Schirmer, Elizabeth Wilson, and Eli Zaretsky.[3] This work has mostly examined current welfare programs from a variety of theoretical perspectives and, if a summary of a divergent literature is possible, suggests that the welfare state incorporates long-lasting political tensions in that it reproduces and reinforces profound social inequities between groups while also improving the material conditions of beneficiaries. By and large, this work is not focused on the origins of welfare policies and the welfare state. The existing histori-

123

cal work does not typically compare programs designed for men with those designed for women.

There has been little convergence between the state formation research and the feminist critiques of the welfare state. Indeed, it is striking that while the questions asked by both groups of scholars may occasionally run parallel to each other, the sources used in analysis rarely overlap. When the concerns that motivate these researchers are examined together, an important and provocative set of questions emerges. Is the state gendered and if so how? How can theories of state formation and theories of the welfare state illuminate one another? Arising from feminist theories of difference, how do gender, race, and class intersect in the creation of the United States welfare state?[4] What is the role of comparative case studies of welfare programs in contributing both to an understanding of events and to a more richly elaborated social theory?

The sum of these questions, and others like them, is more an agenda for interdisciplinary research than the subject of a single essay. The more focused aim of this work is to initiate a critical reconceptualization of the origins of the U.S. welfare state. Specifically, I shall present the beginnings of a historically grounded argument for viewing U.S. welfare policy and ultimately the welfare state as fundamentally divided into two channels, one originally designed for white industrial workers and the other designed for impoverished, white, working-class widows with young children.[5] In important ways the ideology and administrative forms of the two-channel welfare state predate the New Deal, having their origins in the Progressive era. In this period, benefits devised for mostly male wage workers were strongly linked to welfare capitalism and scientific management, while those devised for a select group of mothers (impoverished widows with young children) were linked to the poor law tradition and the administrative practices of the Charity Organization Society movement. A good image for organizing these findings is that industrialists set the terms for the male, work-based parts of the welfare state while their wives, through charity organization work, set the terms for the female, motherhood-based segments.[6] Both the creation of a two-channel welfare state and the tensions between the intersection of motherhood and wage work can be seen in the first successful benefit programs in the United States: Workmen's Compensation and Mothers' Aid. These programs had different ideologies, clienteles, principles of entitlement, and administrative styles and they set the tone for the Social Security Act, which in turn greatly reinforced the gender, racial, and class organization of the welfare state.

To discuss these issues the essay is organized into two parts. The first section briefly covers the methodology that guided the study. The second part, the main body of the text, is a theoretical and historical elaboration of the thesis presented. The chapter tries not only to present its conclusions but also to articulate the many connected issues and unanswered questions.

METHODOLOGY

The proper methodologies for examining far-reaching social phenomena have consistently posed problems for social scientists and historians.[7] In an era where behavioralism is still a dominant paradigm, two of the traditional methodological problems are the role of case studies and the uses of historical analysis in interpretation and theory building. Compared to the experimental designs and statistical analyses possible with large populations and large numbers of narrowly defined measurements, narrative case studies present a "degrees of freedom" problem, that is, too many observations on a limited number of cases.[8] Similarly, historical analysis creates a serious problem in the philosophy of behavioral sciences. In many statistical techniques time is either objectified into a variable or treated exogenously. Such views allow for more simplified statistical models but do not adequately aid in thinking about complex social processes that develop over decades, if not longer.

Behavioralism presents another sociology of knowledge problem, less discussed in the social sciences than in history. The behavioral revolution in the social sciences undermined disciplinary confidence in the role of argumentation and narrative in representing events, evaluating evidence, and building theory. Historians Natalie Zemon Davis and Bonnie Smith are examining the history of narrative and its relation to the professionalization of academic disciplines, especially history and the social sciences.[9] They suggest that positivism came to discredit both traditional forms of narrative and narration as a creative act.[10]

Against the backdrop of these issues, some scholars presented approaches to comparative historical studies based on the logic of argumentation and to a lesser extent the style of presentation. Implicit in this work was the belief that the logic of comparison was at least as powerful in producing understanding as were the results of statistical analyses. This view parallels the belief in experimental social sciences that the research design yields more to explanation than do particular statistical analyses. In 1980, Theda Skocpol and Margaret Somers presented an analysis of the "logics in use" in comparative history: comparative history as the parallel demonstration of theory, comparative history as contrasts of context, and comparative history as macrocausal analysis.[11]

This research uses a combination of two approaches: contrast-oriented and macrocausal comparative historical techniques. Contrast-oriented comparative history emphasizes, according to the authors, the differences between and among cases. Using case histories that highlight a contrast, this approach focuses on historical integrity and is used to discourage, some might say puncture, ever-inclusive theoretical formulations of social processes. On the other hand, "comparative history as macro-causal analysis. . .uses comparative history primarily for the purpose of making causal inferences about macro-level structures and processes."[12] The purpose is to use historical cases to advance theoretical understanding in an implicitly inductive manner. The method used here is based on the premise that, in the contrast-oriented manner, an undifferentiated, decontextualized view of welfare policy and the welfare state, that is, a view that does not recognize the primacy of the gender, race, and class of the clients for whom programs are designed, is overly general. The case studies of Workmen's Compensation and Mothers' Aid elaborate the relevant similarities and differences in the programs' ideologies, social premises, methods of proving eligibility, and administrative styles, with the aim, in the macroanalytical tradition, of rethinking social theory for state and welfare state formation.

GENDER, RACE, CLASS AND THE U.S. WELFARE STATE

Examining welfare policies and the welfare state requires beginning with definitions. In the United States, the concepts "welfare policy" and "the welfare state" are often employed without precision. For some policy analysts with an interest in programmatic change, the welfare state is discussed as merely the sum of all welfare policies, where policies are defined as programs and their ideological orientations.[13] In this usage, the word "state" is not connected to the politics of state formation or activity, where the "state" is more rigorously defined as "the site of autonomous official action" including decision making, planning, and creating and mobilizing a bureaucratic infrastructure for implementation.[14] The distinction between welfare policy and the welfare state is crucial because it allows us to assert that there have been public welfare policies before the advent of the welfare state. Further, it can be argued that the content of early welfare policies and their administrative arrangements have left their marks on the development of the U.S. welfare state, with its capacity for governmentally defining programs and delivering benefits.

But these definitions leave other questions unanswered. It is more difficult to agree on what programs and approaches define welfare policy than it is to separate definitions of welfare policy and the welfare state.[15] By convention, in the United States welfare policy consists of those public programs providing money, goods in kind, or services that are made available to offset regularly occurring events outside the control of individuals.[16] The ideology underpinning these programs is that collective responses at least partially funded and managed by government are necessary to meet the loss of income experienced due to old age, disability, unsupported motherhood, fluctuations in the business cycle, and the phases of capitalist development. In Western and Eastern Europe, welfare policy also includes at least partial payment of medical expenses and income support for the sick, but these kinds of benefits are only available through public means for the poor and the aged in the United States. Similarly, conventional definitions of U.S. welfare policy usually do not include corporate benefits or programs run, if not necessarily financed, by the voluntary sector.

This definition of welfare policy is both employed and critiqued in this study. The criticisms include the fact that most of welfare policy, as defined previously, assumes a lifetime of steady work for wages, which has been neither the practice nor the ideal for most women (of all races) nor the possibility for many men of color.[17] In addition, the exclusion of certain programs and protections from the conventional definition of welfare policy is troubling. Educational institutions and programs, job formation and training programs, and laws protecting collective bargaining and regulating the conditions of labor provide at minimum the "flanking subsystems" of the more readily acknowledged welfare policies.[18] These other programs help to define the size of the labor force, the composition of the reserve army of the unemployed, and the relationship between groups of workers and types of labor: productive, domestic, and reproductive.

In a series of wide-ranging and important articles, Theda Skocpol, John Ikenberry, and Ann Shola Orloff have transformed scholarly thinking on the origins of the U.S. welfare state.[19] The authors agree with the widely held view that the Great Depression ushered in the welfare state acknowledging, however, that early welfare policies existed beforehand. The authors sought new answers to the perennial question, Why was the United States so late in establishing its welfare state in comparison with Western European countries? Reversing the question for a moment, this body of literature reports that social policies, especially national schemes of social insurance, developed comparatively early in some Western European countries because, in the first instance, political parties needed to recruit newly enfranchised members of the electorate and because, in the second instance, policies could be developed and administered through existing politically neutral national bureaucracies, themselves a remnant of the autocratic past. Applying these criteria to the U.S. case, the authors reject as inaccurate or incomplete any explanations for the late development of the U.S. welfare state based on the strength and persistence of liberal values, differential rates of industrialism, or differential power of the working class.

Skocpol, Ikenberry, and Orloff demonstrate that the United States did not meet the political and administrative necessities of creating a welfare state until the mid-1930s. The reasons, they assert, rest in part on the comparatively early franchise of white men, which was largely completed by 1840. The early creation of what social scientists routinely, though erroneously, call a "mass electorate" helped to create patronage-based rather than programmatic parties. (Programmatic parties developed in part to woo the waves of voters that periodically washed into the European electorate as the franchise was sequentially liberalized for men.) The authors further argue that Americans distrusted the corruption of public officials that accompanied patronage-based parties. The citizenry was unwilling to countenance the distribution of public benefits by public officials. A federal system of powerful states, and a concomitantly weak national government with a relatively small permanent bureaucracy in Washington and underdeveloped national administrative capacities, completed the list of political liabilities that inhibited the systematic development and adoption of welfare policies and the creation of the welfare state.

Administrative underdevelopment and the corruption of political parties in the United States kept the one large "welfare" program of the nineteenth century—Civil War Pensions—from becoming the entering wedge for social insurance in the twentieth century. The Civil War Pension system was a large enterprise. In 1912, it had 860,000 beneficiaries (covering *two-thirds* of the white native-born men over age sixty-five outside the South) and cost $153 million.[20] These pensions were, however, a product of the patronage-based parties. They were not intended to be an instrument of social amelioration (though they certainly acted as one); they did not rest on a belief of collective responsibility for commonly experienced economic dislocation; their administrative irregularities were widely known and deplored; and they offered the model of a pension fully funded from the general revenue at a time when joint employee-employer insurance systems, some with additional public revenue contributions, were the typical policy in Western Europe.[21]

It was not until the nation faced the crisis of the Great Depression that enough of these obstacles could be overcome and that welfare state building, through the vehicle of the Social Security Act, could begin. Uniform, nationally administered programs for all major types of problems and constituencies were suggested during the development of the Social Security Act. As finally passed, however, the law reflected the political considerations of a federal system of government and the weight of existing state-level welfare programs:

In the formation of America's unemployment insurance system, all of the nationalizing pressures inside and around the Roosevelt administration had to give way before the practical institutional obstacles built into the federalism and separation of powers inherent in the overall American state structure. . . . The basic administrative shape of other major elements to go into the immediate legislative proposals [for the Social Security Act]—a national old-age insurance system, and federal grants-in-aid to help support state-level, need-based programs (especially) for old people and dependent children —simply aroused much less controversy. Many state-level programs offering old-age pensions and "mothers' pensions" (actually for dependent children) were already in existence by the early 1930s, so federal subsidization rather than direct administration by the national government was taken for granted—all the more because Roosevelt would never for a moment have countenanced direct national "welfare" expenditures not backed up by contributory taxes from the potential recipients.[22]

The state capacities approach does not emphasize any aspects of the composition of clientele. This is not due to assuming incorrectly that all members of the working class were equally the beneficiaries of welfare programs. The authors acknowledge that early welfare programs assisted the most integrated members of the industrial working class in the United States: northern white men employed in mining, heavy manufacturing, and transportation and, to a lesser extent, their widows.[23] But as always the interest is in state formation. Elsewhere Skocpol specifies that the economic class interests of both the working class and capitalists shaped and were shaped by the particularly American forms of state development, as well as culture and politics to the extent that these things can be separated. Wide geographical distances and a federal system made it difficult for both workers and owners to establish national movements and institutions designed to benefit from centralized action and planning.[24] But even this limited discussion of class is not extended to other groups. Perhaps because the main thrust of the new state-building literature is comparing state formation among and between nations, the literature has not turned its own comparative methodology toward the consequences of gender and race on questions of welfare state formation within one country.

A feminist commentary on the political and administrative approach to the origins of the welfare state must surely begin with a series of What if? questions. What if the United States had really had mass-based political parties? What if women had achieved the franchise in 1878 when the "Anthony Amendment" was first introduced in Congress by California Senator A.A. Sargent?[25] Or, more interestingly, what if women had won the vote in, say, 1890, when the National American Woman Suffrage Association was formed, *and* the 1890s had not brought about the systematic disenfranchisement of southern blacks? Would these new groups of voters have been integrated into patronage-based political parties? Would they have posed a programmatic challenge for the parties? Would that challenge have altered the climate for social reform? And would any change in party program have been sufficient to overcome the underdeveloped administrative capacities of government, capacities so necessary to the establishment of welfare programs? None of these scenarios was remotely likely, but taken together, they alert us to the gender and race components of the process of political incorporation driving welfare state formation.

On a more concrete level, feminist critiques of the welfare state are widely divergent in their approaches and often quite theoretical in their presentation. Liberal, radical, socialist, and Marxist feminists each bring a specific perspective.[26] As suggested earlier, a major concern of this literature is that the welfare state simultaneously reinforces profound social inequities between groups, especially but not only the sexes, while also beginning to ameliorate the financial distress of beneficiaries. At the heart of the various approaches is a concern for how different types of labor are related to one another; how laboring, broadly defined, is related to political and economic power; and whether or not the state works to reproduce or alter labor-power relationships.

The concept "labor" is often divided into three categories: *productive* labor, located in or out of the home, where individuals make items or deliver services for household consumption, exchange, or to earn money; *domestic* labor, which maintains a household; and *reproductive* labor, which includes the bearing and raising of children.[27] In principle, both women and men can perform any type of labor, except of course the bearing of children. But in practice, all societies create a sexual division of labor, though the specific content of the division varies from culture to culture and within cultures by age, race, caste, and class. It is generally held that part of the sexual division of labor is a sexually assigned difference in access to political and economic rights and resources. At the macrosocial level, this sexual division of labor does not empower women and men equally. Nannerl O. Keohane, drawing on the work of Michelle Rosaldo, describes the inequality this way:

The public realm, across cultures and over the centuries, has been male-centered to an extent unparalleled in other parts of human social life. Virtually all offices charged with responsibility for making or carrying out decisions that affect an entire society have been held by men. Women have seldom exercised authority over groups containing men of equivalent age and social class. Anthropologists confirm the universality of this truth in different kinds of societies. As Shelly Rosaldo put it recently: "Women may have ritual powers of considerable significance to themselves as well as men, but women never dominate in rites requiring the participation of the community as a whole. I know of no case where men are required to serve as an obligatory audience to female ritual of political performance." [28]

This set of general findings leads us to look beyond macrosocial patterns and ask, What were labor-power relations between the sexes at the time of the first wave of U.S. benefit programs? The answer must encompass the connections between gender relations, political processes, and economic activity during the Progressive period. This period was characterized by significant political volatility, changes in party politics for white men, and the demands for political incorporation by women. These demands were themselves embedded in the ideology of separate spheres and the reality of separate female and male political institutions. Viewed this way, it is not surprising that a two-channel welfare state developed.

The details of these relations, like all discussions of the Progressive period, resist simple specification.[29] The two powerful locally based parties of the nineteenth century waned in a period when men's political and economic interests were no longer mostly community based. (But though less powerful, these parties remained male institutions, even though their roles in male civic rituals changed.) Male voter turnout declined markedly. At the same time, as historian Paula Baker writes, "Men increasingly replaced or supplemented electoral participation with the sorts of single-issue, interest-group tactics women had long employed."[30] Both customary and legal racial separation continued to increase in this period, further limiting the opportunities for official political participation of black men, especially in the South.

Simultaneously, the first twenty years of this century witnessed the increasing power of several mass movements promoting (mostly white) women's empowerment. These movements focused on empowerment both in the family and in public life. These efforts drew upon and supported such powerful women's institutions as the Women's Christian Temperance Union, the National American Woman Suffrage Association, the National Womans' Party, parts of the Settlement movement (notably Hull House), women's colleges, and women's social and religious organizations of all kinds. White women depended significantly on these mostly separate women's institutions to create the organizational, material, and psychological basis for political activism.[31] Black women, denied access to many institutions established by white women, more frequently used a combination of all-women's and mixed-sex groups (especially churches) as a springboard for political action, action that for both groups defended and undercut gender relations premised on separate spheres.[32]

The ideology of separate spheres retained profound resonance in the years before World War I.[33] It argued that women and men had separate but complementary interests, skills, and abilities and gave many women a vehicle for political action through images of moral guardianship analogous to motherhood and civic housekeeping analogous to domestic responsibilities. For some women's organizations, the rhetoric of moral guardianship and civic housekeeping became a method of reconciling traditional family relations and support for women's incursions into public space, and even support for the vote. But throughout this period, the tension between the individualistic liberal egalitarian quality of suffrage and the interest in using the vote, symbolically or actually, as a mechanism to strengthen women's power within *existing* gender relations was never far from the surface, as the competing strategies and beliefs of the National American Woman Suffrage Association and National Womans' Party demonstrate.[34]

The changes in political activities were closely connected to rapid industrialization and increased urbanization. From the point of view of individuals, the principal characteristic of industrialization was the growth of wage labor. By 1920, well into the consolidation of industrial capitalism, manufacturing and mechanical employees (the largest occupational group of wage earners) comprised 30.8 percent of the labor force.[35] Wage laborers and the poor who hoped to join them had for several generations faced a very uncertain income. They routinely experienced unemployment and underemployment as well as severe external pressures on wage rates from an "oversupply" of labor and the lack, in most instances, of strong unions.[36]

The race and gender composition of manufacturing and mechanical workers conveys a great deal about the general composition of wage earners. In 1920, 32.5 percent of whites and 18.4 percent of blacks were employed in these industries. But another perspective on this labor force is also necessary. Only 6.9 percent of this occupational group was black.[37] In other words, the manufacturing labor force was overwhelmingly white. Recognizing that black men were often denied industrial jobs, commentators like Kelly Miller wrote that "the [empowerment] stronghold of the Negro hitherto has been his ability to do crude work along the lines where the white man did not care to compete."[38] Miller also noted that urban black women had high rates of employment, though mostly in domestic positions.

In 1920, men outnumbered women four to one in the labor force. In manufacturing and mechanical pursuits, men outnumbered women twenty to one. Women were still heavily concentrated in domestic and personal service work. Almost 26 percent of employed women worked in service jobs, compared to 22.6 percent employed in manufacturing.[39] Black and white women were concentrated in different types of employment. Jacqueline Jones reports that southern black women often preferred industrial labor to the low wages and scrutiny of domestic work in white women's homes.[40] But manufacturing work was hard for black women to get. The cotton textile industry, for example, had a virtually all-white labor force. Early in industrialization, northern, native-born white women fared better in getting manufacturing jobs. As the decades passed, many of those foreign-born white women who had held domestic servant jobs gradually moved into manufacturing, being replaced in domestic service by newly migrated black women.[41]

These trends can be augmented by information on marital status and household composition. Overall, in 1900 only 5.6 percent of married women worked, a figure that rose to 10.7 percent in 1910, where it hovered for two decades.[42] More married black women worked than married white women, out of dire necessity. Southern black women, whose labor was especially insecure and arduous, had the interest and the need to resist both proletarianization and the close control of domestic work and would occasionally be "absent" from their paid jobs for family and community reasons. Such a strategy "amounted to resistance to . . . a long history of enforced economic and racial subservience."[43] The value of their domestic work to their households and the demands of childbearing and child rearing required all wage-earning mothers to develop strategies for accommodating the "double day."

The middle-class, white, Protestant ideology of Progressive America glorified mothering and, importantly, identified women's interests as largely equivalent to children's interests. Paradoxically, this glorification occurred at the same time educators were suggesting that the skills of motherhood were not merely natural but also needed tutelage.[44] In this ideology, especially as it was expressed at the popular level by magazines like *Good Housekeeping* and the *Delineator*, paid work and mothering did not intersect.[45] This ideology carried with it not only a recognition of the double burden of domestic responsibility and paid employment facing working mothers but also the clear possibility of vastly restricting women's lives to the domestic sphere. Moreover, the ideology helped to solidify motherhood and children's needs as the major legitimate metaphor with which to discuss women's interests in the political realm.

WORKMEN'S COMPENSATION AND MOTHER'S AID

A comparative history of Workmen's Compensation and Mothers' Aid elaborates how the political, economic, and household conditions of the Progressive period gave rise to a two-channel welfare state. Workmen's Compensation was a program developed for the white northern men employed in heavy industry, even though it always covered some female workers. Workmen's Compensation set the tone for the first channel of the welfare state, which was male, judicial, public, and routinized in origin. In comparison, Mothers' Aid was originally designed for the white impoverished widows of men like those eligible for Workmen's Compensation. It set the tone for the second channel of the welfare state, which was female, administrative, private, and nonroutinized in origin.

At the turn of the century, much of American industry ran on a model of unchecked, ruthless competition. In heavy industry, competition and dangerous production processes exacted an enormous toll. In a year-long study of heavy industry in Allegheny County (Pittsburgh), Pennsylvania, undertaken in 1907–1908, Crystal Eastman found that there were 195 industrial deaths among 70,000 steel workers, 125 industrial deaths among 50,000 railroaders, and 71 industrial deaths among 20,000 miners. In addition to the fatalities, which totaled 526, a three-month study of hospital records revealed that 509 workers required hospitalization for nonfatal work-related injuries.[46] On a national scale, popular writers reported that an average of 328 railroad workers were killed in industrial accidents *each month* from 1888 to 1908, and an estimated 35,000 workers were killed and 536,000 injured due to their employment each year.[47] The drive for Workmen's Compensation arose from public outrage over these figures, especially in comparison to much lower figures in Western Europe.

Light manufacturing did not receive as much attention when journalists like William Hard brought industrial accidents to public attention. But these industries, like cotton textiles, employed large numbers of white women and girls and faced fairly high rates of injury, especially among girls under sixteen. A study undertaken by the Department of Labor in 1907 and 1908 of the 126 cotton textile mills keeping records on accidents revealed 1,241 injuries in a one-year period out of a labor force of 64,571. Just over 25 percent of the accident victims were women in a labor force that was almost 40 percent female.[48]

Businessmen as much as workers had a need to regularize and limit the social and economic costs of industrial accidents. As the death and injury toll increased, the costs of acquiring employers' liability insurance rose dramatically. Nationally, U.S. businesses paid $200,000 in premiums in 1887, a figure that rose to $35 million in 1912.[49] The increasing cost of insurance in part reflected the expansion of manufacturing and the rise in the number of workers. But increasing costs were also a function of increasing liability caused by the fact that manufacturers were losing their common-law protections against responsibility for industrial accidents.

In the nineteenth century, employers were protected from tort liability in industrial accidents by three common-law defenses: the fellow servant doctrine, the assumption of risk, and contributory negligence. The fellow servant doctrine asserted that a fellow employee was responsible for the negligence of other workers and had a duty to inform himself or herself of the possible bad work habits of colleagues and endeavor to correct them. The assumption of risk doctrine allowed notice of dangerous conditions by employers to absolve them of their liabilities on the grounds that workers had been alerted to the risks they faced and willingly assumed them. Likewise, the courts disallowed any claims where workers had contributed in any way to the situation that caused the accident. Unions lobbied vigorously against these defenses, especially the fellow servant doctrine, and began to have some successes in state legislatures, especially in limiting this defense in the railroad industries, the favorite whipping boy in many agriculturally dominated state legislatures.[50]

With their legal defenses diminishing, some businesses were willing to look for a way to predict, regularize, and limit their liabilities. The businesses most interested in regularizing accident costs included technology-intensive growth industries like steel, automobiles, petroleum refining, railroads, copper, business machines, and agricultural implements. All of them had undergone national integration of production, enjoyed oligopolistic conditions, and were capital rather than labor intensive. Their capital-intensive financial structure made them more insulated from pressures to keep the total wage bill, including insurance, extremely low.[51]

The original vehicle for designing this policy was the American Association for Labor Legislation, a proto-corporatist group of reform-minded capitalists from large businesses, labor leaders, social reformers, and a few politicians. Later in the effort the flag was also carried by the National Civic Federation (NCF), a similarly constituted group that had more consistent support from union leaders. Samuel Gompers, who had participated in the NCF, had initially been skeptical of Workmen's Compensation and only came to support it after he realized there was a national consensus for it.[52] Moreover, labor was not united in wanting to give up the right to sue employers, an option that had been retained in the English Workmen's Compensation law. Many local unions favored that approach, which did not get much attention from reform politicians.[53] The best law in the eyes of many reformers would have eliminated tort liability in a system that replaced a high percentage of wages over a reasonably long period of time in a system of state-managed if not state-financed insurance. Not surprisingly, the laws that were passed often used private insurance, replaced a low percentage of wages for a short duration, and, importantly, employed a formulaic approach to responding to long-term disability.

For less serious accidents, Workmen's Compensation functioned like a poorly paid sick leave. After a waiting period, a successful claimant received some small percentage of his or her wages. Long-term disability was handled differently, being reimbursed according to a dismemberment schedule, yielding a flat sum for the loss of an arm or a leg, etc. These schedules were attacked as a "product of guesswork and 'crude bargaining.' "[54] They did have the virtue of greatly routinizing the decision rules for assigning benefits. Routinized decision rules allow for the same funding decision to be made easily by different officials.

The routinization of decision rules about eligibility deserves more attention. Comparing the administrative origins, ideologies, and practices of early welfare policies solidifies the understanding of a two-channel welfare state. The administrative style of Workmen's Compensation blends judicial forms with procedures borrowed from the scientific management school of business management, which was adopted by many large corporations in the Progressive period. It is important to remember that Workmen's Compensation was designed to replace a tort liability system. By accepting Workmen's Compensation, beneficiaries gave up their right to sue employers for damages. Once a method to negotiate constitutional issues was devised in 1912, nonsouthern states adopted Workmen's Compensation with great rapidity.[55] By 1920, forty-two states and three territories passed Workmen's Compensation laws. The administration of each state's program was greatly facilitated by the publication in 1914 and revision in 1920 of Samuel A. Harper's *The Law of Workmen's Compensation*, a digest presenting Illinois' pioneering law, a case commentary on its provisions, and, importantly, a *model set of forms*, forty-six in all (!), covering almost every aspect of the Workmen's Compensation process.[56]

Three qualities of this group of forms are especially important because they alert us to themes in administrative design. First, the forms are legal in layout and origin, and they reflect the fact that the Illinois Industrial Commission, which had jurisdiction and oversight of Workmen's Compensation cases, had a quasijudicial character. This judicial quality leads to the second characteristic to the forms as a whole: they are intended to be public documents in the way that most other legal documents presenting judicial decisions are intended to be open to public scrutiny. This does not mean that the records of the commission were not treated with care, but merely that there is a clear physical and cultural presumption of publicness, itself a norm associated with the political place and power of men.

The third quality of these forms is the extent to which they demonstrate that Workmen's Compensation rests on a set of established, routinized decision rules. The tables for computing wage replacement and the extent of disability, which are part of Harper's book but which have not necessarily been available to claimants, can be seen implicitly in forms that refer to weekly wages, medical expenses, and extent of injuries.[57] Even time is rationalized by the decision rules and through the forms. Successful claimants knew how long they would receive payments and at what level, a clear break from the temporal and fiscal uncertainties of relief under the poor laws or through charity organization activities.

The administrators of Workmen's Compensation used these forms in a bureaucracy whose structure and practices were in part modeled on the scientific management school of corporate administration. Beginning at the turn of the century, large corporations cushioned from price competition began to experiment with corporate welfare. The administrative model they used came from the scientific management movement, which organized personnel relations on the principle of " 'cold blooded science' rather than sentimentalism." [58] The drive for the new organizational form was fueled by the national integration of technology-dependent industries, increased dependence on continuous production processes, and geographically widespread production and distribution, all of which required higher levels of uniform administration.[59] The businessmen and lawyers who promoted Workmen's Compensation and staffed organizations like the Illinois Industrial Commission looked to the law and scientific management when they needed to create new bureaucracies in an age of underdeveloped governmental capacities.

Workmen's Compensation set a course that other social insurance programs followed and, indeed, improved upon. In fact, the hallmark of social insurance eligibility became straightforward decision criteria in the service of highly routinized decision making and dispassionate, if not exactly scientific, management. This was and is the administrative style linked with work-based benefits. For many years the vast majority of direct beneficiaries of these programs were white men. Contemporary research clearly shows that routinized decision rules, and concomitantly simpler application procedures, contribute markedly to client satisfaction with insurance programs and reinforce the social legitimacy of the clients as being deserving of their benefits.[60] Hence, in Workmen's Compensation, we see the confluence of the major elements of the first channel in the welfare state: socially legitimate, standardized decision criteria supporting insurance programs whose eligibility is based on the wage work employing white men. The legalism of Workmen's Compensation did not carry over to the social insurance programs of the New Deal, but the public, male quality did.

Industrial accidents, not to mention industrially related disease, took their toll on families. The death or disability of a breadwinner was an economic as well as personal catastrophe. If a mother were left without the income of a male breadwinner, her family suffered tremendously. If she needed to support her family aided only by her children's income, she was at a wage disadvantage compared to a man working the same number of hours. If she worked in a manufacturing job, her wages would average only two-thirds of her male counterparts.[61] Manufacturing work was difficult to find and it took single mothers away from their homes, creating a crisis of supervision for children.[62] Thus many women chose to do piece work or to take in boarders. Both types of work yielded lower income than most jobs performed outside the home, and taking in boarders could put both the women and their children in danger of possible sexual exploitation.[63]

Charity arrangements in the Progressive period often exacerbated these problems. Beginning in 1877, a number of large eastern cities did away with public outdoor relief, that is, publicly provided goods or services to the poor in their own homes. The new local policies more or less exclusively favored institutional care in alms houses or orphanages, institutions that originally developed with surprising rapidity and endurance in the antebellum period. Institutional care was augmented by a system of private charities making *small,* short-term gifts to noninstitutionalized people. In many cities their relief work came to be monitored by Charity Organization Societies, whose tasks were to register, track, and refer poor people in need. These societies also popularized the role of "friendly visitors," who examined the cause of each family's want. Personal visits and administrative control, rather than relief, "formed the basis of . . . [a] 'science' of . . . therapeutics that was supposed to relieve philanthropy of sentimentality and indiscriminate almsgiving." [64] Hence the administrative style of the Charity Organization Society movement is called "Scientific Charity." Neither institutionalization nor piecemeal private relief coordinated by social workers offered solutions to the dilemma of work and child supervision confronting single mothers, however.

Although institutionalization was a popular policy in the nineteenth century, the public became increasingly unwilling to mix children with other paupers and demanded the creation of separate orphanages for children.[65] By the Progressive era, the label orphanages was misleading, since, as Ann Vandepol writes, "These asylums quickly developed into the major social mechanism for sustaining children of low-income parents faced with unemployment, financial collapse, or death of a male breadwinner. At many asylums, half-orphans (children with one parent alive) outnumbered full orphans by a wide margin. In California by 1900 there were 5,399 half-orphans and only 959 full orphans housed in institutions throughout the state." [66] Some charity workers and reformers much preferred foster care to placing children of indigent families in asylums or orphanages. Homelike settings were believed to be better at molding character than institutional care. Similarly, education rather than child labor was viewed as better for children, and in the long run, family finances. Settlement-house Progressives like Florence Kelley and Jane Addams favored keeping a child in his or her own home, and in school, if possible.

"School pensions" were the first policies designed to respond to keeping children of widows in school without forcing families to forgo the children's earnings.[67] The grants were only available on a very limited basis in a few jurisdictions. Moreover, school pensions did not fully address the tensions between earning a living and supervising one's children that were felt by single mothers. What were single mothers with young children to do? Theirs was an extreme dilemma of dependency, on male income, on children's income, and on their obligations to care for children and be housekeepers.

The movement for the more universal, in-home support of the children of impoverished widows received a national platform at the 1909 White House Conference on Children, whose report stated that "children of parents of worthy character . . . who are without the support of normal breadwinners, should as a rule by kept with their parents, such aid being given as may be necessary to maintain suitable homes for the rearing of children." [68] Though a preference for supervision over wage earning was expressed in the conference, the Resolutions Committee stopped short of supporting public outdoor relief for mothers with dependent children. Even Homer Folks was not yet convinced of the propriety of public aid to single mothers with children at this time.[69] Folks' position demonstrates the power of the Charity Organization Society movement's opposition to public outdoor relief, which they felt encouraged laziness and dependency. Charity Organization spokespeople Mary E. Richmond and Edward T. Devine further condemned Mothers' Aid in that it was neither a pension given for past service nor a universal support for all mothers, as a proper policy might have suggested.[70] So too, the Charity Organization Society opponents of Mothers' Aid could not help but have known that this program would signal the loss of the hegemony over defining the forms of relief.

The Charity Organization Society movement lost its battle against Mothers' Aid. Mothers' Aid had wide popular support among the General Federation of Women's Clubs and the National Congress of Mothers and Parent-Teacher Associations. Mark H. Leff describes their membership as "principally middle-aged, middle-class, poorly educated married women. These women sensed a waning influence in an emerging industrial system that created a new social hierarchy." These groups worked with the National Consumers' League, some suffrage groups, and the Women's Christian Temperance Union to pass state laws. They were successful as an effort of women organized for women, working with the aid of sympathetic male politicians.[71] Most of this organizing predates national suffrage, although activity in states that gave women suffrage before the nineteenth Amendment was especially strong. The movement for Mothers' Aid can certainly be seen as part of women's drive for political incorporation, both in the content of the policy and in the effort to win political citizenship.

Unlike Workmen's Compensation, which had a large contingent of working-class leaders, Mothers' Aid was a movement often but not exclusively led by middle-class women in sympathy with working-class and poor women. Middle-class support ranged from the college-educated women of the settlement movement, who saw themselves as part of a workers' movement, to the homemaking women of the organizations described previously. The *Delineator*, a magazine reaching 5,000,000 readers, took on Mothers' Aid as one of its causes.[72] Leff reports that in Chicago immigrants' newspapers with working-class readership supported Mothers' Aid. The American Federation of Labor did endorse a Mothers' Aid revolution in 1911, although Mothers' Aid was never a priority for organized labor.[73] The full role of labor unions needs to be examined at the local level, research that has not yet been done.

The first statewide "Mothers' Aid Law" passed in Illinois in 1911. In point of fact, it was a loosely written law funding needy parents, and it was revised and substantially tightened in 1913. Like many early laws the revised legislation limited eligibility *de facto* to widowed mothers with children under the school-leaving age who could prove both citizenship and three years residence in the county in which they applied.[74] By 1919, thirty-nine states had passed similar laws. As time passed, many states offered benefits to women who were deserted or whose husbands were disabled or incarcerated. The rapid diffusion of Mothers' Aid occurred largely because in twenty-nine states the laws permitted rather than required local governments to give these grants. Similarly, very few states contributed to local payments. Local option and local funding made for highly variable coverage. Local control also meant that local norms dictated client selection. A study undertaken in 1931 by the U.S. Children's Bureau reported that beneficiaries were overwhelmingly white: only 3 percent of clients were black, with another 1 percent being other women of color. The racism practiced in determining beneficiaries varied from place to place, though. Certain areas, like Washington, D.C. and several Ohio counties, granted Mothers' Aid to black women in proportions higher than they were found in that area's population.[75]

In many places the initial implementation of Mothers' Aid fell to the Charity Organization Society or its members, even though these organizations often opposed such laws.[76] The first task confronting administrators was to remove children from child-minding institutions, returning them to their mothers. This action saved the localities the difference between the costs of their institutional care and their home-based care and met the implicit demand of all new welfare policies to save money. Both Workmen's Compensation and Mothers' Aid were promoted as good investments that saved money for taxpayers and society in general.[77]

Not only did opponents often participate in the initial implementation of Mothers' Aid, they also influenced its organization in lasting ways. Scientific Charity's particular view of casework, which was intrusive while attempting to be uplifting, and which allowed for enormous discretion on the part of the caseworkers due to the imprecision of and difficulty in applying eligibility standards, became the administrative hallmark of income-tested benefits for mothers financed by the general revenue. As in the case of Workmen's Compensation, the public sector, in this instance usually the newly created Juvenile Court rather than the Industrial Commission, was administratively inexperienced and underdeveloped.[78] Public officials again looked outside government for administrative models, this time adopting the practices traditionally used by the Charity Organization Societies rather than legalistic forms or the practice of Scientific Management. In 1914, A. E. Sheffield described the intake, decision-making, and monitoring procedures of the Massachusetts Mothers' Aid law this way:

The mother makes application of the overseer of the poor in her place of residence. He investigates her need, fitness, and resources, filling out a blank form which the board has prepared of the purpose, and ending with his recommendation. This information and advice he sends to the state board [of charities]. The supervisor then assigns one of the five women visitors to make a second independent investigation, and reviews the recommendation of the overseer in the light of the two findings. The result of her study of the case, whether approval, disapproval or suggestions on treatment, she embodies in a letter to the overseer in question. In the course of her work she is in constant conference with the superintendent of the adult poor division, a man who has the advantage of many years acquaintance with the individual cases that present some deviation from the usual types, while the committee itself considers special cases and all general questions of policy.[79]

This entitlement process differs notably from the intake procedures used in Workmen's Compensation. In Workmen's Compensation an employee merely had to give notice of the injury to his or her employer. A standard form existed for this report but any written notice containing the required information would suffice[80] (see figure 5.1). The employer then sent a claim to the quasijudicial commission governing the program. The employee also had to undergo a physical examination by a doctor of the employer's choosing, if the employer requested such an examination. The doctor, an external agent appealing to

NO. 40

ILLINOIS INDUSTRIAL COMMISSION

Notice to Employer of Accidental Injury and Claim for
Compensation Therefor

To .... :
        (Write name of employer here.)
        .... :
        (Write address of employer here.)
        You will take notice that the ·undersigned was on the .... day
of ...., A. D. 19.., injured by an accident arising out of and
in the course of his employment, while employed by you at ....,
Illinois.
        Name of employee ....
        Post office address ....
        Relationship to claimant ....
                (State whether notice given by injured person or by dependent.)
        Claim for compensation is for.................................
        Cause of the accident ....
        ....
        Nature of the injury is as follows..............................
        ....
                (Signed:·) ....

NOTE.—This notice must be filled out by the injured workman or someone in his behalf, or in case of his death, by a dependent or dependents, or
someone in their behalf. It should be served upon the employer as soon
as practicable after the accident, and not later, in any event, than thirty
days thereafter. See § 24 of Act.

Figure 5.1. Form for Notice to Employer of Accidental Injury and Claim for Compensation Therefor. This is the least legalistic Workmen's Compensation form, perhaps because it was considered
an internal communication to the employer, who used a separate, more typical form to report to the
Illinois Industrial Commission. Source: Samuel A. Harper, *The Law of Workmen's Compensation*,
Second Edition (Chicago: Callaghan and Company, 1920), 636.

external, "scientific" norms, determined the extent and duration of disability.
The doctor filled out a simple form that was also sent to the commission.[81]
Though the medical decision rules and their application became more complex over the years, the initial intake process in Workmen's Compensation was
quite straightforward compared to Mothers' Aid.[82]

A key difference in the administration of the two programs is that Mothers'
Aid was given in return for an ongoing service rather than in response to a
realized risk. For instance, the administrators of Workmen's Compensation
cared if alcohol contributed to accidents (such claims were denied), but they
did not care, or, more important, they could not control the beneficiary who
spent all of his or her benefits on drink. The behavior of Mothers' Aid beneficiaries, on the other hand, was closely monitored. Thus is was the *capacity
to care* that was supported in Mothers' Aid; or said another way, the program

recognized not only women's economic dependency on men and children for adequate family income but also the dependency of children (and adult men and elderly relatives) on women's domestic and reproductive labor, which had both emotional and material components. This was not, however, a mutually equal dependency.[83]

Moreover, by preferring caring to earning, Mothers' Aid reinforced low-wage work for beneficiaries because the work paying low wages, like in-home clothing assembly or domestic work outside the home, was most likely to meet the requirement that employment not affect supervision. In the early days of Mothers' Aid, the rhetoric of a sharp division between paid work and supervision did not match the reality of beneficiaries' experiences. For example, a 1923 study of the implementation of Mothers' Aid in nine locations showed that 52 percent of mothers receiving aid also worked for wages, certainly not the image of full-time domesticity underpinning the popular political debate.[84] Mothers' Aid reinforced and subsidized low wages for some poor single mothers lacking a man's income.

The Mothers' Aid application and case investigation forms demonstrate the program's commitment to establishing a woman's capacity to care. As a group they represent the continuous, administrative, private, and nonroutinized character of the program. Figures 5.2 and 5.3 reproduce the Illinois (Cook County) Mothers' Aid application and case investigation forms in use in 1919. These forms are typical, even moderate, examples of their genre, chosen to make a comparison with Illinois's model Workmen's Compensation forms, as published in 1920. The Mothers' Aid forms were clearly designed to be part of an ongoing, internal (i.e., private) bureaucratic process. The distant, final, public, and judicial qualities of the set of Workmen's Compensation forms are missing.[85] The U.S. Children's Bureau distributed both examples of Mothers' Aid laws and administrative forms to a well-developed network of activists, educators, and politicians. Thus the administrative practices and forms developed in localities, all of which arose from the ideological and practical necessities of a program requiring long-term monitoring, were widely available.[86]

The eligibility decision rules in Mothers' Aid were not the formulaic past-wages-and-percent-of-disability tables used in Workmen's Compensation. Mothers' Aid administrators did try for clear policies, but the specification of those polities was difficult because they encompassed a large number of variables, many of which were qualitative and defined against the family norms of white, middle-class Protestants. An example of such a variable is the require-

Figure 5.2. Form for application for Mother's Aid from the Juvenile Court of Cook County (Chicago). Source: U. S. Department of Labor, Children's Bureau, *Laws Relating to "Mothers' Pensions" in the United States, Canada, Denmark, and New Zealand*, Legal Series No. 4, Bureau Publication No. 63, 1919, p. 75.

APPLICATION CARD.

Surname..............	Man's first.............	Woman's first...........	Date of application......

Alias.................................	Other names needed for identification......	Social state........

Cross references...

Date.	Res. No.	Street.	Rooms.	Floor.	F. or R.	Rent.	How long.	Sanitary condition.	Landlord or agent. Address.	Dist.

First names.	Date of birth.	Birth-place.	Occupation or school with grade.	Wages.	Left sch. at age of.	Amt. of ins.	Prem.	Cause of death.	Date of death.	Mental or physical defects and illiteracy.	Docket number.
Man.											
1............ Woman's maiden name.											
2............ Children.											
3............ Others in family.						Kinship.	To.	Contributes to family.			
12............											
13............											

Union.	Lodge.	Benefit society.	Other sources of income.	Amt.	Pawns.	Install-ments.	Debts to.	Amt.	For.
		Weekly benefit.							

Race.	Length of time in—			Marriage.			Previous marriage.	Property.
	County.	State.	U. S.	Date.	Place.	By whom.		
Man....								Do you own any?.....
Woman.								What, if any, did your husband leave?.....

Relatives.	Address.	Kinship.	To.	References.	Address.	Connection.	Of.
				Church or Sunday school.		Original religion.	
				Man....................................			
				Woman..................................			
				Children................................			

State of Illinois, County of Cook, ss:

———— being first duly sworn, on oath doth depose and say that the written statements under the various printed headings on the opposite side of this application card were voluntarily made by this affiant and written thereon by direction of this affiant and that the statements thereon, both written and printed, are true in substance and in fact.

Subscribed and sworn to before me this —— day of —— A. D. 19—.

———— ————.

———— ————, Notary Public.

REPORT OF INVESTIGATOR.

Previous addresses.	Rent.	When.	How long.	Previous addresses.	Rent.	When.	How long.

Employer.	Address.	Of No.	Wages.	R., I., or S.	Date. From— To—	Position.	Department.	Foreman.

Agencies and persons interested.	Address.	Capacity.	Date.	Disabilities.	Of No.	Date.
				Accident........................ Chronic physical disability .		
				Epilepsy....................... Insanity...................... Subnormal mind...............		
				Industrial accident........... Occupational disease.........		
Institutional care of.		Of No.	Date.	Tuberculosis....................		
				Venereal disease............... Maternity.....................		
				Imprisonment.................. Death.........................		

Figure 5.3. Form for report of investigator performing the case investigation for applicants for Mother's Aid from the Juvenile Court of Cook County (Chicago). Source: U. S. Department of Labor, Children's Bureau, *Laws Relating to "Mothers' Pensions" in the United States, Canada, Denmark, and New Zealand*, Legal Series No. 4, Bureau Publication No. 63, 1919, p. 76.

ment that mothers be "morally fit," a term that included sexual behavior, use of alcohol and tobacco, presence of boarders, and housekeeping skills. Moreover, administrators and chroniclers of the program experienced a tension over wanting to portray the management of the programs as both scientific and flexible enough to be compassionate. Flexibility and nonroutinized decision rules went hand in hand with repeated scrutiny. Beneficiaries of Mothers' Aid never really knew for certain how long they could maintain their eligibility. Uncertainty over the duration of benefits became a long-standing characteristic of the motherhood channel of welfare policy and the welfare state.

The Aid to Dependent Children system, which nationalized the scope of the

Mothers' Aid programs and partially subsidized them, subsumed the administrative style given to Mothers' Aid by the Charity Organization Society interpreters of the poor law tradition. This administrative style was characterized by moralistic, diffuse decision criteria, high levels of bureaucratic discretion, and many levels of managerial cross-checking. While it was designed to be efficient and accountable, it was also cumbersome and repeatedly intrusive.

The motherhood channel of the welfare state initiated by Mothers' Aid differs from the one cut by Workmen's Compensation in most aspects except race. Through the type of "work" they recognized and the politics of local control, both programs often excluded blacks. This practice was reinforced in the Social Security Act when leaders of the NAACP were unable to convince senators that domestic workers and farm laborers, fully 60 percent of the black labor force in 1930, should be included in categories of employment covered by the old-age insurance program.

The U.S. welfare state has been fundamentally shaped by the legacy of Workmen's Compensation and Mothers' Aid, perhaps quite out of proportion to the original scope of the programs and the good they accomplished. The welfare state has two channels, carved out of a set of a specific gender, race, and class relationships during a period of political volatility and demands for political incorporation by women; supported by an ideology and practice of separate spheres; and institutionalized through different types of administrative capacities of the law and welfare capitalism. The second channel, based on reproductive and domestic labor of white women, took its form from the Charity Organization Societies' social work techniques. The programs on which these channels are based predate the centralized creation of a U.S. welfare state during the New Deal.

These origins should be considered as strongly directing but not binding the events that followed. Gender, race, and class relations and the administrative capacities of American government have changed in the last seventy years, and the force of those changes can be seen by canals that connect the motherhood and wage-work channels of the welfare state. Indeed, the entrance of black women into the motherhood welfare system in the 1950s and 1960s needs to be reconsidered in the light of how this shift fundamentally changed the programs' purposes, and how, paradoxically, this new economic and political "equality" with white women brought a level of direct state control to the lives of black women, about which they had traditionally felt a justifiable ambivalence. Likewise, the dramatic rise in the number of working mothers of all races employed in jobs covered by Social Security indicates all the complexities inherent in a two-channel welfare state predicated on the separation of wage earners and childbearers. Social theory and social policy need to be reexamined in this light.

NOTES

1   David Held et al., eds., *States and Society* (New York: New York University Press,
     1983); Stephen D. Krasner, "Approaches to the State: Alternative Conceptions
     and Historical Dynamics," *Comparative Politics* 16 (1984): 223–46; Eric Nord-
     linger, *On the Autonomy of the Democratic State* (Cambridge, Mass.: Harvard
     University Press, 1981); Stephen Skowronek, *Building a New American State: The
     Expansion of National Administrative Capacities, 1877–1920s* (Cambridge: Cam-
     bridge University Press, 1982); Charles Tilly, *The Formation of the Nation States
     in Western Europe* (Princeton, N.J.: Princeton University Press, 1975).
2   Theda Skocpol, "Bringing the State Back In: Strategies of Analysis in Current
     Research," in *Bringing the State Back In*, ed. Peter B. Evans, Dietrich Ruesch-
     meyer and Theda Skocpol (Cambridge: Cambridge University Press, 1985); Ann
     Shola Orloff and Theda Skocpol, "Why Not Equal Protection? Explaining the
     Politics of Public Social Spending in Britain 1900–1911, and in the United States,
     1880s–1920," *American Sociological Review* 49 (1984): 726–50; Theda Skocpol
     and John Ikenberry, "The Political Formation of the American Welfare State in
     Historical and Comparative Perspective," in *Comparative Social Research: The
     Welfare State, 1883–1983*, vol. 6, ed. Richard F. Tomasson (Greenwich, Conn.:
     JAI Press, 1983); Theda Skocpol and Kenneth Finegold, "State Capacity and
     Economic Intervention in the Early New Deal," *Political Science Quarterly* 97
     (1982): 255–78; Theda Skocpol, "Political Response to Capitalist Areas: Neo-
     Marxist Theories of the State and the Case of the New Deal," *Politics and Society*
     10 (1980): 155–202.
3   Mary McIntosh, "The State and the Oppression of Women," in *Feminism and
     Materialism*, ed. Annette Kuhn and Annmarie Wolpie (London: Routledge and
     Kegan Paul, 1978); Barbara J. Nelson, "Women's Poverty and Women's Citizen-
     ship: Some Political Consequences of Economic Marginality," *Signs* 10 (1984):
     209–31; Barbara J. Nelson, "Family Politics and Policy in the United States and
     Western Europe," *Comparative Politics* 17 (1985): 351–71; Lisa Peattie and Martin
     Rein, *Women's Claims: A Study in Political Economy* (New York: Oxford Univer-
     sity Press, 1983); Virginia Sapiro, "The Gender Basis of American Social Policy,"
     in this volume; Jennifer Schirmer, *The Limits of Reform: Women, Capital and Wel-
     fare* (Cambridge, Mass.: Schenkman, 1982); Elizabeth Wilson, *Women and the
     Welfare State* (London: Tavistock Publications, 1977); Eli Zaretsky, "The Place
     of the Family in the Origins of the Welfare State," in *Rethinking the Family, Some
     Feminist Questions*, ed. Barrie Thorne and Marilyn Yalom (New York: Longman,
     1982).
4   Paula Giddings, *When and Where I Enter: The Impact of Black Women on Race
     and Sex in America* (New York: Bantam, 1984); Hester Eisenstein and Alice
     Jardine, eds., *The Future of Difference* (New Brunswick, N.J.: Rutgers University
     Press, 1980).
5   A word is in order on the racial and ethnic comparisons used in this research.
     Aggregate Census data and program reports for the period I am examining do
     not, as a rule, include material on people of Asian, Hispanic, or Native American
     background. The text compares only the experiences of U.S. blacks and whites.
6   While women were not found in the ranks of industrialists at this time, men were

active in the Charity Organization Society and Settlement movements, rendering the gender distinction between the origins of the two welfare channels more complicated.

7   Charles Tilly, *Big Structures, Large Processes, Huge Comparisons* (New York: Russell Sage Foundation, 1984); Barney G. Glaser and Strauss L. Anselm, *The Discovery of Grounded Theories: Strategies for Qualitative Research* (Chicago: Aldine, 1967).

8   Harry Eckstein, "Case Study and Theory in Political Science," in *Handbook of Political Science*, vol. 7, *Strategies of Industry*, ed. Fred I. Greenstein and Nelson W. Polsby (Reading, Mass.: Addison-Wesley, 1975).

9   Natalie Zemon Davis, "Gender and Genre: Women as Historical Writers, 1400–1820," in *Beyond Their Sex: Learned Women of the European Past*, ed. Patricia H. Labalme (New York: New York University Press, 1980); Bonnie G. Smith, "The Contribution of Women to Modern Historiography in Great Britain, France, and the United States," *American Historical Review* 89 (1984): 709–32. For a discussion of this issue in the policy sciences see Thomas J. Kaplan, "The Narrative Structure of Policy Analysis," *Journal of Policy Analysis and Management* 5 (1986): 761–78; Peter Reuter, "The Social Costs of the Demand for Quantification," *Journal of Policy Analysis and Management* 5 (1986): 807–12.

10   One might argue that one of the informal indicators of the discrediting of narrative in social science is the increasing use of citations within the body of the professional texts, rather than at the bottom of the page or the end of the work. One of the effects of this practice is physically to break up the narrative.

11   Theda Skocpol and Margaret Somers, "The Users of Comparative History in Macrosocial Inquiry," *Comparative Studies in Society and History* 22 (1980): 174–97.

12   Skocpol and Somers, "The Users of Comparative History," 181.

13   Harold L. Wilensky, *The Welfare State and Equality: Structural and Ideological Roots of Public Expenditures* (Berkeley, Calif.: The University of California Press, 1975); Clause Offe, "Social Policy and the Theory of the State," in *Clause Offe: Contradictions of the Welfare State*, ed. John Keane (Cambridge, Mass.: MIT Press, 1984), 88–92.

14   Orloff and Skocpol, "Why Not Equal Protection?" 730–31; Skocpol, "Bringing the State Back In"; Krasner, "Approaches to the State," 224.

15   Michael Shalev, "The Social Democratic Model and Beyond: Two 'Generations' of Comparative Research on the Welfare State," in *Comparative Social Research: The Welfare State*, vol. 6, ed. Richard F. Tomason (Greenwich, Conn.: JAI Press, 1983).

16   The term welfare policy poses its own problems. It is used here as the sum of social policies that meet the conditions described in the text. Another common definition is income-tested, noncontributory programs financed through the general revenue (e.g., AFDC, SSI, Food Stamps). In this usage welfare contrasts to insurance programs. In this text I use the term income-tested for this second definition of welfare.

17   In this century, black and white women experienced many of the same patterns of lifetime employment, varying of course by urban or rural location. The jobs held by black and white women were often different, as were their gross wages,

working conditions, generational mobility to new kinds of jobs, and the fact that black women faced racism. See Jacqueline Jones, *Labor of Love, Labor of Sorrow: Black Women, Work, and the Family from Slavery to the Present* (New York: Basic Books, 1985), 234–35, *et passim*.

18   Offe, "Social Policy and the Theory of the State," 94; Francis G. Castles, *The Social Democratic Image of Society* (London: Routledge and Kegan Paul, 1978); Michael B. Katz, *Poverty and Policy in American History* (New York: Academic Press, 1983), 7.

19   See note 2.

20   I. M. Rubinow, *Social Insurance: With Special Reference to American Conditions* (New York: Henry Holt and Company, 1913), 405–7.

21   Rubinow, *Social Insurance*, 351, 354, 362.

22   Skocpol and Ikenberry, "Political Formation of the American Welfare State," 129–30.

23   In this Orloff and Skocpol, "Why Not Equal Protection?" and Skocpol and Ikenberry, "Political Formation of the American Welfare State" stand apart from a long-standing interest in welfare state research. Shelev, "Social Democratic Model and Beyond" reviews two generations of research on the (re)distributional consequences of welfare programs.

24   Skocpol, "Bringing The State Back In," 25–27.

25   Eleanor Flexner, *Century of Struggle* (New York: Atheneum, 1974), 175.

26   See note 2 and Zillah Eisenstein, *The Radical Future of Liberal Feminism* (New York: Longman, 1981); Joyce Gelb and Marion Lief Palley, *Women and Public Policies* (Princeton, N.J.: Princeton University Press, 1982); Carol Glassman, "Women and the Welfare System," in *Sisterhood is Powerful*, ed. Robin Morgan (New York: Vintage, 1970).

27   Nelson, "Family Politics and Policy," 356; Louise A. Tilly and Joan W. Scott, *Women, Work, and Family* (New York: Holt, Rinehart, and Winston, 1978), 3.

28   Nannerl O. Keohane, "Speaking from Silence: Women and the Science of Politics," in *A Feminist Perspective in the Academy: The Difference It Makes*, ed. Elizabeth Langland and Walter Gove (Chicago: University of Chicago Press, 1981), 87; Michelle Rosaldo, "The Use and Abuse of Anthropology: Reflections on Feminism and Cross-Cultural Understanding," *Signs* 5 (1980): 389–417.

29   Daniel T. Rodgers, "In Search of Progressivism," *Reviews in American History*, vol. 10, no. 4 (1982): 113–32; Paula Baker, "The Domestication of Politics: Women and Political Society, 1878–1920," in this volume; Samuel P. Hays, "Political Parties and the Community-Society Continuum," in *The American Party Systems: Stages of Development*, Second Edition, ed. William Nesbitt Chambers and Walter Dean Burnham (New York: Oxford University Press, 1975).

30   Baker, "The Domestication of Politics," 70.

31   Kathryn Kish Sklar, "Hull House in the 1890s: A Community of Women Reformers," *Signs* 10 (1985): 658–77.

32   Cheryl Townsend Gilkes, " 'Together and in Harness': Women's Traditions in the Sanctified Church," *Signs* 5 (1985): 678–99.

33   Rosalind Rosenberg, *Beyond Separate Spheres: Intellectual Roots of Modern Feminism* (New Haven, Conn.: Yale University Press, 1982), 1–28.

34   William H. Chafe, *Women and Equality* (New York: Oxford University Press, 1977); Carl N. Degler, *At Odds: Women and the Family in America from the Revolution to the Present* (New York: Oxford University Press, 1980); Ellen Carol DuBois, *Feminism and Suffrage: The Emergence of an Independent Women's Movement in America, 1848–1869* (Ithaca, N.Y.: Cornell University Press, 1978).

35   U.S. Department of Commerce, *Statistical Abstract of the U.S.: 1922* (Washington, D.C.: U.S. Government Printing Office, 1923), table no. 51, p. 54. In this discussion the general category Manufacturing and Mechanical Industries is used as a proxy for wage earners. It contains some artisans (e.g., goldsmiths) and some managers but is still the largest group of wage earners. Wage earners are, of course, found in virtually all other large occupational groupings as well.

36   Alexander Keyssar, *Out of Work: The First Century of Unemployment in Massachusetts* (Cambridge, Mass.: Cambridge University Press, 1986).

37   U.S. Department of Commerce, *Statistical Abstract of the U.S.: 1922*, table no. 51, p. 54.

38   Kelly Miller, "The City Negro: Industrial Status," in *The Black Worker: A Documentary History from Colonial Times to the Present*, ed. Philip S. Foner and Ronald A. Lewis (Philadelphia: Temple University Press, 1980), 12.

39   U.S. Department of Commerce, *Statistical Abstract of the U.S.: 1922*, table no. 51, pp. 54, 60.

40   Jones, *Labor of Love, Labor of Sorrow*, 134–35.

41   Lois Scharf, *To Work and To Wed* (Westport, Conn.: Greenwood Press, 1980), 12.

42   William H. Chafe, *The American Woman: Her Changing Social, Economic, and Political Roles* (London: Oxford University Press, 1972), 56.

43   Jones, *Labor of Love, Labor of Sorrow*, 135.

44   Sheila M. Rothman, *Women's Proper Place* (New York: Basic Books, 1978), 97–134.

45   William Hard, "Financing Motherhood," in *Mothers' Pensions*, ed. Edna Bullock (White Plains and New York: H. W. Wilson Co., 1915); Frederic C. Howe and Marie Jenny Howe, "Pensioning the Widow and the Fatherless," in Bullock, *Mothers' Pensions*, 1915.

46   Roy Lubove, *The Struggle for Social Security, 1900–1935* (Cambridge, Mass.: Harvard University Press, 1968), 46.

47   James Weinstein, *The Corporate Ideal in the Liberal State: 1900–1918* (Boston: Beacon Press, 1968), 40.

48   U.S. Department of Labor, *Report on Condition of Women and Child Wage-Earners in the United States*, vol. 1, *Cotton Textile Industry* (Washington, D.C.: United States Government Printing Office, 1910), 349. To my knowledge no study exists comparing women's and men's experience of industrial accidents either before or after the advent of Workmen's Compensation.

49   Lubove, *Struggle for Social Security*, 51.

50   Weinstein, *Corporate Ideal*, 41–43; Skocpol and Ikenberry, "Political Formation of the American Welfare State," 106–15; Lawrence M. Friedman and Jack Ladinsky, "Social Change and the Law of Industrial Accidents," in *American Law and the Constitutional Order: Historical Perspectives*, ed. Lawrence M. Friedman and Harry N. Scheiber (Cambridge, Mass.: Harvard University Press, 1978); Robert

Asher, "Failure and Fulfillment: Agitation for Employers' Liability Legislation and the Origins of Workmen's Compensation in New York State," *Labor History* 24 (1983): 198–222.

51 Edward Berkowitz and Kim McQuaid, "Businessman and Bureaucrat: Evolution of the American Social Welfare System, 1900–1940," *Journal of Economic History* 38 (1978): 120–42; Samuel Cohn, *The Process of Occupational Sex-Typing: The Feminization of Clerical Labor in Great Britain* (Philadelphia: Temple University Press, 1985), 36–64.

52 Weinstein, *Corporate Ideal*, 48; Nuala McGann Dresher, "The Workmen's Compensation and Pension Proposal in the Brewing Industry, 1910–1912: A Case Study in Conflicting Self-Interest," *Industrial Labor Relations Review* 24 (1970): 14, 32–46.

53 Lubove, *Struggle for Social Security*, 59.

54 Lubove, *Struggle for Social Security*, 59.

55 Hace Sorel Tishler, *Self-Reliance and Social Security, 1870–1917* (Port Washington, N.Y.: Kennikat Press, 1971); Lubove, *Struggle for Social Security*.

56 Samuel A. Harper, *The Law of Workmen's Compensation*, Second Edition (Chicago: Callaghan and Company, 1920), 591–643.

57 See especially form no. 10, "Application for Adjustment of Claim," Harper, *Law of Workmen's Compensation*, 601–3.

58 Berkowitz and McQuaid, "Businessman and Bureaucrat," 120–27.

59 Edward Berkowitz and Kim McQuaid, *Creating the Welfare State: The Political Economy of Twentieth Century Reform* (New York: Praeger, 1980).

60 Barbara J. Nelson, "Client Evaluations and Social Programs," in *The Public Encounter: Where State and Citizen Meet*, ed. Charles T. Goodsell (Bloomington, Ind.: Indiana University Press, 1981); Barbara J. Nelson, "Clients and Bureaucracies: Applicant Evaluations of Public Human Service and Benefit Programs," American Political Science Association Meetings, New York, 1979.

61 Mark Aldrich and Randy Albeda, "Determinants of Working Women's Wages During the Progressive Era," *Explorations in Economic History* 17 (1980): 323–41.

62 Linda Gordon, "Single Mothers and Child Neglect, 1880–1920," *American Quarterly* vol. 37, no. 2 (1985): 173–92. "Single mothers" is a contemporary term and not one that these women would have used for themselves. They would have described themselves as widowed or deserted, or less frequently, divorced.

63 Gordon, "Single Mothers and Child Neglect."

64 Walter I. Trattner, *From Poor Law to Welfare State* (New York: Free Press, 1974), 85.

65 Fewer institutions of all kinds were available for black children. See, for example, Gary B. Kremer and Linda Rea Gibbens, "The Missouri Home for Negro Girls: The 1930s," *American Studies* 24 (1983): 77–93.

66 Ann Vandepol, "Dependent Children, Child Custody, and Mothers' Pensions," *Social Problems* 29 (1982): 221–35.

67 L. A. Halbert, "The Widows Allowance Act in Kansas City," in *Mothers' Aid*, ed. Edna Bullock (White Plains and New York: H. W. Wilson Co., 1915).

68 *Proceedings of the Conference on the Care of Dependent Children*, S. Doc. 721 (Washington, D.C.: United States Government Printing Office, 1909), 9–10.

69   Janet Marie Wedel, *The Origins of State Patriarchy During the Progressive Era: A Sociological Study of the Mothers' Aid Movement*, Sociology Department (Washington University, Ph.D. Dissertation, 1975), 283–84.

70   Lubove, *Struggle for Social Security*, 102; Frederic Almy, "Public Pensions to Widows: Experiences and Observations Which Lead Me to Oppose Such a Law," in *Selected Articles on Mothers' Pensions*, ed. Edna D. Bullock (White Plains and New York: H. W. Wilson Co., 1915), 155.

71   Mark H. Leff, "Consensus for Reform: The Mother's-Pension Movement in the Progressive Era," *Social Service Review* 47 (1973): 397–29.

72   Wedel, *Origins of State Patriarchy*, 299.

73   Leff, "Consensus for Reform", 407.

74   Edith Abbott and Sophonisba P. Breckenridge, *The Administration of the Aid-to-Mothers Law in Illinois*, Legal Series No. 7, Bureau Publication No. 82 (Washington, D.C.: U.S. Department of Labor, Children's Bureau, 1921), 12.

75   U.S. Department of Labor, Children's Bureau, *Mothers' Aid, 1931*, Bureau Publications No. 22 (Washington, D.C.: U.S. Government Printing Office, 1933), 13–14.

76   Wedel, *Origins of State Patriarchy*, 330; T. J. Edmonds and Maurice P. Hexter, "State Pensions to Mothers in Hamilton County, Ohio," in *Selected Articles on Mothers' Pensions*, ed. Edna D. Bullock (White Plains and New York: H. W. Wilson Co., 1915), 5.

77   Wedel, *Origins of State Patriarchy*; Katz, *Poverty and Policy*.

78   For a discussion of the role of the courts (though not specifically the juvenile court) in state formation see Skowronek, *Building a New American State*.

79   A. E. Sheffield, "Administration of the Mothers' Aid Law in Massachusetts," in *Selected Articles on Mothers' Aid Pensions*, 73.

80   Harper, *Law of Workmen's Compensation*, 450–58.

81   Harper's *Law of Workmen's Compensation* compendium of forms does not include one to be used as a model for doctors to report their findings. Such forms did exist prior to 1920, at least in Minnesota, where the archives of Workmen's Compensation claims include a Physicians Certificate asking seven questions and allowing no more than three lines for each answer.

82   Saad Z. Nagi, *Disability and Rehabilitation: Legal, Clinical, and Self-Concepts and Measurement* (Columbus, Ohio: Ohio State University Press, 1969).

83   Sapiro, "Gender Basis of American Social Policy."

84   Florence Nesbitt, *Standards of Public Aid to Children in Their Own Homes*, Bureau Publication No. 118 (Washington, D.C.: U.S. Department of Labor, Children's Bureau, 1923), 11–13.

85   There were Mothers' Aid forms that were not only legalistic looking but actual legal documents, such as the petition to the juvenile court for Mothers' Aid funds. These documents ratified and transmitted decisions made elsewhere.

86   Laura A. Thompson, *Laws Relating to Mothers' Pensions in the United States, Canada, Denmark, and New Zealand*, Legal Series No. 4, Bureau Publication No. 63 (Washington, D.C.: U.S. Department of Labor, Children's Bureau, 1919).

CHAPTER 6

Representations of Gender: Policies to "Protect" Women Workers and Infants in France and the United States before 1914

JANE JENSON

At the end of the nineteenth century both France and the United States experienced a fundamental restructuring of economic relations. France was finally industrializing, at the same time as the long depression of 1873–95. The United States was beginning to overtake Britain as the industrial model for the world and concentration of capital was reshaping social conditions. Both countries experienced, as a result, a moment of profound uncertainty about social and political relations, and reformers campaigned to have the state regulate the effects of urbanization, immigrant labor forces, declining birth rates, restructuring industry, and economic uncertainty. French and American politicians and social activists spoke in apocalyptic terms of social instabilities.

Out of this moment of social change came many of the programs that we now identify with the 'welfare state.' As this article demonstrates, the characteristics of such programs and thus their implications for constituting and sustaining unequal class and gender relations—as well as other social relations—cannot simply be read off the large-scale changes occurring in many industrial societies at the time. Rather, to understand the specific ways that state welfare contributed to the constitution and maintenance of unequal relations of class and gender we must locate these programs in the politics of that time, assessing the relationship between strategies of many actors—including political parties, social movements and parts of the state—and the policy outcomes.

The strategies chosen, in turn, were the consequence of a wide range of resources available to actors, including the representations of proper social relations that they deployed. To the extent that any actor was powerful enough to prevail in shaping state policies, its representation of social relations became embedded in the policy, via the delineation of goals and forms of programs. As a result, we can understand how representations of social relations continue through time, borne on the policies constituted out of political struggle. It is, therefore, conflict over such representations as part of the strategic resources of actors and as a crucial aspect of policy outcomes that provides the analytic focus of this article.

In France and the United States at the end of the nineteenth century, both countries' political discourses were rich in competing representations of gender and class identities, and debates over the proper roles for women and workers (as well as immigrants, races, etc) were heated. Out of these two quite similar situations of economic uncertainty came state policies that contained quite dissimilar representations of gender relations, resulting in quite different forms of those gender identities. In France, such identities included the possibility—and indeed at times the assumption—of the validity and importance of women's paid work, both for single and married women. The French state created policies that reflected this assumption and that facilitated women's performance of the dual roles of worker and mother. Legislation protecting both working women and mothers and infants developed within the labor code, reflecting a certain societal agreement that if women workers were not exactly the same as men, women *were* nonetheless workers. In the United States, by contrast, policies did not reflect the same assumption about the possibility of combining two roles, and "two-channel" state programs took form, which addressed men as workers and women as mothers.[1] The rest of this article explicates the grounds for this difference, via an examination of the history of workplace and maternal and infant protection in the two countries and by locating the initiatives in a general process by which new representations of gender relations came to be embedded in state policies, particularly during moments of economic restructuring.

In both France and the United States, infant mortality and public health were major social problems, linked in people's minds not only to labor force needs and national honor but also to fears about social instability more generally. By the late nineteenth century French demographers announced that the rate of population growth was dropping dramatically. Concerned groups of all sorts considered depopulation a threat to the nation, particularly in the event of another war with Germany. The American birth rate also declined throughout the nineteenth century, so that by the 1890s only France's was lower.[2]

By 1900, most European countries had enacted legislation to prohibit women from working in industry for limited periods before and/or after giving birth. France was an exception to this international trend until 1913 legislation provided a potential prenatal and a compulsory postnatal leave for women working in "all industrial and commercial establishments." Most important, a daily allowance to compensate for lost wages became available for eight weeks before and after childbirth to "all women of French nationality who habitually work for wages outside the home, whether as a worker, an employee, or a domestic," if their personal means were limited.[3] Dispute over this allowance held up the legislation until 1913, but it was finally passed after a debate that stressed the needs of the state. Until 1945 paid maternity leaves represented the primary state effort to decrease infant mortality rates and improve the health of newborns.

In France, the explanation preferred by demographers and other social policy experts for infant mortality was a too-hasty return to work by new mothers because of their poverty, not maternal occupation per se. By the 1890s, demographers had found that 45 percent of infant deaths in the first year of life occurred within the first month, and they concluded that leaves of four to eight weeks would substantially alter mortality rates. Observing women's continued work during the last part of their pregnancies (thus provoking premature births, underweight newborns, difficult deliveries, maternal weakness, etc.), and their insistence on returning to work immediately after delivery (thus leaving their newborns to be fed bottled milk and cared for by others less careful than the natural mother and risking postpartum complications that threatened the health and long-term fertility of the mother), agitation for various types of leaves took place between 1886 and 1913, when compulsory paid leaves were finally written into labor legislation. The emphasis on leaves clearly reflected a widely shared assumption that women's participation in the paid labor force, even after marriage and during childbearing years, was widespread, inevitable, and even desirable. Yet, something had to be done so that women could combine both their productive and reproductive activities. Some representatives of capital and both revolutionary and reformist workers' organizations mobilized alongside nationalists, social Catholics, and feminists to demand, with different rationales, a state policy.[4]

Although state initiative relied on the development of a program of maternity leaves, France also had other organizations and programs devoted to infant health. Here too multiple efforts were made to reconcile work and childbearing. For example, public and private charitable organizations sought out needy working and unemployed women and provided them with payments in exchange for a commitment to keep their babies at home and to breast-feed.[5] There were well-baby clinics, associations to make payments to mothers who nursed for an extended period, and voluntary associations that established milk stations.[6] Nursing stations, crèches in factories, and state-provided child care in the schools from the age of three also reflected these concerns.[7] Moreover, as the authors of the concluding report of the first International Congress of

Gouttes de Lait in Paris in 1905 clearly understood, the ability to nurse was class-related. Poor women who worked were in greatest need of pure milk for their babies.[8]

The question of infant health also concerned the reformers who advocated regulation of the hours of women's work. In 1892, fifty years after enactment of the Factory Acts in Britain, the first laws limiting the hours of women's work finally passed the French legislature.[9] In essence, the laws permitted women to work eleven hours, including one hour of rest, and prohibited night work (between 9 P.M. and 5 A.M.). There were, of course, exceptions to this prohibition for some kinds of occupations, for some times of year, and for some industries. Moreover, the legislation excluded the family workshop. In 1900 the coverage of the law was extended to include men working in the same unit of production and a uniform maximum of eleven hours was set, with the eventual goal of ten.[10]

Reduction of women's hours of work was always part of a larger demand by the labor movement to reduce hours. Beginning in the last decades of the nineteenth century trade unions struck over shorter hours and mobilized for state actions, especially in 1890–91, 1904–06, and 1919, when eight-hour legislation came to France. Socialist leaders proposed shorter hours as a means of solving many social ills; the campaign was a direct response to the effects of economic restructuring and social problems. Thus, an eight-hour day was supposed to alleviate structural unemployment, reduce the psychological and physical impact of intensifying and unskilled work, eliminate overproduction, increase time for family life (in particular by giving the father more time with his family), and result in healthier workers.[11] But it was not only the labor movement that advocated reduced hours. Social Catholics and radical republicans, including employers, also argued that a general reduction of working time would increase efficiency and productivity.[12]

A first breach in the opposition to reduced hours came, then, with the 1892 law regulating women's and children's hours. The grounds used for "protecting" some of the population were that they were the ones without political rights and thus without resources to protect themselves through workplace or political actions. Arguments about lack of rights overwhelmed references to women's physical infirmities—particularly menstruation—which also were sometimes cited as a reason making shorter hours desirable.[13] Also embedded in the discussion was the notion that shorter hours would enable women to do housework and look after their children better. Indeed, in exploring the "need" for shorter hours and no night work, studies inquired into the effects of long days and night work on infant feeding. In this way, the great concern with natalism linked up the "protection" of women workers.

The need for more time for families to spend together, especially with the children, provided the core theme used by both labor movement activists and businessmen in this discussion. Social peace and national well-being were supposedly hostage to long hours, which left children unsupervised, homes disrupted (thus encouraging men to seek solace in the café), and infants without proper food.[14] The goal was always to gain this reform for all workers, and granting it to women was claimed as a breach that would of necessity widen in the future.[15] The men could, and did, ride to leisure on the skirts of the women.

The development of "protective" legislation in the United States took a quite different course. The trade unions did not lead the movement for the legislative reduction of hours; the craft-dominated American Federation of Labor (AFL) preferred a collective bargaining strategy and officially opposed state regulation. This meant bargaining employer by employer and by the late nineteenth century many male workers had negotiated reduced hours. It was those parts of the reform movement concerned with the social conditions of women, of which feminists were a most prominent segment, that insistently advocated legislative restrictions on the hours and occupations women could work. As a result, women's protection had an uneven history until the landmark case of *Muller v. Oregon*, decided by the Supreme Court in 1908.[16] This case provided the justification, which lasted until the 1970s, for differential treatment of women and men workers. *Muller* accepted the protection of women workers, in terms of hours and conditions of work, because women were *different* from men, physically and in their social roles.

This view of protection emerged in a period when laissez-faire liberalism was at its height in American legal doctrine. Freedom of contract, set out in the similarly landmark case of *Lochner v. New York* in 1905, dominated the Court's understanding of labor relations. Since *Lochner* found it "unreasonable" to limit the hours of work of male bakers, the National Consumers' League and Louis Brandeis, who prepared the arguments in the *Muller* case, were forced to argue within the Court's discourse and demonstrate that limitation of women's hours was, by contrast, "reasonable." They did this by marshaling statistical and anecdotal material from around the world to "demonstrate" that long hours and night work were detrimental to women's long-term health, an argumentation strategy labeled the Brandeis Brief. The brief made two simultaneous arguments. One, drawn from the emerging scientific literature on work, claimed a link between fatigue, overwork, and low productivity; short hours were simply more efficient. Another argued that long hours and night work threatened the health and well-being of the "mothers of future generations."

The Court's opinion particularly stressed the latter, writing into *Muller* the notion that there were innate and inherent differences between women and men, which meant that women would always need protection, even if it infringed freedom of contract.[17] For men, however, with their different biology and social responsibilities, *Lochner* held that permissable protection depended upon the strong demonstration of extraordinary conditions of work. In this case, the requirement of "reasonableness" had come to depend on differentiating women and men, and the Court became fixated on the idea.

The decisions about the protection of women in the United States were also linked to the second area of investigation here—maternal and infant protection —and the effects of long hours and night work on rates of infant mortality were prominently discussed in *Muller*. Nevertheless, the United States did not develop leaves, paid or unpaid, for pregnant women and/or new mothers. For example, in 1916 the American Association for Labor Legislation proposed a federal law to provide maternity benefits modeled on the Northern European examples. Any woman earning less than $100 a month (i.e., most women working for wages) would have received two-thirds of her wages from an employer-employee-government fund plus free medical care for two weeks before and six weeks after delivery, on the condition she did not work in that period.[18] The law did not pass, opposed by employers who argued it was not necessary because they did not think women worked after marriage. Despite the theme of the nation's need for babies, which characterized the period of World War I especially, few calls for leaves were heard.

The belief that motherhood was woman's primary mission could have been used as an argument in support of federal maternity benefits. The same belief, however, was a rationale for ignoring the plight of women who could not take time off from work to recuperate or to nurse, or who feared they would lose their jobs if they did so. Women who were both mothers and workers were not supposed to exist. They were invisible.[19]

As proposals for maternity leaves fell by the wayside, greater attention in both public and private programs turned to infant protection and reformers directed most of their efforts towards infant care, particularly to combating diarrhea, the number-one cause of infant mortality. Two kinds of initiatives developed. One was the provision of pure and/or sterilized milk to mothers who did not nurse, through a system of milk stations. The second was programs, established first by municipalities and then extended, to purify the milk supply available to consumers. Both private philanthropists and state officials promoted these efforts.[20] In the United States there was, at first, less emphasis on teaching mothers the importance of breast-feeding than in the European movements for infant health:

While Americans especially were apt to measure their success by the number of bottles of milk which had been distributed, Budin [a leading French specialist active in the infant-care movement], in contrast, tended to measure the success of his Consultation by the number of mothers who were breast feeding.[21]

Such efforts to educate mothers about breast-feeding depended on a more holistic understanding of the issue, including the needs of mothers for care during and after pregnancy. This understanding penetrated American debates only in the second decade of the twentieth century.[22] When the discussion did begin it tended to focus on providing proper, "scientific" medical care and teaching women to feed their babies better, whether at the breast or on the bottle.

As a result, just as in other programs like those for Mothers' Aid, policies of infant and maternal protection institutionalized two channels of state welfare, one for working men and one for mothers.[23] American women who crossed the boundaries—working mothers—found no programs to meet their needs.[24] Whereas in France the representation of gender relations displayed an assumption that women worked for wages and that restrictions on hours should apply to all workers, in the United States assumptions about gender made working mothers invisible and encouraged state policies that separated the policy channels in which women and men's social roles developed. How can we understand this cross-national difference in state policies? Why did two states in similar periods of social uncertainty develop quite different policies directed towards working women and mothers?

GENDERING EFFECTS IN THE POLITICS
OF THE THIRD REPUBLIC

The nineteenth century in France brought economic upheavals.[25] Industrial production, export growth, and the expansion of free waged labor all occurred in a context characterized by economic and political liberalism.[26] But this did not continue. By the end of the century political parties, trade unions, and social movements for reform, including a feminist movement, emerged to provide support for a common political discourse centered around the general identity of *citizen-producer*. The consolidation of a common discourse followed from a shared analysis of the social and economic instability and misery, which the French termed the "social question." Numerous politicians, trade unionists, feminists, social theorists, and state experts explored the conditions of French society, especially in Paris and other cities, and discovered misery, squalour, immorality, starvation, prostitution, and infant mortality.[27] Economic and political liberalism seemed to create unbearable costs, not only for individuals but for the nation too.

Embedded in this discourse of economic and social crisis was a particular representation of gender and gender relations. In the discourse on the social question "*femmes isolées* [single women] represented the domain of misery, a world of turbulent sexuality, subversive independence and dangerous insubordination. They embodied the city itself."[28] Social observers pointed to the failure of the wage system to pay women enough to support even themselves; women with children were in substantially worse straits. Thus, women's poverty represented everyone's poverty and their misery was feared both for its own sake and because of the apprehension that it would lead to social and political instability.

Associated with this attention to economic misery as the crucible of social problems was the fear of depopulation. Concern about saving the children of the poverty stricken, which had prompted the development of facilities for abandoning children as well as child care for working women (e.g., in the state nursery schools [*écoles maternelles*]), became a hysteria about national decline after the defeat by Germany and the loss of Alsace-Lorraine.[29] Here, too, a sense that the social changes of the nineteenth century, and especially the ideology of liberalism that had given meaning to it, were at the root of the problem informed popular and expert perceptions of the real decline in population size. Therefore, within the concern about depopulation was an analytic link to the economic system, which people thought to be guaranteeing neither reproduction of the labor force nor a powerful nation state.[30]

By the end of the nineteenth century politics in the Third Republic had made hegemonic a universalizing identity, which can be labeled citizen-producer. Generalization of this identity involved accepting industrial society but allocating a great deal of authority to the state. French statism, so powerful since the days of Colbert, took on new meaning. The new notion of citizenship brought politics that incorporated new social strata and immigrants and led to the organization of a new political form, the political party based on mass mobilization. A consequence was consolidation of democratic politics and defeat of conservative nationalism by the combined republican forces. The Dreyfus Affair was symbolically important because at that moment a large segment of the French petite bourgeoisie, the class that was the linchpin of the new politics, detached itself from the clerically based nationalism that had so influenced the first decades of the Third Republic. Unions, cooperatives, and professional societies, as well as single-issue movements, all assumed the new identity of citizen-producer. An alliance of these groups was expressed in practice as well as made possible by a series of important reforms in these crucial decades, which gave some stability to relations both in the workplace and in the broader society through social policy.

Embedded in this universalistic identity were certain ideas about gender relations that shaped and limited the identities that women, seeking their own political and social emancipation—their own access to citizenship, in particular—could mobilize. One result of the discourse about the social question was that social reformers carried in their doctrines an understanding of gender relations and these ideas were crucial components of the reform package.[31] Moreover, although the universe of political discourse contained a wide range of feminist positions, all of which jostled each other in the effort to shape the meaning systems of the coming century, feminists who were comfortable with the terms of the citizen-producer identity and who could manipulate the discourse surrounding it were most influential within the movements for social reform.

The feminist movement reconstituted after the defeat of the Commune in 1871 was pluralistic. One important strand, led by Léon Richer and Maria Deraismes, insisted that feminism was "reasonable, realistic, and centred on the reform of civil rights." It demanded equality in order to allow women to fulfil their obligations as wives and mothers, as well as to receive a better education and exercise an "interesting" profession.[32] Political rights, basically the vote, were not a central goal of this feminism, which focused more on the development of women's civil rights in a society ordered by the Napoleonic Code, according to which the husband was officially the patriarchal head of the family unit. Other strands of feminism, closer to the workers' movement, demanded education, better working conditions, and higher wages for women.

These foci reflected the fact that the most politically influential feminism at the time was deeply embedded in anticlericalism, which organized the politics of both the center and left in these years.[33] The strong Free Mason movement supported several feminist groups both materially and ideologically. Socialist feminists depended upon as well conflicted with the anticlerical workers' movement. It was, in large part, the feminists' ability to speak to or in the discourse of their allies that ordered the influence of the multitude of strands of feminism present in the universe of political discourse. Those who fit well with the vision of republican men (demanding, for example, secular education for girls, expanded civil rights for married women, or protection of infants for the nation) or socialist men (demanding, for example, greater unionization, higher wages, and protection of all workers) fared the best. Those feminists for whom political rights were a central goal found few allies and were marginal to a discourse producing an identity in which citizenship rights remained unabashedly male. Hubertine Auclert is the best representative of this strand. Her socialist feminism advocating complete equality, and thus suffrage too, came to grief because republicans of all stripes feared that female suffrage would reinforce the church and thus bring about the political defeat of the republican forces.[34] The effect of this balance of power within the women's movement was that pre-1914 feminists paid a good deal of attention to the conditions of women's work but less to their right to vote.

As a movement of resistance, however, feminism's fate rested not only on the actions of women but also on the practices of its political allies and their understandings of gender relations. One of these allies was the labor movement, which was an active promoter of both protection for working mothers and of reduced hours for all workers.[35] The labor movement was dominated by, but never exclusively concentrated among, skilled workers who tended to be men, but it included women as well. Therefore, while women workers were not numerous in the trade unions, they were present in both unions and parties. The acceptance of limited hours for women was part of a long-term strategy for reduced hours for everyone, which the labor movement sought.

By the beginning of the twentieth century, the French labor movement had moved beyond a simple protectionist position to include one of revolutionary syndicalism. Revolutionary syndicalism brought with it the dominance of a broader and more egalitarian discourse on women's role.[36] Committed to a class revolutionary stance, and confronted with rising rates of female employment and capital's frequent preference for women over men, the Confédération Générale du Travail (CGT) moved to organize rather than try to block women from participation in the paid labor force.[37] The Couriau Affair was a crucial turning point for the labor movement. In this 1913 controversy, the upper levels of the CGT disciplined the Lyon Printers' Federation for denying union membership to a female printer, Emma Couriau, and for expelling her husband because he refused to forbid her to seek work and union membership. The dispute was resolved only after the intervention of feminists and the national labor movement in a local controversy. The resolution in the direction of equality and acceptance of working women's rights was tremendously influential for the whole movement.[38]

The consequence of the strategic choice made in the Couriau Affair was far-reaching. The inclusion of women in unions became a political task of the first order, so that women could be brought around to support the revolutionary goals of the union movement. Similarly, confronted with capital's resort to women workers in order to reduce wage bills, the French unions instituted a strategy of emphasizing increases in the salaries of the lowest paid, as well as introducing into political discourse the mobilizing demand of equal pay for equal work. If employers could no longer pay women less than men, women would not threaten men's jobs. Moreover, unions' mobilizing actions would solidify the commitment of women to the goals of societal transformation, which the revolutionary union movement promoted. This strategy of solidarity did not divide the working class by gender, and the assumption of the "unnaturalness" of women's employment was not systematically promoted by the unions or their political allies. As the debates around infant protection and hours legislation revealed, for French unions and the social reformers close to them, the world imagined was one in which women were not necessarily confined to the home. Rather, the imagined ideal was one in which there was sufficient time for both work and family, for leisure and for home life.

The effect of politics *within* the labor movement was that consequential choices were made about gender relations and these choices had implications for the identity that working women might adopt. As well, within the struggles *between* labor and capital there was a struggle between working women and men about the gender self-presentation that the developing class would make.

The outcome was not given in advance nor was the result imposed on women, who were present in the struggles (although never in equal numbers); it was the result of concrete struggles in concrete situations.[39]

But it was not only unions and left-wing parties that contributed gendering effects. The doctrine of Solidarism, which much influenced the Radicals and other republicans, was another important source. In brief, Solidarism as social theory stressed the reciprocal rights and duties of citizens and state. Citizens owed each other, and ultimately the state, loyalty because they were inextricably bound in interdependency (solidarity). Society, composed of these links of rights and duties, resembled a contract. In this way, the philosophy provided middle-class reformers with a rationale for social programs that laid the foundation for the early welfare state. The society envisaged in this social theory was very different from one of pure liberalism or from a class society. Solidarism was a philosophy of the petite bourgeoisie, still economically and politically dominant in the Third Republic.[40] Moreover, Solidarism united not only the political organizations of these classes but also the growing corps of state experts, university-based social theorists, and reforming Catholics influenced by *Rerum Novarum*. Crucial to Solidarism was a vision in which society consisted not of individuals but of collectivities. Associative action including collective action in mutualism, syndicalism, and cooperatives was central to Solidarism as was the idea of the family as the basic social unit.

A direct consequence of the form politics took at the end of the nineteenth century was in shaping bourgeois feminism. The "solution" of Solidarism and the left-center alliance that came out of the Dreyfus Affair gave life to the identity of citizen-producer for women. Bourgeois feminists acted in a political situation in which philosophies of individualism were overwhelmed by the fears of excessive liberalism and the social costs of a laissez-faire state. The Solidarist solution to the social problem of nineteenth-century France effectively undermined any feminism that would have pushed for the simple equality of women. Thus, although organizations did exist that advocated such a reform and, therefore, although the identity of independent women did exist within the universe of political discourse, the position could gain no purchase to make its identity and its organization visible or viable.

Instead, the only viable feminism was the faction that joined the alliance of radical republicans, coming to that position as a result of support for freemasonry, or anticlericalism, or the rights of man, which continued to exclude women. In that alliance, however, the position of women was extremely contradictory. On the one hand, their male colleagues did support emancipatory reforms and some important ones were instituted. On the other hand, the social doctrine that provided the glue uniting political forces in the early Third Republic assigned a separate and not necessarily equal role to women, elevating the family to the status of fundamental social unit.

Therefore, feminists were caught in a dilemma. If they wished to improve women's situation, which was after all their primary goal, they were compelled to operate with the terms of the prevailing discourse. But, using a discourse much influenced by the identity of citizen-producer, feminists emphasized women's duties to the nation and helped institutionalize the identity of citizen-producer, accepting that women's most important product would be children for the *patrie*.[41] It was never the case that children were to be the only product of women, however; women would and should work for wages. In that sense the identity of citizen-producer could be taken up by women who saw themselves both as workers and mothers, and this identity was sustained by state policies like infant protection and hours legislation. Absent from this configuration, however, was any identity that defined women as different from men based simply on sexual difference, not maternity, and that promised them greater equality, even in difference.

The identity of citizen-producer accommodated women but in limited ways; it was the translation of a quite particular understanding of gender relations in which women's place was in the family although not necessarily in the home. Working women, as working men, owed their first loyalty to the family and through it to the state. Other more individualistic collective identities disappeared from view. They had been present as alternatives in the past, however, and they continued to live on in the shadow world of the universe of political discourse as did more critical class identities. In the meantime, state programs addressed women as workers *and* as mothers, albeit through the family. Many of the policies for maternal and infant protection were intended to strengthen the family, rather than to address the needs of women per se, while hours legislation for women was to be the opening wedge for workers gaining greater control over their working conditions.

GENDERING EFFECTS IN THE PRE-1914 UNITED STATES

In France the identity of citizen-producer was in large part institutionalized by a political process organized through the legislature, which provided the focus of politics. The lack of workplace recognition of unions and workers made party politics and legislative reforms crucial as the route to reforms. Moreover, the highly centralized state, tightly linked to Paris, left little space for regional variations in political programs. In the United States, federalism and a political ideology of liberalism had encouraged the nineteenth-century development of what has been called a "state of courts and parties," a form that had become by the last decades of the century inappropriate to the new economic and social conditions. This state of courts and parties was one in which legislatures were less important as organizers of politics than were the courts, especially the Supreme Court, and political parties.[42]

At the time the economy was undergoing increasing concentration and industrial capitalism acquired technological sophistication. By the last decade of the nineteenth century the United States was the world's first industrial power and manufacturing was generating more of the national income than agriculture. This new emphasis on manufacturing was accompanied by massive immigration, urbanization, and the development of a huge mass market. At the same time, labor was scarce and skilled workers commanded relatively high wages and had some workplace power. But the high production costs associated with labor processes requiring skilled labor, and the pressures for lower costs coming from an increasingly large domestic market, led to new production techniques that allowed substitution of unskilled workers for skilled ones.[43]

Political changes accompanied these economic developments. National-level bureaucratic state institutions already familiar in Western European countries finally took form in the United States. Out of the crises, class conflict, and complexity of those years came a series of new regulatory and bureaucratic bodies that replaced to some extent courts and political parties as the mediators of state-society relations.[44] An impasse was broken. But the new institutions that took form did not fall from heaven; they were produced by political conflicts that occurred within the old institutions of the state of courts and parties. And, the new was profoundly marked by the old.

The courts, in particular, continued to play a substantial role. While recognizing the continent-wide scale of the economic order and the need for governing authority, the courts had earlier appropriated the mantle of rational policy makers for themselves. In particular,

with constitutional laissez-faire, the Court sought to sharpen the boundaries between the public and private spheres, to provide clear and predictable standards for gauging the scope of acceptable state action, and to affirm with the certainty of fundamental law the prerogatives of property owners in the marketplace.[45]

Therefore, any efforts at reform would engage the courts, which had appropriated for themselves the right to act as economic arbiters. As a result, all efforts to redesign the state by making it more subject to bureaucratic controls had to pass through the courts and were therefore subject to its definition of proper state involvement. In this way these new bodies encountered difficulties that undermined their effectiveness.[46]

The impact of this requirement of working within the discourse of the courts is very clear in the case of the legislation regulating women's hours of work. As described previously, *Muller* was grounded in a discourse of difference, founded in biological differences between women and men. Only with that argumentation was the Supreme Court willing to bypass its standard of "freedom of contract." Similar efforts by the National Consumers' League or other reformers to introduce workplace regulation foundered on the Court's insistence on upholding its definition of laissez-faire liberalism.

Nevertheless, this was a moment of political change, out of which eventually came a newly strengthened federal government. In the process, a large number of actors jockeyed for position to define the future of American politics and state/society relations. Out of that jostling in a moment of economic and social restructuring and political debate came a doubly bifurcated identity that might be labeled *"specialized citizenship."* A first dichotomy was between workplace and political identities, as the realms of work and politics separated. This was in many ways a classic vision of liberal democracy, dividing the world functionally so that the economy and politics appeared to be separate activities. Economic relations were to operate on the basis of "market principles" while political activity for distribution of goods and services was rationalized as improving the market at the margin when distortions occurred. Thus, the state was to be an inspector, limit monopolies, and provide help for those who could not compete. In addition, this discourse incorporated much optimism about technological progress and the mutability of economic and social conditions through the application of science and technology.

A second dichotomy divided the political realm, driving a gender cleavage deep into the notions of citizenship rights. Whereas in France in these years the fundamental social unit was the family, headed by a man in whom exclusive citizenship rights resided, emerging notions of American women's citizenship were individualistic but founded on a concept of "difference," which transferred into politics and especially new social programs notions of female qualities of nurture and maternity that had earlier sustained a strict gender divide between "private" and "public" realms. In this way, the two channels for state welfare, which conceived of workers as male and women as nonwaged mothers, began to take form as feminist reformers, in alliance with male reformers, pressed for new state actions.

The feminist movement as a whole contributed important terms to the doubly bifurcated identity of specialized citizenship. Feminism in the early twentieth century extended the emphasis of the nineteenth-century women's movement on equal rights. In doing so it placed a great deal of stress on programs and practices that would increase women's individuality while newly recognizing the heterogenity that characterized women's situations. As differences among women increased as a result of the rising rates of labor force participation, the expansion of the service sector, immigration rates from diverse countries, and urbanization, the assumption of a common experience of "woman" was unsustainable. Therefore, the theme of variation within a common identity of women emerged.[47]

In this process feminists made use of a complicated discourse. They argued, of course, for a common human condition. This was the legacy of and the founding rock of their liberalism. Out of that argument came the claim for citizenship rights, especially suffrage. Simultaneously, however, feminists employed a discourse of difference, one that described, even defined, women as more nurturing, more maternal, more caring than men.[48] The injection of this female perspective into the political world would improve it immensely, they insisted, and women needed the vote to make such improvements happen.[49] Making such claims to citizenship for a particular group, feminists were identifying women as an important—a special—segment of the American political process, one that had hitherto been excluded but that deserved a place.

The gendering effects of the doubly bifurcated identity were that women's identity came to depend on their position as mothers of the future generation, their citizenship entailing a different responsibility to the collectivity than men. Citizenship was gendered, in other words, along biological lines. Women were highly visible, both as the proponents of reform of state welfare programs and as objects of reform, but their identity was overdetermined by their potential for maternal nurturing in both the private and public realms.

The birth-control movement was an important source of this discourse about motherhood as women's vocation. Women reformers in the United States had long paid attention to the question of control over reproduction. Indeed it was a more widely shared goal than even the suffrage.[50] In the nineteenth century voluntary motherhood, that is, sexual abstinence by couples, was the fundamental principle of the American birth-control movement. Only through the exercise of this kind of self-control could women be freed from unwanted sex and repeated and punishing pregnancies and families from the costs of too many children. Yet, by the first decades of the twentieth century, voluntary motherhood was attacked by those concerned about race suicide.[51] Middle-class women who tried to control their reproduction were accused of contributing to the decline of Yankee stock and the values on which "the nation had been built." In other words, the fears of the consequences of immigration and high birthrates among first-generation immigrants resulted in a turn against the women who had advocated birth control as a central political reform. Responding to this vicious attack, the birth-control movement adopted a discourse about motherhood and the possibilities of "motherhood as a career." This discourse was intended to confront head-on the vicious attacks of the race-suiciders. Yet, a consequence was to make even more invisible women who were not full-time mothers and to reinforce the notion that women's duty to the nation passed exclusively through their maternal roles.

Another important location for feminist politics was in the Progressive movement, which represented the reforming zeal of middle-class America, disgusted by corrupt politics, which had "perverted" American institutions, and by the emerging evidence of the consequences of unregulated market forces. Reform of institutions and practices was needed to put the American system back on an even keel. The Progressives challenged old-style party politics, and in doing so they helped to provide the glue for a new kind of politics that defined an altered role for the state within the pluralistic politics of contending groups.

This politics was not only deeply influenced by the claims and actions of women, but it was also vilified by its opponents as representing an effeminate form of politics. At first, the very notion of such reform, in which the state, rather than market forces or political parties, took responsibility for relieving poverty or other forms of misery was rejected as "unmanly" politics. In the end, "feminized" policies did develop, coming out of a privatized sector of philanthrophic organizations led by women, which provided the models for the first social programs.[52] In this way, American state welfare was more a victory of women reformers and their allies than of any working-class organization.

Progressive reformers shared an optimism about "progress" and technological improvements. Because Progressives believed that simplistic acceptance of market-driven outcomes led to a series of unfortunate, albeit unintended, effects, they demanded greater state regulation. This regulation ranged from trust-busting and the empowerment of new regulatory agencies to the campaigns for governmental inspection of food processing. Embedded in this political position was a great deal of faith in technical achievement and technocrats acting in the state if necessary. Infant protection, in this way, developed a programmatic identity that maximized the role of science and medicine in producing healthy babies. The widely distributed sterilized bottle became the symbol of the diffusion of "scientific" child care from doctors to middle-class mothers to working-class mothers.[53]

The National Consumers' League (NCL) was a central actor in the Progressive movement. It sought out the weaknesses in the system, the places where the particularly needy were being abandoned. Originally, the NCL had identified all workers as needing protection from long hours and bad working conditions but the opposition of the trade unions and the courts soon turned its focus towards women and children. Subsequently, in making claims on behalf of such groups, via practices like the Brandeis Brief, the NCL contributed to rather than challenged the link between women and maternity and their separateness from men.[54]

Disputes over the length of the working day rocked the American economy at this time; however, with the growth of the American Federation of Labor in the last decades of the nineteenth century workers gained some power in the production process and they sought redress for their workplace grievances and demands almost exclusively through collective bargaining, while organizing for political action in neighborhood-based political parties.[55] Such a privatized regulation of the wage relation involved primarily skilled workers or workers whose industrial production could be labeled skilled. Because regulation of wage relations for other kinds of workers was less institutionalized, such workers suffered all the effects of uncertainty and lack of a living wage. Many such workers were women and only in the first decades of the twentieth century did their situation begin to stabilize, basically through state regulation of hours and conditions of work, gained through the political struggles of reform movements, often led by women.

The union movement, dominated by men, feared the effects of female employment on their own wages. The solution the unions chose was to seek "protective" legislation, which would limit women's labor force participation, and simultaneously to bargain hard for the family wage.[56] This support for legislative action was one of the few times the AFL departed from its preferred strategy of eschewing political action for workplace bargaining. The low levels of organization of women workers provided the rationale.

Given their understanding of the proper gender division of labor as well as organized labor's usual focus on workplace struggles, it is hardly surprising that labor leaders did not play a role in the demand for maternal and infant protection. For them the family remained a "private" realm to be regulated by men and women without union or state guidance. At the same time, any actions that might encourage more women workers were to be avoided, because, according to the AFL, the unorganized women would only drive down men's wages, thus making it more difficult for them to support their wives and children. The logic was tight and it clearly excluded the notion that women's paid work was to be encouraged.

Some organization of working women before World War I did, of course, occur. Important in organizing women was the Women's Trade Union League (WTUL), composed of middle-class and working-class women who encouraged unionization. After numerous efforts to set up union locals and affiliate them to the AFL, the WTUL recognized a series of obstacles.[57] One was that it had difficulty fitting women's work into the skill categories the AFL was willing to recognize, and therefore male-dominated unions sometimes rejected applications for affiliation.[58] But, at the same time the WTUL's long-standing commitment to the AFL made it impossible for the organization to advocate another form of unionism, especially since the AFL suspected the WTUL leaders' (usually of middle-class origin) credentials as supporters of workers. In addition, the league encountered the same difficulties establishing permanent unions among a diverse and transient labor force that other organizers had described. Therefore, eventually the WTUL began to place less emphasis on organizing women and more on protective legislation. Its analysis shifted from one that stressed the commonalities of female and male workers expressed through their hoped-for affiliation in the same unions towards an emphasis on the differences of women workers.

In the United States then, organizations like the AFL and WTUL as well as the dominant streams of feminism contributed to the discursive and practical constitution of an identity for working women different from men's and one that made women's supposed special qualities their credentials for protection. Women, according to male unionists, were temporary workers removed from the labor force by marriage. Their extraordinary workplace weakness derived from their lack of unionization, which in turn permitted an exception to the usual union practice of insisting on making gains in the workplace rather than through legislation.[59] For the WTUL women workers were also different from men, caught up in family and work situations that led to their unusual exploitation. The way to deal with the problem, for the WTUL, was to stress the differences and make demands for protective legislation.

In political debate women's needs and potential contributions were described as a potential for maternal nurturing. Unmarried working girls were the "mothers of the future" and as such they required protective legislation to safeguard their futures. Yet, this resort to the state transgressed the very rules of separation of work and politics that characterized the dominant terms in American politics at the time. "Real" workers bargained privately in nonpartisan unions. Workers who made claims on the state did no more than to reconfirm their "otherness." Moreover, because there was little confirmation of women's identity as workers, working "girls" were considered exceptions (because they were temporary workers) while married working women became invisible. Entering the political realm in this way, women's identity became overdetermined by biology and it became prey to discursive construction by other actors, like the courts, which saw women simply as mothers.

The feminist movement that had grown out of the nineteenth-century woman's movement was confounded by these notions of specialized citizenship. The feminist movement in the early twentieth century became entangled in a contradiction. Because work and politics were separated and there was little call, either by trade unions or reformers, for the state to regulate the conditions of work, when feminists agitated for protective legislation for women at work or in maternity, they solidified popular notions of women as mothers, as "other" than workers, as minors. This classing of women as "wards of the state" put them in the same category as children, native peoples, and others often considered without the capacity of caring for themselves. Thus, within the terms of American political discourse, as long as women remained in need of state protection they could never be full participants in the polity.

This contradiction confronted the feminist movement with a difficult choice. If it stressed the "special nature" of "femaleness," the result was to help embed gender differences in the heart of the welfare programs, a difference according to which male citizens were fully adult workers and citizens and female citizens were mothers for the nations. If feminists argued strictly for equality in the real world of a segmented labor force, hostile unions and bosses, and a Court driven by an ideology of "freedom of contract" women's lives would continue to be difficult. This resulting tension over strategy held back American feminists after 1920.[60]

The practical effect of stressing an identity of difference is seen in the ways that protective legislation, women's work, and suffrage intertwined discursively before 1914. Feminists were central actors not only in suffrage organizations but also in the National Consumers' League and the WTUL. In both these latter bodies, the demand for the vote for women became a central political position providing the grounds for alliance. Indeed it was the recognition of women's increasing work force activity that provided an important link in the suffragists' liberalism. Since one of the arguments against women's political rights was their economic and social dependence, the rise in labor force participation could only lay that argument to rest. Thus, for suffragists, an alliance with working women was crucial.[61] For organizations concerned about work and women, then, the possible strength deriving from expanded political rights also became crucial. The belief that with the vote came political power encouraged many women reformers to combine demands for protective legislation with demands for suffrage. In this alliance, the vote emerged as a primary goal, a tool for reform, whereas in France, the forces of the Left not only feared female suffrage as strengthening the church but also as undermining a Solidaristic society of families whose male head could represent the whole. Thus eventually the American suffrage movement succeeded in gaining citizenship rights for women earlier than in France and women did participate, even before gaining the vote, in the design of American social programs. Yet the cost of victories was that a two-channel welfare system was created, with women's lives limited by the state's willingness to confine them to a single social role.

CONCLUSION

This article has explored the representations of gender and the resulting identities for female and male citizens that took shape in France and the United States at the end of the nineteenth century. In neither country did these identities emerge magically or even simply out of political debates. Each developed as solutions to problems faced by economic, social, and political institutions, which in resolving them made use of the representations of gender within their own world views. One result was that such representations were further strengthened by being embedded in the policies of emerging state welfare programs. In France, concerns about demographic "catastrophe" as well as a social doctrine of Solidarism provided the impetus for state policies that sought to accommodate women's work and maternity. In the United States in contrast middle-class Progressivism and a feminist movement emphasizing women's "nurturing" qualities acted in a situation in which actors looked to the state only in exceptional circumstances. The social programs that developed in these years reflected such differences.

Throughout this story, all actions for social programs took place within a context in which representations of gender—and the identities that followed from these representations—were crucial organizers of the political terrain. In France working women, both single and married, were commonplace and state programs for protection of women and children reflected a widely shared acceptance of this social fact. The newly forged universalizing identity of citizen-producer incorporated the idea that citizens produced both in the workplace and in the home. The duality of women's citizenship roles was crucial in the way welfare policy took form, with programs to meet women's needs as workers and mothers inscribed in labor legislation. Yet, notions of citizenship in this paradigm were not individualized, so that forces for reform could simultaneously advocate greater workplace rights for women while opposing female suffrage. Women, as individual actors, remained enclosed and invisible within the family. It was always the family that needed both healthy and rested parents if it were to produce the nation's babies.

In the United States, by contrast, a doubly bifurcated identity emerged, based on the liberal-democratic assumption of a separation between politics and work as well as the public/private dichotomy. American women were invisible as workers for everyone but those who argued for their "exceptional" needs. Women's citizenship rights were claimed almost exclusively because of their supposed maternal qualities. Absent was an identity for working women or for women unencumbered by nurturing responsibilities. Consequences of this particular collective identity for women are seen in "two-channel" welfare programs, which addressed women as mothers and men as workers, as well as constituting state welfare as a feminized realm, responding to the politics of women and their allies.

At this time of the prehistory of the "welfare state" in these two countries, then, the collective identities available to women differed. The nature of interwar politics, especially feminist politics, was marked by this difference.[62] Each provided points of strength and points of weakness. Operating within the interstices of the universe of political discourse, which provided them with differentially limited space for maneuver, French and American women continued after 1914 to search for the route towards emancipation, liberation, and equality in difference.

NOTES

Research for this work was supported by SSHRCC grant #410-86-0238 and the Center for International Affairs, Harvard University. For comments on earlier drafts I am grateful to Linda Gordon, Laura Levine Frader, and Sonya Michel.

1 The argument about two-channel welfare programs in the United States is developed in Barbara Nelson, "The Origins of the Two-Channel Welfare State: Workmen's Compensation and Mothers' Aid," this volume.

2 Linda Gordon, *Woman's Body, Woman's Right: A Social History of Birth Control in America* (New York: Viking, 1976), 48.

3 This discussion of the details of infant protection draws frequently from Mary Lynn Stewart (-McDougall), "Protecting Infants: The French Campaign for Maternity Leaves, 1890s–1913," *French Historical Studies*, vol. XIII, 79–105. The prenatal allowance required a medical certificate that continued employment would endanger the mother or unborn child. No restrictions but need applied to postnatal benefits. In 1919 35 percent of the new mothers of Paris met the means test, despite the miniscule sum being paid. Françoise Thébaud, "Donner la vie: Histoire de la maternité en France entre les deux guerres," *Thèse de Troisième Cycle*, Paris VII, 1982, 88.

4 Few participants in the policy debate—the demographic and medical experts who collected the data on infant mortality, the women or men workers, the social reformers who agitated for the payment, the capitalists who established private programs and promoted public ones, and the politicians and trade unionists who debated the specifics of the programs—thought that a poor working woman could count on a male wage to carry her through even a limited unpaid maternity leave.

5 For example, state efforts to reduce child abandonment, and thus to raise the birthrate (since so many children left to asylums died quickly), included a small amount of monetary aid and larger amounts of material help to poor mothers, whether single or married. Yet the intent of the program was that women would continue to earn their livings. Thus, in the Department of the Seine (Paris), by the late 1880s, municipal officials were willing to pay a poor mother the whole cost of a wet nurse (the same amount as the average weekly wage of an unskilled working woman) in order to discourage unmarried mothers from giving up their babies. The rest of the costs of maintaining herself and child were to be earned, however. See Rachel Fuchs, "Morality and Poverty: Public Welfare for Mothers in Paris, 1870–1900," *French History*, vol. 2, no. 3, 290–94, 304; Thébaud, "Donner la vie," 87.

6 Perhaps the best known of these milk services was the *Goutte de Lait*, established in 1894, but many maternity hospitals and private charities had similar services. The goals were the same: encourage breast-feeding, teach the importance of well-baby consultations, and provide sterilized artificial feeding when breast-feeding was impossible. As each *Goutte de Lait* said, bottled milk was *"faute de mieux."* John Blake, "Origins of Maternal and Child Health Programs," in *The Health of Women and Children* (New York: Arno, 1977; originally published in 1953), 9–11.

7 The first crèches dated from 1844 and expanded rapidly in number in the nine-

teenth century as places to care for the children of working mothers. The goal was to eliminate "baby-farming," or the system of wet-nursing in which the babies lived with the nurse. The *Loi Roussel* of 1874 was a similar effort. Blake, "Origins," 5. On American wet-nursing, which was essentially part of the "servant problem," see Janet Golden, "Trouble in the Nursery: Physicians, Families and Wet Nurses at the End of the Nineteenth Century," in *"To Toil the Livelong Day":* *America's Women at Work, 1780–1980*, ed. Carol Groneman and Mary Beth Norton (Ithaca, N.Y.: Cornell University Press, 1987).

8 Blake, "Origins," 21. It is important to note that many of these programs were neutral on questions of the woman's morality; they were only concerned that she would use the public assistance to care for the child. Thus, women who were unmarried or were involved with a man (or even several sequentially) were eligible for assistance as long as they demonstrated "maternal affection." One important indicator of such affection was willingness to breast-feed. Fuchs, "Morality and Poverty," 297–98. This focus on the child's welfare and willingness to condone parental "immorality" carried through into the post-1945 welfare state. See Jane Jenson, "Friend or Foe: Women and State Welfare," in *Becoming Visible: Women in European History*, ed. Renate Bridenthal, Claudia Koonz, and Susan Stuard (Boston: Houghton-Mifflin, 1987), 543–44.

9 This law also regulated children's work, but I will not give the specifics of those restrictions for reasons of parsimony.

10 For a more detailed description of the regulations, as they affected women, see Marilyn Boxer, "Protective Legislation and Home Industry: The Marginalization of Women Workers in Late Nineteenth-Early Twentieth Century France," *Journal of Social History*, vol. 20, no. 1 (1986): 45–65. Her argument is that the result of this "protective" legislation was to marginalize the female labor force by encouraging homework. Since all workers' hours were being reduced over these years, this "single factor" explanation is hard to accept.

11 For details of this campaign see Gary S. Cross, "The Quest for Leisure: Reassessing the Eight-Hour Day in France," *Journal of Social History*, vol. 18, no. 2 (1984): 195–216.

12 Mary Lynn Stewart (-McDougall), "Paternalism, Patriarchy and Protection: The Rhetoric of Labor Reform, 1880s and 1890s," paper presented to the Annual Meeting of French Historical Studies, Columbia, South Carolina, March 1988, 4–5.

13 Stewart (-McDougall), "Paternalism, Patriarchy and Protection," 9 and *passim*.

14 Cross' citation in "The Quest for Leisure," 202, from a later union campaign to protect against encroachments on the eight-hour day, can stand for the theme of the whole movement: If the eight-hour day was lost, not only would wages decrease but the worker would "lose dignity," would not "be able to educate himself or his family, and women would have 'to return to the slavery of housework after a longer workday'."

15 Some feminists were the major opponents of this two-stage strategy because they thought the immediate effect would be to close women out of higher-paying jobs. See Boxer, "Protective Legislation and Home Industry," 52–53.

16   This analysis of *Muller v. Oregon* is from Judith A. Baer, *The Chains of Protection: The Judicial Response to Women's Labor Legislation* (Westport, Conn.: Greenwood, 1978); Susan Lehrer, *Origins of Protective Labor Legislation For Women, 1905–1925* (Albany: State University of New York, 1987).

17   Ann Corinne Hill, "Protection of Women Workers and the Courts: A Legal Case History," *Feminist Studies*, vol. 5, no. 2 (1979): 247–73.

18   Richard W. Wertz and Dorothy C. Wertz, *Lying-In: A History of Childbirth in America* (New York: The Free Press, 1977), 224–25. Between 1910 and 1920, six states did pass legislation limiting women's work during pregnancy, but the federal law that would have made the schemes workable did not pass. Sheila B. Kamerman, Alfred J. Kahn, and Paul Kingston, *Maternity Policies and Working Women* (New York: Columbia University Press, 1983), 33.

19   Wertz and Wertz, *Lying-In*, 224. On the appeal to the national need and the wartime importance of babies, see p. 209 and also Grace L. Meigs, "Maternal Mortality from all Conditions Connected with Childbirth in the United States and Certain Other Countries," in *The Health of Women and Children* (New York: Arno, 1977; originally published by U.S. Department of Labor, Children's Bureau, 1917).

20   Blake, "Origins," 13ff. and Wertz and Wertz, *Lying-In*, 202ff.

21   Blake, "Origins," 22.

22   Blake, "Origins," 36; Meigs, "Maternal Mortality," 9; Wertz and Wertz, *Lying-In*, 202.

23   In the case of Mothers' Aid pensions, which began in some states by 1911, there was a distinct shift in antipoverty policy away from day nurseries and other programs that permitted mothers to work towards programs that foreclosed the category of working mother, reflecting the relative emptiness of that identity set. For more details see Sonya Michel, "From Civic Usefulness to Federal Maternalism," paper presented at the Berkshire Conference of Women's Historians, Wellesley College, June 1987.

24   The structure of even the educational programs clearly reflect this silence around working women. The use of philanthropic or municipal milk stations as the primary mechanism for "outreach" for educating new mothers assumed women were free in the daytime to visit the station and pass time following its programs. French programs not only distributed milk through such stations but also agitated for the establishment of nursing rooms in factories, as well as crèches and organized instructional programs in factories and in the evenings.

25   The description of the economic conditions of nineteenth-century France, unless otherwise noted, is based on Robert Boyer, "Wage Formation in Historical Perspective: The French Experience," *Cambridge Journal of Economics* 3 (1979): 104ff.

26   The development of the labor market was encouraged by the *Loi Le Chapelier* (1791), which forbid all collective action and established the principle of individual but not collective freedom of producers to sell their products. For a half a century the *Loi Le Chapelier* denied wage earners any possibility of collectively defending their own interest. This law codified an "atomistic" labor market, thus institutionalizing a system of competitive regulation. Nevertheless, a purely

atomistic or completely "liberal" labour market did not persist. By the end of the century a set of institutions and actors that gave shape to a more collectively determined wage relation replaced it.

27 In the debates about pauperism and pauperization in the nineteenth century, three issues were intertwined: the inescapable growth of wage labor, the inadequacy of workers' wages, and their aleatory character, which maintained workers in a situation of uncertainty. See Henri Hatzfeld, *Du Paupérisme à la sécurité sociale: Essai sur les origines de la sécurité sociale en France, 1850–1940* (Paris: Armand Colin, 1971), 25.

28 Joan W. Scott, " 'L'Ouvrière! Mot impie, sordide . . .' Women Workers in the Discourse of French Political Economy, 1840–1860," in *The Historical Meaning of Work*, ed. Patrick Joyce (Cambridge: Cambridge University Press, 1987), 126.

29 For details about population trends as well as the analysis of the problem see Karen Offen, "Depopulation, Nationalism and Feminism in Fin-de-Siècle France," *American Historical Review* (June 1984).

30 The link to industrialization was explicit in the programs designed to cope with depopulation, especially the payments made to working women to stay at home for a period after the birth of their babies. See Jane Jenson, "Gender and Reproduction: Or, Babies and the State," *Studies in Political Economy*, no. 20 (1986): 17–20.

31 For example, Emile Zola, whose polemic, *J'accuse*, began the Dreyfus Affair, used his time in exile to write his novel *Fecondité*. This celebration of the archtypical French family of an artisan-turned-farmer and his fruitful wife and daughters, was part of Zola's multifaceted effort to instruct the French population on its duties in the dizzying circumstances of social change. Offen, "Depopulation," 663 discusses this in more detail.

32 Madeleine Rebérioux et al., "Hubertine Auclert et la question des femmes à 'l'immortel congrès' (1879)," *Romantisme: Revue du dix-neuvième siècle*, nos. 13–14 (1976): 133.

33 Offen, "Depopulation," 652.

34 Rebérioux, "Hubertine Auclert." For a detailed description of the opposition to expanded female suffrage in the interwar years, led by the Radicals, but quietly accepted by the Socialists, see Jane Jenson, "Changing Discourse, Changing Agendas: Political Rights and Reproductive Policies in France," in *The Women's Movement of Western Europe and the USA: Consciousness, Political Opportunity and Public Policy*, ed. Mary Katzenstein and Carol Mueller (Philadelphia: Temple University Press, 1987).

35 In early nineteenth-century France, utopians like Saint Simon and Fourier, with their commitment to the emancipation of women, were ousted in conflict within the labor movement by the followers of Proudhon, whose strict gender-based division of labor gave women the famous choice between being "housewives or harlots." Thus, by mid-century, emancipatory feminism was overwhelmed. But Proudhonism lost its hegemony in the latter part of the century.

36 Charles Sowerwine, "Workers and Women in France before 1914: The Debate over the Couriau Affair," *Journal of Modern History*, vol. 55, 9 (1983): 412.

37 There was never the same emphasis on the family wage in France as in the United

States, even in the nineteenth century. The family wage was advocated by a few union activists, but its definition was quite different in France. The family wage meant a family income sufficient to support any size family, *no matter the number of children*. In other words, it was a concept that made no reference to the activities or earning potential of women; it was directed towards the needs of children.

38 Sowerwine, "The Coriau Affair"; Marie-Hélène Zylberberg-Hocquard, *Féminisme et syndicalisme en France* (Paris: Anthropos, 1978), chap. III.

39 In Britain the exclusion of women from the workplace occurred earlier, when the trade union movement became dominated by a discourse of the family wage, protection of women and children, and separate spheres. Jenson, "Babies and the State," 31.

40 On Solidarism, see John Weiss, "Origins of the French Welfare System: Poor Relief in the Third Republic, 1871–1914," *French Historical Studies*, vol. XIII, no. 1 (Spring 1983): 47–78; J. E. S. Hayward, "The Official Social Philosophy of the French Third Republic: Léon Bourgeois and Solidarism," *International Review of Social History* 6 (1961): 19–48.

41 They did insist, of course, that women's rights had to be expanded if they were to perform their duties, and feminists demanded improvements in the conditions . of maternity, women's education, and working conditions. See Offen, "Depopulation," 652.

42 For the development of this conceptualization see Stephen Skowronek, *Building a New American State: The Expansion of National Administrative Capacities, 1877–1920* (Cambridge: Cambridge University Press, 1982).

43 Martin Shefter, "Trade Unions and Political Machines: The Organization and Disorganization of the American Working Class in the Late Nineteenth Century" in *Working-Class Formation: Nineteenth-Century Patterns in Western Europe and the United States*, ed. Ira Katznelson and Aristide Zolberg (Princeton, N.J.: Princeton University Press, 1986), 199ff.

44 Skowronek, *Building a New American State*, Part II, Introduction.

45 Skowronek, *Building a New American State*, 41.

46 A second limit was the politicization by parties of the bureaucracy, which weakened the initial design of a merit-based civil service. On both aspects, see Skowronek, *Building a New American State*, 166ff.

47 This argument provides the major theme in Nancy Cott, *The Grounding of Modern Feminism* (New Haven, Conn.: Yale University Press, 1987), Introduction.

48 Gordon, *Woman's Body, Woman's Right*, 99ff.

49 This double discourse clearly characterized the nineteenth-century woman movement, as Cott describes it. It also extended into pre-1914 feminism. As Cott writes: "By that time [1910] suffragists were as likely to argue that women deserved the vote *because* of their sex—because women as a group had relevant benefits to bring and interests to defend in the polity—as to argue that women deserved the vote *despite* their sex." *The Grounding of Modern Feminism*, 29.

50 Gordon, *Woman's Body, Woman's Right*, xv.

51 Gordon, *Woman's Body, Woman's Right*, chap. 6.

52 On the accusation of effeminacy, see Paula Baker, "The Domestication of Politics: Women and American Political Society, 1780–1920," this volume.

53 For a discussion of "scientific motherhood" and its diversion into the discourse of "race suicide," see Gordon, *Woman's Body, Woman's Right*, 129ff.

54 Nancy Cott argues that the link between Progressive politics and the woman's movement was around the discourse of difference. *The Grounding of Modern Feminism*, 21.

55 This is the main thesis of Shefter, "Trade Unions and Political Machines."

56 See Lehrer, *Origins of Protective Labor Legislation*, 126, 142, and chap. 7 *passim*. The labor movement was the leader in demands for protective legislation for women until 1890. After that middle-class reformers directed the campaign. See Baer, *The Chains of Protection*, 33.

57 This analysis of the WTUL is primarily from Nancy Schrom Dye, "Feminism or Unionism? The New York Women's Trade Union League and the Labor Movement," *Signs* 3, nos. 1–2 (1975): 111–25; Lehrer, *Origins of Protective Legislation*, chap. 6.

58 The difficulties that the WTUL encountered in fitting women's skills into the recognized skill categories used by the AFL reflects the long-standing gender conflict over who will define skill. For a discussion of the gendering effects of such definitional struggles see Jane Jenson, "The Talents of Women, The Skills of Men: Flexible Specialization and Women," in *The Transformation of Work?*, ed. Stephen Wood (London: Unwin Hyman, 1989).

59 But for the AFL, the most important gain women could make would come when their husbands negotiated a family wage through collective bargaining. See Lehrer, *Origins of Protective Labor Legislation*, 142–44.

60 Cott, *The Grounding of Modern Feminism*, chap. 8.

61 Cott, *The Grounding of Modern Feminism*, 24.

62 For an examination of the legacies of these strengths and weaknesses in contemporary French feminism see Jenson, "Friend or Foe."

CHAPTER 7

Family Violence, Feminism, and Social Control

LINDA GORDON

In studying the history of family violence, I found myself also confronting the issue of social control, incarnated in the charitable "friendly visitors" and later professional child protection workers who composed the case records I was reading. At first I experienced these social-control agents as intruding themselves unwanted into my research. My study was based on the records of Boston "child-saving" agencies, in which the oppressions of class, culture, and gender were immediately evident. The "clients" were mainly poor, Catholic, female immigrants. (It was not that women were responsible for most of the family violence but that they were more often involved with agencies for reasons we shall see.) The social workers were exclusively well educated and male and overwhelmingly White Anglo-Saxon Protestant (WASP). These workers, authors of case records, were often disdainful, ignorant, and obtuse —at best, paternalistic—toward their clients.

Yet, ironically, these very biases created a useful discipline, showing that it was impossible to study family violence as an objective problem. Attempts at social control were part of the original definition and construction of family violence as a social issue. The very concept of family violence is a product of conflict and negotiation between people troubled by domestic violence and social-control agents attempting to change their supposedly unruly and deviant behavior.

In this essay I want to argue not a defense of social control but a critique of its critiques and some thoughts about a better, feminist framework. I would like to make my argument as it came to me, through studying child abuse and neglect. Nine years ago when I began to study the history of family violence, I assumed I would be focusing largely on wife beating because that was the target of the contemporary feminist activism, which had drawn my attention to the problem. I was surprised, however, to find that violence against children represented a more complex challenge to the task of envisioning feminist family policy and a feminist theory of social control.

SOCIAL CONTROL

Many historians of women and the family have inherited a critical view of social control, as an aspect of domination and the source of decline in family and individual autonomy. In situating ourselves with respect to this tradition, it may be useful to trace very briefly the history of the concept. "Social control" is a phrase usually attributed to the sociologist E. A. Ross. He used the phrase as the title of a collection of his essays in 1901, referring to the widest range of influence and regulation societies imposed upon individuals.[1] Building on a Hobbesian view of human individuals as naturally in conflict, Ross saw "social control" as inevitable. Moving beyond liberal individualism, however, he argued for social control in a more specific, American Progressive sense. Ross advocated the active, deliberate, expert guidance of human life not only as the source of human progress but also as the best replacement for older, familial, and communitarian forms of control, which he believed were disappearing in modern society.

Agencies attempting to control family violence are preeminent examples of the kind of expert social-control institutions that were endorsed by Ross and other Progressive reformers. These agencies—the most typical were the Societies for the Prevention of Cruelty to Children (SPCCs)—were established in the 1870s in a decade of acute international alarm about child abuse. They began as punitive and moralistic "charitable" endeavors, characteristic of nineteenth-century elite moral purity reforms. These societies blamed the problem of family violence on the depravity, immorality, and drunkenness of individuals, which they often traced to the innate inferiority of the immigrants, who constituted the great bulk of their targets. By the early twentieth century, the SPCCs took on a more ambitious task, hoping not merely to cure family pathology but also to reform family life and child raising. Describing the change slightly differently, in the nineteenth century, child protection agents saw themselves as paralegal, punishing specific offenses, protecting children from specific dangers; in the early twentieth century, they tried to supervise and direct the family lives of those considered deviant.

The view that intervention into the family has increased, and has become a characteristic feature of modern society, is now often associated with Talcott Parsons's writings of the late 1940s and 1950s. Parsons proposed the "transfer of functions" thesis, the notion that professionals had taken over many family functions (e.g., education, child care, therapy, and medical care). Parsons's was a liberal, optimistic view; he thought this professionalization a step forward, leaving the family free to devote more of its time and energy to affective relations. There was already a contrasting, far more pessimistic, interpretation, emanating from the Frankfurt school of German Marxists, who condemned the decline of family autonomy and even attributed to it, in part, the horrors of totalitarianism.

The latter tradition, critical of social control, has conditioned most of the historical writing about social-control agencies and influences. Much of the earlier work in this mid-twentieth-century revival of women's history adopted this perspective on social control, substituting gender for class or national categories in the analysis of women's subordination. In the field of child saving in particular, the most influential historical work has adopted this perspective.[2] These critiques usually distinguished an "us" and a "them," oppressed and oppressor, in a dichotomous relation. They were usually functionalist: they tended to assume or argue that the social-control practices in question served (were functional for) the material interests of a dominant group and hindered (were dysfunctional to) the interests of the subordinate. More recently, some women's historians have integrated class and gender into this model, arguing that the growth of the state in the last 150 years has increased individual rights for prosperous women but has only subjected poor women to ever greater control.[3] Alternatively, women's historians represent social control as half of a bargain in which material benefits—welfare benefits, for example—are given to those controlled in exchange for the surrender of power or autonomy.[4]

The development of women's history in the last decade has begun to correct some of the oversimplifications of this "anti–social-control" school of analysis. A revival of what might be called the Beardian tradition (after Mary Beard) recognizes women's activity—in this case, in constructing modern forms of social control.[5] Historians of social work or other social-control institutions, however, have not participated in the rethinking of the paradigm of elite domination and plebian victimization.[6]

The critique of the domination exercised by social work and human services bureaucracies and professionals is not wrong, but its incompleteness allows for some serious distortion. My own views derive from a study of the history of family violence and its social control in Boston from 1880 to 1960, using both the quantitative and qualitative analysis of case records from three leading child-saving agencies.[7] Looking at these records from the perspective of children and their primary caretakers (and abusers), women, reveals the impoverishment of the anti–social-control perspective sketched previously and its inadequacy to the task of conceptualizing who is controlled and who is controlling in these family conflicts. A case history may suggest some of the complexities that have influenced my thinking.

In 1910 a Syrian family in Boston's South End, here called the Kashys, came to the attention of the Massachusetts Society for the Prevention of Cruelty to Children (MSPCC) because of the abuse of the mother's thirteen-year-old girl.[8] Mr. Kashy had just died of appendicitis. The family, like so many immigrants, had moved back and forth between Syria and the United States several times; two other children had been left in Syria with their paternal grandparents. In this country, in addition to the central "victim," whom I shall call Fatima, there was a six-year-old boy and a three-year-old girl, and Mrs. Kashy was pregnant. The complainant was the father's sister, and indeed all the paternal relatives were hostile to Mrs. Kashy. The MSPCC investigation substantiated their allegations: Mrs. Kashy hit Fatima with a stick and with chairs, bit her ear, kept her from school, and overworked her, expecting her to do all the housework and to care for the younger children. When Fatima fell ill, her mother refused to let her go to the hospital. The hostility of the paternal relatives, however, focused not only on the mother's treatment of Fatima but mainly on her custody rights. It was their position that custody should have fallen to them after Mr. Kashy's death, arguing that "in Syria a woman's rights to the care of her chn [abbreviations in original] or the control of property is not recognized." In Syrian tradition, the paternal grandfather had rights to the children, and he had delegated this control to his son, the children's paternal uncle.

The paternal kin, then, had expected Mrs. Kashy to bow to their rights; certainly her difficult economic and social situation would make it understandable if she had. The complainant, the father's sister, was Mrs. Kashy's landlady and was thus in a position to make her life very difficult. Mrs. Kashy lived with her three children in one attic room without water; she had to go to the ground level and carry water up to her apartment. The relatives offered her no help after her bereavement and Mrs. Kashy was desperate; she was trying to earn a living by continuing her husband's peddling. She needed Fatima to keep the house and care for the children.

When Mrs. Kashy resisted their custody claims, the paternal relatives called in as a mediator a Syrian community leader, publisher of the *New Syria*, a Boston Arabic-language newspaper. Ultimately the case went to court, however, and here the relatives lost as their custody traditions conflicted with the new preference in the United States for women's custody. Fatima's wishes were of no help to the agency in sorting out this conflict, because throughout the struggle she was ambivalent: sometimes she begged to be kept away from her mother, yet when away, she begged to be returned to her mother. Ultimately, Mrs. Kashy won custody but no material help in supporting her children by herself. As in so many child abuse cases, it was the victim who was punished: Fatima was sent to the Gwynne Home, where—at least so her relatives believed—she was treated abusively.

If the story had stopped there one might be tempted to see Mrs. Kashy as relatively blameless, driven perhaps to episodes of harshness and temper by her difficult lot. But thirteen years later, in 1923, a "school visitor" brought the second daughter, now sixteen, to the MSPCC to complain of abuse by her mother and by her older, now married, sister Fatima. In the elapsed years, this second daughter had been sent back to Syria; perhaps Mrs. Kashy had had to give up her efforts to support her children. Returning to the United States eighteen months previously, the girl had arrived to find that her mother intended to marry her involuntarily to a boarder. The daughter displayed blood on her shirt, which she said came from her mother's beatings. Interviewed by an MSPCC agent, Mrs. Kashy was now openly hostile and defiant, saying that she would beat her daughter as she liked.

In its very complexity, the Kashy case exemplifies certain generalizations central to my argument. One is that it is often difficult to identify a unique victim. It should not be surprising that the oppressed Mrs. Kashy was angry and violent, but feminist rhetoric about family violence has often avoided this complexity. Mrs. Kashy was the victim of her isolation, widowhood, single motherhood, and patriarchal, hostile in-laws; she also exploited and abused her daughter. Indeed, Mrs. Kashy's attitude to Fatima was patriarchal: she believed that children should serve parents and not vice versa. This aspect of patriarchal tradition served Mrs. Kashy. But, in other respects, the general interests of the oppressed group—here the Syrian immigrants—as expressed by its male, *petit bourgeois* leadership, were more inimical to Mrs. Kashy's (and other women's) aspirations and "rights" than those of the elite agency, the MSPCC. Furthermore, one can reasonably surmise that the daughters were also actors in this drama, resisting their mother's expectations as well as those of the male-dominated community, as New World ideas of children's rights coincided with aspirations entirely their own. None of the existing social control critiques can adequately conceptualize the complex struggles in the Kashy family, nor can they propose nonoppressive ways for Fatima's "rights" to be protected.

FEMINISM AND CHILD ABUSE

Feminist theory in general and women's history in particular have moved only slowly beyond the "victimization" paradigm that dominated the rebirth of feminist scholarship. The obstacles to perceiving and describing women's own power have been particularly great in issues relating to social policy and to family violence, because of the legacy of victim blaming. Defending women against male violence is so urgent that we fear women's loss of status as deserving, political "victims" if we acknowledge women's own aggressions. These complexities are at their greatest in the situation of mothers because they are simultaneously victims and victimizers, dependent and depended on, weak and powerful.

If feminist theory needs a new view of social control, thinking about child abuse virtually demands it. Child abuse cases reveal suffering that is incontrovertible, unnecessary, and remediable. However severe the biases of the social workers attempting to "save" the children and reform their parents—and I will have more to say about this later—one could not advocate a policy of inaction in regard to children chained to beds, left in filthy diapers for days, turned out in the cold. Children, unlike women, lack even the potential for social and economic independence. A beneficial social policy could at least partly address the problem of wife beating by empowering women to leave abusive situations, enabling them to live in comfort and dignity without men, and encouraging them to espouse high standards in their expectations of treatment by others. It is not clear how one could empower children in analogous ways. If children are to have "rights" then some adults must be appointed and accepted, by other adults, to define and defend them.

Women, who do most of the labor of child care, have the strongest emotional bonds to children, fought for and largely won rights to child custody over the last 150 years. Yet women are often the abusers and neglecters of children. Indeed, child abuse becomes the more interesting and challenging to feminists because in it we meet women's rage and abuses of power. Furthermore, child abuse is a gendered phenomenon, related to the oppression of women, whether women or men are the culprits, because it reflects the sexual division of the labor of reproduction. Because men spend, on the whole, so much less time with children than do women, what is remarkable is not that women are violent toward children but that men are responsible for nearly half of the child abuse. But women are always implicated because even when men are the culprits, women are usually the primary caretakers who have been, by definition, unable to protect the children. When protective organizations remove children or undertake supervision of their caretakers, women often suffer greatly, for their maternal work, trying as it may be, is usually the most pleasurable part of their lives.

Yet in the last two decades of intense publicity and scholarship about child abuse, the feminist contribution has been negligible. This silence is the more striking in contrast to the legacy of the first wave of feminism, particularly in the period 1880 to 1930, in which the women's rights movement was tightly connected to child welfare reform campaigns. By contrast, the second wave of feminism, a movement heavily influenced by younger and childless women, has spent relatively little energy on children's issues. Feminist scholars have studied the social organization of mothering in theory but not the actual experiences of child raising, and the movement as a whole has not significantly influenced child welfare debates or policies. When such issues emerge publicly, feminists too often assume that women's and children's interests always coincide. The facts of child abuse and neglect challenge this assumption as does the necessity sometimes of severing maternal custody in order to protect children.

PROTECTING CHILDREN

Child abuse was "discovered" as a social problem in the 1870s. Surely many children had been ill-treated by parents before this, but new social conditions created an increased sensitivity to the treatment of children and, possibly, actually worsened children's lot. Conditions of labor and family life under industrial capitalism may have made poverty, stress, and parental anger bear more heavily on children. The child abuse alarm also reflected growing class and cultural differences in beliefs about how children *should* be raised. The anti-cruelty-to-children movement grew out of an anti-corporal-punishment campaign, and both reflected a uniquely professional-class view that children could be disciplined by reason and with mildness. The SPCCs also grew from widespread fears among more privileged people about violence and "depravity" among the urban poor; in the United States, these fears were exacerbated by the fact that these poor were largely immigrants and Catholics, threatening the WASP domination of city culture and government.

On one level, my study of the case records of Boston child-saving agencies corroborated the anti-social-control critique: the work of the agencies did represent oppressive intervention into working-class families. The MSPCC attempted to enforce culturally specific norms of proper parenting that were not only alien to the cultural legacy of their "clients" but also flew in the face of many of the economic necessities of the clients' lives. Thus, MSPCC agents prosecuted cases in which cruelty to children was caused, in their view, by children's labor: girls doing housework and child care, often staying home from school because their parents required it; girls and boys working in shops, peddling on the streets; boys working for organ grinders and lying about their ages to enlist in the navy. Before World War I, the enemies of the truant officers were usually parents, not children. To immigrants from peasant backgrounds it seemed irrational and blasphemous that adult women should work while able-bodied children remained idle. Similarly, the MSPCC was opposed to the common immigrant practice of leaving children unattended and allowing them to play and wander in the streets. Both violated the MSPCC's norm of domesticity for women and children; proper middle-class children in those days did not—at least not in the cities—play outside on their own.

The child savers were attempting to impose a new, middle-class urban style of mothering and fathering. Mothers were supposed to be tender and gentle and above all, to protect their children from immoral influences; the child savers considered yelling, rude language, or sexually explicit talk to be forms of cruelty to children. Fathers were to provide models of emotional containment, to be relatively uninvolved with children; their failure to provide adequate economic support was often interpreted as a character flaw, no matter what the evidence of widespread, structural unemployment.

MSPCC agents in practice and in rhetoric expressed disdain for immigrant cultures. They hated the garlic and olive oil smells of Italian cooking and considered this food unhealthy (overstimulating, aphrodisiac). The agents were unable to distinguish alcoholics and heavy drinkers from moderate wine and beer drinkers, and they believed that women who took spirits were degenerate and unfit as mothers. They associated many of these forms of depravity with Catholicism. Agents were also convinced of the subnormal intelligence of most non-WASP and especially non–English-speaking clients; indeed, the agents' comments and expectations in this early period were similar to social workers' views of black clients in the mid-twentieth century. These child welfare specialists were particularly befuddled by and disapproving of nonnuclear child-raising patterns: children raised by grandmothers, complex households composed of children from several different marriages (or, worse, out-of-wedlock relationships), children sent temporarily to other households.

The peasant backgrounds of so many of the "hyphenated" Americans created a situation in which ethnic bias could not easily be separated from class bias. Class misunderstanding, moreover, took a form specific to urban capitalism: a failure to grasp the actual economic and physical circumstances of this immigrant proletariat and subproletariat. Unemployment was not yet understood to be a structural characteristic of industrial capitalism. Disease, overcrowding, crime, and—above all—dependence were also not understood to be part of the system, but, rather, were seen as personal failings.

This line of criticism, however, only partially uncovers the significance of child protection. Another dimension and a great deal more complexity are revealed by considering the feminist aspect of the movement. Much of the child welfare reform energy of the nineteenth century came from women and was organized by the "woman movement."[9] The campaign against corporal punishment, from which the anti-child-abuse movement grew, depended upon a critique of violence rooted in feminist thought and in women's reform activity. Women's reform influence, the "sentimentalizing" of the Calvinist traditions,[10] was largely responsible for the softening of child-raising norms. The delegitimation of corporal punishment, noticeable among the prosperous classes by mid-century, was associated with exclusive female responsibility for child raising, with women's victories in child custody cases, even with women's criticisms of traditionally paternal discipline.[11]

Feminist thinking exerted an important influence on the agencies' original formulations of the problem of family violence. Most MSPCC spokesmen (and those who represented the agency in public were men) viewed men as aggressors and women and children, jointly, as blameless victims. However simplistic, this was a feminist attitude. It was also, of course, saturated with class and cultural elitism: these "brutal" and "depraved" men were of a different class and ethnicity than the MSPCC agents, and the language of victimization applied to women and children was also one of condescension. Nevertheless, despite the definition of the "crime" as cruelty to children, MSPCC agents soon included wife beating in their agenda of reform.

Even more fundamentally, the very undertaking of child protection was a challenge to patriarchal relations. A pause to look at my definition of patriarchy is necessary here. In the 1970s a new definition of that term came into use, first proposed by Kate Millett but quickly adopted by the United States feminist movement: patriarchy became a synonym for male supremacy, for "sexism." I use the term in its earlier, historical, and more specific sense, referring to a family form in which fathers had control over all other family members—children, women, and servants. This concept of a patriarchal family is an abstraction, postulating common features among family forms that differed widely across geography and time. If there was a common material base supporting this patriarchal family norm (a question requiring a great deal more study before it can be answered decisively), it was an economic system in which the family was the unit of production. Most of the MSPCC's early clients came from peasant societies in which this kind of family economy prevailed. In these families, fathers maintained control not only over property and tools but also, above all, over the labor power of family members. Historical patriarchy defined a set of parent-child relations as much as it did relations between the sexes, for children rarely had opportunities for economic independence except by inheriting the family property, trade, or craft. In some ways mothers, too, benefited from patriarchal parent-child relations. Their authority over daughters and young sons was important when they lacked other kinds of authority and independence, and in old age they gained respect, help, and consideration from younger kinfolk.

The claim of an organization such as an SPCC to speak on behalf of children's rights, its claim to the license to intervene in parental treatment of children, was an attack on patriarchal power. At the same time, the new sensibility about children's rights and the concern about child abuse were symptoms of a weakening of patriarchal family expectations and realities that had already taken place, particularly during the eighteenth and early nineteenth centuries in the United States. In this weakening, father-child relations had changed more than husband-wife relations. Children had, for example, gained the power to arrange their own betrothals and marriages and to embark on wage work independent of their fathers' occupations (of course, children's options remained determined by class and cultural privileges or the lack of them, inherited from fathers). In contrast, however, wage labor and long-distance mobility often made women, on balance, more dependent on husbands for sustenance and less able to deploy kinfolk and neighbors to defend their interests against husbands.

Early child protection work did not, of course, envision a general liberation of children from arbitrary parental control or from the responsibility of filial obedience. On the contrary, the SPCCs aimed as much to reinforce a failing parental/paternal authority as to limit it. Indeed, the SPCC spokesmen often criticized excessive physical violence against children as a symptom of inadequate parental authority. Assaults on children were provoked by children's insubordination; in the interpretation of nineteenth-century child protectors, this showed that parental weakness, children's disobedience, and child abuse were mutually reinforcing. Furthermore, by the turn of the century, the SPCCs discovered that the majority of their cases concerned neglect, not assault, and neglect exemplified to them the problems created by the withdrawal, albeit not always conscious or deliberate, of parental supervision and authority (among the poor who formed the agency clientele there were many fathers who deserted and many more who were inadequate providers). Many neglect and abuse cases ended with *children* being punished, sent to reform schools on stubborn child charges.

In sum, the SPCCs sought to reconstruct the family along lines that altered the old patriarchy, already economically unviable, and to replace it with a modern version of male supremacy. The SPCCs' rhetoric about children's rights did not extend to a parallel articulation of women's rights; their condemnation of wife beating did not include endorsement of the kind of marriage later called "companionate," implying equality between wife and husband. Their new family and child-raising norms included the conviction that children's respect for parents needed to be inculcated ideologically, moralistically, and psychologically because it no longer rested on an economic dependence lasting beyond childhood. Fathers, now as wage laborers rather than as slaves, artisans, peasants, or entrepreneurs, were to have single-handed responsibility for economic support of their families; women and children should not contribute to the family economy, at least not monetarily. Children instead should spend full-time in learning cognitive lessons from professional teachers, psychological and moral lessons from the full-time attention of a mother. In turn, women should devote themselves to mothering and domesticity.

FEMINISM, MOTHERING, AND INDUSTRIAL CAPITALISM

This child-raising program points to a larger irony—that the "modernization" of male domination, its adaptation to new economic and social conditions, was partly a result of the influence of the first wave of feminism. These first "feminists" rarely advocated full equality between women and men and never promoted the abolition of traditional gender relations or the sexual division

of labor. Allowing for differences of emphasis, the program just defined constituted a feminist as well as a liberal family reform program in the 1870s.
Indeed, organized feminism *was* in part such a liberal reform program, a program to adapt the family and the civil society to the new economic conditions
of industrial capitalism, for consciously or not, feminists felt that these new
conditions provided greater possibilities for the freedom and empowerment of
women.

To recapitulate, child protection work was an integral part of the feminist
as well as the bourgeois program for modernizing the family. Child-saving
had gender as well as class and ethnic content, but in none of these aspects
did it simply or homogeneously represent the interests of a dominant group
(or even of the composite group of WASP elite women, that hypothetical
stratum on which it is fashionable to blame the limitations of feminist activity). The antipatriarchalism of the child protection agencies was an unstable
product of several conflicting interests. Understanding this illuminates the influence of feminism on the development of a capitalist industrial culture even
as feminists criticized the new privileges it bestowed on men and its degradation of women's traditional work. The relation of feminism to capitalism and
industrialism is usually argued in dichotomous and reductionist fashion: either
feminism is the expression of bourgeois woman's aspirations, an ultimate individualism that tears apart the remaining noninstrumental bonds in a capitalist
society; *or,* feminism is inherently anticapitalist, deepening and extending the
critique of domination to show its penetration even of personal life and the allegedly "natural." Although there is a little truth in both versions, at least one
central aspect of feminism's significance for capitalism has been omitted in
these formulations—its role in redefining family norms and particularly norms
of mothering.

Changes in the conditions of motherhood in an industrializing society were
an important part of the experiences that drew women to the postbellum feminist movement. For most women, and particularly for urban poor women,
motherhood became more difficult in wage labor conditions. Mothers were
more isolated from support networks of kin, and mothering furthered that isolation, often requiring that women remain out of public space. The potential
dangers from which children needed protection multiplied, and the increasing
cultural demands for a "psychological parenting" increased the potential for
maternal "failure." [12] These changes affected women of all classes, while, at
the same time, motherhood remained the central identity for women of all
classes. Childbirth and child raising, the most universal parts of female experience, were the common referents—the metaphoric base of political language
—by which feminist ideas were communicated.

As industrial capitalism changed the conditions of motherhood, so women
began to redefine motherhood in ways that would influence the entire culture.

They "used" motherhood simultaneously to increase their own status, to promote greater social expenditure on children, and to loosen their dependence
on men, just as capitalists "used" motherhood as a form of unpaid labor.
The working-class and even sub-working-class women of the child abuse case
records drew "feminist" conclusions—that is, they diagnosed their problems
in terms of male supremacy—in their efforts to improve their own conditions of
mothering. In their experiences, men's greater power (economic and social),
in combination with men's lesser sense of responsibility toward children, kept
them from being as good at mothering as they wanted. They responded by
trying to rid themselves of those forms of male domination that impinged most
directly on their identity and work as mothers and on children's needs as they
interpreted those needs.

But if child protection work may have represented *all* mothers' demands, it
made *some* mothers—poor urban mothers—extremely vulnerable by calling
into question the quality of their mothering, already made more problematic
by urban wage labor living conditions, and by threatening them with the loss of
their children. Poor women had less privacy and therefore less impunity in their
deviance from the new child-raising norms, but their poverty often led them to
ask for help from relief agencies, therefore calling themselves to the attention
of the child-saving networks. Yet poor women did not by any means figure
only on the victim side, for they were also often enthusiastic about defending
children's "rights" and correcting cruel or neglectful parents. Furthermore,
they used an eclectic variety of arguments and devices to defend their control of their children. At times they mobilized liberal premises and rhetoric to
escape from patriarchal households and to defend their custody rights; they
were quick to learn the right language of the New World in which to criticize
their husbands and relatives and to manipulate social workers to side with them
against patriarchal controls of other family members. Yet at other times they
called upon traditional relations when community and kinfolk could help them
retain control or defend children. Poor women often denounced the "intervention" of outside social control agencies like the SPCCs but only when it suited
them, and at other times they eagerly used and asked such agencies for help.

Let me offer another case history to illustrate this opportunistic and resource-
ful approach to social control agencies. An Italian immigrant family, which
I will call the Amatos, were "clients" of the MSPCC from 1910 to 1916.[13]
They had five young children from the current marriage and Mrs. Amato had
three from a previous marriage, two of them still in Italy and one daughter
in Boston. Mrs. Amato kept that daughter at home to do housework and look
after the younger children while she earned money doing piece rate sewing at
home. This got the family in trouble with a truant officer, and they were also
accused, in court, of lying to Associated Charities (a consortium of private
relief agencies), saying that the father had deserted them when he was in fact

living at home. Furthermore, once while left alone, probably in the charge of a sibling, one of the younger children fell out of a window and had to be hospitalized. This incident provoked agency suspicions that the mother was negligent.

Despite her awareness of these suspicions against her, Mrs. Amato sought help from many different organizations, starting with those of the Italian immigrant community and then reaching out to elite social work agencies, reporting that her husband was a drunkard, a gambler, a nonsupporter, and a wife beater. The MSPCC agents at first doubted her claims because Mr. Amato impressed them as a "good and sober man," and they blamed the neglect of the children on his wife's incompetence in managing the wages he gave her. The MSPCC ultimately became convinced of Mrs. Amato's story because of her repeated appearance with severe bruises and the corroboration of the husband's father, who was intimately involved in the family troubles and took responsibility for attempting to control his son. Once the father came to the house and gave his son "a warning and a couple of slaps," after which he improved for a while. Another time the father extracted from him a pledge not to beat his wife for two years!

Mrs. Amato wanted none of this. She begged the MSPCC agent to help her get a divorce; later she claimed that she had not dared take this step because her husband's relatives threatened to beat her if she tried it. Then Mrs. Amato's daughter (from her previous marriage) took action, coming independently to the MSPCC to bring an agent to the house to help her mother. As a result of this complaint, Mr. Amato was convicted of assault once and sentenced to six months. During that time Mrs. Amato survived by "a little work and . . . Italian friends have helped her." Her husband returned, more violent than before: he went at her with an axe, beat the children so much on the head that their "eyes wabbled [sic]" permanently, and supported his family so poorly that the children went out begging. This case closed, like so many, without a resolution.

The Amatos' case will not support the usual anti-social-control interpretation of the relation between oppressed clients and social agencies. There was no unity among the client family and none among the professional intervenors. Furthermore, the intervenors were often dragged into the case and by individuals with conflicting points of view. Mrs. Amato and Mrs. Kashy were not atypical in their attempts to use "social control" agencies in their own interests. Clients frequently initiated agency intervention; even in family violence cases, where the stakes were high—losing one's children—the majority of complaints in this study came from parents or close relatives who believed that their own standards of child raising were being violated.[14]

In their sparring with social work agencies, clients did not usually or collectively win because the professionals had more resources. Usually no one decisively "won." Considering these cases collectively, professional social work overrode working-class or poor people's interests, but in specific cases the professionals did not always formulate definite goals, let alone achieve them. Indeed, the bewilderment of the social workers (something usually overlooked because most scholarship about social work is based on policy statements, not on actual case records) frequently enabled the clients to go some distance toward achieving their own goals.

The social-control experience was not a simple two-sided tradeoff in which the client sacrificed autonomy and control in return for some material help. Rather, the clients helped shape the nature of the social control itself. Formulating these criticisms about the inadequacy of simple anti-social-control explanations in some analytic order, I would make four general points.

First, the condemnation of agency intervention into the family, and the condemnation of social control itself as something automatically evil, usually assumes that there can be, and once was, an autonomous family. On the contrary, no family relations have been immune from social regulation.[15] Certainly the forms of social control I examine here are qualitatively and quantitatively different, based on regulation from "outside," by those without a legitimate claim to caring about local, individual values and traditions. Contrasting the experience of social control to a hypothetical era of autonomy, however, distorts both traditional and modern forms of social regulation.

The tendency to consider social control as unprecedented, invasive regulation is not only an academic mistake. It grew from nineteenth-century emotional and political responses to social change. Family autonomy became a symbol of patriarchy only in its era of decline (as in 1980s' New Right rhetoric). Family "autonomy" was an oppositional concept in the nineteenth century, expressing a liberal ideal of home as a private and caring space in contrast to the public realm of increasingly instrumental relations. This symbolic cluster surrounding the family contained both critical and legitimating responses to industrial capitalist society. But as urban society created more individual opportunities for women, the defense of family autonomy came to stand against women's autonomy in a conservative opposition to women's demands for individual freedoms. (The concept of family autonomy today, as it is manipulated in political discourse, mainly has the latter function, suggesting that women's individual rights to autonomous citizenship will make the family more vulnerable to outside intervention). The Amatos' pattern, a more patriarchal pattern, of turning to relatives, friends, and, when they could not help, Italian-American organizations (no doubt the closest analogue to a "community" in the New World), was not adequate to the urban problems they now encountered. Even the violent and defensive Mr. Amato did not question the right of his father, relatives, and friends to intervene forcibly, and Mrs. Amato did not appear shocked that her husband's relatives tried, perhaps successfully, to hold her forcibly in her marriage. Family autonomy was not an expectation of the Amatos.

Second, the social-control explanation sees the flow of initiative going in only one direction: from top to bottom, from professionals to clients, from elite to subordinate. The power of this interpretation of social work comes from the large proportion of truth it holds and also from the influence of scholars of poor people's movements who have denounced elite attempts to blame "the victims." The case records show, however, that clients were not passive but, rather, active negotiators in a complex bargaining. Textbooks of casework recognize the intense interactions and relationships that develop between social worker and client. In the social work version of concern with countertransference, textbooks often attempt to accustom the social worker to examining her or his participation in that relationship.[16] This sense of mutuality, power struggle, and intersubjectivity, however, has not penetrated historical accounts of social work/social-control encounters.

Third, critics of social control often fail to recognize the active role of agency clients because they conceive of the family as a homogeneous unit. There is an intellectual reification here that expresses itself in sentence structure, particularly in academic language: "The family is in decline," "threats to the family," "the family responds to industrialization." Shorthand expressions attributing behavior to an aggregate such as the family would be harmless except that they often express particular cultural norms about what "the family" is and does, and they mask intrafamily differences and conflicts of interest. Usually "the family" becomes a representation of the interests of the family head, if it is a man, carrying an assumption that all family members share his interests. (Families without a married male head, such as single-parent or grandparent-headed families, are in the common usage broken, deformed, or incomplete families and thus do not qualify for these assumptions regarding family unity). Among the clients in family violence cases, outrage over the intervention into the family was frequently anger over a territorial violation, a challenge to male authority; expressed differently, it was a reaction to the exposure to others of intrafamily conflict and of the family head's lack of control. Indeed, the interventions actually *were* more substantive, more invasive, when their purpose was to change the status quo than if they had been designed to reinforce it. The effect of social workers' involvement was often to change existing family power relations, usually in the interest of the weaker family members.

Social work interventions were often invited by family members; the inviters, however, were usually the weaker members of a family power structure, women and children. These invitations were made despite the fact, well known to clients, that women and children usually had the most to lose (despite fathers' frequent outrage at their loss of face) from MSPCC intervention because by far the most common outcome of agency action was not prosecution and jail sentences but the removal of children, an action fathers dreaded less than mothers. In the immigrant working-class neighborhoods of Boston the MSPCC became known as "the Cruelty," eloquently suggesting poor people's recognition and fear of its power. But these fears did not stop poor people from initiating contact with the organization. After the MSPCC had been in operation ten years, 60 percent of the complaints of known origin (excluding anonymous accusations) came from family members, the overwhelming majority of these from women with children following second. These requests for help came not only from victims but also from mothers distressed that they were not able to raise their children according to their own standards of good parenting. Women also maneuvered to bring child welfare agencies into family struggles on their sides. There was no Society for the Prevention of Cruelty to Women, but in fact women like Mrs. Amato were trying to turn the SPCC into just that. A frequent tactic of beaten, deserted, or unsupported wives was to report their husbands as child abusers; even when investigations found no evidence of child abuse, social workers came into their homes offering, at best, help in getting other things women wanted—such as support payments, separation and maintenance agreements, relief—and, at least, moral support to the women and condemnation of the men.[17]

A fourth problem is that simple social-control explanations often imply that the clients' problems are only figments of social workers' biases. One culture's neglect may be another culture's norm, and in such cultural clashes, one group usually has more power than the other. In many immigrant families, for example, five-year-olds were expected to care for babies and toddlers; to middle-class reformers, five-year-olds left alone were neglected, and their infant charges deserted. Social-control critiques are right to call attention to the power of experts not only to "treat" social deviance but also to define problems in the first place. But the power of labeling, the representation of poor people's behavior by experts whose status is defined through their critique of the problematic behavior of others, coexists with real family oppressions. In one case an immigrant father, who sexually molested his thirteen-year-old daughter, told a social worker that that was the way it was done in the old country. He was not only lying but also trying to manipulate a social worker, perhaps one he had recognized as guilt-ridden over her privileged role, using his own fictitious cultural relativism. His daughter's victimization by incest was not the result of oppression by professionals.

FEMINISM AND LIBERALISM

The overall problem with virtually all existing critiques of social control is that they remain liberal and have in particular neglected what feminists have shown to be the limits of liberalism. Liberalism is commonly conceived as a political and economic theory without social content. In fact, liberal political and economic theory rests on assumptions about the sexual division of labor and on notions of citizens as heads of families.[18] The currently dominant left-wing tradition of anti–social-control critique, that of the Frankfurt school, merely restates these assumptions, identifying the sphere of the "private" as somehow natural, productive of strong egos and inner direction, in contrast to the sphere of the public as invasive, productive of conformity and passivity. If we reject the social premises of liberalism (and of Marx), that gender and the sexual division of labor are natural, then we can hardly maintain the premise that familial forms of social control are inherently benign and public forms are malignant.

Certainly class relations and domination are involved in social control. Child protection work developed and still functions in class society, and the critique of bureaucracies and professionalism has shown the inevitable deformation of attempts to "help" in a society of inequality, where only a few have the power to define what social order should be. But this critique of certain kinds of domination often serves to mask other kinds, particularly those between women and men and between adults and children. And it has predominantly been a critique that emphasizes domination as opposed to conflict.

Social work, and, more generally, aspects of the welfare state have a unique bearing on gender conflicts. Women's subordination in the family, and their struggle against it, not only affected the construction of the welfare state but also the operations of social-control bureaucracies. In fact, social-control agencies such as the MSPCC, and more often, individual social workers, did sometimes help poor and working-class people. They aided the weaker against the stronger and not merely by rendering clients passive. Social work interventions rarely changed assailants' behavior, but they had a greater impact on victims. Ironically, the MSPCC thereby contributed more to help battered women, defined as outside its jurisdiction, than it did abused children. Industrial capitalist society gave women some opportunity to leave abusive men because they could earn their own livings. In these circumstances, even a tiny bit of material help, a mere hint as to how to "work" the relief agencies, could turn these women's aspirations for autonomy into reality. Women could sometimes get this help despite class and ethnic prejudices against them. Italian-American women might reap this benefit even from social workers who held derogatory views of Italians; single mothers might be able to get help in establishing independent households despite charity workers' suspicions of the immorality of their intentions. Just as in diplomacy the enemy of one's enemy may be *ipso facto* a friend, in these domestic dramas the enemy of one's oppressor could be an ally.

These immigrant clients—victims of racism, sexism, and poverty, perhaps occasional beneficiaries of child welfare work—were also part of the creation of modern child welfare standards and institutions. The welfare state was not a bargain in which the poor got material help by giving up control. The control itself was invented and structured out of these interactions. Because many of the MSPCC's early "interventions" were in fact invitations by family members, the latter were in some ways teaching the agents what were appropriate and enforceable standards of child care. A more institutional example is the mothers' pension legislation developed in most of the United States between 1910 and 1920. As I have argued elsewhere, the feminist reformers who campaigned for that reform were influenced by the unending demands of single mothers, abounding in the records of child neglect, for support in raising their children without the benefit of men's wages.[19]

The entire Progressive era's child welfare reform package, the social program of the women's rights movement, and the reforms that accumulated to form the "welfare state" need to be reconceived as not only a campaign spearheaded by elites. They resulted also from a powerful if unsteady pressure for economic and domestic power from poor and working-class women. For them, social work agencies were a resource in their struggle to change the terms of their continuing, traditional, social control, which included but was not limited to the familial. The issues involved in an anti–family-violence campaign were fundamental to poor women: the right to immunity from physical attack at home, the power to protect their children from abuse, the right to keep their children—not merely the legal right to custody but the actual power to support their children—and the power to provide a standard of care for those children that met their own standards and aspirations. That family violence became a social problem at all, that charities and professional agencies were drawn into attempts to control it, were as much a product of the demands of those at the bottom as of those at the top.

Still, if these family and child welfare agencies contributed to women's options, they had a constricting impact too. I do not wish to discard the cumulative insights offered by many critiques of social control. The discrimination and victim blaming women encountered from professionals was considerable, the more so because they were proffered by those defined as "helping." Loss of control was an *experience,* articulated in many different ways by its victims, including those in these same case records. Often the main beneficiaries of professionals' intervention hated them most, because in wrestling with them one rarely gets what one really wants but rather another interpretation of one's needs. An accurate view of the meanings of this "outside" intervention into the family must maintain in its analysis, as the women clients did in their strategic decisions, awareness of a tension between various forms of social control and the variety of factors that might contribute to improvements in personal life. This is a contradiction that women particularly face, and there is no easy resolution of it. There is no returning to an old or newly romanticized "community control" when the remnants of community rest on a patriarchal power structure hostile to women's aspirations. A feminist critique of social control must contain and wrestle with, not seek to eradicate, this tension.

NOTES

Because this paper distills material I have been musing on throughout my work on my book about family violence (*Heroes of Their Own Lives: The History and Politics of Family Violence: Boston 1880–1960* [New York: Viking/Penguin, 1988]), and my intellectual debts are vast. Several friends took the time to read and help me with versions of this essay, including Ros Baxandall, Sara Bershtel, Susan Stanford Friedman, Allen Hunter, Judith Leavitt, Ann Stoler, Susan Schechter, Pauline Terrelonge, Barrie Thorne; I am extremely grateful. Elizabeth Pleck took time out from her own book on the history of family violence to give me the benefit of her detailed critique. I had help in doing this research from Anne Doyle Kenney, Paul O'Keefe, and Jan Lambertz in particular. Discussions with Ellen Bassuk, Wini Breines, Caroline Bynum, Elizabeth Ewen, Stuart Ewen, Marilyn Chapin Massey, and Eve Kosofsky Sedgewick helped me clarify my thoughts.

1   E. A. Ross, *Social Control* (New York, 1901).

2   A few examples follow: Anthony M. Platt, *The Child Savers: The Invention of Delinquency* (Chicago: University of Chicago Press, 1969); Barbara Ehrenreich and Deirdre English, *For Her Own Good: One Hundred and Fifty Years of the Experts' Advice to Women* (Garden City, N.Y.: Anchor/Doubleday: 1978); Christopher Lasch, *Haven in a Heartless World: The Family Besieged* (New York: Basic Books, 1977) and his *The Culture of Narcissism: American Life in an Age of Diminishing Expectations* (New York: Norton, 1979); Jacques Donzelot, *The Policing of Families*, trans. Hurley (New York: Pantheon, 1979); Barbara M. Brenzel, *Daughters of the State: A Social Portrait of the First Reform School for Girls in North America, 1856–1905* (Cambridge: MIT Press, 1983); Stuart Ewen, *Captains of Consciousness: Advertising and the Social Roots of the Consumer Culture* (New York: McGraw-Hill, 1976); Daniel T. Rodgers, *The Work Ethic in Industrial America, 1850–1920* (Chicago: University of Chicago Press, 1974); Nigel Parton, *The Politics of Child Abuse* (New York: St. Martin's Press, 1985).

3   Eileen Boris and Peter Bardaglio, "The Transformation of Patriarchy: The Historic Role of the State," in *Families, Politics, and Public Policy: A Feminist Dialogue on Women and the State*, ed. Irene Diamond (New York: Longman, 1983), 70–93; Judith Areen, "Intervention between Parent and Child: A Reappraisal of the State's Role in Child Neglect and Abuse Cases," *Georgetown Law Journal* 63 (March 1975): 899–902; Mason P. Thomas, Jr., "Child Abuse and Neglect, pt. 1: Historical Overview, Legal Matrix, and Social Perspectives," *North Carolina Law Review* 50 (February 1972): 299–303.

4   John H. Ehrenreich, *The Altruistic Imagination: A History of Social Work and Social Policy in the United States* (Ithaca: Cornell University Press, 1985).

5   Alice Kessler-Harris, *Out to Work: A History of Wage-Earning Women in the United States* (New York: Oxford University Press, 1982), esp. chap. 7; Gwendolyn Wright, *Moralism and the Modern Home: Domestic Architecture and Cultural Conflict in Chicago, 1873–1913* (Chicago: University of Chicago Press, 1980); Kathryn Sklar, "Hull House As a Community of Women in the 1890s," *Signs* 10 (Summer 1985); Susan Ware, *Beyond Suffrage: Women in the New Deal* (Cambridge: Harvard University Press, 1981).

6   Exceptions include Michael C. Grossberg, "Law and the Family in Nineteenth-Century America" (Ph.D. diss., Brandeis University, 1979); Boris and Bardaglio, "The Transformation of Patriarchy."

7   The agencies were the Boston Children's Service Association, the Massachusetts Society for the Prevention of Cruelty to Children, and the Judge Baker Guidance Center. A random sample of cases from every tenth year was coded and analyzed. A summary of the methodology and a sampling of findings can be found in my "Single Mothers and Child Neglect, 1880–1920," *American Quarterly* 37 (Summer 1985): 173–92.

8   Case code no. 2044.

9   In Boston the MSPCC was called into being largely by Kate Gannett Wells, a moral reformer, along with other members of the New England Women's Club and the Moral Education Association. These women were united as much by class as by gender unity. Wells, for example, was an antisuffragist, yet in her club work she cooperated with suffrage militants such as Lucy Stone and Harriet Robinson, for they considered themselves all members of a larger, loosely defined but nonetheless coherent community of prosperous, respectable women reformers. This unity of class and gender purpose was organized feminism at this time. See New England Women's Club Papers, Schlesinger Library; MSPCC Correspondence Files, University of Massachusetts/Boston Archives, folder 1; Arthur Mann, *Yankee Reformers in the Urban Age* (Cambridge: Harvard University Press, 1954), 208.

10 Ann Douglas, *The Feminization of American Culture* (New York: Knopf, 1977).

11 For examples of the growing anti-corporal-punishment campaign, see Lyman Cobb, *The Evil Tendencies of Corporal Punishment As a Means of Moral Discipline in Families and School* (New York, 1847); Mrs. C. A. Hopkinson, *Hints for the Nursery* (Boston, 1863); Mary Blake, *Twenty-Six Hours a Day* (Boston: D. Lothrop, 1883); Bolton Hall, "Education by Assault and Battery," *Arena* 39 (June 1908): 466–67. For historical commentary, see N. Ray Hiner, "Children's Rights, Corporal Punishment, and Child Abuse: Changing American Attitudes, 1870–1920," *Bulletin of the Menninger Clinic* 43, no. 3 (1979): 233–48; Carl F. Kaestle, "Social Change, Discipline, and the Common School in Early Nineteenth-Century America," *Journal of Interdisciplinary History* 9 (Summer 1978): 1–17; Myra C. Glenn, "The Naval Reform Campaign against Flogging: A Case Study in Changing Attitudes toward Corporal Punishment, 1830–1850," *American Quarterly* 35 (Fall 1983): 408–25; Robert Elno McGlone, "Suffer the Children: The Emer-

gence of Modern Middle-Class Family Life in America, 1820–1870" (Ph.D. diss., University of California at Los Angeles, 1971).

12 Nancy Chodorow and Susan Contratto, "The Fantasy of the Perfect Mother," in *Rethinking the Family: Some Feminist Questions*, ed. Barrie Thorne and Marilyn Yalom (New York: Longman, 1982); Joseph Goldstein, Anna Freud, and Albert J. Solnit, *Beyond the Best Interests of the Child* (New York: Free Press, 1973); *Before the Best Interests of the Child* (New York: Free Press, 1979).

13 Case code no. 2042.

14 To this argument it could be responded that it is difficult to define what would be a parent's "own" standards of child raising. In heterogeneous urban situations, child-raising patterns change rather quickly, and new patterns become normative. Certainly the child welfare agencies were part of a "modernization" (in the United States called Americanization) effort, attempting to present new family norms as objectively right. In the poor neighborhoods, however, poverty, crowding, and the structure of housing allowed very little privacy, and the largely immigrant clients resisted these attempts and retained autonomous family patterns, often for several generations. Moreover, my own clinical and research experience suggests that even "anomic" parents, or mothers, to be precise, tend to have extremely firm convictions about right and wrong child-raising methods.

15 Nancy Cott, for example, has identified some of the processes of community involvement in family life in eighteenth-century Massachusetts, in her "Eighteenth-Century Family and Social Life Revealed in Massachusetts Divorce Records," *Journal of Social History* 10 (Fall 1976): 20–43; Ann Whitehead has described the informal regulation of marital relations that occurred in pub conversations in her "Sexual Antagonism in Herefordshire," in *Dependence and Exploitation in Work and Marriage*, ed. Diana Leonard Barker and Sheila Allen (London: Longman, 1976), 169–203.

16 For example, see William Jordan, *The Social Worker in Family Situations* (London: Routledge & Kegan Paul, 1972); James W. Green, *Cultural Awareness in the Human Services* (Englewood Cliffs, N.J.: Prentice-Hall, 1982); Alfred Kadushin, *Child Welfare Services* (New York: Macmillan, 1980), chap. 13.

17 Indeed, so widespread were these attempts to enmesh social workers in intrafamily feuds that they were responsible for a high proportion of the many unfounded complaints the MSPCC always met. Rejected men, then as now, often fought for the custody of children they did not really want as a means of hurting their wives. One way of doing this was to bring complaints against their wives of cruel treatment of children, or the men charged wives with child neglect when their main desire was to force the women to live with them again. Embittered, deserted wives might arrange to have their husbands caught with other women.

18 Zillah Eisenstein, *The Radical Future of Liberal Feminism* (New York: Longman, 1981); Joan B. Landes, "Hegel's Conception of the Family," (125–44) and Mary Lyndon Shanley, "Marriage Contract and Social Contract in Seventeenth-Century English Political Thought" (80–95), both in *The Family in Political Thought*, ed. Jean Bethke Elshtain (Amherst: University of Massachusetts Press, 1982).

19 See my "Single Mothers and Child Neglect," *American Quarterly* 37 (Summer 1985): 173–92.

CHAPTER 8

Struggle Over Needs: Outline of a Socialist-Feminist Critical Theory of Late-Capitalist Political Culture

NANCY FRASER

Need is also a political instrument, meticulously prepared, calculated and used.

—Michel Foucault[1]

In late-capitalist, welfare state societies, talk about people's needs is an important species of political discourse. We argue, in the United States, for example, about whether the government should provide for citizens' needs. Thus, feminists claim that there should be state provision of parents' day-care needs, while social conservatives insist on *children's* needs for their mothers' care, and economic conservatives claim that the market, not the government, is the best institution for meeting needs. Likewise, Americans also argue about whether existing social welfare programs really do meet the needs they purport to satisfy or whether, instead, they misconstrue the latter. For example, right-wing critics claim that Aid to Families with Dependent Children destroys the incentive to work and undermines the family. Left critics, in contrast, oppose workfare proposals as coercive and punitive, while many poor women with young children say they want to work at good-paying jobs. All these cases involve disputes about what exactly various groups of people really do need and about who should have the last word in such matters. In all these cases, moreover, needs-talk is a medium for the making and contesting of political claims. It is an idiom in which political conflict is played out and through which inequalities are symbolically elaborated and challenged.

Talk about needs has not always been central to western political culture; it has often been considered antithetical to politics and relegated to the margins of political life. However, in welfare state societies, needs-talk has been institutionalized as a major vocabulary of political discourse.[2] It coexists, albeit often uneasily, with talk about rights and interests at the very center of political life. Indeed, this peculiar juxtaposition of a discourse about needs with discourses about rights and interests is one of the distinctive marks of late-capitalist political culture.

Feminists (and others) who aim to intervene in this culture could benefit from considering the following questions: Why has needs-talk become so prominent in the political culture of welfare state societies? What is the relation between this development and changes in late-capitalist social structure? What does the emergence of the needs idiom imply about shifts in the boundaries between "political," "economic," and "domestic" spheres of life? Does it betoken an extension of the political sphere or, rather, a colonization of that domain by newer modes of power and social control? What are the major varieties of needs-talk and how do they interact polemically with one another? What opportunities and/or obstacles does the needs idiom pose for movements, like feminism, that seek far-reaching social transformation?

In what follows, I outline an approach for thinking about such questions rather than proposing definitive answers to them. What I have to say falls into five parts. In the first section, I suggest a break with standard theoretical approaches by shifting the focus of inquiry from needs to discourses about needs, from the distribution of need satisfactions to "the politics of need interpretation." And I propose a model of social discourse designed to bring into relief the contested character of needs-talk in welfare state societies. In the second section, I relate this discourse model to social-structural considerations, especially to shifts in the boundaries between "political," "economic," and "domestic" spheres of life. In the third section, I identify three major strands of needs-talk in late-capitalist political culture, and I map some of the ways in which they compete for potential adherents. In the fourth section, I apply the model to some concrete cases of contemporary needs politics in the United States. Finally, in a brief conclusion, I consider some moral and epistemological issues raised by the phenomenon of needs-talk.

THE POLITICS OF NEED INTERPRETATION:
A DISCOURSE MODEL

Let me begin by explaining some of the peculiarities of the approach I am proposing. In my approach, the focus of inquiry is not needs but rather *discourses* about needs. The point is to shift our angle of vision on the politics of needs. Usually, the politics of needs is understood to concern the distribution of satisfactions. In my approach, by contrast, the focus is *the politics of need interpretation*.

The reason for focusing on discourses and interpretation is to bring into view the contextual and contested character of needs claims. As many theorists have noted, needs claims have a relational structure; implicitly or explicitly, they have the form "A needs x in order to y." Now, this structure poses no problems when we are considering very general or "thin" needs such as food or shelter *simpliciter*. Thus, we can uncontroversially say that homeless people, like everyone else in nontropical climates, need shelter in order to live. And most people will infer that governments, as guarantors of life and liberty, have a responsibility to provide for this need. However, as soon as we descend to a lesser level of generality, needs claims become far more controversial. What, more "thickly," do homeless people need in order to be sheltered from the cold? What specific forms of provision are implied once we acknowledge their very general, thin need? Do homeless people need forbearance to sleep undisturbed next to a hot air vent on a street corner? A space in a subway tunnel or a bus terminal? A bed in a temporary shelter? A permanent home? Suppose we say the latter. What kind of permanent housing do homeless people need? Rental units in high rises in center city areas remote from good schools, discount shopping, and job opportunities? Single-family homes designed for single-earner, two-parent families? And what else do homeless people need in order to have permanent homes? Rent subsidies? Income supports? Jobs? Job training and education? Day care? Finally, what is needed, at the level of housing policy, in order to insure an adequate stock of affordable housing? Tax incentives to encourage private investment in low-income housing? Concentrated or scattered site public housing projects within a generally commodified housing environment? Rent control? Decommodification of urban housing?[3]

We could continue proliferating such questions indefinitely. And we would, at the same time, be proliferating controversy. That is precisely the point about needs claims. These claims tend to be nested, connected to one another in ramified chains of "in-order-to" relations. Moreover, when these chains are unravelled in the course of political disputes, disagreements usually deepen rather than abate. Precisely how such chains are unravelled depends on what the interlocutors share in the way of background assumptions. Does it go without saying that policy designed to deal with homelessness must not challenge the basic ownership and investment structure of urban real estate? Or is that a point at which people's assumptions and commitments diverge?

It is the implication of needs claims in contested networks of in-order-to relations that I call attention to when I speak of the politics of need interpretation. Thin theories of needs that do not undertake to explore such networks cannot shed much light on the politics of needs. Such theories assume that the politics of needs concerns only whether various predefined needs will or will not be provided for. As a result, they deflect attention from a number of important political questions.[4] First, they take the *interpretation* of people's needs as simply given and unproblematic; they thus occlude the interpretive dimension of needs politics, the fact that not just satisfactions but *need interpretations* are politically contested. Second, they assume that it is unproblematic who interprets the needs in question and from what perspective and in the light of what interests; they thus overlook the fact that *who* gets to establish authoritative, thick definitions of people's needs is itself a political stake. Third, they take for granted that the socially authorized forms of public discourse available for interpreting people's needs are adequate and fair; they thus neglect the question whether these forms of public discourse are skewed in favor of the self-interpretations and interests of dominant social groups and, so, work to the disadvantage of subordinate or oppositional groups; they occult, in other words, the fact that the means of public discourse themselves may be at issue in needs politics. Fourth, such theories fail to problematize the social and institutional logic of processes of need interpretation; they thus neglect such important political questions as: where in society, in what institutions, are authoritative need interpretations developed? and what sorts of social relations are in force among the interlocutors or cointerpreters?

In order to remedy these blindspots, I propose a more politically critical, discourse-oriented alternative. I take the politics of need interpretation to comprise three analytically distinct but practically interrelated moments. The first is the struggle to establish or deny the political status of a given need, the struggle to validate the need as a matter of legitimate political concern or to enclave it as a nonpolitical matter. The second is the struggle over the interpretation of the need, the struggle for the power to define it and, so, to determine what would satisfy it. The third moment is the struggle over the satisfaction of the need, the struggle to secure or withhold provision.

Now, a focus on the politics of need interpretation requires a model of social discourse. The model I have developed foregrounds the multivalent and contested character of needs-talk, the fact that in welfare state societies we encounter a plurality of competing ways of talking about people's needs. The model theorizes what I call "the socio-cultural means of interpretation and communication" (MIC). By this I mean the historically and culturally specific ensemble of discursive resources available to members of a given social collectivity in pressing claims against one another. Included among these resources are the following:

1. the officially recognized idioms in which one can press claims; for example, needs-talk, rights-talk, interests-talk;

2. the vocabularies available for instantiating claims in these recognized idioms; for example, therapeutic vocabularies, administrative vocabularies, religious vocabularies, feminist vocabularies, socialist vocabularies;

3. the paradigms of argumentation accepted as authoritative in adjudicating conflicting claims; thus, with respect to needs-talk, how are conflicts over the interpretation of needs resolved? By appeals to scientific experts? By bro-

kered compromises? By voting according to majority rule? By privileging the interpretations of those whose needs are in question?

4. the narrative conventions available for constructing the individual and collective stories that are constitutive of people's social identities;

5. modes of subjectification; the ways in which various discourses position the people to whom they are addressed as specific sorts of subjects endowed with specific sorts of capacities for action; for example, as "normal" or "deviant," as causally conditioned or freely self-determining, as victims or as potential activists, as unique individuals or as members of social groups.[5]

In late-capitalist welfare state societies, there are a plurality of forms of association, roles, groups, institutions, and discourses. Thus, the means of interpretation and communication are not all of a piece. They do not constitute a coherent, monolithic web but rather a heterogeneous field of diverse possibilities and alternatives.

In fact, in welfare state societies, discourses about needs typically make at least implicit reference to alternative interpretations. Particular claims about needs are "internally dialogized"; implicitly or explicitly they evoke resonances of competing need interpretations.[6] They therefore allude to a conflict of interpretations. For example, groups seeking to restrict or outlaw abortion counterpose "the sanctity of life" to the mere "convenience" of "career women"; thus, they cast their claims in terms that refer, however disparagingly, to feminist interpretations of reproductive needs.[7]

Of course, late-capitalist societies are not simply pluralist. Rather, they are stratified, differentiated into social groups with unequal status, power, and access to resources, traversed by pervasive axes of inequality along lines of class, gender, race, ethnicity, and age. And the MIC in these societies are also stratified; they are organized in ways that are congruent with societal patterns of dominance and subordination.

It follows that we must distinguish those elements of the MIC that are hegemonic, authorized, and officially sanctioned, on the one hand, from those that are nonhegemonic, disqualified, and discounted, on the other hand. Some ways of talking about needs are institutionalized in the central discursive arenas of late-capitalist societies: parliaments, academies, courts, and mass circulation media. Other ways of talking about needs are enclaved as socially marked subdialects and normally excluded from the central discursive arenas. For example, moralistic and scientific discourses about needs associated with AIDS are well represented on government commissions; in contrast, gay and lesbian rights activists' interpretations of those needs are largely excluded.

From this perspective, needs-talk appears as a site of struggle where groups with unequal discursive (and nondiscursive) resources compete to establish as hegemonic their respective interpretations of legitimate social needs. Dominant groups articulate need interpretations intended to exclude, defuse, and/

or coopt counterinterpretations. Subordinate or oppositional groups, on the
other hand, articulate need interpretations intended to challenge, displace,
and/or modify dominant ones. In neither case are the interpretations simply
"representations." In both cases, rather, they are acts and interventions.

NEEDS DISCOURSE: BETWEEN THE POLITICAL,
THE ECONOMIC, AND THE DOMESTIC

Now I should like to situate the discourse model I have just sketched with
respect to some social-structural features of late-capitalist societies. Here, I
seek to relate the rise of politicized needs-talk to shifts in the boundaries separating "political," "economic," and "domestic" dimensions of life. However,
unlike many social theorists, I shall treat the terms "political," "economic"
and "domestic" as cultural classifications and ideological labels rather than as
designations of structures, spheres, or things.[8]

Let me begin by noting that the terms "politics" and "political" are highly
contested and they have a number of different senses. In the present context,
the two most important senses are the following. First, there is the institutional
sense in which a matter is deemed "political" if it is handled directly in the
institutions of the official governmental system, including parliaments, administrative apparatuses, and the like. In this sense, what is "political"—call it
"official-political"—contrasts with what is handled in institutions like "the
family" and "the economy," which are defined as being outside the official-
political system, even though they are in actuality underpinned and regulated
by it. Second, there is the discourse sense in which something is "political" if
it is contested across a range of different discursive arenas and among a range
of different publics. In this sense, what is "political"—call it "discursive-
political" or "politicized"—contrasts both with what is not contested in public
at all and also with what is contested only by and within relatively specialized,
enclaved, and/or segmented publics. These two senses are not unrelated. In
democratic theory, if not always in practice, a matter does not usually become
subject to legitimate state intervention until it has been debated across a wide
range of discourse publics.

In general, there are no a priori constraints dictating that some matters
simply are intrinsically political and others simply are intrinsically not. As a
matter of fact, these boundaries are drawn differently from culture to culture
and from historical period to historical period. For example, reproduction became an intensely political matter in the 1890s in the United States amid a
panic about "race suicide." By the 1940s, however, there was a consensus
that birth control was a "private" matter. Finally, with the emergence of the
women's movement in the 1960s, reproduction was repoliticized.[9]

However, it would be misleading to suggest that, for any society in any period, the boundary between what is political and what is not is simply fixed or given. On the contrary, this boundary may itself be an object of conflict. For example, struggles over Poor Law "reform" in nineteenth-century England were also conflicts about the scope of the political. And as I shall argue shortly, one of the primary stakes of social conflict in late-capitalist societies is precisely where the limits of the political will be drawn.

We can better understand such conflict if we examine some presuppositions and implications of the discourse sense of "politics." Recall that this sense stipulates that a matter is "political" if it is contested across a range of different discursive arenas and among a range of different discourse publics. Note, therefore, that it depends upon the idea of discursive publicity. However, in this conception, publicity is not understood in a simple unitary way as the undifferentiated opposite of discursive privacy. Rather, publicity is understood differentiatedly, on the assumption that it is possible to identify a plurality of distinct discourse publics and to theorize the relations among them.

Clearly, publics can be distinguished along a number of different axes, for example, by ideology (the readership of *The Nation* versus the readership of *The Public Interest*), by stratification principles like gender (the viewers of "Cagney and Lacey" versus the viewers of "Monday Night Football") and class (the readership of the *New York Times* versus that of the *New York Post*), by profession (the membership of The American Economic Association versus that of The American Bar Association), or by central mobilizing issue (the Nuclear Freeze movement versus the "Pro-Life" movement).

Publics can also be distinguished in terms of relative power. Some are large, authoritative, and able to set the terms of debate for many of the rest. Others, by contrast, are small, self-enclosed, and enclaved, unable to make much of a mark beyond their own borders. Publics of the former sort are often able to take the lead in the formation of hegemonic blocs: concatenations of different publics that together construct "the common sense" of the day. As a result, such leading publics usually have a heavy hand in defining what is "political" in the discourse sense. They can politicize an issue simply by entertaining contestation concerning it, since such contestation will be transmitted as a matter of course to and through other allied and opposing publics. Smaller, counter-hegemonic publics, by contrast, generally lack the power to politicize issues in this way. When they succeed in fomenting widespread contestation over what was previously "nonpolitical," it is usually by far slower and more laborious means. In general, it is the relative power of various publics that determines the outcome of struggles over the boundaries of the political.

Now, how should we conceptualize the politicization of needs in late-capitalist societies? Clearly, this involves processes whereby some matters break out of zones of discursive privacy and out of specialized or enclaved publics so as to become foci of generalized contestation. When this happens, previously taken-for-granted interpretations of these matters are called into question, and heretofore reified chains of in-order-to relations become subject to dispute.

What are the zones of privacy and the specialized publics that previously enveloped newly politicized needs in late-capitalist societies? What are the institutions in which these needs were enclaved and depoliticized, where their interpretations were embedded in networks of in-order-to relations that simply went without saying?

In late-capitalist societies, what is "political" is normally defined in contrast to what is "economic" and "domestic" or "personal." Thus, we can identify two principal sets of institutions here that depoliticize social discourses. They are, first, domestic institutions, especially the normative domestic form, namely, the modern, male-headed, nuclear family; and, second, official-economic capitalist system institutions, especially paid workplaces, markets, credit mechanisms, and "private" enterprises and corporations.[10] Domestic institutions depoliticize certain matters by personalizing and/or familializing them; they cast these as private-domestic or personal-familial matters in contradistinction to public, political matters. Official-economic capitalist system institutions, on the other hand, depoliticize certain matters by economizing them; the issues in question here are cast as impersonal market imperatives or as "private" ownership prerogatives or as technical problems for managers and planners, all in contradistinction to political matters. In both cases, the result is a foreshortening of chains of in-order-to relations for interpreting people's needs; interpretive chains are truncated and prevented from spilling across the boundaries separating "the domestic" and "the economic" from "the political."

Clearly, domestic and official-economic system institutions differ in many important respects. However, in *these* respects they are exactly on a par with one another: both enclave certain matters into specialized discursive arenas; both thereby shield such matters from generalized contestation and from widely disseminated conflicts of interpretation. As a result, both entrench as authoritative certain specific interpretations of needs by embedding them in certain specific, but largely unquestioned, chains of in-order-to relations.

Since both domestic and official-economic system institutions support relations of dominance and subordination, the specific interpretations they naturalize usually tend to advantage dominant groups and individuals and to disadvantage their subordinates. If wife battering, for example, is enclaved as a "personal" or "domestic" matter within male-headed, nuclear families; and if public discourse about this phenomenon is canalized into specialized publics associated with, say, family law, social work, and the sociology and psychology of "deviance"; then this serves to reproduce gender dominance and subordination. Similarly, if questions of workplace democracy are enclaved as "economic" or "managerial" problems in profit-oriented, hierarchically managed paid workplaces; and if discourse about these questions is shunted into specialized publics associated with, say, "industrial relations" sociology, labor law, and "management science"; then this serves to perpetuate class (and usually also gender and race) dominance and subordination.

As a result of these processes, members of subordinated groups commonly internalize need interpretations that work to their own disadvantage. However, sometimes culturally dominant need interpretations are superimposed upon latent or embryonic oppositional interpretations. This is most likely where there persist, however fragmentedly, subculturally transmitted traditions of resistance, as in some sections of the United States labor movement and in the collective historical memory of many African-Americans. Moreover, under special circumstances, processes of depoliticization are disrupted. Then, dominant classifications of needs as "economic" or "domestic," as opposed to "political," come to lose their "self-evidence" and alternative, oppositional, and *politicized* interpretations emerge in their stead.

In any case, family and official-economy are the principal depoliticizing enclaves that needs must exceed in order to become "political" in the discourse sense in late-capitalist societies. Thus, the emergence of needs-talk as a political idiom in these societies is the other side of the increased permeability of domestic and official-economic institutions, their growing inability fully to depoliticize certain matters. The politicized needs at issue in late-capitalist societies, then, are "leaky" or "runaway" needs: they are needs that have broken out of the discursive enclaves constructed in and around domestic and official-economic institutions.

Runaway needs are a species of *excess* with respect to the normative modern domestic and economic institutions. Initially at least, they bear the stamp of those institutions, remaining embedded in conventional chains of in-order-to relations. For example, many runaway needs are colored by the assumption that "the domestic" is supposed to be separated from "the economic" in male-dominated, capitalist societies. Thus, throughout most of United States history, child care has been cast as a "domestic" rather than an "economic" need; it has been interpreted as the need of children for the full-time care of their mothers rather than as the need of workers for time away from their children; and its satisfaction has been construed along the lines of "mothers' pensions" rather than of day care.[11] Here, the assumption of separate spheres truncates possible chains of in-order-to relations that would yield alternative interpretations of social needs.

Where do runaway needs run to when they break out of domestic or official-economic enclaves? I propose that runaway needs enter a historically specific and relatively new societal arena. Following Hannah Arendt, I call this arena "the social" in order to mark its noncoincidence with the family, official-economy, or state.[12] As a site of contested discourse about runaway needs, "the social" cuts across these traditional divisions. It is an arena of conflict among rival interpretations of needs embedded in rival chains of in-order-to relations.

As I conceive it, the social is a switch point for the meeting of heterogeneous contestants associated with a wide range of different discourse publics. These contestants range from proponents of politicization to defenders of (re)depoliticization, from loosely organized social movements to members of specialized, expert publics in and around the social state. Moreover, they vary greatly in relative power. Some are associated with leading publics capable of setting the terms of political debate; others, by contrast, are linked to enclaved publics and must oscillate between marginalization and cooptation.

The social is also the site where successfully politicized runaway needs get translated into claims for government provision. Here, rival need interpretations get translated into rival programmatic conceptions; rival alliances are forged around rival policy proposals; and unequally endowed groups compete to shape the formal policy agenda. For example, in the United States today, various interest groups, movements, professional associations, and parties are scrambling for formulations around which to build alliances sufficiently powerful to dictate the shape of impending welfare "reform."

Eventually, if and when such contests are (at least temporarily) resolved, runaway needs may become objects of state intervention. Then, they become targets and levers for various strategies of crisis management. And they also become the *raisons d'être* for the proliferation of the various agencies comprising the social state.[13] These agencies are engaged in regulating and/or funding and/or providing the satisfaction of social needs. And in so doing, they are in the business of interpreting, as well as of satisfying, the needs in question. For example, the United States social welfare system is currently divided into two gender-linked and unequal subsystems: an implicitly "masculine" social insurance subsystem tied to "primary" labor force participation and geared to (white male) "breadwinners"; and an implicitly "feminine" relief subsystem tied to household income and geared to homemaker-mothers and their "defective" (i.e., female-headed) families. With the underlying (but counterfactual) assumption of "separate spheres," the two subsystems differ markedly in the degree of autonomy, rights, and presumption of desert they accord beneficiaries, as well as in their funding base, mode of administration, and character and level of benefits.[14] Thus, the various agencies comprising the social welfare system provide more than material aid. They also provide clients, and the public at large, with a tacit but powerful interpretive map of normative, differentially valued gender roles and gendered needs. Therefore, the different branches of the social state, too, are players in the politics of need interpretation.[15]

To summarize: in late-capitalist societies, runaway needs that have broken out of domestic or official-economic enclaves enter that hybrid discursive space that Arendt aptly dubbed "the social." They may then become foci of state intervention geared to crisis management. These needs are thus markers of major social-structural shifts in the boundaries separating what are classified as "political," "economic," and "domestic" or "personal" spheres of life.

CONFLICTS OF INTERPRETATION: OPPOSITION, REPRIVATIZATION, AND EXPERTISE

Now I would like to propose a scheme for classifying the many varieties of needs-talk in late-capitalist societies. The point is to identity some distinct types of discourse and to map the lines along which they compete. This in turn will permit us to theorize some basic axes of needs politics in welfare state societies.

I suggest there are three major kinds of needs discourses in late-capitalist societies. First, there are what I call "oppositional" forms of needs-talk, which arise when needs are politicized "from below." These contribute to the crystallization of new social identities on the part of subordinated social groups. Second, there are what I call "reprivatization" discourses, which emerge in response to the first. These articulate entrenched need interpretations that could previously go without saying. Finally, there are what I call "expert" needs discourses, which link popular movements to the state. These can best be understood in the context of "social problem solving," institution building, and professional class formation. In general, it is the polemical interaction of these three strands of needs-talk that structures the politics of needs in late-capitalist societies.[16]

Let us look first at the politicization of runaway needs via oppositional discourses. Here, needs become politicized when, for example, women, workers, and/or peoples of color come to contest the subordinate identities and roles, the traditional, reified, and disadvantageous need interpretations previously assigned to and/or embraced by them. By insisting on speaking publicly of heretofore depoliticized needs, by claiming for these needs the status of legitimate political issues, such persons and groups do several things simultaneously. First, they contest the established boundaries separating "politics" from "economics" and "domestics." Second, they offer alternative interpretations of their needs embedded in alternative chains of in-order-to relations. Third, they create new discourse publics from which they try to disseminate their interpretations of their needs throughout a wide range of different discourse publics. Finally, they challenge, modify, and/or displace hegemonic elements of the means of interpretation and communication; they invent new forms of discourse for interpreting their needs.

In oppositional discourses, needs-talk is a moment in the self-constitution of new collective agents or social movements. For example, in the current wave of feminist ferment, groups of women have politicized and reinterpreted various needs, have instituted new vocabularies and forms of address, and, so, have become "women" in a different, though not uncontested or univocal, sense. By speaking publicly the heretofore unspeakable, by coining terms like "sexism," "sexual harassment," "marital, date, and acquaintance rape," "labor force sex-segregation," "the double shift," "wife-battery," etc., feminist women have become "women" in the sense of a discursively self-constituted political collectivity, albeit a very heterogeneous and fractured one.

Of course, the politicization of needs in oppositional discourses does not go uncontested. One type of resistance involves defense of the established boundaries separating "political," "economic," and "domestic" spheres by means of "reprivatization" discourses. Institutionally, "reprivatization" designates initiatives aimed at dismantling or cutting back social welfare services, selling off nationalized assets, and/or deregulating "private" enterprise; discursively, it means depoliticization. Thus, in reprivatization discourses, speakers oppose state provision of runaway needs and they seek to contain forms of needs-talk that threaten to spill across a wide range of discourse publics. Reprivatizers may insist, for example, that domestic battery is not a legitimate subject of political discourse but a familial or religious matter. Or, to take a different example, that a factory closing is not a political question but an unimpeachable prerogative of "private" ownership or an unassailable imperative of an impersonal market mechanism. In both cases, the speakers are contesting the breakout of runaway needs and trying to (re)depoliticize them.

Interestingly, reprivatization discourses blend the old and the new. On the one hand, they seem merely to render explicit need interpretations that could earlier go without saying. But, on the other hand, by the very act of articulating such interpretations, they simultaneously modify them. Because reprivatization discourses respond to competing, oppositional interpretations, they are internally dialogized, incorporating references to the alternatives they resist, even while rejecting them. For example, although "pro-family" discourses of the social new right are explicitly antifeminist, some of them incorporate in a depoliticized form feminist inspired motifs implying women's right to sexual pleasure and to emotional support from their husbands.[17]

In defending the established social division of discourses, reprivatization discourses deny the claims of oppositional movements for the legitimate political status of runaway needs. However, in so doing, they tend further to politicize those needs in the sense of increasing their cathectedness as foci of contestation. Moreover, in some cases, reprivatization discourses, too, become vehicles for mobilizing social movements and for reshaping social identities.

Doubtless the most stunning example is Thatcherism in Britain, where a set of reprivatization discourses articulated in the accents of authoritarian populism has refashioned the subjectivities of a wide range of disaffected constituencies and united them in a powerful coalition.[18]

Together, oppositional discourses and reprivatization discourses define one axis of needs-struggle in late-capitalist societies. But there is also a second, rather different axis of conflict. Here, the focal issue is no longer politicization versus depoliticization but rather the interpreted *content* of contested needs once their political status has been successfully secured. And the principal contestants are oppositional social movements and organized interests like business, which seek to influence public policy.

For example, today in the United States day care is gaining increasing legitimacy as a political issue. As a result, we are seeing the proliferation of competing interpretations and programmatic conceptions. In one view, day care would serve poor children's needs for "enrichment" and/or moral supervision. In a second, it would serve the middle-class taxpayer's need to get AFDC recipients off the welfare rolls. A third interpretation would shape day care as a measure for increasing the productivity and competitiveness of American business, while yet a fourth would treat it as part of a package of policies aimed at redistributing income and resources to women. Each of these interpretations carries a distinct programmatic orientation with respect to funding, institutional siting and control, service design, and eligibility. And as they collide, we see a struggle to shape the hegemonic understanding of day care that may eventually make its way onto the formal political agenda. Clearly, not just feminist groups but also business interests, trade unions, children's rights advocates, and educators are contestants in this struggle. And they bring to it vast differentials in power.[19]

The struggle for hegemonic need interpretations usually points toward the future involvement of the state. Thus, it anticipates yet a third axis of needs struggle in late-capitalist societies, namely, politics versus administration. Here the principal contestants are oppositional social movements and the experts and agencies in the orbit of the social state.

Recall that "the social" is a site where needs that have become politicized in the discourse sense become candidates for state-organized provision. Consequently, these needs become the object of yet another group of discourses: the complex of "expert," "public policy" discourses based in various "private," "semipublic" and state institutions.

Expert needs discourses are the vehicles for translating sufficiently politicized runaway needs into objects of potential state intervention. And they are closely connected with institutions of knowledge production and utilization.[20] They include: qualitative and especially quantitative social-scientific discourses generated in universities and "think-tanks"; legal discourses generated in judicial institutions and their satellite schools, journals, and professional associations; administrative discourses circulated in various agencies of the social state; and therapeutic discourses circulated in public and private medical and social service agencies.

As the term suggests, expert discourses tend to be restricted to specialized publics. Thus, they are associated with professional class formation, institution building, and social "problem solving." But in some cases, such as law and psychotherapy, expert vocabularies and rhetorics are disseminated to a wider spectrum of educated laypersons, some of whom are participants in social movements. Moreover, social movements sometimes manage to coopt or create critical, oppositional segments of expert discourse publics. For all these reasons, expert discourse publics sometimes acquire a certain porousness. And, expert discourses become the *bridge* discourses linking loosely organized social movements with the social state.

Because of this bridge role, the rhetoric of expert needs discourses tends to be administrative. These discourses consist in a series of rewriting operations, procedures for translating politicized needs into administerable needs. Typically, the politicized need is redefined as the correlate of a bureaucratically administerable satisfaction, a "social service." It is specified in terms of an ostensibly general state of affairs that could, in principle, befall anyone— for example, unemployment, disability, death or desertion of a spouse.[21] As a result, the need is decontextualized and recontextualized: on the one hand, it is represented in abstraction from its class, race, and gender specificity and from whatever oppositional meanings it may have acquired in the course of its politicization; on the other hand, it is cast in terms that tacitly presuppose such entrenched, specific background institutions as wage labor, privatized child rearing, and their gender-based separation.

As a result of these expert redefinitions, the people whose needs are in question are repositioned. They become individual "cases" rather than members of social groups or participants in political movements. In addition, they are rendered passive, positioned as potential recipients of predefined services rather than as agents involved in interpreting their needs and shaping their life conditions.

By virtue of this administrative rhetoric, expert needs discourses, too, tend to be depoliticizing. They construe persons simultaneously as rational utility-maximizers and as causally conditioned, predictable, and manipulable objects, thereby screening out those dimensions of human agency that involve the construction and deconstruction of social meanings.

Moreover, when expert needs discourses are institutionalized in state apparatuses, they tend to become normalizing, aimed at "reforming" or more often stigmatizing "deviance."[22] This sometimes becomes explicit when services incorporate a therapeutic dimension designed to close the gap between clients' recalcitrant self-interpretations and the interpretations embedded in adminis-trative policy.[23] Now the rational utility-maximizer-cum-causally-conditioned-object becomes, in addition, a deep self to be unravelled therapeutically.[24]

To summarize: when social movements succeed in politicizing previously depoliticized needs, they enter the terrain of the social where two other kinds of struggles await them. First, they have to contest powerful organized interests bent on shaping hegemonic need interpretations to their own ends. Second, they encounter expert needs discourses in and around the social state. These encounters define two additional axes of needs-struggle in late-capitalist soci-eties. They are highly complex struggles, since social movements typically seek state provision of their runaway needs even while they tend to oppose administrative and therapeutic need interpretations. Thus, these axes, too, in-volve conflicts among rival interpretations of social needs and among rival constructions of social identity.

POLITICS OR ADMINISTRATION? SOME APPLICATIONS

Now I would like to apply the model I have been developing to some con-crete cases of conflicts of need interpretation. The first example is designed to identify a tendency in welfare state societies to transform the politics of need interpretation into the management of need satisfactions. A second group of examples, by contrast, charts the countertendency from administration to resistance and potentially back to politics.[25]

First, consider the example of the politics of needs surrounding wife bat-tering. Until about fifteen years ago, the term "wife battering" did not exist. When spoken of publicly at all, this phenomenon was called "wife beating" and was often treated comically, as in, "Have you stopped beating your wife?" Linguistically, it was classed with the disciplining of children and servants as a "domestic," as opposed to a "political," matter. Then, feminist activ-ists renamed the practice with a term drawn from criminal law and created a new kind of public discourse. They claimed that battery was not a personal, domestic problem but a systemic, political one; its etiology was not to be traced to individual women's or men's emotional problems but, rather, to the ways these refracted pervasive social relations of male dominance and female subordination.

Thus, feminist activists contested established discursive boundaries and politicized a previously depoliticized phenomenon. In addition, they reinter-preted the experience of battery and posited a set of associated needs. Here, they situated battered women's needs in a long chain of in-order-to relations that spilled across conventional separations of "spheres"; they claimed that, in order to be free from dependence on batterers, battered women needed not just temporary shelter but also jobs paying a "family wage," day care, and affordable permanent housing. Further, feminists created new discourse publics, new spaces, and institutions in which such oppositional need interpretations could be developed and from which they could be spread to wider publics. Finally, feminists modified elements of the authorized means of interpretation and communication; they coined new terms of description and analysis and devised new ways of addressing female subjects. In their discourse, battered women were not addressed as individualized victims but as potential feminist activists, members of a politically constituted collectivity.

This discursive intervention was accompanied by feminist efforts to provide for some of the needs they had politicized and reinterpreted. Activists organized battered women's shelters, places of refuge and of consciousness raising. The organization of these shelters was nonhierarchical; there were no clear lines between staff and users. Many of the counselors and organizers had themselves been battered; and a high percentage of the women who used the shelters went on to counsel other battered women and to become movement activists. Concomitantly, these women came to adopt new self-descriptions. Whereas most had originally blamed themselves and defended their batterers, many came to reject that interpretation in favor of a politicized view that offered them new models of human agency. In addition, these women modified their affiliations and social identifications. Whereas many had originally felt deeply identified with their batterers, they came to affiliate with other women.

This organizing eventually had an impact on wider discursive publics. By the late 1970s, feminists had largely succeeded in establishing domestic violence against women as a legitimate political issue. They managed in some cases to change attitudes and policies of police and the courts and they won for this issue a place on the informal political agenda. Now the needs of battered women were sufficiently politicized to become candidates for publicly organized satisfaction. Finally, in several municipalities and localities, movement shelters began receiving local government funding.

From the feminist perspective, this represented a significant victory, but it was not without cost. Municipal funding brought with it a variety of new, administrative constraints ranging from accounting procedures to regulation, accreditation, and professionalization requirements. As a consequence, publicly funded shelters underwent a transformation. Increasingly, they were staffed by professional social workers, many of whom had not themselves experienced battery. Thus, a division between professional and client supplanted the more fluid continuum of relations that characterized the earlier shelters. Moreover, many social work staff have been trained to frame problems in a quasi-psychiatric perspective. This perspective structures the practices of many publicly funded shelters even despite the intentions of individual staff, many of whom are politically committed feminists. Consequently, the practices of such shelters have become more individualizing and less politicized. Battered women tend now to be positioned as clients. They are increasingly psychiatrized, addressed as victims with deep, complicated selves. They are only rarely addressed as potential feminist activists. Increasingly, the language game of therapy has supplanted that of consciousness raising. And the neutral scientific language of "spouse abuse" has supplanted more political talk of "male violence against women." Finally, the needs of battered women have been substantially reinterpreted. The very far-reaching earlier claims for the social and economic prerequisites of independence have tended to give way to a narrower focus on the individual woman's problems of "low self-esteem." [26]

The battered women's shelter case exemplifies one tendency of needs politics in late-capitalist societies: the tendency for the politics of need interpretation to devolve into the administration of need satisfaction. However, there is also a countertendency that runs from administration to client resistance and potentially back to politics. I would like now to document this countertendency by discussing four examples of client resistance, examples ranging from the individual, cultural, and informal to the collective, political, and formally organized.

1. Individuals may locate some space for maneuver within the administrative framework of a government agency. They may displace and/or modify an agency's official interpretations of their needs, even without mounting an overt challenge. Historian Linda Gordon has uncovered examples of this sort of resistance in the records of child protection agencies during the Progressive era.[27] Gordon cites cases in which women who had been beaten by their husbands filed complaints alleging child abuse. Having involved case workers in their situations by invoking an interpreted need that *was* recognized as legitimate and as falling within the agency's jurisdiction, they managed to interest the case workers in a need that was *not* so recognized. In some cases, these women succeeded in securing intervention under the child abuse rubric that provided them some measure of relief from domestic battery. Thus, they informally broadened the agency's jurisdiction to include, indirectly, a hitherto excluded need. While citing the social state's official definition of their need, they simultaneously displaced that definition and brought it closer in line with their own interpretations.

2. Informally organized groups may develop practices and affiliations that are at odds with the social state's way of positioning them as clients. In so doing, they may alter the uses and meanings of benefits provided by government agencies, even without explicitly calling these into question. Anthropologist Carol Stack has documented examples of this sort of resistance in her study of "domestic kin networks" among poor black AFDC recipients in a midwestern city in the late 1960s.[28] Stack describes elaborate kinship

arrangements that organize delayed exchanges or "gifts" of prepared meals, food stamps, cooking, shopping, groceries, sleeping space, cash (including wages and AFDC allowances), transportation, clothing, child care, and even children. It is significant that these domestic kin networks span several physically distinct households. This means that AFDC recipients use their benefits beyond the confines of the principal administrative category of government relief programs, namely, "the household." Consequently, these clients circumvent the nuclear-familializing procedures of welfare administration. By utilizing benefits beyond the confines of a "household," they alter the state-defined meanings of those benefits and, thus, of the needs they purport to satisfy. At the same time, they indirectly contest the state's way of positioning them as subjects. Whereas AFDC addresses them as biological mothers who belong to deviant nuclear families that lack male breadwinners, they double that subject position with another one, namely, members of socially, as opposed to biologically, constituted kin networks who cooperate in coping with dire poverty.

3. Individuals and/or groups may resist therapeutic initiatives of the social state while accepting material aid. They may reject state-sponsored therapeutic constructions of their life stories and capacities for agency and insist instead on alternative narratives and conceptions of identity. Sociologist Prudence Rains has documented an example of this kind of resistance in her comparative study of the "moral careers" of black and white pregnant teenagers in the late 1960s.[29]

Rains contrasts the ways the two groups of young women related to therapeutic constructions of their experience in two different institutional settings. The young, middle-class white women were in an expensive, private, residential facility. This facility combined traditional services, such as seclusion and a cover for "good girls who had made a mistake," with newer therapeutic services, including required individual and group counseling sessions with psychiatric social workers. In these sessions, the young women were addressed as deep, complicated selves. They were encouraged to regard their pregnancies not as simple "mistakes" but, rather, as unconsciously motivated, meaningful acts expressive of latent emotional problems. This meant that a girl was to interpret her pregnancy—and the sex that was its superficial cause—as a form of acting out, say, a refusal of parental authority or a demand for parental love. She was warned that, unless she came to understand and acknowledge these deep, hidden motives, she would likely not succeed in avoiding future "mistakes."

Rains documents the process by which most of the young white women at this facility came to internalize this perspective and to rewrite themselves in the psychiatric idiom. She records the narratives they devised in the course of rewriting their "moral careers." For example:

When I first came here I had it all figured out in my mind that Tom . . . had kind of talked me into it and I gave in. I kind of put it all on him. I didn't really accept my own part of it. . . . [H]ere they stressed a lot that if you don't realize why you're here or why you ended up here and the emotional reasons behind it, that it will happen again. . . . I feel now that I have a pretty full understanding of why I did end up here and that there was an emotional reason for it. And I accept my part in it more. It wasn't just him (p. 93).

This narrative is interesting in several respects. As Rains notes, the exchange of a "mistake" view of the past for a psychiatric view provided certain comforts: the new interpretation "did not merely set aside the past but accounted for it, and accounted for it in ways which allowed girls to believe they would act differently in the future" (p. 94). Thus, the psychiatric view offers the pregnant teenager a model of agency that seems to enhance her capacity for individual self-determination. On the other hand, the narrative is highly selective, avowing some aspects of the past while disavowing others. It plays down the narrator's sexuality, treating her sexual behavior and desires as epiphenomenal "manifestation[s] of other, deeper, and nonsexual emotional needs and problems" (p. 93). In addition, it defuses the potentially explosive issue of consent versus coercion in the teenage heterosexual milieu by excusing Tom and by revising the girl's earlier sense that their intercourse was not consensual. Moreover, the narrative forecloses any question as to the legitimacy of "premarital sex," assuming that for a woman, at least, such sex is morally wrong. Finally, in light of the girls' declarations that they will not need contraceptives when they return home and resume dating, the narrative has yet another meaning. Encapsulating a new awareness of deep emotional problems, it becomes a shield against future pregnancies, a prophylactic. Given these elisions in the story, a skeptic might well conclude that the psychiatric promise of enhanced self-determination is largely illusory.

The relative ease with which Rains's white teenagers internalized the therapeutic interpretation of their situation stands in stark contrast with the resistance offered by her black subjects. The young black women were clients in a nonresidential municipal facility providing prenatal care, schooling, and counseling sessions with a psychiatric social worker. The counseling sessions were similar in intent and design to those at the private residential facility; the young women were encouraged to talk about their feelings and to probe the putative, deep emotional causes of their pregnancies. However, this therapeutic approach was much less successful at the public facility. The young black women resisted the terms of the psychiatric discourse and the language game of question and answer employed in the counseling sessions. They disliked the social worker's stance of nondirectiveness and moral neutrality—her unwillingness to say what *she* thought—and they resented what they considered her intrusive, overly personal questions. These girls did not acknowledge her right to question them in this fashion, given that they could not ask "personal" questions of her in turn. Rather, they construed "personal questioning" as a privilege reserved to close friends and intimates under conditions of reciprocity.

Rains documents several dimensions of the young black women's resistance to the "mental health" aspects of the program. In some instances, they openly challenged the rules of the therapeutic language game. In others, they resisted indirectly by humor, quasi-deliberately misunderstanding the social worker's vague, nondirective, yet "personal" questions. For example, one girl construed "How did you get pregnant?" as a "stupid" question and replied, "Shouldn't you know?" (p. 136).

Some others subjected the constant therapeutic "How did it feel?" to an operation that can only be called "carnivalesque." The occasion was a group counseling session for which the case worker was late. The young women assembled for the meeting began speculating as to her whereabouts. One mentioned that Mrs. Eckerd had gone to see a doctor. The conversation continued:

> "To see if she's pregnant."
> "She probably thinks that's where you get babies."
> "Maybe the doctor's going to give her a baby. . . ."
> Bernice then started doing an imitation interview pretending she was a social worker asking questions of a pretend-pregnant Mrs. Eckerd, "Tell me, how did it feel? Did you like it?"
> This brought a storm of laughter, and everybody started mimicking questions they supposedly had had put to them. Someone said, "She asked me did I want to put my baby for adoption, and how did it feel?"
> When Mrs. Eckerd finally arrived, May said, "Why do social workers ask so may questions?"
> Mrs. Eckerd said, "What kind of questions do you mean, May?"
> Bernice . . . said, "Like 'How did it feel?' "
> There was an uproar over this (p. 137).

Thus, Rains's black subjects devised a varied repertoire of strategies for resisting expert, therapeutic constructions of their life stories and capacities for agency. They were keenly aware of the power subtext underlying their interactions with the social worker and of the normalization dimension of the therapeutic initiative. In effect, these young black women blocked efforts to inculcate in them white, middle-class norms of individuality and affectivity. They refused the case worker's inducements to rewrite themselves as psychologized selves, while availing themselves of the health services at the facility. Thus, they made use of those aspects of the agency's program that they considered appropriate to their self-interpreted needs and ignored or sidestepped the others.

4. In addition to informal, ad hoc, strategic, and/or cultural forms of resistance, there are also more formally organized, explicitly political, organized

kinds. Clients of social welfare programs may join together *as clients* to challenge administrative interpretations of their needs. They may take hold of the passive, normalized, and individualized or familialized identities fashioned for them in expert discourses and transform them into a basis for collective political action. Frances Fox Piven and Richard A. Cloward have documented an example of this kind of resistance in their account of the process by which AFDC recipients organized the welfare rights movement of the 1960's.[30] Notwithstanding the atomizing and depoliticizing dimensions of AFDC administration, these women were brought together in welfare waiting rooms. It was as a result of their participation as clients, then, that they came to articulate common grievances and to act together. Thus, the same welfare practices that gave rise to these grievances created the enabling conditions for collective organizing to combat them. As Piven put it, "the structure of the welfare state itself has helped to create new solidarities and generate the political issues that continue to cement and galvanize them."[31]

CONCLUSION: ON RELATIVISM AND RIGHTS

Let me conclude by flagging some issues that are central to this project but that I have not yet discussed in this essay. In this essay, I have concentrated on social-theoretical issues at the expense of moral and epistemological issues. But the latter are very important for a project, like mine, which aspires to be a *critical* social theory.

My analysis of needs-talk raises two very obvious and pressing philosophical issues. One is the question whether and how it is possible to distinguish better from worse interpretations of people's needs. The other is the question of the relationship between needs claims and rights. Although I cannot offer full answers to these questions here, I would like to indicate something about how I would approach them. I want also to try to situate my views in relation to contemporary debates among feminist theorists.

Feminist scholars have demonstrated again and again that authoritative views purporting to be neutral and disinterested actually express the partial and interested perspectives of dominant social groups. In addition, many feminist theorists have made use of poststructuralist approaches that deny the possibility of distinguishing warranted claims from power plays. As a result, there is now a significant strand of relativist sentiment within feminist ranks. At the same time, many other feminists worry that relativism undermines the possibility of political commitment. How, after all, can one argue against the possibility of warranted claims while oneself making such claims as that sexism exists and is unjust?[32]

This issue about relativism surfaces in the present context in the form of the question: Can we distinguish better from worse interpretations of people's needs? Or, since all need interpretations emanate from specific, interested locations in society, are all of them equally compromised?

I claim that we *can* distinguish better from worse interpretations of people's needs. To say that needs are culturally constructed and discursively interpreted is not to say that any need interpretation is as good as any other. On the contrary, it is to underline the importance of an account of interpretive justification. However, I do not think that justification can be understood in traditional objectivist terms as correspondence, as if it were a matter of finding the interpretation that matches the true nature of the need as it really is in itself independent of any interpretation.[33] Nor do I think that justification can be premised on a preestablished point of epistemic superiority, as if it were a matter of finding the one group in society with the privileged "standpoint."[34]

Then what *should* an account of interpretive justification consist of? In my view, there are at least two distinct kinds of considerations such an account would have to encompass and to balance. First, there are procedural considerations concerning the social processes by which various competing need interpretations are generated. For example, how exclusive or inclusive are various rival needs discourses? How hierarchical or egalitarian are the relations among the interlocutors? In general, procedural considerations dictate that, all other things being equal, the best need interpretations are those reached by means of communicative processes that most closely approximate ideals of democracy, equality, and fairness.[35]

In addition, considerations of consequences are relevant in justifying need interpretations. This means comparing alternative distributive outcomes of rival interpretations. For example, would widespread acceptance of some given interpretation of a social need disadvantage some groups of people vis-à-vis others? Does the interpretation conform to rather than challenge societal patterns of dominance and subordination? Are the rival chains of in-order-to relations to which competing need interpretations belong more or less respectful, as opposed to transgressive, of ideological boundaries that delimit "separate spheres" and thereby rationalize inequality? In general, consequentialist considerations dictate that, all other things being equal, the best need interpretations are those that do not disadvantage some groups of people vis-à-vis others.

In sum, justifying some interpretations of social needs as better than others involves balancing procedural and consequentialist considerations. More simply, it involves balancing democracy and equality.

What, then, of the relationship between needs and rights? This, too, is a controversial issue in contemporary theory. As Elizabeth Schneider's paper in this volume indicates, critical legal theorists have argued that rights claims work against radical social transformation by enshrining tenets of bourgeois individualism.[36] Meanwhile, some feminist moral theorists suggest that an orientation toward responsibilities is preferable to an orientation toward rights.[37] Together, these views might lead some to want to think of needs-talk as an alternative to rights-talk. On the other hand, many feminists worry that left-wing critiques of rights play into the hands of our political opponents. After all, conservatives traditionally prefer to distribute aid as a matter of need *instead* of right precisely in order to avoid assumptions of entitlement that could carry egalitarian implications. For these reasons, feminist activists and legal scholars like Schneider have sought to develop and defend alternative understandings of rights.[38] Their approach might imply that suitably reconstructed rights claims and needs claims could be mutually compatible, even intertranslatable.[39]

Very briefly, I align myself with those who favor translating justified needs claims into social rights. Like many radical critics of existing social welfare programs, I am committed to opposing the forms of paternalism that arise when needs claims are divorced from rights claims. And unlike some communitarian, socialist, and feminist critics, I do not believe that rights-talk is inherently individualistic, bourgeois-liberal, and androcentric. That is only the case where societies establish the *wrong* rights, for example, where the (putative) right to private property is permitted to trump other, social rights.

Moreover, to treat justified needs claims as the bases for new social rights is to begin to overcome obstacles to the effective exercise of some existing rights. It is true, as Marxists and others have claimed, that classical liberal rights to free expression, assembly, and the like are "merely formal." But this says more about the social context in which they are currently embedded than about their "intrinsic" character. For, in a context devoid of poverty, inequality, and oppression, formal liberal rights could be broadened and transformed into substantive rights, say, to collective self-determination.

Finally, I should stress that this work is motivated by the conviction that, for the time being, needs-talk is with us for better or worse. For the foreseeable future, political agents, including feminists, will have to operate on a terrain where needs-talk is the discursive coin of the realm. But, as I have tried to show, this idiom is neither inherently emancipatory nor inherently repressive. Rather, it is multivalent and contested. The larger aim of my project is to help clarify the prospects for democratic and egalitarian social change by sorting out the emancipatory from the repressive possibilities of needs-talk.

NOTES

A longer version of this essay appears in Nancy Fraser, *Unruly Practices: Power, Discourse, and Gender in Contemporary Social Theory* (Minneapolis: University of Minnesota Press, 1989). © University of Minnesota Press. I am grateful for helpful comments from Sandra Bartky, Linda Gordon, Paul Mattick, Frank Michelman, Martha Minow, Linda Nicholson, and Iris Young. The Mary Ingraham Bunting Institute of Radcliffe College provided crucial financial support and a utopian working situation.

1   Alan Sheridan, trans., *Discipline and Punish: The Birth of the Prison* (New York: Vintage, 1979), 26.

2   In this paper, I shall use the terms "welfare state societies" and "late-capitalist societies" interchangeably to refer to the industrialized countries of Western Europe and North America in the present period.

3   Decommodification of housing could mean socialized ownership or, alternatively, occupant ownership combined with a nonmarket mechanism for determining values during transfers (e.g., price controls).

4   A recent example of the kind of theory I have in mind is David Braybrooke, *Meeting Needs* (Princeton N.J.: Princeton University Press, 1987). Braybrooke claims that a thin concept of need "can make a substantial contribution to settling upon policies without having to descend into the melee" (p. 68). Thus, he does not take up any of the issues I am about to enumerate.

5   The expression "mode of subjectification" is inspired by Foucault, although his term is "mode of subjection" and his usage differs somewhat from mine. Cf. Michel Foucault, "On the Genealogy of Ethics: An Overview of Work in Progress," in *The Foucault Reader*, ed. Paul Rabinow (New York: Pantheon, 1984), 340–73. For another account of this idea of the socio-cultural means of interpretation and communication, see Nancy Fraser, "Toward a Discourse Ethic of Solidarity," *Praxis International* 5, no. 4 (January 1986): 425–29.

6   The expression "internally dialogized" comes from Mikhail Bakhtin. See "Discourse in the Novel," in *The Dialogic Imagination: Four Essays by M.M. Bakhtin*, translated by Caryl Emerson and Michael Holquist (Austin, Tex.: University of Texas Press, 1981), 259–422.

7   For a very interesting study of this antiabortion discourse, see Kristin Luker, *Abortion and the Politics of Motherhood* (Berkeley: University of California Press, 1984).

8   I owe this formulation to Paul Mattick. For a thoughtful discussion of the advantages of this sort of approach, see his "On *Feminism as Critique*" (unpublished manuscript).

9   Linda Gordon, *Woman's Body, Woman's Right* (New York: Viking, 1976).

10 Throughout this paper, I refer to paid workplaces, markets, credit systems, etc., as "*official*-economic system institutions" so as to avoid the androcentric implication that domestic institutions are not also "economic." For a discussion of this issue, see my "What's Critical About Critical Theory? The Case of Habermas and Gender," in Fraser, *Unruly Practices*.

11 See Sonya Michel, "American Women and the Discourse of the Democratic Family in World War II" in *Behind the Lines: Gender and the Two World Wars*, ed. Margaret Higonnet, Jane Jenson and Sonya Michel (New Haven: Yale University Press, 1987); Sonya Michel, "Children's Interests/Mothers' Rights: A History of Public Child Care in the United States" (unpublished manuscript).

12   See Hannah Arendt, *The Human Condition* (Chicago: The University of Chicago Press), especially chap. 2, 22–78. However, it should be noted that my view of "the social" differs significantly from Arendt's. Whereas she sees the social as a one-dimensional space wholly under the sway of administration and instrumental reason, I see it as multivalent and contested. Thus, my view incorporates some features of the Gramscian conception of "civil society."

13   Of course, the social state is not a unitary entity but a multiform, differentiated complex of agencies and apparatuses. In the United States, the social state comprises the welter of agencies that make up especially the Departments of Labor and of Health and Human Services—or what currently remains of them.

14   For an analysis of the gendered structure of the United States social welfare system, see my "Women, Welfare and the Politics of Need Interpretation," in Fraser, *Unruly Practices*; Barbara Nelson, "The Origins of the Two-Channel Welfare State: Workmen's Compensation and Mothers' Aid," this volume; Barbara Nelson, "Women's Poverty and Women's Citizenship: Some Political Consequences of Economic Marginality," *Signs* 10 (1984): 209–31; Diana Pearce, "Women, Work and Welfare: The Feminization of Poverty," in *Working Women and Families*, ed. Karen Wolk Feinstein (Beverly Hills, Calif.: Sage Publications, 1979).

15   For an analysis of United States social welfare agencies as purveyors and enforcers of need interpretations, see my "Women, Welfare and the Politics of Need Interpretation" in Fraser, *Unruly Practices*.

16   This picture is at odds with the one implicit in the writings of Foucault. From my perspective, Foucault focuses too single-mindedly on expert, institution-building discourses at the expense of oppositional and reprivatization discourses. Thus, he misses the dimension of contestation among competing discourses and the fact that the outcome is a resultant of such contestation. For all his theoretical talk about power without a subject, then, Foucault's historical practice is surprisingly traditional in treating expert institution builders as the only historical subjects.

17   See the chapter on "Fundamentalist Sex: Hitting Below the Bible Belt" in Barbara Ehrenreich, Elizabeth Hess, and Gloria Jacobs, *Re-making Love: The Feminization of Sex* (New York: Anchor Books, 1987). For a fascinating account of "postfeminist" women incorporating feminist motifs into born-again Christianity, see Judith Stacey, "Sexism by a Subtler Name? Postindustrial Conditions and Postfeminist Consciousness in the Silicon Valley," *Socialist Review* (1987): 7–28.

18   See Stuart Hall, "Moving Right," *Socialist Review* (January–February 1981): 113–37. For an account of new right reprivatization discourses in the United States, see Barbara Ehrenreich, "The New Right Attack on Social Welfare," in Fred Block, Richard A. Cloward, Barbara Ehrenreich, and Frances Fox Piven, *The Mean Season: The Attack on the Welfare State* (New York: Pantheon Books, 1987), 161–95.

19   I am indebted to Teresa Ghilarducci for this point (personal communication).

20   In *Discipline and Punish*, Michel Foucault provides a useful account of some elements of the knowledge production apparatuses that contribute to administrative redefinitions of politicized needs. However, Foucault overlooks the role of social movements in politicizing needs and the conflicts of interpretation that arise between such movements and the social state. See note 16.

21   Cf. the discussion of the administrative logic of need definition in Jürgen Haber-
     mas, *Theorie des kommunikativen Handelns*, Band II, *Zur Kritik der funktionalis-
     tischen Vernunft* (Frankfurt am Main: Surhkamp Verlag, 1981), 522–47.

22   See Foucault, *Discipline and Punish*, for an account of the normalizing dimensions
     of social science and of institutionalized social services.

23   Jürgen Habermas discusses the therapeutic dimension of welfare state social ser-
     vices in *Theorie des kommunikativen Handelns*, Band II, *Zur Kritik der funktiona-
     listischen Vernunft*, 522–47.

24   In *Discipline and Punish*, Michel Foucault discusses the tendency of social-
     scientifically informed administrative procedures to posit a deep self. In *The His-
     tory of Sexuality*, Volume I, *An Introduction*, trans. Robert Hunley (New York:
     Vintage, 1978), he discusses the positing of a deep self by therapeutic psychiatric
     discourses.

25   For the sake of simplicity, I shall restrict the examples treated to cases of contes-
     tation between two forces only, where one of the contestants is an agency of the
     social state. Thus, I shall not consider examples of three-sided contestation, nor
     examples of two-sided contestation between competing social movements.

26   For an account of the history of battered women's shelters, see Susan Schechter,
     *Women and Male Violence: The Visions and Struggles of the Battered Women's
     Movement* (Boston: South End Press, 1982).

27   Linda Gordon, "Family Violence, Feminism, and Social Control," in this vol-
     ume; Linda Gordon, *Heroes of Their Own Lives: The Politics and History of Family
     Violence, Boston 1880–1960* (New York: Viking Press, 1988).

28   Carol B. Stack, *All Our Kin: Strategies for Survival in a Black Community* (New
     York: Harper & Row, 1974).

29   Prudence Mors Rains, *Becoming an Unwed Mother: A Sociological Account* (Chi-
     cago: Aldine Atherton, 1971). In what follows, all citations are to this edition and
     page numbers appear in the text following quotations. I am indebted to Kathryn
     Pyne Addelson for bringing Rains's work to my attention.

30   Frances Fox Piven and Richard A. Cloward, *Regulating the Poor: The Func-
     tions of Public Welfare* (New York: Vintage Books, 1971), 285–340 and *Poor
     People's Movements* (New York: Pantheon Books, 1979). Unfortunately, Piven
     and Cloward's account is gender-blind and, as a consequence, androcentric. For
     a feminist critique, see Linda Gordon, "What Does Welfare Regulate? A Review
     Essay on the Writings of Frances Fox Piven and Richard A. Cloward," *Social Re-
     search* 55, no. 4 (Winter 1988): 610–30. For a more gender-sensitive account of
     the history of the NWRO, see Guida West, *The National Welfare Rights Movement:
     The Social Protest of Poor Women* (New York: Praeger Publishers, 1981).

31   Frances Fox Piven, "Ideology and the State: Women, Power, and the Welfare
     State," in this volume.

32   For the view that objectivity just is the mask of domination *tout court*, see
     Catharine A. MacKinnon, "Feminism, Marxism, Method, and the State: An
     Agenda for Theory," *Signs* 7, no. 3 (Spring 1982): 515–44. For the view that
     relativism undermines feminism, see Nancy Hartsock, "Rethinking Modernism:
     Minority vs. Majority Theories," *Cultural Critique* (Fall 1987): 187–206. For

a good discussion of the tensions among feminist theorists on this issue (which does not however, in my view, offer a persuasive resolution), see Sandra Harding, "The Instability of the Analytical Categories of Feminist Theory," *Signs* 11, no. 4 (1986): 645–64. For a discussion of related issues raised by the phenomenon of postmodernism, see Nancy Fraser and Linda Nicholson, "Social Criticism without Philosophy: An Encounter between Feminism and Postmodernism," *Theory, Culture & Society* 5 (1988): 373–94.

33 For a critique of the correspondence model of truth, see Richard Rorty, *Philosophy and the Mirror of Nature* (Princeton: Princeton University Press, 1979).

34 The "standpoint" approach has been developed by Nancy Hartsock. See her *Money, Sex and Power: Toward a Feminist Historical Materialism* (New York: Longman, 1983). For a critique of Hartsock's position, see Harding, "The Instability of the Analytical Categories of Feminist Theory."

35 In its first-order normative content, this formulation is Habermassian. However, I do not wish to follow Habermas in giving it a transcendental or quasi-transcendental metainterpretation. Thus, while Habermas purports to ground "communicative ethics" in the conditions of possibility of speech understood universalistically and ahistorically, I consider it a contingently evolved, historically specific possibility. See Jürgen Habermas, *The Theory of Communicative Action*, volume one, *Reason and the Rationalization of Society*, trans. Thomas McCarthy (Boston: Beacon Press, 1984); *Communication and the Evolution of Society*, trans. Thomas McCarthy (Boston: Beacon Press, 1979), and *Moralbewusstsein und kommunikatives Handeln* (Frankfurt: Suhrkamp Verlag, 1983).

36 Elizabeth M. Schneider, "The Dialectic of Rights and Politics: Perspectives from the Women's Movement," in this volume.

37 For arguments for and against this view see the essays in E. F. Kittay and Diana T. Meyers, eds., *Women and Moral Theory* (New Jersey: Rowman and Littlefield, 1987).

38 In addition to Schneider, "The Dialectic of Rights and Politics," see Martha Minow, "Interpreting Rights: An Essay for Robert Cover," *The Yale Law Journal* 96 no. 8 (July 1987): 1860–915; Patricia J. Williams, "Alchemical Notes: Reconstructed Ideals from Deconstructed Rights," *Harvard Civil Rights Civil Liberties Law Review* 22, no. 2 (Spring 1987): 401–33.

39 I owe this formulation to Martha Minow (personal communication).

CHAPTER 9

The Dialectic of Rights and Politics: Perspectives from the Women's Movement

ELIZABETH M. SCHNEIDER

INTRODUCTION: THE DEBATE ON RIGHTS

The nature of legal rights has long been a subject of interest to legal scholars and activists.[1] Recently, dialogue on the issue has intensified, provoked by numerous critiques of liberal rights, particularly by Critical Legal Studies (CLS) scholars. These recent critiques have tended to view rights claims and rights consciousness as distinct from and frequently opposed to politics and as an obstacle to the political growth and development of social movements groups.

The idea that legal rights have some intrinsic value is widespread in our culture. A rights claim can make a statement of entitlement that is universal and categorical. This entitlement can be seen as negative because it protects against intrusion by the state (a right to privacy), or the same right can be seen as affirmative because it enables an individual to do something (a right to choose whether to bear a child). Thus, a rights claim can define the boundaries of state power and the entitlement to do something and, by extension, provide an affirmative vision of human society. Rights claims reflect a normative theory of the person, but a normative theory can see the rights-bearing individual as isolated or it can see the individual as part of a larger social network. Recently, legal scholars, in particular CLS and feminist scholars, have debated the meanings of rights claims and have questioned the significance of legal argumentation focused on rights.

CLS scholars question whether rights claims and rights discourse can facilitate social reconstruction. Some CLS scholars argue that liberalism is premised on dichotomies, such as individual and community or self and other, that divide the world into two mutually exclusive spheres. Rights claims only perpetuate these dichotomies, which, to CLS scholars, limit legal thinking and inhibit necessary social change. CLS scholars base their critique of rights on the inherently individualistic nature of rights under legal liberalism, the "reification" of rights generally, and the indeterminate nature of rights claims. Other CLS scholars argue that rights are "permeated by the possessive individualism of capitalist society."[2] Because rights "belong" to individuals—rights rhetoric portrays individuals as "separated owners of their respective bundles of rights—they are necessarily individualistic."[3] This notion of ownership delimits the boundaries of state authority from that of individual autonomy, the self from other. Rights discourse tends to overemphasize the separation of the individual from the group and thereby inhibits an individual's awareness of her connection to and mutual dependence upon others.

CLS scholars also see rights discourse as taking on a "thing-like" quality —a fixed and external meaning—that "freezes and falsifies" rich and complex social experience.[4] This "attribution of a thing-like or fixed character to socially constructed phenomena," called reification, "is an essential aspect of alienated consciousness, leading people to accept existing social orders as the inevitable 'facts of life'."[5] This process thus gives people a sense of "substitute connection" and an illusory sense of community that disables any real connection.[6] Finally, these scholars see rights claims as indeterminate because argumentation based on rights does not solve the problem of how to resolve conflicts between rights and cannot transform social relations.

CLS scholars criticize the use of rights claims by social movement groups on related grounds. They argue that this use can keep people passive and dependent upon the state because it is the state that grants them their rights. Legal strategies based on rights discourse, then, tend to weaken the power of a popular movement by allowing the state to define the movement's goals. Rights discourse obscures real political choice and determination. Further, it fosters social antagonisms by magnifying disagreement within and conflicts between groups over rights. From a strategic perspective, then, reliance on rights by social movements can be politically debilitating.

Some feminist critiques of rights also see rights claims as formal and hierarchical—premised on a view of law as patriarchal. From this perspective, law generally, and rights particularly, reflect a male viewpoint characterized by objectivity, distance, and abstraction. As Catharine MacKinnon, a leading exponent of this position writes, "Abstract rights will authorize the male experience of the world."[7] The critiques usefully emphasize the indeterminacy of rights and the ways in which rights discourse can reinforce alienation and passivity. Both critiques highlight the ways in which rights discourse can become divorced from political struggle. They appropriately warn us of the dangers social movements and lawyers encounter when relying on rights to effect social change.

But both critiques fail to take account of the complex, and I suggest dialectical, relationship between the assertion of rights and political struggle in social movement practice. They see only the limits of rights and fail to appreciate the dual possibilities of rights discourse. Admittedly, rights discourse can reinforce alienation and individualism and can constrict political vision and debate. But, at the same time, it can help to affirm human values, enhance political growth, and assist in the development of collective identity.

Failing to see that both possibilities exist simultaneously, these critiques have rigidified, rather than challenged, the classic dichotomies of liberal thought— law and politics, individual and community, and ultimately, rights and politics. Radical social theory, such as CLS and feminist scholarship, must explore the dialectical dimensions of each dichotomy, not reinforce the sense that the dichotomies are frozen and static. Radical social theory must explain how these dichotomies can be transcended.

DIALECTICS AND PRAXIS AS METHODOLOGY: THE EXAMPLES OF FEMINIST THEORY AND FEMINIST LEGAL PRACTICE

The concept of dialectics has shaped much of contemporary social theory and has developed different meanings and uses. Most significantly here, it stands for the idea of the process, connection, and opposition of dualities and for subsequent change and transcendence. The dialectical approach that I use explores the process that connects ideas that appear to be in opposition to one another. One "moment" in the process gives rise to its own negation, and "out of this negativity, emerges a 'moment' which at once negates, affirms, and transcends the 'moment' involved in the struggle." [8] Thus, any idea may be both what it appears to be and something else at the same time; the idea may contain the seeds of its own contradiction, and ideas that appear to be in opposition may really be the same or connected. At any given "moment," ideas may appear to be connected or in opposition because this connection or opposition exists in only one stage of a larger process. The dialectical process is not a mechanical confrontation of an opposite from outside but an organic emergence and development of opposition and change from within the "moment" or idea itself.

The critiques of rights that I have described suffer from an analysis that divorces theory from practice. Rights are analyzed in the abstract, viewed as static—as a form of legal theory separate from social practice—and then criticized for being formal and abstract. My approach to rights views theory and practice as dialectically related, and I look to the philosophical concept of praxis to describe this process. The fundamental aspect of praxis is the active role of consciousness and subjectivity in shaping both theory and practice and the dynamic interrelationship that results. As Karl Klare has explained, law making can be a form of praxis; it can be constitutive, creative, and an expression of "the embeddedness of action-in-belief and belief-in-action." [9] For purposes of this article, my focus on praxis impels me to explore how rights claims can flow from and express the political and moral aspirations of a social movement group, how rights claims are experienced or perceived in social movement practice, and how rights discourse impacts on social movement practice generally.

A feminist philosophical orientation as well as my experience shape my approach to rights. Feminist theory is characterized by an emphasis on the interrelationship of theory and practice. It emphasizes the value of direct and personal experience as the place that theory should begin, as embodied in the phrase "the personal is political." This phrase reflects the view that the realm of personal experience, the "private" that has always been trivialized, particularly for women, is an appropriate and important subject of public inquiry, and that the "private" and "public" worlds are inextricably linked. The notion of consciousness raising as feminist method flows from this insight. In consciousness-raising groups, learning starts with the individual and personal (the private), moves to the general and social (the public), and then reflects back on itself with heightened consciousness through this shared group process. Feminist theory thus reveals the social dimension of individual experience and the individual dimension of social experience.

Feminist theory involves a particular methodology, but it also has a substantive viewpoint and political orientation. Recognizing the links between individual change and social change means understanding the importance of political activity, not just theory. Theory emerges from practice and practice then informs and reshapes theory.

Of the many cases on which I worked at the Center for Constitutional Rights, one, *State v. Wanrow,* stands out for me because it so clearly demonstrates that legal argumentation that expresses the concerns of a social movement can assist in the political development of that movement. A jury convicted Yvonne Wanrow, a Native American woman, of second-degree murder for shooting and killing a white man named William Wesler, whom she believed had tried to molest one of her children. Wesler had entered her baby-sitter's home uninvited when Wanrow and her children were there. Wanrow, who had a cast on her leg and was using crutches at the time, claimed that, based on her perceptions of the danger created by Wesler, she had acted in self-defense. The trial court, however, instructed the jury to consider only the circumstances "at or immediately before the killing" when evaluating the gravity of the danger the defendant faced,[10] even though Wanrow claimed that she had information that led her to believe that Wesler had a history of child molestation and had previously tried to molest one of her children. The trial court also instructed the jury to apply the equal force standard, whereby the person claiming self-defense can only respond with force equal to that which the assailant uses. Wesler had not been carrying a gun.

Center lawyers became involved in the case on appeal to the Washington Supreme Court. Reading the trial transcript, we realized that the judge's instructions prevented the jury from considering Yvonne Wanrow's state of mind, as shaped by her experiences and perspective as a Native American woman, when she confronted this man. The jury had not been presented with evidence concerning the lack of police protection generally in such situations, the pervasiveness of violence against women and children, the effect on Wanrow of her knowledge of Wesler as a child molester, and Wanrow's belief that she could only defend herself with a weapon. Moreover, the judge's instructions to the jury directed the jury to apply the equal force standard and not to consider Wanrow's perspective when evaluating her claim of self-defense. Consequently, our decision to challenge the sex bias in the law of self-defense —as reflected in these instructions—was formed from the insight that Yvonne Wanrow's perspective as a Native American woman had to be included in the courtroom.

We developed the legal argument for women's "equal right to trial," which challenged sex bias in the law of self-defense, based upon our knowledge of the particular problems women who killed men faced in the criminal justice system: the prevalence of homicides committed by women in circumstances of male physical abuse or sexual assault; the different circumstances in which men and women killed; myths and misconceptions in the criminal justice system concerning women who kill as "crazy"; the problems of domestic violence, physical abuse, and sexual abuse of women and children; the physical and psychological barriers that prevented women from feeling capable of defending themselves; and stereotypes of women as unreasonable. If the jury did not understand Yvonne Wanrow's experience and the way in which it shaped her conduct, it could not find her conduct to have been reasonable and therefore an appropriate act of self-defense. Since the jury would not be able to consider this defense, Wanrow, then, could not be treated fairly.

On appeal Wanrow's conviction was reversed. A plurality of the court voted to reverse on the ground that the trial court's instructions violated Washington law in three ways. First, the instruction that limited the jury's consideration to the circumstances "at or immediately before the killing" misconstrued Washington law. Properly construed, state law allowed the jury to consider Wanrow's knowledge of the deceased's reputation, prior aggressive behavior, and all other prior circumstances, even if that knowledge were acquired long before the killing. Second, the instruction concerning equal force misstated state law and denied Wanrow equal protection:

The impression created—that a 5'4" woman with a cast on her leg and using a crutch must, under the law, somehow repel an assault by a 6'2" intoxicated man without employing weapons in her defense, unless the jury finds her determination of the degree of danger to be objectively reasonable—constitutes a separate and distinct misstatement of the law and, in the context of this case, violates the respondent's right to equal protection of the law.[11]

Third, the trial court's instructions failed to direct the jury to consider the reasonableness of Wanrow's act *from Wanrow's perspective,* or, in other words, "seeing what [s]he sees and knowing what [s]he knows." [12] The Washington Supreme Court affirmed a standard of self-defense based on the individual defendant's perception, as required by Washington law, and underscored the need for this standard by recognizing the existence of sex bias in the law of self-defense generally.

The respondent was entitled to have the jury consider her actions in the light of her own perceptions of the situation, including those perceptions which were the product of our nation's "long and unfortunate history of sex-discrimination." . . . Until such time as the effects of that history are eradicated, care must be taken to assure that our self-defense instructions afford women the right to have their conduct judged in light of the individual physical handicaps which are the product of sex discrimination. To fail to do so is to deny the right of the individual woman involved to trial by the same rules which are applicable to male defendants.[13]

Thus, the political insights into sex bias in self-defense that could help to explain Yvonne Wanrow's situation arose out of legal formulation and argumentation. But the legal argument concerning the "equal right to trial" grew out of a political analysis of sex discrimination that the legal team shared, discussed, and applied to the particular case. The legal argumentation brought together diverse strands of feminist analysis and theory concerning sex-biased treatment of women in the criminal justice system.

This legal argumentation reflected a perspective that feminist activists, lawyers, and writers were beginning to express and share. Further, aspects of this argument were asserted at the same time in other courts in different cases. The rights formulation reflected the political analysis and activity of women's groups concerned with violence against women, the treatment of women within the criminal justice system, and the work of defense committees organizing around particular women defendant's cases. It was a formulation that made sense to many women on an experiential level.

In this sense, the legal formulation grew out of political analysis, but it also pushed the political analysis forward. The particular legal focus on sex bias in the law of self-defense, and on the absence of a women's perspective in the courtroom, clarified feminist analysis of the problems facing women who kill. It explained why both women defendants and lawyers representing them were more likely to claim insanity or impaired mental state rather than assert self-defense. The legal formulation thus moved the political work to a different level, raising the political question of what a woman's perspective might be and what equal treatment would look like. It focused further legal work on the disparate hurdles that limited women defendants' choice of defense—particularly the various ways in which women's experiences were excluded from the courtroom—and laid the foundation for political and legal strategies to remedy the problems created by this exclusion.

What has become known as women's self-defense work is now an established part of both feminist litigation and legal literature. Many courts have now accepted the view that there is sex bias in the law of self-defense. Still, the ongoing legal work in this area teaches us new lessons. It demonstrates the difficulty courts have in hearing women's experiences and modifying the law to take them into account. Some courts that have applied the insight reflected in the equal trial argument have unwittingly recreated the very sex stereotypes of female incapacity that women's self-defense work was intended to overcome. But these new dilemmas of feminist theory can also help to clarify issues, sharpen debate, and deepen insight into these matters.

Wanrow exemplifies the way in which the legal formulation of rights emerging from political analysis and practice can be expressive. It demonstrates the way a rights claim initially flows from political analysis and then becomes the basis for a more self-reflective political analysis. The rights formulation is part of an ongoing process of politics. The rights claim is a "moment" in that process in which the political vision emerges from within the claim of rights. This experience of praxis, then, provides a framework for my analysis of rights and politics.

Recent rights critics have emphasized appropriate caution concerning the use of rights discourse to further political struggle. There is always a risk that a political struggle will be so fixed on rights discourse or winning rights in courts that it will not move beyond rights and will freeze political debate and growth. But it can also be a means to articulate new values and political vision. The way in which a social movement group uses the rights claim and places it in a broader context affects the ability of rights discourse to aid political struggle. Rights discourse and rights claims, when emerging from and organically linked to political struggle, can help to develop political consciousness, which can play a useful role in the development of a social movement.

Rights discourse can express human and communal values; it can be a way for individuals to develop a sense of self and for a group to develop a collective identity. Rights discourse can also have a dimension that emphasizes the interdependence of autonomy and community. It can play an important role in defining the goals of a political struggle, particularly during the early development of a social movement.

COMMUNAL RIGHTS

Staughton Lynd has developed the idea of rights as "communal," infused with the values of community, compassion, and solidarity.[14] Although he focuses on some rights as particularly communal, such as section 7 of the National Labor Relations Act and the First Amendment to the United States Constitution, he argues in favor of fighting for the communal content of as many rights as possible and challenging the zero-sum perspective on rights generally. He looks to the historical context in which a right develops as a primary force shaping the particular collective aspect of the right. The communal dimension of a claim of right may differ depending on the social and political context in which the right claim emerges and the way in which formulation of the right reflects a corresponding political vision. For example, Lynd's view of the right to engage in collective activity under section 7 of the National Labor Relations Act as a paradigmatic communal right is based on his perception of this right as "derived from the actual character of working-class solidarity and accordingly a right that foreshadows a society in which group life and individual self-realization mutually reinforce each other." [15] Lynd's understanding of the collective aspect of rights has several dimensions. He maintains that a right developed in the context of a social movement struggle may have a collective cast to it. Further, the exercise of rights by an individual can expand the ability of the larger group to exercise their rights generally. Finally, Lynd suggests that the concept of the inalienability of rights—that an individual cannot give up a right because it belongs to the group—is premised on an underlying assumption based on the communal aspect of rights. Lynd's analysis, then, provides a framework to challenge the notion that rights claims must necessarily be articulated and perceived as the property of rights-bearing individuals.

INDIVIDUAL SELFHOOD AND COLLECTIVE IDENTITY

Another aspect of a dialectical view of rights is the role that rights discourse can play in individual self-development and collective identity. Carol Gilligan's work in charting differences between male and female moral and psychological development provides a basis for exploring this issue. Listening to the voices of the women she interviewed, Gilligan hears a morality based on responsibility, connection, and caretaking, rather than separation. Gilligan posits that there are different paths to maturity, which are roughly tied to gender. During development, men emphasize individuation and autonomy. Women, on the other hand, emphasize caretaking and connection with others.

Gilligan suggests that at an early stage of development men will more likely seek to resolve moral dilemmas and conflict through the use of rights. She sees rights as abstract, formal, and hierarchical and as a means of resolving problems through an emphasis on separation and the individual. Women's morality of care and responsibility differs from the male model because it emphasizes context, connection, and relationship. In this morality, problems are resolved, in what Gilligan calls a "web"-like manner, by considering all the people involved in the situation and the connections between them. Gilligan believes this approach challenges the "premise of separation" underlying the notion of rights.[16] She sees these two approaches as not simply different from, but potentially threatening to, one another. Mature moral and psychological development for both sexes would seek to synthesize moral perspectives based on both rights and responsibilities.

For this reason, Gilligan suggested that the assertion of rights can play a particularly important role in women's moral development. This psychological process of moral rights assertion has several facets. It allows women to consider their own needs directly and care for themselves, not just care for others. But instead of resting on an individually centered, hierarchically based concept of rights, rights assertion in this context takes on a different character and moves beyond a formal "paralyzing injunction not to hurt others." [17] Gilligan described it in the following way:

Thus, changes in women's rights change women's moral judgments, seasoning mercy with justice by enabling women to consider it moral to care not only for others but for themselves. The issue of inclusion first raised by the feminists in the public domain reverberates through the psychology of women as they begin to notice their own exclusion of themselves. When the concern with care extends from an injunction not to hurt others to an ideal of responsibility in social relationships, women begin to see their understanding of relationships as a source of moral strength. But the concept of rights also changes women's moral judgment by adding a second perspective to the consideration of moral problems, with the result that judgment becomes more tolerant and less absolute.[18]

Gilligan outlines a process of moral development for women that moves from an emphasis on selflessness and care for others, to a recognition of self and autonomy, and then to a self-reflective understanding of the way in which self and other are interconnected. She suggests that assertion of rights, particularly women's rights, can play a crucial role in the transformation of women's sense of self. Public assertion of women's legal rights reverberates in the consciousness of individual women. This process of differentiation through women's assertion of their own rights provides a basis for women to distinguish self from other. This enables women to exercise genuine responsibility, while at the same time, because people can "experience relationship only insofar as we differentiate other from self," to recognize the interrelationship of self and other.[19] Gilligan suggests that, in this way, assertion of rights for women in the context of women's morality of caretaking and responsibility can transform and enhance women's moral development.

Gilligan also suggests a further transformative dimension of women's experience with rights. She implies that assertion of women's rights can provide women with a sense of collective identity, a sense that self and other are connected. Assertion of rights by women can thus change the process by which rights are asserted and the way they are experienced.

Gilligan's suggestion that the psychological experience and social function of rights assertion may perform different developmental tasks for men and women may be overbroad in its link to gender. But the sense of self-definition and collective identification that Gilligan details is, nevertheless, an important aspect of rights claims, as is the linking of public assertion of legal rights to psychological and moral development. The assertion of rights claims and the use of rights discourse may thus not be purely individual—it can link the individual to a broader social group. In this sense, rights discourse can play a role in transcending the dichotomy of individual and community.

INTERDEPENDENT RIGHTS

Gilligan implies that the gender-linked oppositions of rights and care-based morality can be transcended in dialectical fashion in a third stage of development in which both men and women see the importance and interconnection of rights and responsibilities. She also suggests that rights discourse in this third stage, modified by what she perceives as characteristically female concerns regarding context, care, and connection, might be different.

Gilligan imagines that this third stage of development will be based upon the synthesis of male and female voices—those of rights and responsibilities. The discourse is no longer either simply about justice or simply about caring; rather it is about bringing them together to transform the domain. Although feminist scholars have questioned whether this third stage is really transformative, Gilligan's vision of rights articulated in this different voice has stimulated attempts by legal scholars to reimagine rights and to conceive of them as "interdependent."

For example, in a number of articles Martha Minow has sought an understanding of rights that resolves the tension between autonomy and caretaking. She explores reconstructive visions of rights shaped by a "conception of self . . . [that locates] each individual within social networks [where] membership helps constitutes the 'I', and belonging is essential to becoming." [20] Minow attempts to redefine the substance of purportedly individualistic rights by positing a right to connection, by developing the interconnection of rights and responsibilities, and by suggesting that rights claims can focus on the social and economic preconditions for rights.

William Simon's article on welfare rights, which contrasts the New Deal social work jurisprudence of welfare rights with the contemporary New Property conception of rights, suggests a similar perspective, which he calls "regenerative."[21] Simon sees the New Property conception of rights as reincarnating classical legalist view of rights based on the protection of individual independence and self-sufficiency from the collective power of the state. In contrast, he suggests that rights in New Deal social work jurisprudence differed from the classical model because they challenged this distinction between the individual and the community and reflected a norm of interdependence. Rights were used as part of a dialectical process of political development and a means of education for the welfare claimant. Rights claims were a means by which people on welfare came to understand their goals and a way for the individual claimant to get involved in political activity, to have greater participation in the process of decision making, and to have a more articulate understanding of her interests.

Rights in this context became a way to have a dialogue, a conversation; they "facilitated the beginning and middle as well as the conclusion of analysis."[22] In contrast with classical liberal conceptions of rights, this conception implicated collective concerns and reflected the "social or communal dimension of the self and of legal entitlement."[23] Rights claims were made "for" something, not only against other and the state.[24] Simon's description implies that the process by which the rights claims were developed and articulated and the interdependent content of the rights must be related. It suggests that the communal dimension of the right helped to shape the role that rights played for the welfare claimant and the rights-enforcing social worker.

Kenneth Karst's effort to reconstruct constitutional law as a "jurisprudence of interdependence" is similarly premised on Gilligan's work. Karst accepts Gilligan's dichotomy of rights and care-based systems of moral development as fundamentally male and female, and he uses this opposition as a framework to reimagine constitutional law and litigation. Karst seems to accept the notion of rights as historically hierarchical and individualistic, but he wants to synthesize rights with care so as to develop "a conception of justice that recognize[s] our interdependence."[25] He understands that concepts of rights and the language of rights will still be necessary to further this process, but he seeks to infuse rights-talk with the values of the web and to modify rights-dominated constitutional litigation to take greater account of the morality of care.

Karst seeks to synthesize these perspectives by looking for ways in which the male experience of rights can be creatively "feminized" and modified in litigation.[26] He suggests that legal argumentation should include a broader social, institutional, and political perspective; a closer focus on the particular human context of a case; the use of intuition and experience as the basis for the articulation of rights; and the use of vocabulary that particularizes and names experience. Significantly, he observes that this may be particularly possible in the area of sex-discrimination litigation.

The notions of interdependent rights that these various theorists have envisioned are efforts to redefine the substance of rights claims and the process of rights assertion so as to modify and transform the individualistic dimensions of rights. They are efforts to reimagine rights shaped by a vision of self that Gilligan posits as female—a sense of self based upon connection instead of separation or distance. These views of interdependent rights emphasize the ability of rights discourse to express human values and affirm the creative, expressive, and connective possibilities of rights.

RIGHTS AS CONVERSATION

The theoretical efforts discussed previously focused on the way that rights connected to political struggle can be part of an ongoing conversation and can have a character, content, and meaning that is more communal because they reflect the very political struggle from which they emerged. This political context might affect both the process by which rights are articulated as well as the content of the rights themselves: what the rights mean to individuals and members of the group who claim them at a particular time, and how they are understood and experienced at that time. However, even if rights discourse is understood as part of a process of political education and mobilization, how do we ensure that the articulation of rights claims will truly assist in that larger process? How can we be sure that if rights discourse dominates the conversation of politics, the conversation will ever move beyond rights? We must take seriously Peter Gabel's caution that rights can substitute the illusion of community for a more authentic and genuine sense of community. A preoccupation with or excessive focus on rights consciousness can reinforce alienation or powerlessness and weaken the power of popular movements. In and of themselves, rights claims are not a basis for building a sustained political movement, nor can rights claims perform the task of social reconstruction.

If rights claims can provide a sense of selfhood and collective identity and start political conversation, a series of questions should be raised to help guide our evaluation of the use of rights claims in a given context. Does the use of legal struggle generally and rights discourse in particular help build a social movement? Does articulating a right advance political organizing and assist in political education? Can a right be articulated in a way that is consistent with the politics of an issue or that helps redefine it? Does the transformation of political insight into legal argumentation capture the political visions that underlie the movement? Does the use of rights keep us in touch with or divert us from consideration of and struggle around the hard questions of political choice and strategy? Does it keep the movement passive or help it begin to act? Does it help the movement to determine what it really wants? Does it limit or constrain the movement's vision of what might be possible? These questions will shape our inquiry as we examine the women's rights experience.

WOMEN'S RIGHTS AND FEMINIST STRUGGLE

Recent experience with claims of legal rights for women suggests the importance of understanding the relationship between rights and political struggle from a dialectical perspective. There is a richly textured process by which a social movement group articulates political demand through a rights claim, which then affects the development of the group. Most significantly, the experience of the women's rights movement simultaneously reveals the communal possibilities of rights and underscores the limits of political strategy focused on rights. This part briefly examines four areas of women's rights work that highlight this experience: equality, reproductive rights, sexual harassment, and legal treatment of battered women.

RIGHTS CLAIMS AND DISCOURSE IN THE WOMEN'S MOVEMENT

Over the last twenty years, claims for women's rights have increasingly been used to articulate political demand for equality and for change in gender roles. The public nature of such legal rights assertion is especially significant because of the private nature of discrimination against women. The locus of women's subordination is frequently the private sphere—the home and family—which is perceived as isolated and experienced in isolation. Women also tend to see individual fault rather than to identify a systemic pattern of social discrimination. Thus, public claims of legal rights help women to overcome this sense of privatization and of personal blame, which has perpetuated women's subordination.

Formulations of women's rights emerged from the women's movement itself, from the experiences of women, and from feminist theory. This integration of experience and theory reflected in rights claims was heightened by the fact that at the same time notions of women's rights were articulated, the number of women in the legal profession was increasing dramatically. Many of the women lawyers who have focused on women's rights work entered law school because of the women's movement or were drawn into the women's movement during law school. These women, then, articulated rights claims in a dual capacity as lawyers and as activists. Lawyering was not "other" to these women but rather a deepening process of identification, self-reflection, and connection with others (both women clients and lawyers), which mirrored the experience of the movement itself.

Perhaps for this reason, women's rights litigation has involved several important aspects of Karst's reconstructed constitutional litigation: the use of experience and intuition as starting point and guide, the creative use of both political and social contexts, and the exploration of the human impact and context of the case in concrete terms. Much women's rights litigation has implemented a strategy that uses amicus curiae briefs to present these broader perspectives to ensure that women's voices are heard in court.

In addition, the advocacy process itself has had a significant effect in mobilizing women for political action. For women who have historically been excluded from public life and political action, activity in the public sphere helps to transcend the public and private dichotomy. It also helps women learn skills that are necessary to organize and mobilize political support. In this sense, the struggle for rights has enabled women to become politically active and to gain power.

At the same time, the women's movement's experience with rights suffers from some of the problems discussed by rights critics. First, in some sense the idea of equal rights, although radical in conception, has not captured the scope and depth of the feminist program. Rights claims do not effectively challenge existing social structures. Reflecting on the reproductive rights experience, Rosalind Petchesky has written:

> The concept of "rights," [is,] in general, a concept that is inherently static and abstracted from social conditions. Rights are by definition claims staked within a given order of things. They are demands for access for oneself, or for "no admittance" to others; but they do not challenge . . . the social relations of production and reproduction. The claim for "abortion rights" seeks access to a necessary service, but by itself it fails to address the social relations and sexual divisions around which responsibility for pregnancy and children is assigned. In real-life struggles, this limitation exacts a price, for it lets men and society neatly off the hook.[27]

Second, the articulation of a right can, despite a movement's best efforts, put the focus of immediate political struggle on winning the right in court. The concreteness and immediacy of legal struggle tends to subsume the more diffuse role of political organizing and education.

Third, since women's rights formulations oblige the state to act, serious questions about the appropriate role of the state in the context of women's rights have emerged, given feminist skepticism over the ability of the state to help women.

Finally, despite some substantive gains in the legal treatment of women, rights claims generally have had only limited success in the courts. For example, even though women's rights to reproductive choice have improved, access to those rights for poor women and especially poor women of color has not been adequately protected.

Yet in some areas of women's rights, there have been important victories for individual women, for women as a class, and for the development of substantive legal doctrine. Public consciousness of sex discrimination in the law, for example, has increased. Looking at the gains and losses together, I believe that the struggles around legal rights have moved the women's movement forward.

RIGHTS TO EQUALITY AND REPRODUCTIVE CHOICE

The women's rights movement articulated women's right to equal treatment as a claim of equal protection under the Fourteenth Amendment, and women's rights to procreative freedom as a claim of liberty and privacy under the due process clause of the Fourteenth Amendment. The way in which equality and reproductive rights issues were formulated by women and distorted and limited by the courts raises serious questions about how rights claims affect social movements.

The issue of equal treatment poses the theoretical problem of sameness and difference. Equal protection of the law is guaranteed only to those who are similarly situated. Thus, the issue for equality theory is comparative—who is the same as whom. In deciding this issue of comparability, difficult questions must be considered concerning whose standards are the norm, whether women and men really are different, what differences are real (biologically based or socially constructed), and whether these differences, if they do exist, really matter.

The comparative equal rights approach has had limited political and doctrinal success in the courts and legislatures. The equal rights vision was substantially limited by the defeat of the federal equal rights amendment. Because both the public and the courts viewed the equal rights amendment as a litmus test of political support for the women's movement, its defeat affected the movement nationally, even though on the state level, state equal rights amendments have had greater success. Further, despite efforts by feminist litigators to formulate women's rights claims as if no differences existed between men and women, the Supreme Court has read in differences. Finally, the Supreme Court has viewed equality claims as distinct from reproductive choice claims. Despite the vigorous efforts of feminist litigators to argue that pregnancy discrimination violates equality principles, the Supreme Court has held that since the capacity to become pregnant is "unique" to women, rules concerning pregnancy do not violate equal protection.[28] Thus, despite widespread acknowledgement by the women's movement of the centrality of pregnancy and reproductive choice to women's subordination, pregnancy and reproductive choice have been seen by the Court as problems of equality.

The movement for reproductive choice played a critical role in the early development of the women's movement. In the early 1970s large groups of women organized to demonstrate against state laws that criminalized abortion and to challenge abortion laws in the courts. Although feminists articulated this "women's right" as a right to liberty, the Supreme Court in *Roe v. Wade* decided the issue on privacy grounds. Thus, in *Roe*, a woman's right to choose whether to have an abortion was seen as a woman's private decision, which left her free from state and medical interference in the first trimester but allowed the state's interest in the decision in the first trimester; the state's interest in the decision was allowed to increase in the second trimester and eventually outweigh her interest in the third trimester.

The articulation of women's claims to equality and reproductive choice have had an important ideological effect, but the doctrinal evolution of these rights, as the reproductive rights example suggests, has muddied their meaning. First, feminist commentators widely believe that the Court's distinct theoretical articulation of reproductive control as a right to privacy separate from equality constrains political analysis on both a practical and ideological level and reinforces ideological separation of deeply interrelated oppression.

Second, feminist commentators find the very articulation of the women's right to procreative freedom as a matter of privacy to be problematic, because it reinforces and legitimizes the public and private dichotomy that historically has been damaging to women. For women, the domestic sphere and sexuality —primary areas of subordination—have been viewed as private and unregulated. Although the right has a powerful collective dimension, which could be used to emphasize group values as well as to develop the strands of individual autonomy, as interpreted by the Court, it is primarily individualistic in that it simply protects an individual's right to choose. Most significantly, analyzing the right to reproductive choice as a right of privacy emphasizes the process of decision making, which entails a balancing of interests throughout the term of the pregnancy, rather than the importance of abortion itself, which concerns the control that a woman should have over her own body and life decisions.

Nevertheless, winning the right to procreative choice in the Supreme Court certainly helped many women regardless of the particular doctrinal formulation developed. Winning it as a right of privacy may have given some activists a false sense of security, but it has led others to greater insights into the mutable nature of the legal right to choose.

Ultimately, women's rights formulations by both feminists and the courts are best considered from a dialectical perspective. On an ideological level, the formulation of women's rights in both the equality and reproductive rights contexts has simultaneously expanded and limited our perspective on women's subordination. In both contexts, the articulation of the right allowed new contradictions to unfold.

The equal rights focus of the contemporary women's movement is a good example. The contemporary women's movement grew out of the civil rights struggle. Thus, there was a strategic orientation to analogize to the civil rights experience, this time struggling to include sex within the ambit of the Fourteenth Amendment and to ensure passage of the Equal Rights Amendment.

This emphasis on equality rights, however understandable, arguably narrowed the movement's focus and constricted its vision of possible change. It caused women to analyze their experience from a comparative perspective and to stress political debate over equal treatment with men, rather than over empowerment, self-actualization, or "women-centered" perspectives generally. This limitation on the scope of equality rights was also encouraged by the fact that many of the plaintiffs raising and benefiting from equal rights claims were men. The factual context of much litigation that featured an individual plaintiff's attempt to "get" something from society, such as military dependents' benefits, increased Social Security, property tax exemptions, or admission to a sex-segregated nursing school, appeared to narrow the focus of equality rights even further.

Moreover, because the women's movement articulated its equality concerns using a rights language that frequently becomes symbolic and reified, the movement's ability to account for the range of potential political strategies and to determine appropriate reforms in any given area became more difficult. The equal rights perspective also made it easier for women to avoid the complex question of biological and social differences. Finally, some argue that the pervasiveness of an equality perspective contributed to an emphasis within the women's movement on the "symbolic" equality of rules that reflected formal, as opposed to substantive, fairness and justice.[29]

Nevertheless, the struggle over equal rights was a useful development for the women's movement. Through it the women's movement acquired a broader and clearer understanding of what it wanted, what obstacles it faced, how deep the phenomenon of sexism went, and how hard it was to affect meaningful change. The development of an equality perspective enabled women to understand the tenacity of "neutral" standards based on male experience and legitimized discussion of equality within public discourse.

By providing a public vehicle for expressing what women want, the rights struggle clarified and heightened the debates within the movement itself and then turned these insights back into theory. For instance, even though the efforts of feminist litigators to treat pregnancy as an equality issue failed in the courts, the Pregnancy Discrimination Act was passed as a result of efforts based on feminist legal argumentation to fit pregnancy into a discrimination model—Title VII. Now, however, the Pregnancy Discrimination Act's equal treatment model has been challenged on the ground that it bars employers from taking account of women's special needs for maternity leave. Thus, at each stage of the process, contradictions have emerged that have clarified differences and moved the debate to new levels.

Both the right to equality and the right to reproductive choice are rights derived from the contexts of political struggle and feminist organization. Both rights emerged from a radical feminist vision that equality was not limited to formal legal treatment or assimilation of women into male roles but rather required the radical restructuring of society. The expression of these visions began with the formulation of rights claims in the courts. Yet even though these visions have neither been nor could be achieved in the courts, their introduction through rights claims started the "conversation" in society at large about women's roles and women's subordination under the law.

The radical impulse behind the notion of women's equality and reproductive control, then, is powerful. By concretizing an abstract idea and situating it within women's experience, these rights claims did not simply "occupy" an existing right but rather modified and transformed the nature of the right. These claims, then derived from concrete struggle and political vision, articulate a notion of collective experience. They do not simply reflect an individual woman's claim, but rather they have a communal dimension that can expand opportunities for women as a class.

SEXUAL HARASSMENT AND BATTERING

Both the concept of sexual harassment and the notion of legal protection for battered women emerged directly from feminist thinking on issues of sexuality in the 1970s. Both areas suggest the importance of legal thinking tied to political struggle and to the experience of women themselves.

The history of sexual harassment is an important example of the creative development of rights. The experience of what is now called sexual harassment did not even have a name until feminist thinkers provided it with one. Widely practiced, it was viewed as a normal and inevitable activity of men when exposed to female co-workers. The idea of sexual harassment as a harm, and as an experience that was not simply normal, private, or individual to one woman, was developed through the work of feminist theorists and litigators. This work gave formerly private and hidden experience a public dimension and so legitimized it as a subject of public discourse.

Sexual harassment defined an injury to an individual woman and to women as a class from a woman's perspective. The concept of sexual harassment and the definition of harm that developed reflected the methodology of consciousness raising applied to law.

At the same time, the articulation of claims of sexual harassment has led to new problems, arising in part because of the very gains realized in the recognition of sexual harassment as a cognizable wrong. These new dilemmas concern the scope of employer liability, visions of women as sexual victims, not actors, and victim precipitation. These tensions highlight important concerns that can then reshape theory and so push feminist analysis forward.

In the 1970s, projects to help battered women suddenly appeared throughout the United States, and by the 1980s a real national battered women's movement existed. Legal claims emerging from this abuse sought to change police practices, develop legislation to criminalize battering, enforce the victim's rights, and increase a victim's protection and legal options. Some of these legislative reforms made particularly creative connections between battering and patriarchy as, for example, state legislation that used money from marriage license fees to fund battered women's shelters. The claim that women had a right not to be battered, a right to require husbands to leave the house, and a right to get orders of protection emerged from the efforts of feminist activists and thinkers to define the problem of battering.

Both the articulation of the right to be free from sexual harassment and claims for legal protection of battered women appear more affirmative and less problematic than the previous rights struggle over equality. Is it because the political message and demand of these claims is narrower, simpler, or clearer? Is it because these claims have done better, thus far, in the courts? Or is it because the development of these legal rights is at an earlier stage than that of equality and reproductive rights? Sexual harassment and battered women's rights theory exposed new harms and expanded understanding by labeling these previously private issues as public harms. Moreover, the scope of both rights as articulated by feminist litigation was broad. For example, sexual harassment claims did not simply rest on the employment treatment of individual women but rather on a broader understanding of how a workplace environment can be tainted by sexual harassment and innuendo, and therefore harm all women who work there. In addition, the claims as articulated recognized the connection between the individual and collective components of the claim. Similarly, in the battering context, the idea that women needed *ex parte* orders of protection and that police owed a duty of care to battered women transcended the individual dimension of the claim and illuminated the problems of patriarchy, because it was premised on the view that women not have the same access to the courts as do men.

Further, the articulation of these rights claims developed feminist theory in several important ways. For example, in the battered women's movement, claims of right in both civil and criminal contexts raised important questions for feminists about how to view the state. The claims sharpened debate over the role of law in modifying the public and private dichotomy, especially given the historic absence of law in the area of domestic relations generally. Debates over whether feminists should support criminalization and other reform efforts within the criminal justice system to ameliorate the problem of battering clarified the need for a feminist theory of the state that neither expressly relied upon nor rejected it. These debates underscored the ideological function of criminalization in defining battery as a public and not a private harm, and heightened the movement's analysis of reforms for battered women. For instance, reforms could focus on the individual "bad" man, or the individual woman's "victimization," but they then would not address the shared experience of battered women, the common problems of patriarchy, the conditions that create or perpetuate violence against women, or the economic and social resources— jobs, child care, housing—that battered women need to free themselves from dependence.

Some within the battered women's movement have been sensitive to these tensions and have recognized the need for litigation and legal reforms in the context of political organizing and education. These advocates have sought to consider reform efforts within a theoretical framework that focuses on the political effect and message of these efforts. Such an approach evaluates a reform based on whether it helps to redress the balance of power within the family, emphasize the broader experience of sex discrimination within the family (rather than individual victimization), and challenge the public and private dichotomy. Most significantly, this approach evaluates whether a particular reform helps to strengthen the women's movement and organize more women. This approach underscores the role that rights claims can play in furthering political development.

In both the areas of sexual harassment and legal treatment of battered women, rights claims have strengthened public consciousness on the issues and illuminated broader political perceptions of patriarchy and sexual subordination. The women's movement has begun to reshape the law in women's terms and has thus exposed new dilemmas and challenges. This effort to reshape law through the articulation of legal rights has been an important aspect of the political struggle around these issues.

A DIALECTICAL PERSPECTIVE RECONSIDERED

The women's movement's experience with rights shows how rights emerge from political struggle. The legal formulation of the rights grew out of and reflected feminist experience and vision and culminated in a political demand for power.

This analysis of the women's rights movement, shaped by an understanding of praxis, reveals a conception of both the process through which rights are formulated as well as the content of the rights themselves. The process has been "regenerative" as rights were developed in the "middle," not at the "end," of political dialogue. Rights were the product of consciousness raising and were often articulated by both political activists and lawyers translating and explaining their own experiences. Further, rights asserted in the context of the women's movement enabled women to develop an individual and collective identity as women and to understand the connection between individual and community. The articulation of rights, then, has been a means of protecting, reflecting, and building upon a burgeoning sense of community developing within the women's movement.

The context of these rights contained both individual and communal dimensions. In this sense, as Lynd's formulation suggests, these rights did not simply relate to individual women but expanded the opportunities for women as a class. Litigation over reproductive rights, sexual harassment, and battering illuminated the common experiences of women by establishing individual women's entitlement to relief.

Admittedly, claims for equal rights have not captured the experience of women as a class as effectively as the other rights claims detailed previously. Although these claims for equal rights have been shaped and defined to some degree by collective experience, they appear to have a weaker collective and stronger individual dimension. Further, equality litigation itself has not focused on the social and economic preconditions for equal treatment. Thus, although these cases attacked important stereotypes affecting women as a class, they communicated the sense that an equal right perspective only affords individual women access to treatment as males.

In fairness, it could be said that the content of women's rights in all these areas was "traditional" and individualistic. But this characterization minimizes the importance of context. Since rights in the women's movement experience emerged in the middle of "conversation," and began a process of articulating political vision connected to political program, their meaning and content have been closely tied to the political practice of the women's movement. If the rights claim is part of a larger process and the movement believes that the rights claim expresses its vision, the claim is likely to have a greater impact on the movement itself. If the movement sees rights claims as an integral part of the struggle, but not the exclusive focus, the process of rights assertion will more likely activate, rather than pacify, the social movement.

Indeed, the content of women's rights claims suggests Karst's jurisprudence of interdependence. Rights language was not simply "occupied." The source of the claims, women's experience, modified the substance of the claims themselves. Feminist litigation has reflected many of the aspects that Karst discusses—creativity, experience, intuition, and the use of a broader political and social context. Perhaps the ladder of rights can, in some contexts, be reshaped by the web of connection. Perhaps rights, in some contexts, can truly be interdependent or at least can have interdependent dimensions.

Assertion of equal rights, reproductive rights, and rights to be free from sexual harassment and battering assisted political organizing and education in the women's movement. Rights discourse encouraged the articulation of feminist vision and furthered the process of political assertion. In this sense, legal formulations of these rights laid the basis for the further articulation of women's demands. By challenging notions of equality, for example, women sought to enter the world of public citizenship. But the persistence of separate spheres of work and family divided along gender-based lines, and the tenacity of female responsibility for child rearing, emerged as limitations to that world. Nonetheless this language of equality stimulated the different visions and strategies that the legal formulation of this problem, the debate over equal/special treatment of pregnancy, has eventually revealed.

But once a right is articulated, or even won, the issues change. How will the right be applied? How will it be enforced? Women's rights have been necessary for the political development of women, particularly because they combat the privatization of women's oppression. However, rights, although they must vigorously be fought for, cannot perform the task of social reconstruction. The present economic crisis for women in this country underscores the need for a radical redefinition of social and economic responsibility and a restructuring of work and family that would transform the lives of women, particularly the many women who live in poverty. Rights, even rights that are interdependent, can only begin to help people organize themselves and identify with larger groups.

The experience of rights in the women's movement supports the need for a perspective on rights and politics grounded in a dialectical sensibility, a view that allows us to acknowledge both the universal, affirming, expressive, and creative aspects of rights claims and at the same time, maintain a critical impulse towards rights. We must hold on to and not seek to deny the contradictions between the possibilities and the limits of rights claims and discourse. In the women's movement, a wide range of feminist activists and commentators have participated in a broad critique of rights analysis, both on theoretical and practical levels. A common theme of these critiques has been the need to strengthen legal challenges for equal rights while at the same time not limiting our vision to a narrow conception of rights. We need to continue to strive for a political strategy that expresses a politics and vision of social reconstruction sensitive to women's real concerns. Legal strategy must be developed in the context of political strategy. It should attack formal doctrinal barriers, which inhibit the recognition of the interconnectedness of women's oppression and look at the particular factual context of discrimination in shaping legal responses.

A struggle for rights can be both a vehicle of politics and affirmation of who we are and what we seek. Rights can be what we make of them and how we use them. The experience of rights assertion in the women's movement can move us forward to a self-reflective recognition of the importance and the limitations of political and legal strategy that utilizes rights.

NOTES

The research and writing of this article were supported with grants from the Brooklyn Law School Faculty Summer Research program. Earlier versions were presented at the Conference on the Second Sex at the University of Pennsylvania (1984), Eighth and Ninth Annual Meetings of the Conference on Critical Legal Studies in Washington, D.C. (1984) and Chestnut Hill, Massachusetts (1985), and the Feminist Legal Theory Workshop at the University of Wisconsin Law School–Madison (1985).

The ideas discussed in this essay reflect the influence of many people. Arthur Kinoy, Nancy Stearns, and Rhonda Copelon shaped my view of rights as a lawyer; Ed Sparer's work persuaded me to look at these questions from a theoretical perspective; and continuing dialogue with Martha Minow has encouraged and strengthened me to enter the conversation on rights. I am particularly grateful to the many people who shared their ideas and responses with me: Katharine Bartlett, Margaret Berger, Rhonda Copelon, Martha Fineman, Lucinda Finley, Mary Joe Frug, Marsha Garrison, Linda Gordon, Joel Handler, Dirk Hartog, Bailey Kuklin, Kathleen Lahey, Sylvia Law, Isabel Marcus, Carrie Menkel-Meadow, Frances Olsen, Deborah Rhode, Jack Schlegel, Carol Stack, Nadine Taub, David Trubek, and Wendy Williams. Sylvia Law's support and generosity helped me work. Christina Clarke, Jim Williams, Judith Chananie, Linda Feldman, and Kathleen Turley provided helpful research assistance. Joel Kosman has been an unusually skilled and sensitive editor.

1   An expanded, fully referenced, and footnoted version of this article appeared in *New York University Law Review* 61 (October 1986): 589–652. For reasons of space, we have retained here only references for direct quotations.

2   Staughton Lynd, "Communal Rights," *Texas Law Review* 62 (1984): 1417, 1418.

3   Frances Olsen, "Statutory Rape: A Feminist Critique of Rights Analysis," *Texas Law Review* 63 (1984): 393.

4   Peter Gabel and Duncan Kennedy, "Roll Over Beethoven," *Stanford Law Review* 36 (1984): 3–6.

5   Peter Gabel and Paul Harris, "Building Power and Breaking Images: Critical Legal Theory and the Practice of Law," *New York University Review of Law and Social Change* 11 (1982/83): 373, *n. 10.*

6   Peter Gabel, "The Phenomenology of Rights-Consciousness and the Pact of the Withdrawn Selves," *Texas Law Review* 62 (1984): 1580.

7   Catharine MacKinnon, "Feminism, Marxism, Method and the State: Toward Feminist Jurisprudence," *Signs* 8 (1983): 658.

8   Richard Bernstein, *Praxis and Action* (Philadelphia: University of Pennsylvania Press, 1971), 20–21.

9   Karl Klare, "Law-Making as Praxis," *Telos* 40 (1979): 124, *n. 5.*

10 *State v. Wanrow*, 88 Wash. 2d, 234, 559 P.2d, 555.

11 Ibid., 240, 559 P.2d 558–59.

12 Ibid., 238, 559 P.2d, 557 (citing *State v. Dunning*, 8 Wash. App. 340, 342, 506 P.2d 321, 322 [1973]).

13 Ibid., 240–41, 559 P.2d, 559.

14 Lynd, "Communal Rights," 1418–19.

15 Ibid., 1419.

16 Carol Gilligan, *In a Different Voice: Psychological Theory and Women's Development* (Cambridge: Harvard University Press, 1982), 28, 38, 54, 57.

17 Ibid., 149.

18 Ibid., 149.

19 Ibid., 63.

20 Martha Minow, " 'Forming Underneath Everything that Grows': Towards a History of Family Law," *Wisconsin Law Review* (1985): 819, 894.

21 William Simon, "The Invention and Reinvention of Welfare Rights," *Maryland Law Review* 44 (1985): 1.

22 Ibid., 15.
23 Ibid., 13.
24 Ibid., 17.
25 Kenneth Karst, "Woman's Constitution," *Duke Law Journal* (1984): 495.
26 Ibid., 504–5.
27 Rosalind Pollack Petchesky, *Abortion and Woman's Choice: The State, Sexuality, and Reproductive Freedom* (New York: Longman, 1984), 7.
28 *Geduldig v. Aiello*, 417 U.S. 484, 492–97 (1974).
29 Martha Fineman, "Implementing Equality: Ideology, Contradiction and Social Change: A Study of Rhetoric and Results in the Regulation of the Consequences of Divorce," *Wisconsin Law Review* (1983): 885.

CHAPTER 10

Ideology and the State: Women, Power, and the Welfare State

FRANCES FOX PIVEN

INTRODUCTION

Much of the feminist literature of the last few years evinces an almost categorical antipathy to the state. Among socialist feminists, the antipathy is signaled by the use of such terms as *social patriarchy* or *public patriarchy* to describe state policies that bear on the lives of women.[1] And among cultural feminists, it takes form in the nostalgic evocation of the private world of women in an era before state programs intruded on the family.[2]

There is irony in this. While some feminist intellectuals characterize relationships with the state as "dependence," women activists turn increasingly to the state as the arena for political organization and influence. At least as important, the intellectual animus toward the state flies in the face of the attitudes of the mass of American women evident in survey data. While the data show most women are opposed to a defense buildup and presumably, therefore, hostile to the military aspects of state power, in domestic policy areas they evidently believe in a large measure of state responsibility for economic and social well-being, suggesting a belief in the strong and interventionist state that some feminist intellectuals abjure.[3]

Of course, activist women may be erring "liberals," and popular attitudes, including the attitudes of women, can be wrong. But in this instance, I think it is an undiscriminating antipathy to the state that is wrong, for it is based on a series of misleading and simplistic alternatives. On the one hand, there is the possibility of power and autonomy; on the other, dependence on a controlling state. But these polarities are unreal: All social relationships involve elements of social control, and yet there is no possibility for power except in social relationships. In fact, I think the main opportunities for women to exercise power today inhere precisely in their "dependent" relationships with the state, and in this article I explain why.

Before I turn directly to this issue, I want to consider the shift in the political beliefs signaled by the gender gap, for I think it important, as well as evidence of my main contentions about power. The media has bombarded us with information on the gap and also has given us our main explanation, attributing the new cleavage of opinion and voting behavior between men and women to the policies of the Reagan administration.[4] This is not wrong, for the Reagan policies may well have had a catalytic effect on the expression of women's political attitudes. The organized women's movement has also been given credit for generating the gap, and despite the poor match between the largely middle-class constituency of the movement and the cross-class constituency of the gap, and between the issues emphasized by the movement and the issues that highlight the gap, this is probably not entirely wrong either.[5] Nevertheless, I think a development of this scale is likely to have deeper sources than have heretofore been proposed. I will conclude that those roots are in the expanding relationships women have developed with the state and in the new possibilities for power yielded by those relationships. But because the connection between beliefs and this new institutional relationship is not simple and direct, I want first to evaluate and give due weight to other influences on the shift in political opinion that has occurred among women.

Rather than showing the imprint of the women's movement, with its clearly modernizing tendencies, the emphasis on peace, economic equality, and social needs associated with the gender gap suggests the imprint of what are usually taken as traditional female values. This oft-made observation suggests the gender gap is not a fleeting response to particular current events but has deep and authentic roots. At the same time, traditional values of themselves cannot account for this development. The caretaking values of women are old, but the sharp divergence between women and men is entirely new. However much tradition may color the politics of women, the fact that traditional values associated with the family are now being asserted as public values is a large transformation. Or, as Kathy Wilson told a *New York Times* reporter on the occasion of the convening of the National Women's Political Caucus in 1983, "Women are recognizing that their private values are good enough to be their public values." More than that, the beliefs associated with the gender gap are specifically about the obligations of government to protect these values. Women are asserting that the state should represent women, in their terms.

All of this suggests the possibility that a major transformation of consciousness is occurring on a scale that argues powerful historical forces must be at work, whatever the precipitating role of current administration policies. While the comparisons may seem at first glance too grand, I think the public articulation and *politicization* of formerly insular female values may even be

comparable to such historic developments as the emergence of the idea of
democratic rights among the small farmers of the American colonies and the
preindustrial workers of England and France, or the emergence of the conviction among industrial workers at different times and places of their right to
organize and strike. Each of these ideological developments reflected the inter-
play of traditional and transforming influences. And each brought enormous
political consequences in its wake.

CHANGE IN THE OBJECTIVE CIRCUMSTANCES OF WOMEN

Ideas about social life are formed out of memory and experience. They reflect
the inherited interpretations of the past and the adaptation of those interpretations to take account of new conditions. Thus the gender gap simultaneously
reflects the influence of women's traditional beliefs and the transformation
of those beliefs in response to radical changes in the objective circumstances
of American women. Changes in the family, the labor market, and the state
are altering the opportunities and constraints that confront women as political
actors. The very scale of these institutional shifts demands new interpretations
of social reality and lends weight to my contention that a major ideological
transformation is underway.

One large change is in the family. Rising rates of divorce and separation,
combined with growing numbers of women who bear children but do not
marry, mean that fewer and fewer women are in situations that even outwardly
resemble the traditional family. Moreover, even those women who remain
within traditional families now confront the possibility, if not the probability,
of separation or divorce and the near certainty of a long widowhood. Even
within those shrinking numbers of apparently traditional families, relations
have been altered by the fact that many no longer rely exclusively on the wages
earned by men.

Even taken by itself, we should expect this large change in circumstance
to have consequences for the politics of women. The firm contours of the insular and patriarchal family narrowly limited the options for action available
to women, but that kind of family also created options for action, for exercising power in family relations, no matter how convoluted the ways. Now these
options are contracting. And even when they exist, the old forms of female
power have almost surely been weakened. As Barbara Ehrenreich argues, men
in general are increasingly "liberated" from their obligations under the moral
economy of domesticity and, thus, wield the threat of desertion or divorce.[6]

But if the traditional family relations gave women some limited options for
action, in the larger sense these relations made women dependent on men and,
therefore, subject to them, even for access to the public world. It should not
be surprising, therefore, that the political opinions of women followed those

of men so closely in the past. The family was indeed an institution of social control, as of course all institutions are.

Changes in family structure, together with the inability of families to maintain themselves on the wages earned by men, meant that more and more women, like peasants before them, were forced to enter the labor market. Women became wage workers on a mass scale. Whatever this actually meant in the lives of women, it clearly meant that women had entered the mainstream of ideas about power simply because most of those ideas are about marketplace power. There are few analysts indeed who do not think the economic resources and opportunities for organization generated by market relations are the critical resources for power. In this very broad sense, the Left tradition is not different. For nearly a century, Left intellectuals have looked almost exclusively to production relations as the arena in which popular power could be organized and exercised. Production, by bringing people together as workers in mass-production industries, generated the solidarities that made collective action possible. And, once organized, workers in the mass-production industries also gained leverage over capital.

But the prospects for women generated by their mass entry into the labor market are neither so simple nor so happy. The situation is, of course, different for different women. For those who are better educated, liberation from the constraints of the family has meant an opportunity to move into and upward in the realms of the market and politics. These women, among whom I count myself, have tried to shake themselves free of the old moral economy of domesticity and in their place developed new ideas to name their new opportunities and aspirations. These are the ideas of the women's movement, ideas about liberation, modernization, and market success. That movement not only took advantage of burgeoning opportunities for women in government, business, law, and medicine,[7] it helped create those opportunities. In this sense, changes in objective circumstances and ideology were interactive, as I think they always are. If new ideas reflect new conditions, new ideas in turn may well lead people to act in ways that help shape those conditions.

But most women did not become lawyers, nor will they. Most women, forced to sell their labor, sold it in the expanding low-wage service sector as fast-food workers, or hospital workers, or office cleaning women where, perhaps as a result of the influx of vulnerable women workers, wages and working conditions actually deteriorated over the last decade.[8] The stability of the ratio of female earnings to male earnings, *despite the large gains made by some women,* is striking evidence of the weak position of these workers.[9] They are located in industries where unionization has always been difficult and where those unions that did form realized few gains because widely scattered work sites made organization difficult, and a ready supply of unemployed workers weakened the strike power. The prospect of long-term, high levels of unemployment in the American economy makes it less likely than ever that these structural barriers, which prevented unionization and the use of the strike power in the past, can now be overcome.

Nor is it likely that women will gradually enter the manufacturing industries where workers did succeed in unionizing, if only because these industries are shrinking. New jobs are being created not in steel, autos, or rubber, but in fast foods, data processing, and health care. Of course, even if this were not so, even if women were likely to enter the smokestack industries in large numbers, it would be too late, for international competition and robotization have combined to crush the fabled power of mass-production workers. In fact, the broad shifts in the American economy from manufacturing to services and from skilled work to unskilled work mean that the possibilities for the exercise of popular power in the workplace are eroding for both men and women.

Women are losing their old rights and their limited forms of power within the family while in the marketplace, their position is weak, and prospects for improvement through individual mobility or the development of collective power are grim. These circumstances have combined to lead women to turn to the state, and especially to the expanding programs of the welfare state. Income supports, social services, and government employment partly offset the deteriorating position of women in family and economy and have even given women a measure of protection and therefore power in the family and economy. In these ways the state is turning out to be the main recourse of women.

The relationship of women to the welfare state hardly needs documenting. Women with children are the overwhelming majority among the beneficiaries of the main "means-tested" income maintenance programs, such as AFDC, food stamps, and Medicaid.[10] Moreover, the numbers of women affected by these programs are far greater than the numbers of beneficiaries at any one time, for women in the low-wage service and clerical sectors of the labor force turn to welfare state programs to tide them over during family emergencies or their frequent bouts of unemployment. Older women, for their part, depend on Social Security and Medicare benefits, without which most would be very poor. However inadequately, all of these programs moderate the extremes of poverty and insecurity among women.

More than that, the programs that make women a little less insecure also make them a little less powerless. The availability of benefits and services reduces the dependence of younger women with children on male breadwinners, as it reduces the dependence of older women on adult children. The same holds in the relations of working women with employers. Most women work in situations without unions or effective work rules to shield them from the raw power of their bosses. Social welfare programs provide some shield, for the availability of benefits reduces the fear that they and their children will go hungry and homeless if they are fired.

Women have also developed a large and important relationship to the welfare state as the employees of these programs. The proportion of such jobs held by women has actually increased, even as the total number of social welfare jobs greatly expanded. By 1980, fully 70 percent of the 17.3 million social service jobs on all levels of government, including education, were held by women,[11] accounting for about one-third of all female nonagricultural employment and for the larger part of female job gains since 1960.[12] In these several ways, the welfare state has become critical in determining the lives and livelihood of women. The belief in a responsible state reflected in the gender gap is partly a reflection of this institutional reality. But will this institutional context yield women the resources to participate in the creation of their own lives as historical actors? Can it, in a word, yield them power?

WOMEN AND POLITICAL POWER

Very little that has been written about the relationship of women to the state suggests we look to it for sources of power. To the contrary, the main characterization is of a state that exercises social control over women, supplanting the eroding patriarchal relations of the family with a patriarchal relationship with the state. In my opinion, the determination to affirm this conclusion is generally much stronger·than the evidence for it. Even in the nineteenth century, state policies had a more complicated bearing on the situation of women. Thus, while it is clearly true that changes in family law that granted women some rights as individuals, including the right to own property, did not overcome their subordination, that is hardly evidence that the state by these actions was somehow moving "toward a new construction of male domination." [13] This kind of argument is even more strongly made with regard to welfare state programs. From widows' pensions and laws regulating female labor in the nineteenth century to AFDC today, state programs that provide income to women and children, or that regulate their treatment in the marketplace, are condemned as new forms of patriarchal social control. Now there is surely reason for not celebrating widows' pensions as emancipation or AFDC either. These programs never reached all of the women who needed support (widows' pensions reached hardly any), the benefits they provided were meager, and those who received them were made to pay a heavy price in pride. Similarly, government regulation of family and market relations never overcame economic and social discrimination and in some instances reinforced it. But perhaps because some income would seem to be better than none, and even weak regulations can be a beginning, the definitive argument of the social control perspective is not that the welfare state is weak and insufficient, but that involvement with government exacts the price of dependence, somehow robbing women of their capacities for political action. It seems to follow that the massive expansion of these programs in the past two decades and the massive involvement of women and their children in them is cause for great pessimism about the prospects for women exerting power on the state.

In general, I think this mode of argument is a reflection of the eagerness with which we have embraced a simplistic "social control" perspective on institutional life, straining to discover how every institutional change is functional for the maintenance of a system of hierarchical relations and, therefore, evidence of the power of ruling groups. Of course, ruling groups do have power, they do try to exercise social control, and they usually succeed, at least for a time. But they are not all-powerful. They do not rule entirely on their terms, and they do not exercise social control without accommodations. Even then, the institutional arrangements that achieve social control are never entirely secure, for people discover new resources and evolve new ideas, and sometimes these resources and ideas are generated by the very arrangements that, for a time, seemed to ensure their acquiescence.

The critique of the welfare state developed by radical feminists was surely strongly influenced by a major Left analysis of these programs. Overall, and despite the complexities in some of their arguments, some on the Left disparaged social welfare programs as functional not for the maintenance of patriarchy but for the maintenance of capitalism. Where in other arenas there was sometimes readiness to see that institutional arrangements had been shaped by class conflict, and even to see a continuing capacity for class struggle, in the arena of social welfare there was mainly social control. In part, this reflected the view, almost axiomatic among many on the Left, that the only authentic popular power is working-class power arising out of production relations. It was at least consistent with this axiom to conclude that welfare state programs weakened popular political capacities and in several ways. The complicated array of program and beneficiary categories, combined with regressive taxation, fragmented working-class solidarity; the programs provided puny benefits but considerable opportunities for coopting popular leaders and absorbing popular energies; and the very existence of social welfare programs distracted working people from the main political issue, which, of course, was the control of capital. In this view, the welfare state was mainly understood as an imposition from above.

But I do not think the evolution of the American welfare state can be understood as the result only or mainly of a politics of domination. Rather it was the result of complex institutional and ideological changes that occurred in American society and of the complex and conflictual politics associated with these changes. Over the course of the last century, the role of government (particularly the federal government) in American economic life progressively enlarged. This development was largely a reflection of the demands of businessmen in an increasingly concentrated economy. But it had other consequences beyond creating the framework for industrial growth. As government penetration of the economy became more pervasive and more obvious, *laissez-faire* doctrine lost much of its vigor, although it still echoed strongly in the rhetoric of politicians. Few analysts dispute the significance of the doctrine in the American past. It was not that the actual role of government in the economy was so restricted, for the record in that respect is complicated. Rather, the doctrine of limited government was important because it restricted the spheres in which democratic political rights had bearing. Eventually, however, the doctrine became untenable. The political ideas of Americans gradually changed in reflection of a changing reality. An economy increasingly penetrated by government gave rise to the wide recognition of the role of the state in the economy and a gradual fusion of ideas about economic rights and political rights.[14]

This shift in belief is evident in a wealth of survey data that show that Americans think government is responsible for reducing economic inequality, for coping with unemployment, for supporting the needy, for, in short, the economic well-being of its citizens. It is also evident in electoral politics, as Edward R. Tufte's analyses of the efforts of political leaders to coordinate the business cycle with the election cycle make evident,[15] and as do exit poll data on the popular concerns that generated electoral shifts in the 1980 election.[16]

Ideas undergird political action. The emerging recognition that government played a major role in the economy, and that the democratic right to participate in government extended to economic demands, increasingly shaped the character of political movements. Beginning with the protests of the unemployed, the aged, and industrial workers in the Great Depression, to the movements of blacks, women, and environmentalists in the 1960s and 1970s, government became the target of protest, and government action to redress grievances arising in economic spheres became the program. The gradually expanding American welfare state was mainly a response to these movements. It is not by any means that the movements were the only force in shaping the welfare state. On the one hand, the success of the protestors was owed to the growing legitimacy of their demands among a broader public and the threat they therefore wielded of precipitating electoral defections if government failed to respond. On the other hand, the programs that responded to protest demands were limited and modified by other powerful interests, mainly by business groups who resisted the programs or worked to shape them to their own interests. Nevertheless, popular movements were a critical force in creating and expanding the welfare state.[17]

If the welfare state was not an imposition, if it was forged at least in part by a politics from below, what then will be its consequences over the longer run for the continued exercise of political force from below? This of course is the main question raised by the social control thesis, and it is of enormous significance for women given their extensive involvement with the welfare state. Thus far, that involvement is not generating acquiescence. To the contrary, the expectations of government revealed by the gender gap, as well as the indignation and activism of women's organizations in reaction to the policies of the Reagan administration, are not the attitudes of people who feel themselves helpless. Rather, they suggest that women think they have rights vis-à-vis the state and some power to realize those rights. If, however, the wide involvement of women in the welfare state as beneficiaries and workers erodes their capacities for political action, then what we are witnessing is a deluded flurry of activity that will soon pass.

But perhaps not. Perhaps this is the beginning of women's politics that draws both ideological strength and political resources from the existence of the welfare state. One sense in which this may be so is that the welfare state provides some objective institutional affirmation of women's political convictions. I said earlier that the welfare state was in large part a response to the demands of popular political movements of both men and women. These movements, in turn, had been made possible by changes in the relationship of government to the economy, which had encouraged the idea that democratic rights included at least some economic rights. Once in existence, the social programs strengthen the conviction that economic issues belong in political spheres, and that democratic rights include economic rights. In particular, the existence of the social programs are, for all their flaws, an objective and public affirmation of the values of economic security and nurturance that connect the moral economy of domesticity to the gender gap.

This kind of affirmation may well strengthen women for political action. To use a phrase suggested by Jane Jenson in connection with the rise of the French women's movement, the "universe of political discourse" helps determine the likelihood and success of political mobilizations.[18] One can see the criticality of the universe of political discourse or ideological context in determining not only the success but the scale of past expressions of oppositional politics among women. For example, the participation of women in the food riots of the eighteenth and nineteenth centuries reflected the centrality of nurturance to women (as well as their institutional access to the markets, where collective action could take place). But perhaps women were able to act as they did on so large a scale because their distinctive values as women were reinforced by the traditional belief, held by men and women alike, that the local poor had a prior claim on the local food supply. By contrast, when middle-class women reformers in the nineteenth-century United States tried to "bring homelike nurturing into public life," they were pitted against the still very vigorous doctrines of American *laissez-faire*.[19] Not only were their causes largely lost, but their movement remained small, failing to secure much popular support even from women. The situation is vastly different today. The women reformers who are mobilizing now in defense of social welfare programs are not isolated voices challenging a dominant doctrine. The existence of the welfare state has contributed to the creation of an ideological context that has given them substantial influence in the Congress as well as mass support from women.

Women have also gained political resources from their relationship with the state. One critical resource would appear to be of very long standing. It is, quite simply, the vote and the potential electoral influence of women, given their large numbers. Of course, that resource is not new, and it is not owed to the welfare state. Women have been enfranchised for over six decades, but the promise of the franchise was never realized for the reason that women followed men in the voting booth as in much of their public life. Only now, with the emergence of the gender gap, does the promise of electoral power seem real.

Part of the reason for the new significance of women's electoral power is in the institutional changes I have described. The "breakdown" of the family, while it stripped women of old resources for the exercise of power within the family, nevertheless freed women to use other resources. In fact, I think the breakdown of any institutional pattern of social control can generate resources for power, Charles Tilly and other resource mobilization theorists notwithstanding. Tilly is partly right to scorn the long-held view that social dislocation of itself explains political movements.[20] His sweeping dismissal of the disorganization perspective, however, leads him to ignore the resources sometimes yielded people by what is usually viewed as social disorganization. The disintegration of particular social relations may well mean that people are released from subjugation to others and thus freed to use resources that were previously effectively suppressed. The breakdown of the plantation system in the United States, for example, meant that rural blacks were removed from the virtually total power of the planter class, and only then was it possible for them to begin to use the infrastructure of the black Southern church as a focus for political mobilization.

Similarly, only as women were at least partly liberated from the overweening power of men by the "breakdown" of the family has the possibility of electoral power become real. The scale of the gender gap and the fact that it has grown and held in the face of the Reagan administration's ideological blunderbuss suggests the enormous electoral potential of women. This, of course, was the media's preoccupation and the preoccupation of the contenders in the 1984 election. But its importance is almost surely larger and more lasting. Not only did the partisan gender gap reemerge in the 1988 election, but the spread between men and women on the key issues of war and peace and government responsibility for economic well-being also held.[21] Women have the potential of moving into the forefront of electoral calculations in part because they are an enormous and growing constituency. Demographic trends and long-term trends in electoral participation have combined to produce several more million female than male voters. And that enormous constituency is showing a historically unprecedented coherence and conviction that, I have argued, is intertwined with the development of the welfare state. This electorate could change the politics of the welfare state, although not by itself.

The welfare state has generated other political resources that, it seems fair to say, are mainly women's resources. The expansion of social welfare programs has created a far-flung and complex infrastructure of agencies and organizations that are so far proving to be a resource in the defense of the welfare state and may have even larger potential. The historic involvement of women in social welfare and their concentration in social welfare employment now have combined to make women preponderant in this infrastructure and to give them a large share of leadership positions as well.[22] The political potential of these organizations cannot be dismissed because they are part of the state apparatus. Such organizations, whether public or private, are part of the state, in the elementary sense that they owe their funding to government. Nevertheless, the Byzantine complexity of welfare state organization, reflecting the fragmented and decentralized character of American government generally, as well as the historic bias in favor of private implementation of public programs, may afford the organizations a considerable degree of autonomy from the state. That so many of these organizations have lobbied as hard as they have against the several rounds of Reagan budget cuts is testimony to this measure of autonomy. They did not win, of course. But mounting federal deficits are evidence they did not lose either, and that is something to wonder about.

There is another aspect of the politics generated by this organizational infrastructure that deserves note. The welfare state brings together millions of poor women who depend on welfare state programs. These constituencies are not, as is often thought, simply atomized and, therefore, helpless people. Rather the structure of the welfare state itself has helped to create new solidarities and has also generated the political issues that cement and galvanize these solidarities. We can see evidence of this in the welfare rights movement of the 1960s, where people were brought together in welfare waiting rooms, and where they acted together in terms of common grievances generated by welfare practices. We can see it again today, most dramatically in the mobilization of the aged to defend Social Security. The solidarities and issues generated by the welfare state are, of course, different from the solidarities and issues generated in the workplace. But that difference does not argue their insignificance as sources of power, as the Left often argues, and especially for women who have small hope of following the path of industrial workers.

The infrastructure of the welfare state also creates the basis for cross-class alliances among women. The infrastructure is dominated, of course, by better educated and middle-class women. But these women are firmly linked by organizational self-interest to the poor women who depend on welfare state programs. It is poor women who give the welfare state its *raison d'être* and who are ultimately its most reliable source of political support. Of course, the alliance between the organizational infrastructure and the beneficiaries of the welfare state is uneasy and difficult and sometimes overshadowed by antagonisms that are also natural. Nevertheless, the welfare state has generated powerful cross-class ties between the different groups of women who have stakes in protecting it.

CONCLUSION

The erosion of the traditional family and women's deteriorating position on the labor market has concentrated women in the welfare state. The future of these women, workers and beneficiaries alike, hangs on the future of these programs. They need to defend the programs, expand them, and reform them. They need, in short, to exert political power. The determined and concerted opposition to welfare state programs that has emerged among corporate leaders and their Republican allies and the weak defense offered by the Democratic party suggests that the situation will require a formidable political mobilization by women. The programs of the welfare state were won when movements of mass protest, by raising issues that galvanized an electoral following, forced the hand of political leaders. The defense and reform of the welfare state is not likely to be accomplished by less. There is this difference, however. The electoral and organizational support needed to nourish and sustain the movements through which women can become a major force in American political life is potentially enormous.

NOTES

1 Variations of this argument can be found in Mimi Abramovitz, *Regulating the Lives of Women: Social Welfare Policy From Colonial Times to the Present* (Boston: South End Press, 1988); Eileen Boris and Peter Bardaglio, "The Transformation of Patriarchy: The Historic Role of the State," in *Families, Politics, and Public Policy*, ed. Irene Diamond (New York: Longman, 1983), 70–93; N. Barrett, "The Welfare System as State Paternalism," paper Presented to the Conference on Women and Structural Transformation, Institute of Research on Women, Rutgers University, 1983; Carol Brown, "Mothers, Fathers, and Children: From Private to Public Patriarchy," in *Women and Revolution: A Discussion of the Unhappy Marriage of Marxism and Feminism*, ed. Lydia Sargent (Boston: South End Press, 1981),

239–67; Nancy Fraser, article in this volume; Nancy Holmstrom, " 'Women's Work,' The Family, and Capitalism," *Science and Society* 45 (1981): 186–211; Mary McIntosh, "The State and the Oppression of Women," in *Feminism and Materialism*, ed. Annette Kuhn and AnnMarie Wolpe (London: Routledge and Kegan Paul, 1978), 254–89; Diane Polan, "Toward a Theory of Law and Patriarchy," in *The Politics of Law*, ed. David Kairys (New York: Pantheon, 1982), 294–303; Elizabeth Wilson, *Women and the Welfare State* (London: Tavistock, 1977). Happily, however, some more recent work has begun to explore the political and ideological resources yielded women in and through the welfare state. See, for example, Laura Balbo, "Crazy Quilts: Rethinking the Welfare State from a Women's Point of View," Anette Borchorst and Birte Siim, "Women and the Advanced Welfare State—A New Kind of Patriarchal Power?" and Drude Dahlerup, "Confusing Concepts—Confusing Reality: A Theoretical Discussion of the Patriarchal State," in *Women and the State*, ed. Anne Showstack Sassoon (London: Hutchinson, 1987), 45–71, 128– 57, 93–127; Y. Ergas, "The Disintegrative Revolution: Welfare Politics and Emergent Collective Identities," paper presented to the Conference on the Transformation of the Welfare State: Dangers and Potentialities for Women, Bellagio, Italy, 1983; Helga Maria Hernes, *Welfare State and Women Power: Essays in State Feminism* (Oslo: Norwegian University Press, 1987).

2   Jean Bethke Elshtain, "Feminism, Family and Community," *Dissent* (Fall 1982): 442–50; Jean Bethke Elshtain, "Antigone's Daughters: Reflections on Female Identity and the State," in *Families, Politics, and Public Policy*, 300–311.

3   Attitudes toward defense spending account for a good part of the difference in male and female attitudes that captured public attention during the 1980 election, and that has persisted, although the media's interest has faded somewhat. When economic conditions deteriorated in 1982–83, concern with the military was temporarily displaced by concern with the economy among women. See A. H. Miller and O. Malanchuk, "The Gender Gap in the 1982 Elections." Paper presented to the 38th Annual Conference of the American Association for Public Opinion Research, Buck Hill Falls, Pennsylvania, May 19–22, 1983. Alice S. Rossi also reviews data showing an increase of gender identification among women through the 1970s, see "Beyond the Gender Gap: Women's Bid for Political Power," *Social Science Quarterly* 64 (1983): 718–33. See also M. Schlichting and P. Tuckel, "Beyond the Gender Gap: Working Women and the 1982 Election," paper presented to the 38th Annual Conference of the American Association for Public Opinion Research, Buck Hill Falls, Pennsylvania, May 19–22, 1983, for an examination of differences in the attitudes of married and unmarried and employed and unemployed women, which concludes that the gender gap holds regardless of marital or labor-force status.

4   In her article, "Beyond the Gender Gap," Rossi reviews studies that show the beginning of a gender gap as early as the 1950s. However, exit poll data after the 1980 election revealed an unprecedented 9 percent spread in the voting choices of men and women. In subsequent polls, the spread substantially widened to a 15 percent difference between men and women in response to whether Reagan deserved reelection in a *New York Times* poll reported in December 1983. Moreover,

while male ratings of the president rose with the upturn in economic indicators and the invasion of Grenada, the unfavorable ratings by women remained virtually unchanged.

5   Attitudes about the reproductive and legal rights of women, which have been the central issues of the movement, do not show a gap between male and female respondents in the surveys. Single women, however, are much more likely than men to support the "women's rights" issues.

6   Barbara Ehrenreich, *The Hearts of Men* (New York: Anchor Books, 1983).

7   Where only 4 percent of the nation's lawyers and judges were women in 1971, women accounted for 14 percent in 1981. In the same period, the percentage of physicians who are women rose from 9 to 22 percent, and the percentage of female engineers increased from 1 to 4 percent.

8   E. Rothschild, "Reagan and the Real America," *New York Review of Books*, February 5, 1981, p. 28.

9   See Lisa Redfield Peattie and Martin Rein, *Women's Claims: A Study in Political Economy* (New York: Oxford, 1983) for a review of data on women's participation in the labor force that shows the persistence of part-time and irregular employment as well as the concentration of women in low-paying jobs.

10 About half of all female-headed families, or 3 million, received AFDC in 1979. An almost equal number received Medicaid, and 2.6 million were enrolled in the food stamp program. See Steven P. Erie, Martin Rein, and Barbara Wiget, "Women and the Reagan Revolution: Thermidor for the Social Welfare Economy," in *Families, Politics, and Public Policy*, 94–119.

11 Ibid., 103.

12 Steven P. Erie, "Women, Reagan and the Welfare State: The Hidden Agenda of a New Class War." Paper presented to the Women's Caucus for Political Science, Chicago, Illinois, September 1–4, 1983.

13 Eileen Boris and Peter Bardaglio, "The Transformation of Patriarchy: The Historic Role of the State," in *Families, Politics, and Public Policy*, 70–93, quote from p. 75.

14 Frances Fox Piven and Richard A. Cloward, *The New Class War: Reagan's Attack on the Welfare State and Its Consequences* (New York: Pantheon, 1982).

15 Edward R. Tufte, *Political Control of the Economy* (Princeton, N.J.: Princeton University Press, 1978).

16 See Walter Dean Burnham, "The 1980 Earthquake: Realignment, Reaction, or What?" in *The Hidden Election: Politics and Economics in the 1980 Presidential Campaign*, ed. Thomas Ferguson and Joel Rogers (New York: Pantheon Books, 1981), 98–140, for an excellent discussion of the issues that determined the outcome of the 1980 election. He concludes that worry over unemployment was the critical issue leading voters who had supported Carter in 1978 to defect to Reagan in 1980.

17 Frances Fox Piven and Richard A. Cloward, *Regulating the Poor: The Functions of Public Welfare* (New York: Pantheon, 1971): Frances Fox Piven and Richard A. Cloward, *Poor People's Movements: Why They Succeed, How They Fail* (New York: Pantheon, 1977).

18 Jane Jenson, " 'Success' Without Struggle? The Modern Women's Movement in

France." Paper presented to a workshop at Cornell University on the Women's Movement in Comparative Perspective: Resource Mobilization, Cycles of Protest, and Movement Success, May 6–8, 1983.

19 Dolores Hayden, *The Grand Domestic Revolution* (Cambridge, Mass.: The MIT Press, 1981), 4–5.

20 Charles Tilly, "Food Supply and Public Order in Modern Europe," in *The Formation of Nation States in Western Europe*, ed. Charles Tilly (Princeton, N.J.: Princeton University Press, 1975), 380–455.

21 For a discussion of the gender gap in the 1984 elections, see Ethel Klein, "The Gender Gap: Different Issues, Different Answers," in *The Brookings Review* (Winter 1985): 33–37. See also Arthur Miller, "Gender and the Vote: 1984," in *The Politics of the Gender Gap: The Social Construction of Political Influence*, ed. Carol M. Mueller (Beverly Hills, Calif.: Sage Publications, 1988), 258–82. Miller draws on Carol Gilligan's *In a Different Voice* (Cambridge, Mass.: Harvard University Press, 1982) to explain the persisting gender gap as a reflection of women's distinctive "moral development" and consequent attitudes toward social welfare programs. See also Cynthia Deitch, "Sex Difference in Support for Government Spending," in *The Politics of the Gender Gap*, 192–216, for an analysis of sex differences in attitudes toward social spending. For a summary of the data that emphasize the stable and growing differences between men and women on domestic issues, see Carol M. Mueller, "The Empowerment of Women: Polling and the Women's Bloc," in *The Politics of the Gender Gap*, 16–36. As of June 1988, the partisan gap between women and men looking forward to the 1988 election was 9 percent, according to a series of Gallup polls reported in the *New York Times*.

22 Rossi, in an analysis of the first National Women's Conference at Houston in 1977, reports that 72 percent of the delegates were employed either by government or by nonprofit social welfare organizations. Alice S. Rossi, *Feminists in Politics: A Panel Analysis of the First National Women's Conference* (New York: Academic Press, 1982). See also Rossi, "Beyond the Gender Gap," for a discussion of "insider-outsider" coalitions made possible by government employment. This pattern also exists in European welfare states. See Laura Balbo, Untitled paper, and Y. Ergas, "The Disintegrative Revolution: Welfare Politics and Emergent Collective Identities," papers presented to the Conference on the Transformation of the Welfare State: Dangers and Potentialities for Women, Bellagio, Italy, August 1983; Helga Maria Hernes, *The Role of Women in Voluntary Associations*, preliminary study submitted to the Council of Europe, Steering Committee of Human Rights (CDDH), December 1982.

CHAPTER 11

Welfare Is Not for Women: Why the War on Poverty Cannot Conquer the Feminization of Poverty

DIANA PEARCE

The "other America" described two decades ago by Michael Harrington[1] is a changing neighborhood: men are moving out, while women, many with children, are moving in. As a result, the War on Poverty that grew out of the concern aroused by Harrington and others was built on images and assumptions about the poor that were then, and are even more so today, invalid. The fundamental thesis of this article is that the trend toward the "feminization of poverty"[2] has profoundly altered the needs of today's poor, as well as the nature of public policy required to meet these needs.

Although this discussion could be broadened to encompass all the poor, it will be limited to women-maintained households alone. Statistically, the exclusion of households maintained by single males is unimportant, as less than 8 percent of poor households maintained by a single person fall into this category. But analytically it is quite important, as it is not the lack of two adults that is associated with higher rates of poverty, but the fact that it is a woman alone, struggling to maintain a household on her own, that is so highly correlated with poverty. Households maintained by men or married couples not only have lower than average rates of poverty in 1988—5.9 percent are poor as compared to 10.4 percent of all American families and 33.5 percent of woman-maintained households—but households maintained by men or married couples alone are the only family type that recently experienced a *decrease* in poverty despite the recession.[3]

Keeping in mind this focus on all poor women who maintain households alone, this article will discuss three topics. First, it will detail the nature of the trend toward the feminization of poverty. Second, it will contrast the nature of women's poverty with the nature of our antipoverty programs, with particular emphasis on the ways in which the fundamental assumptions behind welfare are at best inappropriate and at worst institutionalize women's poverty. This discussion will focus on the specific approaches and reforms of the War on Poverty, as an example of how even *reforms* of welfare do not work for poor women. Third, this article will outline the needs of women in poverty and briefly sketch the elements of policy necessary to meet those needs.

THE TREND TOWARD FEMINIZATION OF POVERTY

What is the "feminization of poverty"? Whether as widows, divorcees, or unmarried mothers, women have always experienced more poverty than men. But in the last two decades, families maintained by women alone have increased from 36 percent to 53 percent of all poor families.[4]

During the seventies, there was a net increase each year of about 100,000 poor, woman-maintained families. Between 1979 and 1988, another 998,000 families headed by women became poor. And of the decrease in the number of poor families between 1987 and 1988, over 90 percent occurred to families with male householders.[5] There are now more than 3.6 million families maintained by women alone whose income is below the poverty level.

The relative economic status of families maintained by women alone has also declined, with average income of women-maintained families falling from 51 percent to 46 percent of that of the average male-headed family.[6] Once poor, the woman-maintained family is more likely to stay poor, ten times more likely by one estimate.[7]

These trends are even greater among minorities. Particularly in the seventies, blacks experienced a shift in the burden of poverty from two-parent families to families maintained by women alone, so that now about three-fourths of poor black families are maintained by women alone.[8] Because economic opportunities for minority women are even more dismal than those for majority women, this shift has increased minority poverty and exacerbated racial inequality.

In these changes, two opposite trends stand out. First, several groups that have historically experienced disproportionate rates of poverty have been lifted out of poverty by postwar economic growth or by the development of targeted social programs. Many workers, who used to be labeled "the working poor" by themselves as well as by others, are now economically secure enough to be seen as the working class or the middle class. Older Americans, whose poverty frequently occurred because of a health crisis or the lack of housing, and inadequate Social Security, have been given Medicare, housing targeted specifically for the elderly, and broadened and indexed Social Security benefits. As a result, the overall poverty rate for the elderly is now less than that of the population as a whole.[9]

The opposite is true for families maintained by women alone. Although a decreasing *proportion* of these families has experienced poverty—about one-third of all woman-maintained families are poor today, compared to one-half in the sixties—this gain has been overwhelmed by the large increase in the *numbers* of woman-maintained families, greatly enlarging the "pool" of those at risk of being poor.[10]

Most people are aware that the rise in the divorce rate and the increase in the number of children born out of wedlock has increased the number of single-parent families. But this is also a result of the fact that (1) virtually every woman today is married at some point (94 percent by age sixty-five) and (2) most ever-married women have children (only 6 percent remained childless by ages forty to forty-four in 1980, compared to 20 percent in 1950).[11] In short, more women are mothers and fewer have a mate.

But that avoids the question of why women-maintained households have either not shared in the poverty-reducing prosperity of the fifties and sixties or in the poverty reduction experienced by other high-risk groups. The answer lies in two basic phenomena. First, women's poverty is fundamentally different from that experienced by men, and second, poor women are subjected to programs designed for poor men. Poor women find that these programs are not only inadequate and inappropriate but also lock them into a life of poverty.

UNIQUENESS OF FEMALE POVERTY

While many women are poor for some of the same reasons that men are poor—they live in a job-poor area, they lack the necessary skills or education—much of women's poverty is due to two causes that are basically unique to females. Women often must provide all or most of the support for their children, and they are disadvantaged in the labor market.

CHILD REARING

Women often bear the economic as well as the emotional burden of rearing their children. When a couple with children breaks up, frequently the man becomes single, while the woman becomes a single parent. The poverty rate for households with children has always been greater than that for households that do not have children, and the difference has always been greater for women-maintained households. That gap is increasing: 44.7 percent of women-maintained households with children less than eighteen years old are in poverty compared to about 7.7 percent of households maintained by men who have children living with them.[12]

This differential is in part a product of the fact that many families never receive some or all of the support due them from the absent father. For instance, in 1985, only 43 percent of absent fathers paid child support, and only about half of those paid the full amount.[13] The amounts paid are small as well, averaging only $2,100 annually per family (not per child), at a time when the median family income was over $30,000 per year. According to one study, a father's child support payments averaged less than his car payment.[14] To make matters worse, payments have not kept up with inflation. From 1981 to 1985, the real value of the average payment in constant, inflation-adjusted dollars fell 16 percent.[15]

Public support of dependent children is even more appalling. Using as a standard the amount of money paid a foster mother, we can see that we have always been more generous toward children in two-parent foster homes than toward children in their own single-parent homes. Over the last eight years, however, that ratio has become worse, and now instead of the foster parent getting three times what the AFDC parent gets, the foster parent gets four times that amount. In 1982, the average foster child payment was $197 per month, while the average "extra" payment for an additional AFDC child was $49 per month. In some states, foster parents are paid seven or eight times what the child's own mother is paid to care for that child.[16]

THE LABOR MARKET

The disadvantaged position of women in the labor market is well known—the average woman still earns only about 66 percent of what the average male earns (for full-time work).[17] This figure has changed very little in four decades. In 1988, the average woman college graduate, working full-time throughout the year, earned less than the average male high school graduate.[18]

Equally important, but less well known, is another aspect of women's disadvantage in the labor market: more women than men are unable to obtain regular, full-time, year-round work. Many women, especially mothers seeking to support their households on their earnings, encounter serious obstacles to full participation in the labor market, including inadequate, unavailable, or unaffordable day care and discrimination based on full-time work since only part-time or seasonable work is available to them. As a result, only about 40 percent of women maintaining households alone are full-time, year-round workers, compared to almost two-thirds of male householders. About one-third of women heading families alone, compared to 20 percent of men, are not in the labor force at all.[19]

In addition, women are concentrated in a relatively small number of occupations, many of which are underpaid. Thus, women experience occupational segregation and confinement to the pink-collar ghetto, with limitations on opportunity for income and growth that accompany such segregation. Finally, there are the economic costs of sexual harassment that are almost always borne by the woman alone. Every woman who has lost a promotion, quit to avoid further harassment, or mysteriously walked away from an opportunity has paid an economic as well as a psychic price for being a woman.

Even working, women must work harder to avoid poverty. Thirteen percent of minority women single parents who work full time throughout the year are still poor. This is the same percentage of white male householders who do *not* work at all who are poor. Because of the higher poverty rates for women associated with each level of participation in the labor market, and because fewer women household heads participate fully, having a job is a much less certain route out of poverty for women than for men. Altogether, about 4 percent of families with a working male householder are in poverty, while more than 21.4 percent of families headed by employed women have incomes below the poverty level.[20]

THE WELFARE SYSTEM AND WOMEN'S POVERTY

Our various income support programs have been developed to provide income to individuals and families whose earnings are inadequate to meet their needs. But beyond that basic goal, various income support programs differ greatly in every characteristic, such as the amount of benefits, accessibility, and stigma attached to the benefits. Using such characteristics, these programs can be divided into two broad groups. Programs found in the primary sector are for the "deserving" poor, have been characterized as a right (often, but not always, earned as a result of working), have relatively generous benefits, and are non–means-tested and nonstigmatizing. By contrast, programs in the secondary sector are for the "undeserving" poor and frequently restrict entry and/or eligibility depending on time and geography. These programs require impoverishment in order to receive benefits that are penurious in amount and are stigmatizing.

The programs in both sectors are based on male models—a Male Breadwinner model for the primary sector and a Male Pauper model for the secondary sector. An example of a major program in the primary sector is the unemployment compensation program. This program was designed for a limited group, "regular" workers who were presumed also to be the breadwinners in their families, in which the wife had a supporting role but was not herself in paid employment. The original aim was to help these workers, who through no fault of their own and due to the vagaries of seasonal employment patterns, business cycles, or technological obsolescence, found themselves out of work. The group to be aided by this program was not *all* the unemployed, since "casual" workers or those who worked part-time and/or seasonally had not proved their attachment to the work force and, therefore, were not deserving. Women and other minority workers were not *statutorily* excluded from eligibility for unemployment benefits, but many have been excluded in disproportionate numbers by virtue of their low wages or less than full-time work hours. This has far-reaching consequences for those who are the sole support of their households.

By contrast, the secondary sector is disproportionately composed of women and minorities. In spite of this demographic character, secondary sector programs are built on the Male Pauper model, which has its roots in the sixteenth-century Poor Laws of England, when paupers were ex-soldiers, beggars, and vagabond landless peasants and were mostly men. This model operates on a simple set of principles: most of the poor are poor because they do not work, and most of the poor are able-bodied and could work, therefore, the solution to poverty according to the Male Pauper model is to "put 'em to work." Unlike unemployment compensation, there is little concern for the quality of the job, even its monetary return, or for matching worker skills to jobs with appropriate requirements. Rather, any job will do. When applied to women, such as AFDC mothers in the WIN program, the result is less than positive. First, as we have seen, having a job is, ipso facto, a less certain route out of poverty for women than for men. Second, income from earnings only partially addresses a woman's needs and, therefore, only partially alleviates her poverty. A woman's responsibility for children and/or other dependents results in economic and emotional burdens requiring additional income and fringe benefits for child care and health insurance and flexible or part-time work arrangements that are not available with most jobs.

This dual welfare system is not only inherently discriminatory against women, but it also operates to reinforce her disadvantaged status in the labor market. Economists have developed a theory of institutional barriers in the labor market that conceives of the labor market as a dual system, divided into primary and secondary sectors.[21] In the primary sector, workers hold jobs with relatively high pay and good fringe benefits, better working conditions, and greater security; if they should lose their jobs, they are likely to be compensated relatively generously through unemployment compensation and/or through other programs such as disability (at rates that strive to replace 50 percent of gross wages), plus any private or union supplementary benefits. Although, theoretically, workers in this sector must return to work as soon as possible, the program is designed not only to support the worker (and his or her family) during unemployment but also to enable the worker to conduct a job search that will result in reemployment in a job that will maintain his or her skills, occupational status, and income.

In contrast, workers in the secondary sector find themselves at relatively low-wage jobs with little job security and few fringe benefits. If they lose their jobs, which happens relatively more frequently and unpredictably than in the primary sector, these workers often find themselves ineligible for unemployment compensation. Many women in this circumstance turn to AFDC, the "poor woman's unemployment compensation." Studies show that 90 percent of welfare mothers have worked,[22] many of them recently, and women who apply for public assistance do so only after *both* the labor market and the marriage institution have failed to provide income adequate to support their families. However, they cannot even obtain this help without first impoverishing themselves by exhausting their other resources and savings. Once on welfare, they find it not only penurious in amount and stigmatizing, but they are also pushed to leave as soon as possible, no matter how poor the new job's pay and long-term prospects, how inadequate the child care is, or how difficult the transportation. The secondary welfare sector destroys not only one's incentives but also one's prospect of ever working one's way out of poverty.

Thus the dual welfare system reinforces the disadvantaged position of women in the labor market. Disproportionate numbers of women and minorities are found in the secondary sector. While 87 percent of the recipients of primary benefits are in white families headed by men or married couples, only 3 percent are in families maintained by black women alone.[23] Conversely, women householders account for over two-thirds of secondary sector recipients.[24] As one might expect, there is a great difference in the poverty incidence between the two sectors: while only about 8 percent of those families whose heads are receiving primary sector benefits have poverty level incomes, almost three-fourths of families whose heads receive secondary sector benefits are in poverty.[25] Thus women, particularly minority women, disproportionately experience the impoverishing consequences of the dual welfare system.

THE WAR ON POVERTY'S APPROACH TO POVERTY

The War on Poverty of the 1960s provided the most ambitious and far-reaching set of changes in welfare policy and programs attempted since the New Deal. Unfortunately for women, however, even its most innovative and broad reforms did little to help poor women, for the reforms embodied some of the same assumptions of the Male Pauper and Male Breadwinner models that have always underpinned social welfare programs.

First, as in the classic Male Pauper model analysis, the basic problem of poverty was assumed to be the high rate of joblessness among the poor. Similarly, the solution was perceived to be work. Although this solution took such harsh forms as poorhouse incarceration or forced conscription into the armed forces in the nineteenth century, it was mitigated in the War on Poverty programs by an understanding that many of the poor were inadequately equipped for the job market. Interestingly, however, it was assumed that the overwhelming majority of those who needed jobs, and therefore needed the skills to obtain jobs, were men. Ornati's choice of words is telling: "What makes the poor . . . different . . . is the fact that they lack the personal assets which produce income. . . . What is required then is the enlargement of the personal *patrimony* with which the poor can face the labor market successfully." [26] Sargent Shriver, contrasting the proposed War on Poverty with the then-current programs, stated that the price of not changing was (for the poor) "continuous infancy, subservience and postponement of full responsibility and manhood." [27] The underlying assumption here is that once the poor are properly equipped with skills and obtain employment, their poverty will be alleviated. This assumption, as noted previously, is much less valid for women than for men.

Closely related to the emphasis on the Male Pauper job solution was the War on Poverty's concern with youth, particularly male youth. This focus reflects two underlying beliefs on the part of policy analysts. As with many officials of the past, they saw a strong link between poverty and lawlessness, whether in the form of collective action or individual crime, and, likewise, saw that paid employment dealt with both poverty and crime. Poor women, however, do not pose the same kind of threat to the social order as that posed by poor young men. The concern with young men, and, implicitly, juvenile delinquency, was so strong that the Job Corps was originally designed only for young men, and it was only by congressional action that the exclusion of young women was removed.

A third area of emphasis in the War on Poverty was that of the "culture of poverty." This theory was not necessarily supported by the evidence. The Council of Economic Advisors, for example, reported that only 40 percent of AFDC recipients came from families that had received welfare.[28] Even Oscar Lewis, who originally developed the culture of poverty hypothesis from anthropological work in Latin American countries, stated that he thought that no more than 20 percent of poor American families were in any sense in the grip of a culture of poverty.[29] Nonetheless, this theory exerted a powerful influence on policy makers and led to the development of programs to try to save youth from the culture of poverty. Although never adopted, Ornati's proposal to create comprehensive day-care centers emphasizes this theme:

These day care centers [would provide] them with the health and the higher horizons that the deprived environment of their homes is denying them. . . . Can anyone argue that in our society youngsters brought up in such facilities will share the fate of their parents?[30]

The fourth and fifth themes of the War on Poverty were that the "war" should be comprehensive and that it should be empowering for the poor. These two themes ultimately conflicted and negated each other to some extent. On the one hand, the idea that the war be comprehensive, that it take on all aspects of poverty, including housing, employment, health care, etc., called for coordinated strategy and comprehensive planning. Wars, by their nature, require hierarchy, with generals making broad policy decisions and soldiers implementing the policy. On the other hand, as the Cahns aptly pointed out, such top-down, comprehensive approaches created poverty bureaucracies, which in turn made it difficult to carry out locally responsive and creative antipoverty programs.[31] The compromise that resulted was one in which the much-maligned "maximum feasible participation" of the poor was highly constrained. Local groups, whether as formal participants in poverty agencies or not, were forced to choose from a narrowly constrained menu of professionally prepared policy alternatives and programs.

THE ROLE OF LEGAL SERVICES IN REDUCING WOMEN'S POVERTY

As a part of the War on Poverty "package" legal services for the poor shared its assumptions and ideology about the nature of poverty. Although not as narrowly focused on jobs, youth, and the culture of poverty as were many of the War's programs, legal services shared a parallel concern with increasing the economic power of the poor. It was believed that by providing the kind of legal advocacy to the poor that the rich routinely buy, some of the income inequality between the classes could be addressed. In the area of housing, for example, by representing tenants against landlords, lawyers believed they could help tenants fight their oppression more effectively. Such representation, moreover, was not to be limited to such things as contesting eviction notices but was to be extended to enforcing housing codes, organizing tenants, and creating a whole new body of law.

Even though the majority of those helped by legal services are women, such strategies only partially address the problem faced by poor women. To extend the housing example further, a major problem faced by poor women, particularly minority women, is the isolation experienced by women-maintained families. This is a particularly geographical isolation that limits their mobility opportunities in employment and education and the educational opportunities of their children. This isolation is a product of many factors, including the massive housing projects that produce economically as well as racially segregated communities, employment discrimination that limits women householders' economic leverage in the housing market, credit and mortgage discrimination, and discrimination against families with children in the private rental market.

The last factor is a serious problem for single-parent, women-maintained families. The lack of construction of multifamily, reasonable-cost housing by the private market has led to very low vacancy rates, and this factor combined with the decrease in public subsidies for low- and moderate-income housing and the escalating practices of excluding families with children from

rental housing has produced a national housing crisis for low-income families. Nationwide, a 1980 survey found that 25 percent of all rental units and
63 percent of mobile home parks are unavailable to families with children;
another 50 percent of rental units limit the number, age, etc., of children.[32]
Though discrimination of families with children is now outlawed, it is still
widely practiced; the majority of discrimination complaints being investigated
by the United States Department of H.U.D. under the new 1988 law are those
involving families with children.

The outcome of this housing problem is twofold. First, in some states, such
as Texas and California, the result has been the creation of disproportionately
minority, children's ghettoes. Second, for some families, the housing squeeze
triggers a set of tragic events, starting with the family's living in abandoned
buildings and cars and ending with its breaking up, with the children placed
in foster care and the parents sent to adult shelters for the homeless. In sum,
the housing difficulties faced by poor women, which stem in large part from
the gender and antichild discrimination women experience in both the housing
and labor markets, reflect a need for broad-based remedies that go far beyond
the strategies employed by legal services.

Moreover, even if, miraculously, all barriers to decent housing were removed, the housing problems of poor women would only be partially solved.
The design of housing, public as well as private, and the environment in general is inimical to the needs of women, married as well as single, who wish to
both work in the labor market and take care of their children. Two-thirds of our
housing stock is single-family detached dwellings, and most of it is located far
from paid employment and with little or no public transportation. Public and
subsidized housing has been built without attention to such needs as well; not
only is such housing often geographically isolated, but the concentration of
the poor and the high-rise design make public housing so unsafe that mothers,
even those of teenagers, feel compelled to be home at the end of the school
day and during school vacations to assure their children's safety. Obviously,
this need is incompatible with most full-time employment schedules, even
if mothers' places of employment were located near their residences. These
needs have not been addressed by the usual legal services strategies in the area
of housing or elsewhere.

AN ALTERNATIVE MODEL FOR WOMEN IN POVERTY

One part of the War on Poverty points the way, by analogy, toward the kind
of approach that needs to be developed to deal with women's poverty, and
this is the War on Poverty's civil rights and antidiscrimination policies and
programs. Though not often recognized in the later critiques of the War on
Poverty, its contemporary champions and commentators perceived the effort

to break down racial barriers as fundamental to a successful War on Poverty.[33] Unlike War on Poverty programs in other areas and for other groups, efforts to overcome racial barriers recognized that the problem was systemic, institutionalized, and pervasive. Indeed, the War on Poverty was instrumental in expanding civil rights from the question of freedom to questions of poverty and economic opportunity. Some of the strategies chosen, such as warlike, top-down planning, mirrored civil rights tactics as well, favoring a means of channelling federal aid to local minority communities directly.

Paralleling the civil rights part of the War on Poverty, a program attacking women's poverty must have as its underlying premise that gender discrimination is at the core of women's poverty. But unlike the problem of racial discrimination, those attacking gender discrimination lack constitutional, much less federal legislative, support. Civil rights strategies such as informing minorities of their rights are moot for poor women, because the rights for poor women are weak, poorly defined, and/or nonexistent. Therefore, an essential element is the establishment of rights and entitlements for poor women and their families, such as the right to shelter, income support, equal pay, and quality child care.

Furthermore, the campaign against women's poverty should not be premised, implicitly or explicitly, on a false distinction between those who are economically "independent" and those who are "dependent." Frequently this contrast is drawn between women whose work is in the home, either unpaid or poorly paid (such as housekeepers and child-care workers), versus those whose work is in the marketplace, including some women as well as most men. Those in paid employment outside the home environment could not be "independent" without the support system provided by the home or its surrogates, such as "housewives" and day-care centers. Such workers' "independence" could not occur without the hidden and unrecognized dependence these workers have on others. At the heart of this false dichotomy, of course, is the devaluation of the work that women perform, as those who take care of "dependents" as well as "independents."

Unless this devaluation of women's work and the false distinction between independent and dependent workers is challenged, the welfare system cannot be fundamentally changed. In concrete terms, as long as we accept the denigration of women who take care of dependent children as "dependent," and as long as the welfare problem is termed one of "dependency," then the policy choices are constrained to a set of equally impossible choices for a single mother. She must choose between limiting her paid employment to devote more time to her children or limiting her time with her children in order to take more time for paid employment. Either choice perpetuates her poverty, both of income and of life.

This situation is not as hopelessly abstract and its solutions as utopian as they may appear. For example, it has been suggested that women be compensated for their unpaid work through earnings-sharing proposals for Social Security. The irony, of course, is that under such plans women must wait until they retire to receive recognition, though they may become displaced homemakers twenty years prior to becoming eligible for such benefits. Clearly, women should not be economically punished, but indeed compensated for time taken away from paid employment and devoted to raising the next generation, for such temporary "dependence" is essential to society's ongoing survival.

Equally fundamental, however, to any attempt to address women's poverty is the need to incorporate their perspective. One legal services lawyer relates that, in the early years of his practice while he was traveling around the country, he would talk to welfare mothers about how to exercise their rights to be exempt from workfare programs, only to discover that many of the poor women he spoke to in fact *wanted* to participate in those programs.[34] Although there was much rhetoric in the War on Poverty about empowering the poor, the reality was that the choices presented to those on poverty agency boards representing the poor were very narrow, nor did they reflect the needs of poor women.

Altogether, the viewpoint of women in poverty, and a comprehensive understanding of the dynamics of women's poverty, should be reflected in public policies as well as choices made by advocates. However, it cannot be assumed that advocates for *women* will adequately represent the needs of *poor* women nor that advocates for the *poor* will adequately represent the needs of poor *women*. For example, recently a women's rights organization was asked to testify before a city's wage and hours board on the question of whether the city's minimum wage for household and child-care workers should be raised. The organization declined, citing two reasons. First, the organization stated that it had no policy on the question, which seems to reflect its perspective that, unless a question can be posed as one of rights, it may not be dealt with by legal advocates. Second, the organization responded that this was a question over which their women staff disagreed, for some felt they could not "afford" to pay higher wages to their housekeepers and day-care providers. While this may be interpreted as a situation in which middle-class lawyers' and other professionals' interests conflicted with lower-class clients' interests, it also demonstrates a misunderstanding of the issue at stake. The real issue is one of inadequate pay for *all* women workers, women employers of child-care workers and housekeepers as well as the employees themselves. Moreover, this misunderstanding reflects the view that child care and household work are the responsibility of women, a view that is one of the major sources of poverty for women. What would be the reaction, now or even two decades ago, to the proposal that blacks whose employers are black should be paid less because their *employers* also experience lower wages because of *racial* discrimination?

Thus, any campaign against women's poverty must proceed from certain fundamental principles, one of them being that gender discrimination is a key element behind the feminization of poverty. At the same time, it should not be assumed that all policies designed to eliminate gender discrimination will be effective for low-income women. Conversely, policies not currently on the agenda of either poverty or women's rights organizations, such as unemployment compensation reform, may be central to an agenda dealing with women's poverty.

Although it is uncertain what mechanisms best incorporate the voices of poor women, there are some highly innovative and creative efforts in existence. These efforts incorporate an element missing in older models by simultaneously developing an agenda and empowering the poor to achieve the agenda through organizing around poor women's issues; developing specific and achievable goals; and attempting to achieve these goals by collective, usually political, action. Two such organizations are the Women's Economic Agenda Project in California and the Coalition for Basic Human Needs in Massachusetts. The California project was established as the result of a set of state legislative hearings on the feminization of poverty. As a result of the hearings, a group of women, some long-term advocates, some women who were on welfare or in job training programs who had testified at the hearings, organized at the local and state level around issues of economic justice for women.[35] The Coalition for Basic Human Needs is a statewide organization completely run by welfare recipients, who develop their own agenda pertaining to issues of public assistance.

Developing and advocating agendas by, for, and with poor women that are built around a recognition of interdependence, the value and importance of women's work to society, and the institutional character of gender discrimination is essential. It is especially crucial in a time of attack and retrenchment to have a vision of alternative sets of institutions, programs, and policies that would bring about economic justice for women. Only with a vision can much less major actions be seen as meaningful, no matter how small; only with a vision and a set of principles to guide choices can we decide which small steps to take; only with a vision can welfare and all social policy be made into a system that is controlled by and for women. And with such a vision, it is possible to design a "War on Poverty," and a welfare system, that instead of institutionalizing and perpetuating women's poverty, begins the process of dismantling and reversing the feminization of poverty.

NOTES

1   Michael Harrington, *The Other America* (New York: MacMillan, 1962).
2   Diana Pearce, "The Feminization of Poverty: Women, Work and Welfare," *Urban & Social Change Review* (Winter-Spring 1978): 28–36.

3   Between 1982 and 1983, the number of poor households maintained by men or
    married couples decreased by 26,000, while the number of poor households main-
    tained by women alone increased by 123,000 according to U.S. Bureau of the
    Census, *Money Income and Poverty Status of Families and Persons in the United
    States: 1988*, Series P-60, No. 165 (1989).

4   Ibid.

5   Ibid.

6   Ibid.

7   Martha Hill, "Trends in the Economic Situations of the U.S. Families and Chil-
    dren: 1970–1980." Paper prepared for National Academy of Sciences' Committee
    on Child Development and Research Conference, January 28–29, 1982.

8   U.S. Bureau of the Census, *Money Income: 1988*.

9   Ibid.

10 Ibid.

11 Susan Bianchi and Daphne Spain, *American Women: Three Decades of Change*
    (Washington, D.C.: U.S. Department of Commerce, Bureau of Census, 1983).

12 U.S. Bureau of the Census, *Money Income: 1988*.

13 U.S. Bureau of the Census, *Child Support and Alimony: 1985*, Series P-23, No.
    154.

14 Ibid.; Lucy Yee, "What Really Happens in Child Support Cases: An Empirical
    Study of Establishment and Enforcement of Child Support Orders in the Denver
    District Court," *Denver Law Journal* 57 (1979): 21.

15 U.S. Bureau of the Census, *Child Support*.

16 Testimony by Diana Pearce before the Select Committee on Children, U.S. House
    of Representatives, July 1983.

17 U.S. Bureau of the Census, *Money Income: 1988*.

18 Ibid.

19 Ibid.

20 *Money Income: 1988*.

21 Peter Doeringer & Michael Piore, "Unemployment and the Dual Labor Market,"
    Public Interest 38 (Winter 1975): 67–79.

22 Joel F. Handler and Ellen J. Hollingsworth, *The Deserving Poor: A Study of Welfare
    Administration* (New York: Academic Press, 1971).

23 U.S. Bureau of the Census, *Poverty in the United States: 1986*, Series P-60, No.
    160 (1988).

24 Ibid.

25 Ibid.

26 Oscar Ornati, *Poverty Amid Affluence* (New York: Twentieth Century Fund, 1966),
    88 (emphasis added).

27 Sargent Shriver, "The Poor in Our Affluent Society," in *Poverty In Plenty. Pro-
    ceedings on Conference on Poverty-in-Plenty: The Poor in Our Affluent Society,
    Georgetown University, Washington, D.C., 1964*, ed. George Dunne (New York:
    P.J. Kennedy, 1964).

28 Council of Economic Advisors, "The Problem of Poverty in America," in *Eco-
    nomic Report of the President* (Government Printing Office, January 1964). One
    study shows that having been a child in a family that received AFDC increases the

chances of receipt of welfare by 1.4 times; other studies find that the experience of low income, but not welfare receipt per se, increases the likelihood of welfare receipt as an adult. Greg J. Duncan et al., *Years of Poverty, Years of Plenty* (Ann Arbor: University of Michigan, 1984), 82–83.

29 Oscar Lewis, *La Vida* (London: Panther Books, 1968), 57.

30 Oscar Ornati, *Poverty Amid Affluence*, 84–90.

31 Edgar Cahn and Jean Cahn, "The War on Poverty: A Civilian Perspective," *Yale Law Journal* 73 (1964): 1317; Edgar Cahn and Jean Cahn, "Power to the People or the Profession," *Yale Law Journal* 79 (1970): 1005.

32 Alison Hamm, *Housing Discrimination Against Families with Children* (American Planning Association, May 1984).

33 For example, Hubert Humphrey devoted one entire chapter, and parts of others, to civil rights in his book, Hubert Humphrey, *War on Poverty* (New York: McGraw Hill, 1964).

34 Stephen Wexler, "Practicing Law for Poor People," *Yale Law Journal* 79 (1979): 1049.

35 Women's Economic Agenda Project (WEAP), *An Economic Agenda for Women of California* (Oakland, Calif.: WEAP, 1984).

CHAPTER 12

Black Women and AFDC: Making Entitlement Out of Necessity

TERESA L. AMOTT

During the 1980s, a broad public consensus developed around the idea that "welfare dependency" was a social problem, that this social problem was concentrated among blacks, and that the "disintegration of the black family" was a matter for urgent public concern. Conservatives and liberals supported this consensus and pushed for social policies to lower welfare dependency and promote their definition of stable family life. This essay investigates the relationship between welfare and the rise of black single-parent families, arguing that this relationship is complex and mediated by a number of factors, including structural changes in the economy, shifts in the occupational distribution of black men and women, and political mobilization among black women to secure basic economic rights for themselves and their children.

Welfare need not be seen as a social problem but rather as a vital source of income to single mothers whose economic choices are constrained by the myriad of ways that racism and sexism structure economic life in the United States. Poor women have sought to use welfare as a survival strategy and have organized to expand their entitlement to public support. Their struggles have been more successful in some periods than others, depending upon the extent of their political self-organization, the nature and strength of their opposition, and the economic and political conditions of the period.

Part One of this essay examines the rise in single-parent families in the black community over the past thirty years. More attention has been paid to this phenomenon than virtually any other social or demographic fact of the current welfare and poverty debate.[1] Conservatives claim that a rise in single-parent families has been at once the effect of "misguided social policy" and the single most important cause of poverty among blacks. Liberals, unwilling to blame welfare for the rise of single parenting, nonetheless have been placed on the defensive by the conservative analysis and are unable to put forward a strong defense of welfare entitlement.

Even as we examine the rise in black single-parent families, it is important not to overestimate the importance of family structure in creating poverty. Research by Mary Jo Bane has shown that two out of three black families headed by a woman were poor *before* the family event that made a woman a single mother (divorce, separation, death of the husband, or birth of an out-of-wedlock baby).[2] In addition, the poverty risk for a black two-parent family is more than twice as high as that of a white two-parent family.[3] Still, since the vast majority of adults receiving welfare are single mothers, the growth of single motherhood among blacks deserves some attention here.

Part Two of the essay looks at the extent to which single-parent black families have been able to gain access to the resources of the state through welfare programs in order to support their families. I argue that this access has varied historically, and that today the future of black women and their children is seriously threatened by diminishing access to income support from the state.

In 1983, less than 3 percent of the white population received Aid to Families with Dependent Children (AFDC), the major welfare program for poor families. In contrast, over 17 percent of blacks received AFDC benefits.[4] On the surface, this startling disparity is easily explainable for two reasons: differing poverty rates and differing family structures.

First, blacks are more likely to be poor, and thus potentially eligible for welfare, than whites. The 1983 poverty rate for whites stood at 12.1 percent compared to 35.7 percent for blacks.[5]

But even if we look only at poor people, the disparity persists: 24.3 percent of poor whites received AFDC in 1983, compared to 56.0 percent of poor blacks.[6] This further disparity can be explained by differing family structures of blacks compared to whites, since blacks are more likely than whites to live in the types of families that are eligible for AFDC—families with children that are headed by a woman or by an unemployed or disabled man.

Black families are younger and more likely to contain children than are white families. In 1983, only 48.7 percent of white families had one or more children under eighteen, compared to 59.6 percent of black families. In addition, black families are four times more likely to be headed by a single mother than white families.[7]

Black families are more likely to contain persons with work disabilities or unemployed persons than are white families. In 1983, 7.6 percent of whites were classified as work disabled, compared to 12.5 percent of blacks.[8] And also in 1983, the unemployment rate for whites stood at 8.4 percent, compared to 19.5 percent for blacks.[9]

But these simple facts do not tell the whole story. If we go deeper than these statistics, we can see the ways in which welfare utilization is a race- and gender-specific collective response by poor black single mothers to economic and political conditions that threaten the survival of their children and their communities.[10]

PART ONE: WHY BLACK WOMEN ARE SINGLE MOTHERS

The incidence of female-headed families in the black community has been the subject of much analysis and controversy for years, beginning as far back as the 1930s with claims that the black community was "matriarchal." The Moynihan Report of 1965, for instance, alleged that the breakup of families under slavery had deprived black men of the "normal" provider role, leaving women to run the family.[11] The debate over the black family has been heated, and analysis has been obscured by racist and patriarchal assumptions about what constitutes an appropriate family. In addition, it is not clear whether census data on marital status in the early part of the twentieth century are reliable. However, new research is bringing to light important insights into the ways in which the black family has been shaped by and responded to cultural and economic oppression.

The research indicates that up until the mid-twentieth century, most black families contained two parents.[12] Rose Brewer, reviewing this literature, concludes that black families had two main forms: the first, characterized by the birth of a child prior to marriage and the second, families formed around marriage. Even in the first case, however, a marriage generally took place after the birth of the child.[13] As a result, even as late as 1950, only 18 percent of black families were headed by a woman.[14]

According to the conventional wisdom, the share of black families headed by a woman began a rapid rise starting around 1960. By the mid-1980s, roughly 44 percent of black families were headed by a woman.[15] Starting in the 1970s, divorce, separation, and out-of-wedlock births began to play a larger role in the creation of black female-headed families.[16] This change is the key to the current conservative attack on welfare. Conservatives claim that there was a simultaneous expansion in welfare rolls during this period and conclude that this expansion is the cause of family breakup.

UNDERCOUNTING SINGLE PARENTS

Frances Piven and Richard Cloward have challenged these facts and their conservative interpretation. Through careful analysis of the census data on which information on family structure is based, they conclude that "the growth of black single-parent families had been set in motion by a series of social and economic upheavals that did in fact specifically affect blacks, and that these upheavals were under way long before the AFDC rise."[17] The upheavals to which they refer are the migration of blacks to the North during the 1940s and

1950s and the concentration of black migrants in urban ghettoes characterized by high unemployment.

Like other racial-ethnic peoples who have played an important role as a labor force for capitalism, blacks have migrated often in search of work, and it is clear that such migration can cause disruptions in family and kin networks.[18] The first migration from Africa involved the brutal severing of family and kin connections at gunpoint. Since then, migration for blacks has been a mixture of the push of economic hardship with the pull of economic opportunity in a changing market economy. For instance, as Southern agriculture came to require fewer and fewer manual laborers, black men and women left the South in search of work. During both World Wars, in particular, labor shortages opened up some industrial jobs in the North for black men (and, to a lesser extent, black women).[19]

The waves of migration took millions of blacks out of a predominantly agrarian life-style, sharecropping, in which the raising of children was more easily compatible with employment. While the evidence on the existence of single motherhood during sharecropping is not complete, it is known that extended family networks are more common in agrarian societies, and the presence of extended kin makes it easier for single women to fulfill the demands of child rearing.[20]

We can speculate that as blacks migrated out of southern small towns, the social pressures to marry in the event of an out-of-wedlock conception or birth were weakened. Linda Gordon points out that even though traditional social controls such as "landlords, churches, communities, and families" were weakened by migration, there "is no evidence of any lessening of *maternal* commitment to and supervision of children as a result of this migration."[21] At the same time, however, an extended family was less often available to care for children born to a single mother. In the northern ghettoes, black women found child rearing increasingly difficult. Families lived in crowded, unhealthy quarters, and children were exposed daily, on the streets, to gambling and crime. As one black woman commented about Washington, D.C. in the late 1920s: "I have lived here long enough to know that you can't grow a good potato out of bad ground. Dis sho is bad ground."[22] Although some black mothers worked in their homes, taking in laundry and sewing, many others were forced by need to work outside the home, leaving their children with family, friends, or unattended.

Piven and Cloward contend that black out-of-wedlock births began to rise between 1940 and 1965, but that the young mothers typically lived with their parent or parents and were not counted as single-parent families during this period. As a result, there was substantial undercounting of black single-parent families during a period in which AFDC was not generally available and long before the growth in AFDC rolls. Once AFDC became available through the pressures of these very women organized in urban civil rights and welfare rights movements, many women who had lived with their relatives were able to move into independent living arrangements. This process of moving into one's own apartment, then, made visible a single-parent family that had not previously been counted.

This analysis is confirmed by other research that has failed to uncover any significant causal relationship between AFDC and family structure. There is no conclusive evidence that AFDC promotes the formation of single-parent families through divorce, separation, or out-of-wedlock births. High-benefit states, for instance, do not have a greater share of single-parent families than low-benefit states.[23]

Welfare policies prevent two-parent families from collecting AFDC benefits in half of the states, and this could lead to some marital breakup in order for the mother and children to become eligible. However, this effect is likely to be smaller today than in the past, since surprise visitations to determine whether there is a "man in the house" have been illegal since 1968.[24]

Nor does the availability of welfare seem to have much impact on the child-bearing rates of unmarried women. There has been a rise over the past fifteen years in the proportion of all births that are to unmarried women, some proportion of which is due to a drop in the birthrate to married women. (As a result, the *share* of out-of-wedlock births has risen.) And despite the media attention to teen pregnancy, teen birthrates (births per 1,000 women aged fifteen to nineteen) have been declining steadily since the 1970s.[25]

Welfare does appear to be related to the living arrangements single mothers make. In states with high benefits, for instance, there is some evidence that single mothers move into their own apartments at a greater rate than in states with low benefits. Conservatives point to this as an example of the erosion of "family values," but since women appear to be choosing these separate households, a feminist perspective would see this as enhancing women's autonomy, freeing them from abusive situations and lessening stress on the family unit.

THE DEMOGRAPHIC ARGUMENT

Another important explanation for the presence of single-parent families among blacks is the low ratio of black men to black women. Many black researchers see this as the most important cause of the single-parent family formation in the black community.[26] For instance, there were ninety-nine white men for every one hundred white women in 1979, but only eighty-four black men for every one hundred black women.

This disproportion occurs because men of color have lower life expectancies than white men. In 1983, for instance, more than 40 percent of black men did not survive to the age of sixty-five, compared to only 25 percent of white men, 25 percent of black women, and 15 percent of white women.[27] Blacks are one-

and-one-half to two times as likely as whites to die of heart disease, cancer, diabetes, strokes, and other diseases.[28] The death rate from homicide is six times higher for blacks than for whites.[29] Black (and Hispanic) men also have higher risks of occupational accidents and illnesses since they are consigned to the riskiest jobs in the occupational hierarchy.

Racism in the criminal justice system—expressed through higher arrest, conviction, and sentencing rates—also removes many black and Hispanic men from the community. For instance, blacks make up 39 percent of jail inmates,[30] 37 percent of juveniles in public custody, and 26 percent of those arrested.[31]

Liberals such as William Julius Wilson have recently taken the demographic argument further, citing a decline in the proportion of black men who are employed as a major source of the rise in female-headed families and poverty among black families. Wilson argues that the employment prospects of black men have been worsening since the 1960s. He blames this deterioration on a number of structural changes in the United States economy, including the flight of entry-level jobs from the center cities to the suburbs, the decline in United States manufacturing, and the generally high level of unemployment in the past fifteen years compared to the earlier postwar period.

Wilson constructs a "male marriageable pool index" by counting the number of employed—and thus "marriageable"—men per one hundred women of the same age and race. This index declines between 1960 and 1980 in every region of the country except the West. As a result, Wilson and his coauthors find that "black women, and particularly younger black women, face a shrinking pool of economically stable . . . men."[32]

Wilson shows that this decline is correlated with an increase in the proportion of families maintained by a woman, also in every region except the West. In the Northeast, for instance, the index of marriageable black males declined 11.2 percent between 1960 and 1980, while the proportion of women maintaining families rose 24.4 percent.[33]

Using this evidence, Wilson and others have argued for improved employment and training programs aimed at young men.[34] They claim that as these men become more "marriageable," they are more likely to form stable families, helping to support children and lowering the proportion of families falling into poverty.

FLAWS IN THE DEMOGRAPHIC ARGUMENT

While it is clear that young black men need improved employment and training programs, relying on their subsequent marriages to bring black children out of poverty is wishful thinking. Not all employed black men marry: in 1980, for instance, more than 80 percent of *employed* black men between the ages of sixteen and twenty-four were single, as were nearly 40 percent of employed black men between twenty-five and thirty-four.[35] Providing education, employment, and training—along with needed support services such as child care and health insurance—to young black women as well as men is far more likely to improve the economic status of the black community than focusing on black men alone.[36]

Arguments based on the availability of "marriageable" black men are also flawed in that they ignore the effect of women's autonomy and economic independence on marriage rates. Most of the studies showing that women's income and labor force participation lower the economic costs of marital dissolution have focused on white women. Still, this factor is likely to be important for blacks as well, operating over a longer historical period than the more recent changes in white women's economic and marital status. Black women have historically participated in the labor force at a greater rate than white women. While this independence was only partly chosen, and was partly a result of poverty, it nonetheless provided black women with a greater degree of economic power *relative to black men* than that experienced by most white women relative to white men.[37]

Economist Elaine McCrate has studied the rise of nonmarriage among black and white women between 1956 and 1983. Her work shows that for both groups nonmarriage is correlated with increases in labor force participation and improvements in occupational status.[38] Other work by feminist economists has shown that there was an improvement in black women's economic status, as they moved out of domestic service into blue collar and service jobs, over the same period as the rate of nonmarriage rose.[39] (Prior to the second World War, the majority of black women worked as domestic servants, compared to one-third in 1960 and only 6 percent in 1980.[40])

While Wilson's work does focus attention on the serious economic problems faced by black men, it is unfortunate that his analysis has not yet examined how black women have been affected by the types of structural economic shifts he identifies. Women, in other words, appear to be absent from the demographic argument as agents of their own lives. Wilson appears to regard single-parent families as evidence of the "social disorganization" or "pathology" of the black community.[41] Writing in *The Nation*, Adolph Reed, Jr., castigates Wilson for his "reflexive antifeminism and commitment to the language of social pathology," arguing the following:

The problem is not the social disorganization of the inner-city poor, but Wilson's and others' distaste for, and reluctance to examine the institutional and organizational forms that the inner-city poor, particularly women, have devised to survive and to create meaning and dignity in lives bitterly constrained by forces apparently beyond their control.[42]

Black women have "survived and created meaning and dignity" as single mothers even though social policies in this country have been hostile to such nonnuclear families.[43] These women do not construct their lives as half of a male-breadwinner, female-homemaker pair, but rather they see their roles as *single* mothers as central to their lives. The history of black lesbianism, popularized in the novel *The Color Purple* and uncovered by new scholarship, also attests to the independence of black women who have chosen to live without men.

Living without a male wage earner is, however, financially difficult. Despite the improvements in black women's occupational status since the times when domestic service represented their major option, black women are still likely to be found in low-wage jobs. Income from the state, particularly in the form of AFDC, represents a vital resource to single-parent families. The next part of this paper describes how black women have been, at various times in United States history, denied access to AFDC and how they organized to claim their benefits.

PART TWO: WELFARE AND THE SINGLE-PARENT BLACK FAMILY

If we look closely at welfare utilization among single-parent black families, we see that the pattern of welfare use has varied substantially throughout the twentieth century, and that this period can be divided into three distinct historical regimes. The first, between the establishment of the AFDC program in the late 1930s and the rise of the welfare rights movement of the 1960s, was a period in which access to AFDC and to the other New Deal welfare state programs was sharply restricted for blacks by the exclusion of certain industries from coverage under the programs and by the discriminatory practices of the state agencies that administered AFDC.

The second period, lasting from the 1960s through the mid-1970s and shaped primarily by the National Welfare Rights Organization, was a time in which black women collectively asserted their entitlement to income support and gained a substantial measure of success in forcing the state to acknowledge and act on their entitlement. Many of the restrictive regulations of the first period were struck down and welfare rights activists guided individuals seeking assistance through the complex application process.

The third period, which begins in the middle 1970s and continues to the present, is a period of diminishing access and contested entitlement. Government transfer programs reach fewer and fewer of those in need, and, as a result, progress in combating hunger, homelessness, neonatal mortality, and preventable childhood diseases has stalled.

UNEQUAL ACCESS: 1940s–1950s

At the time of the establishment of AFDC, the southern racial caste system was firmly in place. Southern congressmen, determined to maintain a supply of cheap labor to business interests in the South, insisted that authority to set benefit levels and administer eligibility under the AFDC system be set at the state level, claiming that an earlier version of the Social Security bill violated states' rights.[44] This had the effect, according to Theda Skocpol, of insuring that "blacks in the South could be deprived of adequate welfare assistance. Southern economic interests were left free to enforce labor discipline on their own terms and retain competitive advantages in relation to higher-wage industries in the North."[45] Blacks were also excluded from other aspects of the New Deal by, for example, exempting agricultural and domestic workers from coverage under Social Security and unemployment compensation.[46] The exclusion of blacks, required to bring southern whites into the New Deal coalition, could not continue indefinitely. Skocpol argues that the 1960s War on Poverty resulted from black demands on the Democratic party, demands that could not be ignored as more and more blacks migrated north to urban areas in the 1940s.

Once in the North, black women attempted to apply for AFDC to support their families. Still, "suitable home," "man in the house," and "substitute father" rules continued to be used in many states, both northern and southern, selectively to deny access to AFDC throughout the 1950s.[47] Many of these rules were instituted in the 1950s and resulted in midnight raids that declared large numbers of black and single mothers ineligible. Winifred Bell, in a classic study on AFDC, suggests that suitable home rules were used specifically to limit eligibility for black and single mothers.[48]

WELFARE RIGHTS: 1960s–1970s

Throughout the late 1960s and early 1970s, black women made a series of demands on the state for easier eligibility for AFDC. Most of these demands were voiced through the National Welfare Rights Organization (NWRO), a national network of local chapters that pressed state and federal authorities for a living income, one that would support a mother and her children adequately and in dignity.[49] As a result of welfare rights organizing among the poor, welfare rolls expanded dramatically.[50] Between 1970 and 1973 alone, the average number of recipients rose nearly 50 percent.

Expansion of the system occurred in the context of a growing civil rights movement and the Great Society responses by the Democratic party. The relationship of the NWRO to the social ferment of the 1960s has been explored by many researchers, most notably Frances Fox Piven and Richard Cloward.

One aspect of the welfare rights movement has received little attention: the implicit, and sometimes explicit, feminist content of welfare rights demands. Linda Gordon has argued that the women of the NWRO understood the welfare system from a feminist perspective and saw their struggle as legitimating the nurturing work of child rearing in a system that had devalued that work.[51] Gordon also points out that the feminist character of the welfare rights movement has been ignored because the feminist movement has been seen as predominantly white and middle class in its membership and orientation.

The most telling statement of the feminist nature of the movement is an interview with Johnnie Tillmon, the first chairwoman of the NWRO.

I'm a woman. I'm a black woman. I'm a poor woman. I'm a fat woman. I'm a middle-aged woman. And I'm on welfare. In this country, if you're any one of those things—poor, black, fat, female, middle-aged, on welfare—you count less as a human being. . . . Welfare's like a traffic accident. It can happen to anybody, but especially it happens to women. And that is why welfare is a women's issue. For a lot of middle-class women in this country, Women's Liberation is a matter of concern. For women on welfare it's a matter of survival. . . . The truth is that AFDC is like a supersexist marriage. You trade in *a* man for *the* man. . . . *The* man runs everything. In ordinary marriage, sex is supposed to be for your husband. On AFDC, you're not supposed to have any sex at all. You give up control of your own body. It's a condition of aid. . . . *The* man, the welfare system, controls your money. . . . There are a lot of other lies that male society tells about welfare mothers; that AFDC mothers are immoral, that AFDC mothers are lazy, misuse their welfare checks, spend it all on booze and are stupid and incompetent. If people are willing to believe these lies, it's partly because they're just special versions of the lies that society tells about *all* women.[52]

When poor black women demanded higher welfare benefits and dignified treatment, they were insisting on a revision of the New Deal's systematic exclusion of blacks and a recognition by society of their entitlement, as women and mothers, to public support. Thus the NWRO represented a race- and gender-specific collective strategy to ensure the survival of black women and their children in the oppressive conditions of the postwar urban ghetto.

For reasons that need not be spelled out here, the NWRO was unable to sustain itself past the early 1970s, and as a result, there was no strong national presence of poor women to combat the assault on the welfare state that began in the mid-1970s.

RETRENCHMENT: MID-1970s–PRESENT

As the United States economy began to stagnate in the 1970s, a number of regressive political currents gathered strength for an assault on the political acceptability of entitlement, with devastating consequences for black women and their children. Starting in California, a movement to limit state taxes was able to mobilize the concerns of moderate income citizens over their stagnating earnings. Fundamentalist Christians focused on the erosion of "family values" and the rise in divorce and out-of-wedlock births. Corporations facing falling profit rates sought to impose labor discipline through cutbacks in government programs, sophisticated antiunion campaigns, and demands for deregulation. At the state level, these movements combined to sharply limit the never-strong political support for AFDC.

Since 1973, the number of people on AFDC has remained constant at roughly 10.7 million.[53] At the same time, the number of those potentially eligible—predominantly people living in poor single-mother families—grew substantially. In 1973, nearly 85 percent of children living in poor families collected welfare (AFDC); by 1986, less than 60 percent received benefits.[54] The new limitations of entitlement, discussed following, relied on new versions of the old "moral fitness" arguments, imposing work requirements on longer-term welfare recipients who are deemed to be less deserving of continued state assistance than recipients who leave the welfare rolls within a short period of time. The attack on entitlement was legitimated through research and embedded in new, more restrictive eligibility requirements, culminating in the 1988 passage of the Family Security Act.

The Conservative Attack and the New Consensus

Over the past ten years, there has been an expansion in a body of research purporting to show that the "easy" availability of welfare had caused greater poverty and family breakup among poor people.[55] The research was supported by conservative foundations such as Olin and Scaife and was legitimized by the Reagan administration. For instance, in his 1986 State of the Union Address, President Reagan blamed welfare for "the breakdown of the family" and said the "welfare culture" was responsible for "female and child poverty, child abandonment, horrible crimes, and deteriorating schools."

A White House report on welfare reform laid out the conservative argument with unabashed clarity: the report called AFDC an "enabler—a program which enables women to live without a husband or a job." [56] In other words, conservatives argued that welfare was the cause of poverty and family breakup, rather than the effect, since welfare set up incentives for counterproductive behavior among poor people. Their argument was that welfare sets up incentives for people to have children, to avoid marriage, and to stay out of the labor force. Welfare, they claimed, pays people to have children and not work for pay. Much of this debate focused on the "long-term dependent," a phrase that echoed the simultaneously emerging discussions of a black "underclass" characterized by criminal behavior and out-of-wedlock births and thus functioned as a code word for black. Conservatives such as Charles Murray and economist Glenn Loury claimed that government welfare programs were responsible for the growth of the underclass, creating a class of women who did not hold paying jobs and a class of men who did not take on family responsibilities.

Liberals responded to the conservative attack with a guarded defense of welfare, agreeing that the system did not work and particularly that it failed to provide the proper incentives for self-help among the poor.[57] As a result of their failure to defend the basic principle of entitlement against the conservative argument, liberals formed, along with conservatives, a new consensus for welfare reform during the 1988 congressional session.

The new welfare reform legislation was aimed at making it harder for people to collect welfare and creating incentives for women to enter the workforce. The goal of the new legislation was to place the financial responsibility for children back on the individual family unit rather than on the state. In so doing, the reforms were in line with other "privatization" initiatives of the Reagan era, which diminished the scope of public sector responsibilities.

Limiting Entitlement Through Regulation

During the past decade, increasingly restrictive eligibility requirements held down the number of recipients so that only half of poor families could qualify. A recent study for the Southern Regional Project on Infant Mortality identified some of the ways in which welfare caseloads have been restricted.[58] Looking at application information for 1985–86, the study found that three-fifths of families denied welfare benefits were denied for "Failure to Comply with Procedural Requirements." That means over 1.5 million people were denied welfare benefits last year on procedural grounds. And this number is rising: the number of applications denied for procedural grounds has gone up by 75 percent since 1980.

The southern states were particularly notorious, accounting for 45 percent of denials nationwide but only 35 percent of applications. Within the South, however, there was wide variation: Texas holds the worst record, denying half of all applicants, while North Carolina was the least stingy, denying less than one-tenth of applicants.

The first barrier to collecting AFDC is the application form itself. The form varies from four to fifty-five pages, depending upon the state, and can be very difficult to understand. Required documentation can include Social Security cards for all family members; pay stubs; letters from Social Security, the Veterans Administration, and state Unemployment Compensation offices verifying any income from those sources; bank statements; rent and utility receipts; proof of residency; children's birth certificates; and proof of the absence or disability of a parent. The next barrier is the income test. Thirty-three states and the District of Columbia deny benefits to people if they have other income at or below 50 percent of the federal poverty level ($4,650 yearly income for a family of three). In Alabama, for instance, a family of three with more than $183 in monthly earnings is ineligible for welfare. Nationally, one in five applicants for welfare is denied benefits because their earned income is above the state's limit.

The asset limit is next: another 4 percent of families are denied benefits because they own assets above the federal limits ($1,000 in cash and $1,500 equity in a car). The limit on the car's equity value was established in 1979 and has not been adjusted since then. Simply updating the automobile allowance for inflation would raise the limit to $2,348.

If the applicant successfully leaps through these three hoops, she still needs to wait for the application to be processed. Federal regulations specify that the waiting period cannot exceed forty-five days, but many states, such as Georgia, North Carolina, and South Carolina, take a month or more to process an application. The study points out that this waiting period can significantly increase the health risks for pregnant women waiting to qualify for Medicaid so that they can obtain prenatal care.

Poorer and Poorer

Not only has eligibility tightened, squeezing many poor families off the rolls, but benefits have fallen substantially since the early 1970s. Combined federal, state, and local spending on AFDC has fallen in real terms since the mid-1970s. In 1975, net outlays on AFDC were nearly $17 billion (in 1985 dollars.) By 1986, outlays had fallen to $14.7 billion.[59]

Outlays have fallen because the real value of AFDC benefits has dropped. AFDC benefit levels are set by state legislatures, and no state automatically raises AFDC benefits when prices rise. As a result, the purchasing power of AFDC benefits fell by one-third between 1970 and 1986. (Some states were slightly less stingy. For instance, Wisconsin raised benefits by 10 percent over the rate of inflation in that period. But other states, like Illinois and New Jersey, permitted real benefits to fall by over 50 percent.) Even if we add in the value of food stamps, which are received by most AFDC families, the combined value of AFDC and food stamp benefits still fell an average of 26 percent between 1971 and 1984.[60]

As a result of these cutbacks, government transfer programs are substantially less effective at lifting families out of poverty than in the past. The Center for Budget and Policy Priorities estimates that in 1979, cash benefit programs (primarily AFDC) lifted one in seven black female-headed families out of poverty; by 1987, the fraction had fallen to one in fourteen. The center concludes that over one-third of the increase in poverty since 1979 among black female-headed families with children would not have occurred if government programs had remained at their 1979 eligibility and benefit levels.[61]

The consequences of welfare state retrenchment have been severe. Median income for black female-headed families fell from $10,257 in 1978 to $9,710 in 1987 (in 1987 dollars).[62] Those who are poor are poorer than in any year since 1967. For instance, in 1987, 56 percent of the children in poor black female-headed families lived at family incomes below *half* the federal poverty level ($9,056 for a family of three).[63]

The Workfare Solution

Faced with a crisis in income and eligibility, the response of the conservative-liberal consensus for welfare reform has been to pass the Family Security Act of 1988. Written by Senator Daniel Patrick Moynihan, the act was cosponsored by over forty other senators, including liberals such as Kennedy and Mikulski. It does not mandate a federal minimum benefit or provide any incentive to states that raise benefits. As a result, it does nothing to reverse the steady deterioration of welfare recipients' purchasing power since the early 1970s. Instead, the act is built on the assumption that paid employment will represent a ticket out of poverty for women on welfare. The act mandates that states require participation in education, training, or work programs for certain AFDC recipients. The act sets low age limits for mandatory participation (states would be allowed to require participation in welfare-to-work programs for mothers of children over one year of age) and contains punitive provisions for teen parents (states may require teen parents to live with their parents in order to collect AFDC). The act also requires that states establish "pre-eligibility fraud detection measures" to deny benefits to those suspected of fraudulent applications. These measures could open the door to home visits and other invasions of privacy, losing ground that was won by welfare activists and lawyers for the NWRO years ago.

While implementation of the Family Security Act will take several years, evidence from the existing welfare-to-work programs suggests that the act will not provide meaningful employment opportunities for single mothers. At present, most states offer only short-term training programs, which usually prepare recipients for sex-stereotyped jobs such as nurses' aide or file clerks. The child-care benefits allowed to recipients while they attend training programs are far below the cost of enrolling a child in a day-care center. Finally, the act does not provide funding for permanent health coverage. In Massachusetts, whose program has been considered one of the most successful, a recent survey of recipients placed in jobs showed that only 55 percent had any health coverage where they worked and only 14 percent received benefits paid in full by the employer.[64] Most important, single mothers seeking employment at a living wage face the realities of race- and sex-segmentation in the labor force. Despite the media attention to women in managerial and professional work, nearly nine in ten women continue to work in female-dominated jobs. Some of these, such as teaching and nursing, are relatively high skilled, but others, such as child care and waitressing, pay very low wages. As a result, nearly one-third of black single mothers who worked for pay in 1987 lived below the poverty line. Nearly 17 percent of white single mothers who worked in 1987 lived in poverty.[65]

A program that so fundamentally undermined the notion of entitlement could never have passed Congress during the heyday of the NWRO. Liberals would never have joined the coalition supporting the bill, and conservatives would have found their policy proposals far out of the mainstream.

Welfare rights groups are attempting to organize today so that they can be an effective presence during the period in which the Family Security Act will be implemented at the state level and so that they can monitor the effects of the act on poor women and their children. Their organizing efforts face a difficult challenge.

In this period of restricted eligibility, even applying for welfare at all is a political act, the assertion of an entitlement that the current political climate actively discourages.[66] From such individual political acts, a new welfare rights movement may yet be born.[67]

NOTES

1 Less attention has been paid to Hispanic and other racial ethnic groups, partly because very little information is available on these groups. As a result, this essay focuses on blacks.

2 Mary Jo Bane, "Household Composition and Poverty: Which Comes First?" in *Fighting Poverty: What Works and What Doesn't*, ed. Sheldon H. Danziger and Daniel H. Weinberg (Cambridge, Mass.: Harvard University Press, 1986).

3 U.S. Bureau of the Census, Current Population Reports, Series P-60, No.161, *Money Income and Poverty Status in the United States: 1987 (Advance Data from the March 1988 Current Population Survey)* U.S. Government Printing Office, Washington, D.C., 1988, Table 15, 27.

4 This is the most recent year for which a racial breakdown of AFDC recipients is available. The numbers in this paragraph are calculated from data contained in Committee on Ways and Means, U.S. House of Representatives, *Children in Poverty*, WMCP:99-8, May 22, 1985, p.625, and U.S. Bureau of the Census, *Money Income and Poverty Status of Families and Persons in the United States: 1986 (Advance Report)*, Table 16.

5 U.S. Bureau of the Census, *Money Income and Poverty Status 1986*, Table 16. Data for 1983 are used in this section for comparability with the recipient race data in the first paragraph.

6 Author's calculations from data presented in Committee on Ways and Means, *Children in Poverty*, 625.

7 In 1985, 7.1 percent of white families were single-mother families, compared to 28.7 percent of black and 16.3 percent of Hispanic origin families. Among Hispanics, the incidence of female headship varies widely, with Puerto Rican families the highest, at 34.3 percent, followed by Mexican families at 13.4 percent and other Hispanic (primarily Cuban) at 11.9 percent. U.S. Bureau of the Census, *Statistical Abstract of the United States 1986*, Tables 33, 34, and 38.

8 Ibid., Table 617.

9 Ibid., Table 638.

10 This essay will concern itself only with black women and Aid to Families with Dependent Children. More research is needed to document and analyze Hispanic women's utilization of the welfare system. Since data are only available on Hispanics since 1972, this essay will not address Hispanic women. Nonetheless, the

available data suggest that many of the factors pertaining to black women are also relevant to a research agenda on Hispanic women. For instance, in 1983, 31.2 percent of poor Hispanics received AFDC benefits, 68.4 percent of Hispanic families had children under eighteen, the unemployment rate for Hispanics stood at 13.7 percent, and the poverty rate at 28.0 percent.

11 Daniel P. Moynihan, *The Negro Family: The Case for National Action* (Washington, D.C.: Department of Labor, Office of Policy Planning and Research, 1965).

12 See, for example, Herbert Gutman, *The Black Family in Slavery and Freedom, 1750–1925* (New York: Pantheon Books, 1975); Elizabeth Pleck, "The Two-Parent Household: Black Family Structure in Late Nineteenth-Century Boston," *Journal of Social History* 6 (Fall 1972): 3–31; Carl N. Degler, *At Odds: Women and the Family in America from the Revolution to the Present* (New York: Oxford University Press, 1980).

13 Rose Brewer, "Black Women in Poverty: Some Comments on Female-Headed Families," *Signs* 13, no. 2 (Winter 1988).

14 William Julius Wilson and Kathryn M. Neckerman, "Poverty and Family Structure: The Widening Gap between Evidence and Public Policy Issues," in *Fighting Poverty: What Works and What Doesn't*, ed. Sheldon H. Danziger and Daniel H. Weinberg (Cambridge, Mass.: Harvard University Press, 1986), 235, Table 10.1.

15 In contrast, nearly 12 percent of white families and 25 percent of Hispanic families were headed by a woman.

16 Kathryn Neckerman, Robert Aponte, and William Julius Wilson, "Family Structure, Black Unemployment, and American Social Policy," in *The Politics of Social Policy in the United States*, ed. Margaret Weir, Ann Shola Orloff, and Theda Skocpol (Princeton, N.J.: Princeton University Press, 1988), 399.

17 Frances Fox Piven and Richard A. Cloward, "The Contemporary Relief Debate," in *The Mean Season: The Attack on the Welfare State*, ed. Fred Block, Richard A. Cloward, Barbara Ehrenreich, and Frances Fox Piven (New York: Pantheon Books, 1987), 54.

18 Incidentally, the impact of island-to-continental United States migration on family life helps to explain the higher rate of female headship among Puerto Ricans compared to other Hispanic groups.

19 Jacqueline Jones, *Labor of Love, Labor of Sorrow* (New York: Basic Books, 1985), 156–60 and 235–56.

20 See Linda Gordon, "What Does Welfare Regulate?" *Social Research* 55, no. 4 (Winter 1988).

21 Ibid., 620.

22 Jones, *Labor of Love*, 185.

23 See David T. Ellwood and Lawrence H. Summers, "Poverty in America: Is Welfare the Answer or the Problem," 92–96, and William Julius Wilson and Kathryn Neckerman, "Poverty and Family Structure: The Widening Gap Between Evidence and Public Policy Issues," 249, in *Fighting Poverty: What Works and What Doesn't*, ed. Sheldon H. Danziger and Daniel H. Weinberg (Cambridge: Harvard University Press, 1986).

24 Mimi Abramovitz, *Regulating the Lives of Women: Social Welfare Policy from*

Colonial Times to the Present (Boston: South End Press, 1988), 327.

25   Wilson and Neckerman, "Poverty and Family Structure," 236.

26   See, for example, William Julius Wilson, *The Truly Disadvantaged: The Inner City, the Underclass, and Public Policy* (Chicago: University of Chicago Press, 1987), 83–92 and 95–106; William A. Darity and Samuel L. Myers, "Does Welfare Dependency Cause Female Headship? The Case of the Black Family," *Journal of Marriage and the Family* 46, no. 4 (November 1984): 765–79.

27   U.S. Bureau of the Census, *Statistical Abstract of the United States 1987*, Table 106.

28   Ibid., Table 115.

29   Ibid., Table 119.

30   *Statistical Abstract*, Table 303.

31   Ibid., Table 278.

32   Neckerman, Aponte, and Wilson, "Family Structure," 408.

33   William Julius Wilson, Robert Aponte, and Kathryn Neckerman, "Joblessness versus Welfare Effects," in *The Truly Disadvantaged: The Inner City, the Underclass, and Public Policy*, ed. William Julius Wilson (Chicago: The University of Chicago Press, 1987), 99.

34   Such influential organizations as the Children's Defense Fund and the Ford Foundation have advocated for this policy. See Children's Defense Fund, *Declining Earnings of Young Men: Their Relation to Poverty, Teen Pregnancy, and Family Formation*, Washington, D.C., May 1987, and Gordon Berlin and Andrew Sum, *Toward A More Perfect Union: Basic Skills, Poor Families, and Our Economic Future*, Occasional paper 3, Ford Foundation Project on Social Welfare and the American Future, New York, February 1988.

35   Elaine McCrate, "Labor Market Segmentation and Relative Black/White Teenage Birth Rates," unpublished paper, November 1988.

36   One program that targets low-income teen mothers has shown some promise in improving these mothers' employment prospects. The program combines education, training, family planning, and linkages to adult community women volunteers. See Manpower Demonstration Research Corporation, *The Challenge of Serving Teenage Mothers: Lessons from Project Redirection*, October 1988.

37   One indirect measure of the improving fortunes of black women is provided by economist Peter Boehmer's "community earnings ratio." This measure of black access to earnings relative to whites over the post–World War II period is derived by calculating the percentage of blacks with income multiplied by median black earnings, expressed as a ratio to the same figure for whites. The ratio shows that black men and black women had roughly the same access to earnings relative to whites from 1949 to the 1960s. At that point, black women's earnings improve relative to white women's earnings, while black men's earnings stagnate relative to white men's. See Center for Popular Economics, *Economic Report of the People* (Boston: South End Press, 1986), 48.

38   Elaine McCrate, *The Growth of Nonmarriage Among U.S. Women, 1956–1983*, Unpublished Ph.D. dissertation, University of Massachusetts, Amherst, Massachusetts, 1985.

39 See, for example, Randy Albelda, "Nice Work If You Can Get It: Segmentation of White and Black Women Workers in the Postwar Period," *Review of Radical Political Economics* 17, no. 3 (Fall 1985): 72–85.

40 Julianne Malveaux, "The Political Economy of Black Women," in *The Year Left 2: Toward A Rainbow Socialism*, ed. Mike Davis, Manning Marable, Fred Pfeil, and Michael Sprinker (London: Verso, 1987), 63.

41 See, for example, Wilson, "Cycles of Deprivation and the Ghetto Underclass Debate," in Wilson, *The Truly Disadvantaged*, 3.

42 Adolph Reed, Jr., "The Liberal Technocrat," review of Wilson, *The Truly Disadvantaged, The Nation*, February 6, 1988, 168.

43 See Randy Albelda, "It's All in the Family: How Government Influences Family Life," *Dollars and Sense*, March 1987.

44 See Jill Quadagno, "From Old-Age Assistance to Supplemental Security Income: The Political Economy of Relief in the South, 1935–1972, in *The Politics of Social Policy in the United States*, ed. Margaret Weir, Ann Shola Orloff, and Theda Skocpol (Princeton, N.J.: Princeton University Press, 1988), 235–64; Abramovitz, *Regulating the Lives of Women*, 317.

45 Theda Skocpol, "The Limits of the New Deal System and the Roots of Contemporary Welfare Dilemmas," in *The Politics of Social Policy in the United States*, 303.

46 Skocpol, "The Limits of the New Deal System and the Roots of Contemporary Welfare Dilemmas," and Quadagno, "From Old Age Assistance to Supplementary Security Income," *The Politics of Social Policy in the United States*.

47 Abramovitz, *Regulating the Lives of Women*, 318–23.

48 Winifred Bell, *Aid to Families with Dependent Children* (New York: Columbia University Press, 1965), 93–123.

49 For accounts of the NWRO, see Guida West, *The National Welfare Rights Movement: The Social Protest of Poor Women* (New York: Praeger Publishers, 1981); Frances Fox Piven and Richard A. Cloward, *Poor People's Movements* (New York: Vintage Books, 1979).

50 Piven and Cloward, *Poor People's Movements*.

51 Linda Gordon, "What Does Welfare Regulate?"

52 Johnnie Tillmon, "Welfare is a Women's Issue," *Liberation News Service* (no. 415), February 26, 1972, reprinted in *America's Working Women: A Documentary History—1600 to the Present*, ed. Rosalyn Baxandall, Linda Gordon, Susan Reverby (New York: Vintage, 1976), 355–58.

53 Committee on Finance, U.S. Senate, *Data and Materials Related to Welfare Programs for Families with Children*, S. Prt. 100-20, March 1987, p. 18.

54 Children's Defense Fund, *A Children's Defense Budget: FY 1989*, Washington, D.C., 1988, 266.

55 See, for example, George Gilder, *Wealth and Poverty* (New York: Bantam Books, 1982); Charles Murray, *Losing Ground: American Social Policy 1950–1980* (New York: Basic Books, 1984); Lawrence Mead, *Beyond Entitlement: The Social Obligations of Citizenship* (New York: The Free Press, 1985); Mickey Kaus, "The Work Ethic State," *The New Republic* (July 7, 1986): 22–33.

56   White House Working Group on the Family, *The Family: Preserving America's Future*, November 13, 1986.

57   See, for example, David Ellwood, *Poor Support: Poverty in the American Family* (New York: Basic Books, 1988).

58   This section is based on information from the Southern Governor's Association, *Study of the AFDC/Medicaid Eligibility Process in the Southern States* (Washington, D.C., April 1988).

59   Committee on Finance, 25.

60   Committee on Finance, 378–89.

61   Center on Budget and Policy Priorities, *Still Far From the Dream: Recent Developments in Black Income, Employment and Poverty* (Washington, D.C.: 1988), A-3.

62   Ibid., 15. In comparison, white female-headed family income fell from $17,266 to $16,290.

63   Ibid., 12.

64   Commonwealth of Massachusetts, Department of Public Welfare, "An Analysis of the First 25,000 ET Placements," August 1986.

65   U.S. Bureau of the Census, *Money Income and Poverty Status in the United States: 1987*, Table 19, 37.

66   See Barbara Nelson, "Helpseeking from Public Authorities: Who Arrives at the Agency Door?" *Policy Sciences* 12 (August 1980): 175–92, cited in Gordon, "What Does Welfare Regulate?"

67   Some efforts are already under way to link up the remaining welfare rights local chapters and to build coalitions with organizations representing homeless and unemployed people. Contact the National Welfare Rights Union, 29 McLean, Highland Park, MI 48203.

INDEX

Index

Please remember that this is a library book,
and that it belongs only temporarily to each
person who uses it. Be considerate. Do
not write in this, or any, library book.